George Ball, Vietnam, and the Rethinking of Containment

George Ball, Vietnam, and the Rethinking of Containment

David L. DiLeo

Foreword by

Arthur M. Schlesinger, Jr.

The University of

North Carolina Press

Chapel Hill & London

The paper in this book meets the guidelines for permanence
and durability of the Committee on Production Guidelines for
Book Longevity of the Council on Library Resources.

95   94   93   92   91   5   4   3   2   1

Library of Congress Cataloging-in-Publication Data
DiLeo, David L.
    George Ball, Vietnam, and the rethinking of containment /
by David L. DiLeo.
        p.   cm.
    Includes bibliographical references and index.
    ISBN 0-8078-1936-0 (alk. paper).—ISBN 0-8078-4297-4
(pbk. : alk. paper)
    1. Vietnamese Conflict, 1961–1975—United States.
2. Ball, George W.   3. United States—Foreign relations—1945–
I. Title.
DS558.D55   1991
959.704′3373—dc20   90-12641
                                                           CIP

For Emily.
Even while her own heart labored,
she filled the author's to overflowing.

Contents

Illustrations

Foreword

THE LAST HALF-CENTURY has been a time of turbulence for the world and a time of testing for American foreign policy. Few among those charged with steering the republic through the storms of the twentieth century have been more successful in keeping their heads while all about were losing theirs than the subject of this work.

Though George Ball came out of the isolationist heartland, he somehow had from the start an instinct for the realities of the great world beyond. In 1940, in Chicago, the very citadel of isolationism, he took the interventionist side during the bitter national debate over American policy toward the war in Europe. As a lawyer in the Lend-Lease Administration, he began to prepare for the economic problems of the postwar world. As a director of the United States Strategic Bombing Survey in Europe, he perceived the limitations of air power as a means of winning wars. In the 1950s, as an associate of Jean Monnet, he helped organize the campaign for European integration. In the 1960s, as David L. DiLeo shows in rewarding detail, he vainly but presciently opposed deeper American involvement in the Vietnam War. In the 1970s he warned against the growing identification of American interests with the shah of Iran. In the 1980s he rejected the idea that the United States should give a blank check to the government of Israel. He was among the first in the United States to recognize the historic changes Gorbachev was bringing about in the Soviet empire and to pronounce last rites on the Cold War.

I have known George Ball through most of this turbulent half-century, have worked with him in diverse undertakings in government and in politics, and have continually rejoiced in the company of a wonderfully spirited, cheerful, resourceful, imperturbable, elegant man; so my assessment may be prejudiced. For more detached testimony I cite the message that Roy Jenkins of Great Britain, former chancellor of the Exchequer and former president of the European Community, sent to George Ball's eightieth birthday celebration: "to the man who had been more nearly right on every major foreign policy issue of the past forty-five years than anyone else I know."

DiLeo concentrates on one episode in George Ball's varied career: his opposition as under secretary of state to the escalation of the American role in Vietnam—opposition based on the conviction that Vietnam did not lie within America's zone of vital interest, on doubt that we could achieve military victory on the mainland of Asia, and on skepticism as to whether we had the power or the wisdom to order the world according to our liking. Implicit in Ball's critique of America's Vietnam policy was a reassessment of the premises of the containment doctrine as militarized by the Korean War and codified in that mischievous document, NSC/68.

This illuminating book casts significant light on the way American foreign policy is made, on the debates behind our steady march into the Vietnam quagmire, on the dilemmas of dissent within the executive bureaucracy, and on such larger questions as the post-NSC/68 distortions of the containment policy and the malign consequences of the "credibility" thesis fatally embraced by successive administrations.

As DiLeo makes clear in courteous endnotes, I disagree with certain of his interpretations of the Kennedy administration. President Kennedy did not seem a dedicated Cold Warrior to those who worked with him in the White House. "Let us never negotiate out of fear. But let us never fear to negotiate" was both the distinctive note struck in his inaugural address and the abiding theme of his administration. He remained a skeptic about American military intervention in Vietnam, even in 1962 (as DiLeo records in Chapter 5), reproving George Ball, of all people, for a speech that overstated the extent of the American commitment. And he was keenly aware of the limits of American power. As he put it in November 1961, "We must face the fact that the United States is neither omnipotent nor omniscient—that we are only 6 percent of the world's population—that we cannot impose our will upon the other 94 percent of mankind—that we cannot right every wrong or reverse each adversity—and that therefore there cannot be an American solution to every world problem."

Still, DiLeo is right in saying that John Kennedy and George Ball, though each had regard for the other, never hit it off quite as they should have done; and, of course, as a responsible scholar, DiLeo has every right to his own interpretations. Also, as a responsible scholar, he confronts with candor questions that inevitably arise about George Ball's role: how could a secretary of state and his under secretary disagree so profoundly on so vital an issue as Vietnam and retain mutual respect and affection? how could the under secretary defend publicly policies he opposed privately? how could he attack critics who were only saying aloud what he himself was saying inside the government? was his licensed dissent part of Lyndon Johnson's exercise in manipulation? why did he remain so long in the State Department? why did he not go public after his resignation and challenge a course he so rightly perceived as leading to national disaster?

His great friend Walter Lippmann urged Ball to resign and explain why. Ball responded (as he has written in his memoirs, *The Past Has Another Pattern*) that resignation would serve no useful purpose. It would merely be an act of theater without serious impact on the Vietnam policy, "a non-event—at the most a one-day wonder." If he stayed, he could continue arguing against escalation in Vietnam and deal with pressing problems in the rest of the world that would otherwise be neglected. Balancing the futility of resignation against the utility of what he could still do, he decided to stay, at least for a while. When he finally despaired of any change in course, he went quietly: "How could I publicly attack the war without giving aid and comfort to the enemy?"

One also surmises that, as DiLeo suggests, George Ball was influenced by his vocation as a lawyer. Lawyers are professionally charged with making the best possible public arguments for their clients, even if they privately disagree with what a particular client has done. When lawyers and clients come to the parting of the ways, it would be most unprofessional for the lawyer thereafter to expose and denounce the client. Confidentiality is of the essence in the lawyer-client relationship. And the bar is trained not to let professional adversaries become personal enemies. George Ball acted according to the code of his profession.

Did his vocation as a lawyer affect his life as a diplomat in more fundamental ways? Since representation, advocacy, and negotiation constitute the essence of both professions, there would seem a natural affinity between law and diplomacy. Lawyers have always played a major part in the formulation of American foreign policy. Of the sixty men who have served as secretary of state, fifty have been lawyers. Yet some of our most notable diplomats have deplored the consequences of the legal domination of their trade.

Forty years ago George Kennan, for example, in his influential study *American Diplomacy, 1900–1950*, grieved over "the mind of American statemanship, stemming as it does in so large a part from the legal profession in our country." Kennan called the unduly legalistic approach to international problems "the most serious fault of our past policy formulation." He rejected the notion that it was possible "to suppress the chaotic and dangerous aspirations of governments in the international field by the acceptance of some system of legal rules and restraints." He assailed as an illusion the idea "that, instead of taking the awkward conflicts of national interest and dealing with them on their merits with a view to finding the solutions least unsettling to the stability of international life, it would be better to find some formal criteria of a juridical nature by which the permissible behavior of states could be defined."

George Ball has not suffered from the illusions that Kennan had in mind—the illusions that underlay Wilsonian universalism, the Kellogg Pact, and the exhortations of Cordell Hull. He has never believed that abstract principles can solve concrete problems. Like Kennan, Ball is a member of the Realist school that sees international politics as an unending struggle for power, based on national interest, mediated by diplomacy, and, on tragic occasions, settled by force.

The Realist school saw communism after the war as a problem but did not become obsessive about it. Ball, again like Kennan, understood that, even in its high noon, communism was only one of the world's realities and that in its twilight it would be inconsequential next to such realities as global overpopulation, ecological disaster, nuclear proliferation, religious fundamentalism, and other post–Cold War scourges. For a Realist these new challenges demand new remedies and concerted international action.

The Realist attack on legalism forty years ago was in part perhaps an overreaction to Woodrow Wilson and Cordell Hull. In recent times Realists like Ball and Kennan, exasperated by the spectacle of the American republic acting as a law unto itself in Grenada, Libya, and Panama, take a more benign view of international institutions and the dream of a world of law. Unilateralism is seen as a cardinal sin, and the United Nations, which Ball regarded with impatience when it was immobilized by the Cold War, acquires new potentialities as the Cold War passes into history.

What America should really signify, George Ball observed at the dinner marking his eightieth birthday, "is that we are truly a government of laws and not of men, and by laws we comprehend not merely domestic statutes but international practices based on established principles. This means that the United States should build up the jurisdiction of the World Court and give proper respect to its rulings in order to provide meaning to the phrase 'international law,' instead of indulging our current practice of contumacious defiance.

"In all events we should take a fresh look at the institutions built largely at our initiative through which regional problems can be justly resolved. We should overcome our shameful delinquency and pay up the half billion dollars or more of back dues we owe to the United Nations, and we should recognize that now at long last we have a chance to test for the first time Woodrow Wilson's conception of collective security. . . . What may have seemed fanatic idealism before has now become realistic politics."

Once again, George Ball's instinct deserves America's attention.

Arthur Schlesinger, jr

Acknowledgments

IN SIX YEARS of mixing pleasure with pain, a good many favors were recorded. I first recognize my colleagues and students at San Clemente High School for their cheerful support. A word of special gratitude is due Tony Sisca. He inspired and promoted this work, and his wisdom and friendship have been life-changing. I also wish to thank Betty Lemberg who, from her vantage point at the hub of the wheel, frequently found creative ways to lighten the burdens of the overextended. A diligent gang of young student assistants transformed taped interviews into manageable text, demystified the tangled world of the microcomputer, and performed numberless tasks enabling me to indulge myself in the written word. Special among them are Kristy Marshall, Keith and Barbara Allen, and Carrie Devins. Archivist David C. Humphrey and the Lyndon Johnson Foundation were kind sources of practical and financial assistance.

I am deeply indebted to my mentor at the University of California, Irvine, Keith Nelson, for all his knowledge and experience, which he imparted so freely, and for his labor, which he gave so generously—but mostly for our enduring friendship. He is a gifted teacher and a wise counselor. George Herring, a good distance away at the University of Kentucky, has been a kind source of instruction and sometimes severe criticism, but, in equal measure, a vital source of personal encouragement.

On too many occasions to record, the Honorable George W. Ball was a most gracious host, making himself and the resources of his office available without restriction. His kindness and intellectual honesty can only be noted; they can never be repaid. Ball's skillful assistants, Lee Good Hurford and Karen Vasudeva, faithfully kept a steady stream of documents and answers to inquiries flowing from east to west and tended to me with saintly patience during my visits to Princeton. Ambassador J. Robert Schaetzel and his elegant wife Imogen provided me with a splendid base of operations in Washington, D.C., from which this story could be more fully investigated. Their vision of a more rational world, and their Jeffersonian faith that people might someday create one, are truly inspiring. I am ever grateful for their interest in my work,

xvii

and most particularly for the warm friendship that we developed during this project.

I am most thankful for the opportunity to work with the excellent staff at the University of North Carolina Press. Executive Editor Lewis Bateman never lost confidence in the project—or in me. To the great delight of the reader, Mary Reid patiently undangled modifiers and simplified the complex, while Ron Maner dexterously steered the book through the production stages.

Special notes of gratitude and affection are expressed here to all the members of my family. My parents, Lou and Georgette, tapped the resources of the "private sector" to help fund research excursions and were untiring supporters to the end. Finally, heartfelt thanks to Kris, Tim, and Emily for tolerating my many absences and for making life so spectacular. They couldn't be loved more.

Introduction

VIETNAM. Despite a decade-and-a-half of concerted efforts to fit America's longest war into a strategically and emotionally manageable perspective, it remains difficult to evoke a more puzzling and painful memory. In the manner in which Munich became a metaphor for political disaster in the 1930s, Vietnam reminds a generation of baby-boomers of bitter lessons learned and grievous mistakes made that cannot bear repeating. For admittedly different reasons, "No more Vietnams!" reverberates from both ends of the ideological spectrum. In an era in which small nations have demonstrated the pernicious ability to frustrate larger ones, the Right has become more selective and has forsworn a once-heralded global policy to contain the frontiers of communism. The more self-critical Left has also accepted America's strategic limitations and has dared to admit that the United States behaved arrogantly and recklessly in Southeast Asia.

But interpreting the lessons of this most complex war is not solely the province of the self-proclaimed high priests of geopolitics. Save for those younger Americans shielded by youthful innocence, Vietnam is a palpable experience that is widely and sorrowfully shared throughout the culture. Ghastly visual spectacles from the most destructive air war in history, the names of My Lai, Khe Sanh, Kent State, and countless other horrific microcosms of the Vietnam years linger as disturbing reminders of a protracted national nightmare. For most of the men and women who served their country in Southeast Asia, the rationale for American involvement remains as murky and ambiguous as ever. For those Americans who merely weathered the event in the political arena or watched it on television, the Southeast Asian war has just as permanently fixed itself into memory. Although it has become cliché to assert that Vietnam was the first "television war," it is also true that innumerable visual messages from the distant jungle conflict are durably fixed in the collective memory of the nation. Television effigies have endured as vivid and vital reference points from which Americans have come to evaluate the past quarter-century of military globalism.

Despite the compelling wisdom of the axiom that history never repeats itself, the temptation to find analogues from the Vietnam conflict for current foreign policy challenges remains irresistible. Repeated allusions to the ordeal in Southeast Asia in the deadlocked debate over an anti-Communist policy in Central America during the 1980s, for example, demonstrate that policy elites have yet to fashion a bipartisan foreign policy consensus in the post-Vietnam era comparable to the manner in which both parties uncritically embraced the containment doctrine after the Second World War. The specter of Vietnam was often recalled in deciding how to pressure the Sandinistas in Nicaragua into democratic reform or, more recently, how to quell Columbia's drug lords. Even when George Bush launched "Operation Desert Shield" in the Middle East in the summer of 1990, he did so with the sober realization that "getting out" would be as important to the American people, to the Congress, and to the commentators as "getting in." Once seemingly unbridled, the superpower reflex to commit arms to foreign shores is now unequivocally repressed. Presidential war-making privileges are circumscribed by what came to be a popular revulsion with the Southeast Asian war.

America's complex and arduous involvement in Vietnam bridged two worlds. It began in 1950 at a deep-frozen stage of the Cold War when the brooding omnipresence of an expansionist Communist monolith and ominous symbols like "dominoes" and "bipolarity" overwhelmed strategic thinking. It ended in a polycentric world in which both superpowers discovered the inevitable limits to their control of Third World revolutionary nationalism, narrowed their global agendas, and hailed a warming spring thaw in their bilateral relations. Recalling the ideological clarity of the early Cold War creates the illusion of an intellectual time warp. By present standards, the bipartisan strategic consensus extant among policy officials and elite opinion makers after World War II was extraordinary. The intensity of the conflict with the Axis powers and the advent of the atomic age had given rise to a renewed determination to prevent general wars. Schemes to realize the Wilsonian ideal of global collective security, embodied in the heart of the United Nations charter as well as in less romantic security arrangements such as the North Atlantic Treaty, provided the means.

Without serious question, Americans in and out of government accepted the solemn responsibilities of world leadership believed to be bequeathed to them in 1945 and forged highly ambitious domestic and foreign policies to meet the burdens of global preeminence. Traditional American isolationism, so prominent in the decades between the great twentieth-century wars, was extinguished by a flood tide of postwar diplomacy, military alliances, and economic recovery programs. The mystique of a "Pax Americana Technocratica" colored strategic thinking as the American leadership sought to determine, to a progressively greater degree, the shape of the world order. In the years between the Second World War and direct American participation in Vietnam's civil struggle, the United States systematically expanded its global commitments through mutual security arrangements, unprecedented foreign aid programs, and the construction of a forbidding nuclear umbrella under which it warmly welcomed old allies and recent adversaries.

Not everyone, however, was intoxicated by the beguiling spirits of boundless internationalism. Within the Kennedy and Johnson administrations, Under Secretary of State George W. Ball was conspicuous among those few within the foreign policy Establishment to question America's ability to sustain an "American Peace" on a global scale. Though himself a philosophical and political liberal, eminently cosmopolitan, and imbued with an expansive conception of the national mission, Ball came to be known as "the quiet Realist of foreign policy."[1] In an age when hubris was pandemic in Washington and pious internationalism supplanted the pious pacifism of the years immediately preceding Pearl Harbor, Ball advanced the cautious view that America's ability to influence international events was finite. At a moment in their history when Americans were asked by an ambitious and charismatic leader to "bear any burden, meet any hardship, support any friend, [and] oppose any foe to assure the survival and the success of liberty,"[2] Ball asserted that the nation's foreign policy must respect material and moral limitations. At a time when inventive counterinsurgency warfare theories were becoming intellectually and politically fashionable, he regularly confessed his shrewd skepticism about the use of military power as a political instrument. A highly successful Washington attorney with a considerable national and international reputation, Ball's most celebrated advocacy as a policy officer of the government was his resolute opposition to the Vietnam intervention—a phenomenon which he understood to be the tragic and inevitable consequence of uncritical postwar globalism.

In the period between America's initial military engagements of 1961 to the fall of Saigon in 1975, Ball was an ardent and eloquent critic of the strategic and political doctrines which led the United States to war in Indochina. The working papers of the National Security Council show that he was the single presidential adviser to challenge the course of escalation at each decision-making juncture. Beginning in 1970, with the preliminary revelations of the *Pentagon Papers*, Ball came to be generally recognized, and celebrated, as the most prescient spokesman within the councils of the executive branch during the 1960s and as a statesman who displayed independent courage. Before the initial phases of direct American involvement, he had presaged the course of the war with uncanny precision and squarely faced the geopolitical—and personal—consequences of his strategic analyses.

Ball played what a contemporary newspaper account in the summer of 1966 called "a lonely and extraordinary role" in the top echelons of government, one that "only historians can put in proper perspective."[3] This book will try. What follows is both an analysis of a bureaucrat's highly problematic dissent and a revealing look at a tragic episode in American history during which well-meaning patriots grievously underestimated the capacities of their adversaries and displayed what, in retrospect, appears to have been a naive reliance upon superior material resources. The work is not a narrative of Ball's entire career but a search, from his unique experience and vision, for insights into what he and many after him came to regard as an egregiously flawed policy, begotten by a flawed deliberative process, in the top ranks of the American government.

George Ball is a massive, colorful, and passionate figure. It was frequently tempting to digress into what, in another age, might be referred to as his "swashbuckling" escapades in the fields of international law, national politics, and high finance. Though such a volume is contemplated, this work is not primarily biographical, and only when the less majestic components of the protagonist's character and personal life bear upon the story of his Vietnam dissent are such digressions made. I have attempted, rather, to discover the origins of his heartfelt misgivings about military intervention in Vietnam; to delineate his strategic and political case against Americanization of the war and to analyze the "politics" of his dissent within the Kennedy and Johnson administrations; to chronicle his frustrated search for allies in his effort to reverse America's expanding commitments to a succession of rickety Saigon regimes; to describe his ironic role as an occasional advocate for the hawks; to examine his controversial resignation from the State Department; and, finally, to suggest why he has continually bucked the strategic tides set in motion by America's more conservative foreign policy elites. With this done, the many reasons why Ball is generally recognized as one of the most original and sober strategists of the past quarter-century will be made obvious.

Chapter 1

Origins of Dissent

George has a striking command of both physical and intellectual
resources, as well as a great capacity to analyze
—Jean Monnet

GEORGE WILDMAN BALL, as he gleefully accedes, is a studied curmudgeon.[1] This is decidedly not, however, a self-effacing characterization. It is instead merely an admission to a comely variant of curmudgeonry, accented by the certainty that one is nearly always right, and magnified by history's intimation of concurrence. Sage, content with his full life and varied experience, and still indefatigable in pursuit of ever more realistic formulations of American policy, Ball mercilessly lampoons his intellectual adversaries and, despite his considerable experience in diplomatic quarters, does not suffer fools gladly. He has been called "the unheretical critic of American foreign policy,"[2] and at times his irreverence suggests a close kinship with the republic's iconoclastic and radical critics. But close scrutiny of his career woefully disappoints the debunkers. Though regularly upsetting to Establishment conventions, he is preeminently an Established man. This lawyer-banker-diplomat embraces America's most conservative traditions but is tempered by a generous egalitarian spirit which is quite curious for a person of his means and vocations.

Born in Des Moines, Iowa, in 1909, Ball followed his older brothers through the academic climes of Northwestern University, where he received a Bachelor of Arts degree in 1930 and a Doctor of Law degree in 1933. He married Ruth Murdoch of Pittsburgh, Pennsylvania, in 1934. As a young attorney, he went directly to Washington from law school at the beginning of the New Deal to practice his new trade in the Farm Credit Administration. From 1934 to 1935 he worked in the office of the general counsel of the Treasury Department, and at the end of 1935 he returned to the Midwest to practice law in Chicago until the onset of the Second World War.

1

After Pearl Harbor, Ball again entered government service in Washington and was appointed associate general counsel of the Lend-Lease Administration; a year later, he assumed the same position in the Foreign Economic Administration, of which the Lend-Lease Administration had become a part. In 1944 he was appointed a civilian member of the Air Force Evaluation Board to study the effects of tactical operations in Europe and immediately thereafter was appointed a director of the United States Strategic Bombing Survey based in London, which President Roosevelt had commissioned to assess the economic, political, and physical effects of the strategic air offensive against Germany.

Returning to Washington toward the end of 1945, Ball worked as general counsel of the French Supply Council and shortly afterward became founding partner of a law firm known as Cleary, Gottlieb, Steen, and Hamilton, which by that time had established busy offices in New York, Washington, Paris, and Brussels. As a member of the firm and as a specialist in international law and commercial relations, from 1945 to 1968 he divided his time between Washington and Western Europe, where he played an active role in the preliminary work that led to the creation of the European Coal and Steel Community and later the European Common Market.

Throughout the 1950s, Ball was exceedingly active in Democratic party politics on the national level, principally as an adviser to Illinois governor Adlai Stevenson. With the advent of the Kennedy administration in January 1961, he returned to government service as under secretary of state for economic affairs and within a year was elevated to the office of under secretary of state, the number two position in the U.S. State Department. He served as under secretary until his resignation on September 30, 1966, enjoying a tenure in that position second only to that of Sumner Welles in the administration of Franklin Roosevelt. Upon his resignation from the State Department, Ball joined the investment banking firm of Lehman Brothers, Kuhn, Loeb as a senior partner. In May 1968 he resigned his partnership in the firm at the request of President Johnson and served briefly as U.S. ambassador to the United Nations. He returned to Lehman Brothers in January 1969 and was a senior managing director until his retirement in October 1982.

Throughout his professional career, Ball has received a myriad of awards for distinguished public service. President Johnson honored him with the U.S. Medal of Freedom in 1966; he is an officer in the French Legion of Honor and a Grande Ufficiale of the Order of Merit of the Italian Republic; and he has also been awarded the Belgian Grand Cross of the Order of the Crown. Though nominally retired, he is presently chairman of the International Advisory

Board of AMAX, Inc., chairman of the Advisory Board of Chemical Bank, and a member of the Advisory Board of Princeton University's Woodrow Wilson School of International Relations. Despite the extraordinary demands on his time and energies since 1968, Ball has found time to make countless speeches, address dozens of academic symposia, frequently irritate his political adversaries in hard-hitting editorial pieces, teach, and write five books which are distinguished by their tendency to upset the prevailing assumptions about American foreign policy and to redefine American interests in global affairs.

Although the problem of an American response to "communist aggression" in Vietnam was only one of many strategic dilemmas into which Ball poured his energies and analytical powers, his voice of restraint during that contentious period has come to predominate interpretations of his role in the diplomatic history of the postwar period. Mapping the route by which Ball became the single spokesman within Lyndon Johnson's Vietnam advisory circle to argue against any and all forms of military intervention makes for an intriguing chapter in the story of his dissent. Fundamental questions are suggested at the outset of this pursuit: What are the ideological and intellectual origins of Ball's Vietnam dissent? Of what ideological stuff is this cosmopolitan "One Worlder," still tirelessly devoted to the consolidation of the Western industrial democracies, comprised? What combination of factors catapulted Ball from Des Moines's prairies to Camelot's inner sanctum in 1961? What intellectual and experiential factors predicated his Vietnam dissent? What prompted him to challenge two presidents—and all their senior advisers—on the most consequential issue of the day? What political factors conditioned his dissent? Did professional ambition in any way motivate him to think and behave as he did? Was he, in the course of his dissent, driven by idealism or opportunism? Is his notorious candor a manifestation of personal integrity, or does it reflect a deeply rooted personal and political cynicism? Is he lacking in, or overwhelmed by, principle?

Analysis of Ball's personal and professional life eclipses any doubt that his Vietnam advocacy sprang primarily from an inherited world view and only secondarily from what was at times an episodic—and even compulsive—investigation of Vietnam's internal political dynamics. Insight and ideology garnered from experiences in private and public enterprises antedating his State Department service significantly informed his dissent. Tracing those origins reminds one of the critical relationship between ideology and statecraft and illuminates Ball's "prophecies" within the government during the 1960s. Ironically, though his professional experience endowed him with certain analytical powers, we will see that in important bureaucratic circles it critically diminished the under secretary's capacity to persuade.

Although suggesting a historical correlation between William Jennings Bryan and George Wildman Ball may at first appear strained, a brief comparison sheds significant light on the story. Like Bryan, Ball boldly confronted the Eastern Establishment and his president on the paramount issue of war and peace and bore the cross of in-house dissenter. Like Bryan, he failed to be convincing. Notwithstanding the certainty that too comprehensive a comparison between the two middle western favorite sons is intellectually and historically reckless, Ball's course of action during the Vietnam era brings to mind a contrasting, and instructive, episode from Bryan's career during an earlier chapter in the annals of American foreign relations.

In the aftermath of the *Lusitania* sinking in May 1915, Secretary of State Bryan had urged President Wilson to protest English interference with American shipping at the same time he was denouncing German submarine attacks in order to preserve the integrity of what was then America's trumpeted neutrality. Bryan's much publicized disagreement with Wilson and his protest resignation in June for what he considered Wilson's provocative "Lusitania Note" were acts of conscience, the object and consequence of which was preservation of his personal honor. Bryan had reluctantly concluded that he could no longer work for a president with whom he so vigorously disagreed on such a transcending issue.

Unfortunately, and in the American political system quite predictably, the price Bryan paid for his principled act was consignment to political oblivion in Nebraska. His resignation had little impact on Wilson's eventual policies of "armed neutrality" and, later, armed intervention. The lesson most commonly drawn from this interlude in American statecraft—and one that Ball himself drew—is that when a minister of state and the president openly disagree on the issue of the day, the minister's resignation becomes a political requirement for the administration and an obligation of conscience for the minister. The government maintains coherence, and the cabinet officer his principle. Moreover, exposing disagreements between executives and cabinet members augments public debate and hence provides more balanced government. Ministerial resignation in protest is one of the few practicable checks on a progressively "imperial presidency."

For a different set of reasons, Bryan's successor fared equally poorly. Secretary of State Robert Lansing was diametrically opposed to Wilson's peace policy and openly castigated the substance and style of his diplomacy. Lansing felt Wilson should never have gone to Europe to negotiate a treaty with the

Allies, did not believe in the League of Nations concept, and thought Wilson stubborn and unrealistic. Lansing embraced his office more ardently than his principles, and he continued to be identified with an administration in which he had lost effectiveness. As a consequence of his public disclaimers of Wilson's policies, Lansing was humiliated by the president, who refused to include him in a single substantive negotiation at the Paris Peace Conference. Instead of conducting affairs of state, Lansing expended his energies explaining policies with which he was known to be in disagreement to a chorus of correspondents well aware of his discord, and discussing his vapid relationship with Wilson. The price Lansing paid for staying on included political impotence and the embarrassment a sitting cabinet official must feel when his integrity is impugned by a cacophonous assembly of journalistic critics.

Ball knew this history and fashioned for himself a more refined, but perhaps equally hazardous, third course. Secretively, and without self-glorifying public disclosure, he challenged American policy in Vietnam while simultaneously striving to retain his principle and dignity. Unlike Bryan, Ball maintained his office in the Johnson administration and continued to very closely identify himself with policies about which he had profound misgivings. In stark contrast to Lansing's experience, Ball's uncompromised public loyalty to two presidents allowed him to maintain his access to "Top Secret" intelligence reports and invitations to the highest levels of discussion on all aspects of the war.

Like Bryan, Ball emerged from the American heartland to become a naysayer in the ranks of the foreign policy elite. Like Bryan's, Ball's assumptions about America's role in world affairs were conditioned by what may be called his region's Democratic conservatism on matters beyond the borders. In a similar manner, his assumptions about domestic statecraft were conditioned by the waning remnants of middle western liberalism and, indeed, a populist affinity for confrontation with the Eastern Establishment. Analysis of Ball's Vietnam dissent then, strangely enough, begins in the American farm belt. In much the same way a veteran or an athlete might proudly brandish a battle scar, Ball demonstratively invokes his Middle American roots for political effect and revels in nostalgic talk of his Spartan political and social origins. What he intimates to be the cultural and intellectual austerity of his early life suggests much about his self-image, his affiliation with the Eastern Establishment which, ironically, he has now come to epitomize, and his portentous relationships with cabinet colleagues during his government service.

Ball's memoirs, *The Past Has Another Pattern* (1982), describes these midwestern roots and discloses his deepest personal sentiments about his family, his professed agnosticism, and his celebrated mentors. His long chronicle of his own colorful past and of American society and diplomacy in the past half-century is good history. Ball offers unique insights into America's reluctance to play a great power role before World War II and into the evolution of the Cold War, and he provides intimate character sketches of America's foreign policy elites. But alas, like memoirs generally, Ball's inevitably tell us more about the author than the individuals about whom, and the events and places about which, they are ostensibly written. Close examination of what he recalled (or what he chose to recall) and the manner in which it was recorded creates a nearly irresistible temptation to lay him out on Freud's couch. A retreat to the safer ground of E. H. Carr's wise caution about memoirs as historical documents provides a sound, though perhaps less esoteric, analytical tool with which to examine Ball's "memoir-as-monograph": "No document," as Carr wrote in his searching examination of the craft of history, "can tell us more than the author of the document thought—what he thought had happened, what he thought ought to happen, or perhaps only what he wanted others to think he thought, or even what he himself thought he thought."[3]

The first window into George Ball is his account of his grandfather, Amos Ball, Sr., whom he describes as a colorful, if not questionable, character. This patriarch ran a hay and feed store in Iowa, which, though less than a stunning economic success, closely linked Ball's family to the political struggles in the excited climate of the agrarian revolt, which were punctuated by the Bryan-McKinley campaign of 1896. Having taken his family to Iowa from Devonshire, England, in the twilight of the nineteenth century, Amos Ball, Sr., raised and nurtured two succeeding generations of Balls in what had been a seedbed of prairie populism and protest against the Eastern Establishment. George Ball, born in Des Moines and raised there until age twelve, evolved socially and intellectually in a liberal agrarian environment and was molded by the rhythms and challenges of middle western life.[4] Though by that time the Middle West was in the final stages of a conservative ferment, Ball has stated that he would still like to think that he was well tuned to the historical political concerns and intellectual instincts of his boyhood home.[5]

Ball writes an admiring portrait of his grandfather, whom he calls "an amateur ecclesiastic" and who, he reports, believed in "the God-ordained superiority of the Englishmen." Subtly couched in his account of his paternal grandfather is a transparent self-identification which exposes his own cultural prejudices. Ball has clearly and regularly expressed his patiently considered view that certain British institutions are aesthetically and functionally superior to those of the United States and other Western European countries, and his own presuppositions about the superior cultural achievement of the Anglo-Saxon race have been known occasionally to be only thinly veiled.[6] Ball has stated many times, for example, that the British cabinet system (and English traditions respecting dissenting politicians, within which resigning ministers maintain their base of political power in Parliament) is a superior institution. Under British rules, Ball claims, his decision to remain in the Johnson administration to fight against the policy of escalation from the inside would have been fundamentally altered. After a protest resignation in England, Ball likes to remind his listeners, the dissenter is not consigned to political oblivion, a fate about which he nurtured a considerable fear.[7]

Repeatedly evidenced in Ball's memoirs and personal papers are innumerable insights into a world view forged upon the ethnocentric convictions he ascribes to his grandfather. They range from innocent sarcasm disparaging the sterility of German architecture[8] to comments on "French pretension and anachronistic dreams of hegemony"[9] and Italian "unreality and wishful thinking."[10] In stark contrast, Ball lavishly describes the United Kingdom as "a garden of quiet beauty and repose"[11] in which, during recent years, "there has been noticed a new spirit of realism pervading all sectors of British society."[12] And when Ball's characterizations of the world outside Europe are analyzed, piercing indictments of nations' inabilities to keep house and less innocent sarcasm are noted. National histories of Asian peoples are metaphorically reduced to "Kung Fu movies" and "comic operetta," and names of Asian leaders are derisively typified as "typographical errors."[13] This Anglophilia is consistent with Ball's latent racial and ethnocentric images of the world and is abundantly clear in his conception of the politically and culturally optimum—and economically rational—ordering of the international system by a handful of Western capitals. Ball's admiration of, and fascination with, the First World (particularly Western Europe) can be measured in inverse proportion to his ambivalence toward the Third World (particularly Southeast Asia).

This should not, however, suggest that Ball's global assumptions are derived from a vulgar racism. Rather, his ambivalence toward the developing nations is evidence of a conception of the world order thoroughly immersed in, and nearly exclusively informed by, classical Western culture. His well-known skepticism about Third World development, for example, is based primarily upon economic and political, and not racial, prejudices. Ball's lifelong friends, particularly those closest to him during the heated intergovernment debates over the Vietnam problem, perceived him then, and continue to understand him, as a "European-American" enamored of Continental refinements, often comparing him to Dean Acheson in social manner and sophistication. Though given at times to innocent ethnic humor, Ball's personal emotional sympathies for the peoples of the less developed countries run as deep as his pessimism about their futures.[14]

Indeed, many have found it intellectually cumbersome to reconcile Ball's domestic political liberalism and an attractively altruistic economic internationalism (especially his warm endorsement of any and all European-American plans to open Western markets to, and forgive the debt of, Third World states) with his presuppositions about world cultures and his unremitting fear of overextending American resources. Ball watchers, including both his friends and adversaries, regard his forward position on civil rights, particularly his well published antiapartheid convictions, his activist role in the advancement of welfare state politics, and his often expressed concern about demographic trends and environmental protection, to be attractive, even if somewhat ironic. An international lawyer and banker whose interests, persuasions, and experiences are expressed and measured in the idiom of the European and American elite, Ball possesses a decidedly progressive and liberal sensibility. He is, in fact, an amalgam, molded from the discordant clays of Middle American idealism and elite cosmopolitanism.[15]

The memoir as self-identification theory may also be tested in Ball's portrait of his father, Amos Ball, Jr. He writes reverently of his father's love for literature, confessing that he absorbed his passion for great books and assimilated what he ruefully describes as his father's "detachment and sense of the ridiculous."[16] Amos Ball, Jr.'s, love of the humanities was infectious, and it most conspicuously conditioned Ball's life interests and style of expression. In contrast to the manner in which many of the under secretary's colleagues approached the Vietnam problem (McNamara and Rusk were always coolly rational, quantitative, and carefully armed with strategic indices), Ball's memorandums and oral arguments tended to be metaphorical, allegorical, and sometimes even lyrical. He describes his father, and, by intimation, himself, as a scholarly and learned man, analytical, unemotional, and distinctively objective in the sense that, like a novelist, he could at will separate himself from his story. And the under secretary was not predictable. He employed a sufficiently varied intellectual range so that he could generate the arguments for boldness when required, while, sometimes in the same day, advocating more dovish views. Ball could, for example, retain a reputation for toughness in the context of the Cyprus civil war by threatening U.S. involvement, while, at the same time, earning a reputation as an apostle of restraint in Vietnam.

Ball's father was a man of considerable positive energy as well as a thinker. Driven by a Protestant work ethic, Amos Ball, Jr., somewhat ruthlessly knifed his way through the ranks of the Standard Oil Corporation and was able to provide George and his older brothers Stuart and Ralph with the full range of the Midwest's educational and professional opportunities. It is abundantly clear from private and candid discussions with family members that Ball's father modeled reasoned objectivity, perseverance, loyalty, and more than a dash of guile. Amos Ball was a successful bureaucratic infighter and aggressive corporate climber who, through a combination of intelligence, hard work, and timely political maneuvers within the company, achieved rank and power.[17]

Contentedly characterizing his family as "a tight microcosm of bookworms," Ball writes that home life during his growing years was decidedly tranquil. Testifying to the primacy of literature in his childhood and young adulthood, Ball reminisces about routinized weekend trips to the public library with his family, "each member with a suitcase appropriate to his or her size and station in life to carry home the week's reading."[18] It is painfully ironic that this idealization of hearth and home flows from the pen of a man whose own family experience has been painfully strained by the unpredictable rhythms of the public's business and whose adult character was demonstrably influenced by various emoluments of power, prestige, and considerable personal wealth. A man of affairs, throughout his career Ball has repeatedly demonstrated the willingness to sacrifice personal serenity and to exhaust himself physically and emotionally in pursuit of grand political objectives—or simply a good bureaucratic fight.

Weighed against accounts of his family's literary and intellectual life, Ball's remarks about his formal education are rendered curious. His description of his undergraduate training provides interesting categories by which Ball's self-image, relationships with his future comrades-in-arms in the Kennedy and Johnson administrations, and, consequently, his Vietnam dissent might be understood. Northwestern, he writes, "was something less than [his] romanticized view of what a great university should be."[19] Despite his own considerable intellectual acumen, to this date Ball remains sensitive to the austerity of his formal secondary and postsecondary education, particularly when compared to others among the "Best and the Brightest." The characterization of his alma mater is only part of a general pattern, abundantly clear in his writings over the years, of a disparaging sarcasm trained upon ivory tower academia. There is a paradoxical relationship between his own notorious pedantry and erudition and a sham anti-intellectualism which he employs in advocacy, which is manifest in social settings, and which occasionally erupts as an ideological reflex.[20]

As an example of Ball's tendency to self-disclosure by psychological projection, he writes that among his father's foibles was an excessive deference to academics. He strategically remarks in the same passage of the memoirs that Lyndon Johnson shared this trait, and he then ruefully employs an anecdote to set himself apart from the Johnson administration's academic elite. Ball recounts an occasion when he was introduced by LBJ to a German foreign minister as an "intellectual," to which he immediately demurred and retorted, "Mr. President, those are fighting words where I come from."[21] In even more irreverent moments, Ball refers to historians as "doctrinaire scribblers," and he relishes invoking Phillip Guedalla's aphorism that "history repeats itself; historians repeat one another." He is particularly hostile to radical scholars who, as he writes, "twist events like pretzels to fit them into the Marxist mold and systematically strip the American experience of any glory or heroism."[22] By his own admission, and despite the hundreds of great classical works of literature, history, and political theory that he has mastered, Ball considers his midwestern common sense his greatest intellectual attribute.

Belying the irreverent and contrived anti-intellectualism he sometimes displays, Ball counts a number of Ph.D.'s among his closest personal friends, and a quite special place is reserved in his heart for his Northwestern University mentor, Bernard De Voto. Accepted into "Benny's" experimental English seminar, Ball enjoyed a special relationship with his favorite professor, and De Voto certainly developed a special personal interest in him, even occasionally canceling class so that they could play tennis. Ball freely admits that De Voto's personal tutelage and comradeship transformed him into "an obnoxious little intellectual snob."[23] Five years after his graduation from Northwestern, Ball sent De Voto a "letter of tribute," thanking him for his role in the "development of [a] critical attitude at a time when it was easier to accept than to question," and crediting his teacher/friend with mitigating what he then termed his "adolescent Babbittry."[24] De Voto's imprint on Ball was life-changing: the teacher insured the student against the slightest doubt that he was the intellectual equal of any man or woman he would encounter during the remainder of his life.

Discounting the curious self-deflating attitude about his academic roots, it is abundantly clear that Ball was proud to have been an honors student in literature at Northwestern. He thought seriously enough about academic life in Evanston, in fact, to edit a literary journal, write poetry, and hoard, as keepsakes from a formative time in his life, syllabi from his literature courses. Throughout his undergraduate matriculation, Ball read and reread distinguished classics, including the Bible, Homer, Shakespeare, various Greek dramas, Aristotle, Plato, Virgil, Dante, the *Nibelungenlied*, medieval narratives, and French romances.[25] Satire, allegory, and paradox shaped Ball's modes of analysis and imbued him with what he likes to call "a keen sense of the absurd"[26] as well as a dense arsenal of recondite metaphors which, to this day, he shamelessly and often evokes. Ball's avuncular and professorial personality, and a delightful ease with people his junior, make for intriguing contemplations about what he would have been like had he pursued an early ambition to earn a Ph.D. in English literature and become a teacher.

But the future diplomat's training in literature also included immersion in the darker intellectual crevasses of the twentieth century through his meticulous study of Siegfried Sassoon, Wilfred Owen, Robert Graves, Sacheverell Sitwell, and Rupert Brooke—all practitioners of a bitterly satirical verse, bitterly denunciatory of war. Ball was deeply impressed with what he calls their "poetry of disillusion."[27] Their graphic images of the First World War's devastation profoundly influenced the 1920s "Lost Generation" readership, and their vivid portrayals shattered any heroic battlefield mythologies to which Ball may have subscribed as a consequence of his unassuming and quite informal study of the war with his brothers. In the formative years from 1929 to 1939 Ball developed a profound personal aversion to war which, as we will see, would later manifest itself in his oral and written arguments in Vietnam advisory group meetings.

A decade later another great conflict left an equally heavy imprint on Ball's intellectual development. The Second World War had a profound psychological impact on him, one which would also surface in the 1960s. A critical component of his Vietnam dissent was, oddly enough, germinated as Hitler's blitz thundered across Poland. Elements of his initial reaction to the outbreak of World War II are unmistakably present in his later skepticism about mixing war and politics. Though not alluded to in his memoirs, perhaps because it was too revealing of a tortured soul at the crossroads of maturity, at the age of thirty Ball introspectively examined the monumental events of September 1939. In what he entitled "Letter Addressed to Myself to be Read on the Day I Enlist," Ball wrote of his deep cynicism about any greater good to be achieved by a resort to arms. The four-page, single-spaced document is replete with numerous interlineations penned by an emotionally shaken young man, nervously searching for a rationale for what he described as "the mad acts" about to engulf the world.[28]

Peculiarly addressing himself, Ball stated in this most private account of September 1939 that he had not yet been beaten by "an angry and restless public opinion" and had "maintained the ability to think clearly." He describes an internal, paradigmatic conflict between "the conditioning of insidious pro-

paganda" and an increasingly "elusive objectivity." He decried the "mechani-
cal nature of modern war," particularly the "objective detachment" of aerial
bombardment, and roundly criticized the role of propaganda as a psychological means of combat. (Perhaps not surprisingly, he regarded British propagan-
dists as less offensive than their German counterparts.) Ball repeatedly lamented the indiscriminate killing resulting from strategic bombing. Raining
explosives from the sky, he writes, had "taken the romance out of war." He
insightfully added that "the passing of individual combat has 'made war
acceptable' and 'less odious'."[29] The letter portends modes of analysis evident
in Ball's Vietnam dissent, in which he would argue that strategic bombing
would, in time, seriously compromise America's moral position in that war
and, worse, would ultimately even undermine efforts to subdue a zealous and
determined enemy.

After 1939, as a second general European war threatened Western civilization, Ball seems to have been mischievously preoccupied by the fashionable
trend for young men to avoid induction. He mused that he might "find a job in
some administrative department" (which he did), "or join the Quakers" (which
he did not do). He openly describes his own mental flirtations with various and
opprobrious schemes to evade the draft, although the expedients to which he
may have given serious consideration remain unclear. He framed the hurriedly
prepared missive "as a warning and a benediction," admitting to being fright-
ened and ashamed by the prospect of participating in the "ghastly unthinkable
hell."[30] Lamenting Europe's troubles and expressing deep regret about the
implications of an inter-European civil war, Ball was patently dubious about
any greater good to be achieved by the United States resorting to arms and
participating in the carnage.

But his September 1939 letter is distinctly not a manifesto of pacifist,
antiwar idealism. In the very same document, Ball philosophically accepts war
as "a necessary evil" and criticizes the America Firsters' pious isolationism.
Albeit reluctantly, he embraces the "just war" doctrine as it was narrowly
applied to the defense of Western civilization. But Ball's theoretical acceptance of armed conflict does not imply a concomitant approval of what he
considered to be the spurious political doctrines supporting it. He roundly
deprecated the "war-mongering" ideology of America's "liberal journals" and
predicted that "industrialists would easily be persuaded to accept participation
in the war in view of their business interests."[31] This analysis presaged Ball's
assumptions about an even more complex war that emerged during the 1960s
and crystallized certain sensitivities which would equip him to analyze, in both
strategic and moral terms, the peculiar American intervention in Southeast

Asia. Without the real and present danger to American security, the Vietnam conflict never took on the characteristics of the "just war" in Ball's analysis, and he would deplore the inflated and irresponsible rhetoric of a crusade against communism to justify its progressively brutal forms.

Ball's polemic on the blitz of Poland is impressive and suggests that the broad contours of his conceptions of war and peace were forged by 1939. There are, however, other aspects of his early career and other character traits that bear upon his analysis of the Vietnam problem. Foremost among them are his unbounded curiosity and ambition. Simply put, Ball's instinct was (and is) to be close to the center of action. Invitations to the hub of activity were always positively and enthusiastically received but, as we will see, not necessarily required. In the Depression and New Deal years, Ball's buoyancy and self-confidence paid professional dividends, leading to rich experiences in politics and political administration and establishing for him a compelling base of experience from which he would later help mold the outlines of a new American foreign policy. Establishment luminaries he befriended and the reputation as a Washington attorney that he established between 1933 and 1945 were significant links to his State Department service. In these years a self-styled middle western hayseed became a cosmopolitan and well-connected Yankee.

Briefly considering a career as an English professor after his graduation in 1930, Ball enrolled at Northwestern Law School and passed the Illinois bar exam in 1933. Having earned the enthusiastic recommendation of his dean, he served the General Counsel's Office of the recently created Farm Credit Administration (FCA) from May 1933 to May 1934.[32] One of the swarm of lawyers who came to Washington to "save capitalism and reorganize the cosmos,"[33] the future diplomat writes of these years in excited terms, describing them as "yeasty," "effervescent," and "supercharged."[34] The New Deal had an enormous impact upon him. Two intimates and lifelong comrades on the liberal barricades have stressed that the chockablock political activity of the early 1930s and work in the penumbra of Franklin Delano Roosevelt left an indelible imprint on him, setting his liberal compass and accelerating his practical experience in the sometimes delicate and hazardous craft of bureaucratic service.[35] There is no question that Ball's political convictions were galvanized during the New Deal era. Save for a single verifiable instance at the end of the 1950s in which, as copublisher of the *Northern Virginia Sun* newspaper, he helped recruit strikebreakers to defeat union printers,[36] Ball, the inviolate bourgeois, has supported what may unhesitantly be characterized as a working class political agenda. Throughout his adulthood he has been a decidedly partisan and activist Democrat and has repeatedly contributed his

talents and treasure to party causes and candidacies across the country.[37] A
political dissection shows that Ball (despite what the character of his retainers
during his law career and his clients during his work as an investment banker
suggests) has consistently embraced the Democratic party's liberal domestic
platform and has made meaningful contributions to its most progressive foreign policy planks.

When Ball worked near the center of New Deal agricultural and monetary
policy in 1934–35, a significant, if enigmatic, friendship began to take form.
By his own admission, one of his four principal mentors—and men he most
admired—was Dean Acheson, then acting secretary of the treasury. Ball and
Acheson first befriended each other on the handball court at Washington's
Hotel Ambassador while Acheson was attempting (unsuccessfully) to apply
the brakes to Roosevelt's 1933 scheme to shore up the dollar through government purchases of gold. Acheson had believed that a stronger dollar would
slow the economic recovery of the United States, which he believed must take
place within the international system. Acheson's liberalism, at least insofar as
international economic matters was concerned, greatly appealed to Ball. Although it was perhaps true that "Ball took Acheson more seriously than
Acheson took Ball,"[38] in the thirty-five years they remained friends and col-
laborators their relationship proved to be mutually nourishing and, in terms of
Ball's professional career, enormously consequential. Ball greatly admired
Acheson's talents as a lawyer and as a diplomat. Though shortly after victory
against the Axis powers he concluded that "Dean was too much the Cold
Warrior for [his] tastes,"[39] he shared Acheson's Atlanticist perspective and
general allegiance to the containment doctrine. Comparing Acheson and Ball,
William Bundy, assistant secretary of state for Far Eastern affairs (and Acheson's son-in-law), once remarked that the two men held remarkably similar
views on the fundamentals of American foreign policy. Though Ball might
himself emphasize their sharp disagreements in key crisis situations, such as
Acheson's quite bellicose and his own quite restrained counsel to Kennedy
during the Cuban missile stand down, Bundy recognizes their essential simili-
tude. "George Ball was not antithetic to the Cold War and all its aspects,"
Bundy has noted, "or even most of its aspects; he believed in it." And even
today, in the post-Vietnam era, Bundy emphasizes Ball's staunch defense of a
militarily strong America: "You won't find George talking about much lower
defense budgets or for not standing up where it was clearly a test case."[40] Ball
heartily endorsed Truman's rescue operations in Greece, Turkey, and Korea,
but he was not swept away by the more hysterical Cold War rhetoric of the
1950s. "Ball was," Bundy adds as a cautionary example, "totally antithetic to

Ball in 1933, the year when he came to Washington as a Farm Credit Administration lawyer. (Photograph courtesy of George W. Ball)

both the universal idealism of the Third World enthusiasts and the John Foster Dulles universal all-points-containment. He just didn't buy those things and he detested Dulles every which way."[41]

Ball's enduring relationship with Acheson was built upon their shared Eurocentric cultural sensibilities and North Atlantic orientation to world affairs, a decidedly WASPish idiom and value universe, notorious erudition, and unbounded self-confidence. In the academic literature about the 1950s and 1960s, Ball and Acheson are frequently identified as prototypical Atlanticists, classical "European-Americans" in the mold of J. Robert Schaetzel, American ambassador to the European Community, John J. McCloy, German high commissioner, and W. Averell Harriman, American ambassador to the Soviet Union. None of these individuals cultivated too great an interest in the Third World—or in those who did. Bundy notes that both Ball and Acheson "accepted the world as it is," but he recalls a significant point of departure between them regarding the manner in which Ball's classical natural rights liberalism, and specifically his deeply rooted abhorrence of anything that tasted of colonialism, shaped his foreign policy views. This element put a small but meaningful distance between the two men. Bundy admits that "political Realism is the way to describe George's approach, just as certainly as it was the approach of the man who had as great an influence on him as anyone, namely Acheson." But there were distinctions. Bundy discerningly adds that "there are shades of Realism." He recognized that "Ball drew different conclusions as to, say, for example, South Africa. Acheson believed that it was in the best interests of the United States to support the white regime, while George had more liberal idealism laced in" to his analysis of the problem. Bundy recalls one of Ball's more pontifical moments: "If you depart from those values [racial equality] you lose the support of your people, you lose support of the Europeans." He argued this point, as Bundy recalls, "at frequent intervals [and] unashamedly."[42]

During the 1950s and 1960s, Ball eagerly embraced a more accelerated pace of decolonization and movement toward self-determination and majority rights than his mentor. At the same time, it was generally understood that both he and Acheson held certain elevated presuppositions about what, in certain diplomatic circles, would be characterized as the "White Man's Club," and that they had concluded very early in their careers that the world's prosperity and security were functions of institutional arrangements made by a half-dozen Western powers. Although the world political scheme would change dramatically in Ball's lifetime, particularly with the multiplication of sovereign states after 1945, he has never strayed very far from the view that a relatively small concert of Western industrial states (now including Japan) holds the key to world prosperity and stability. While not denying basic political and civil rights to former colonial peoples, he still maintains the rather conservative view that a handful of economic powers still set the global political agenda.

Although Ball may have learned a good deal from his association with Acheson in the Roosevelt era, he has freely stated that he was, at the time, "spectacularly ill-equipped" for much of the New Deal work assigned him. The hurried Washington environment was "a bit unreal" to the young lawyer. In the autumn of 1934, compelled to "get back to the Middle West *and touch the earth* [emphasis added],"[43] Ball resigned from the Treasury Department. This candid remark, which reinforces the imprint of regional identification in Ball's intellectual constitution and self-conception, is the single admission of his being dizzied by the complexities of his duties as a twenty-five-year-old New Dealer, which included writing credit applications and negotiating contracts for the sale of government cotton. Given the range and sensitivity of the weighty crises he would confront as under secretary (including missiles in Cuba, a tangled Cyprus negotiation, revolution in central Africa, and a great many knotted issues related to the exceedingly complex "European partnership"), the conspicuous absence of any similar disclosure testifies to Ball's consummate self-confidence. He has stated that he never once doubted his abilities or convictions in any circumstance, and even though Southeast Asia clearly lay outside his primary area of expertise, he dauntlessly affirms that he never doubted for a moment that his instincts or his analyses were correct.[44]

Returning to Chicago in 1934, Ball joined a law firm which, to his chagrin, he soon discovered to be in an advanced state of decay. In contrast to Washington's whirlwind activity, his first days as a private attorney were "humbling and discouraging." In his five years with a firm he chose not to identify in his memoirs, Ball took very little pleasure in litigating so many Depression-related foreclosures and bankruptcies. In 1939 his fortunes and morale turned upward when he took a position at the more prestigious (and remunerative) firm of Sidley, McPherson, Austin, and Harper, in which Adlai Stevenson, the second of his four mentors, was a junior partner.[45] Even in the environment of a successful corporation, however, the law, for both Ball and Stevenson, was sterile. Stevenson biographer John Bartlow Martin emphasizes that exposure to the New Deal had left an indelible mark on both men, and Stevenson's personal letters unmistakably show that he had been intoxicated by the New Deal experience.

Throughout the 1930s, Stevenson had received numerous offers to return to government service. Satisfied with none of them, but still quite restless, he cathartically threw himself into numerous philanthropic, political, and civic activities. One, Stevenson's intimate connection with the Chicago Council on Foreign Relations, directly and powerfully influenced the development of Ball's career. During the period 1938–41, as a protégé of Stevenson, the future under secretary of state first turned his attention to international affairs by "faithfully attending" the Chicago council's Friday luncheons.[46] As the organization's chairman, Stevenson had a well-established reputation as a gifted speaker and thoughtful policy analyst. Ball's friendship with Stevenson acquainted him with many foreign policy figures in the Establishment who were connected to the Chicago council. Through their law practice and Chicago council membership, and its connection with the parent organization, the Council on Foreign Relations in New York, a thirty-five-year friendship and close political collaboration commenced. Ball became one of Stevenson's principal political and foreign policy advisers, chaired campaign committees in 1952, 1956, and 1960, and maintained a very close relationship with Stevenson until his death in 1965. Although their friendship in the 1960s was at times strained by their somewhat divergent ideologies, particularly their contrasting views on the developing world, Ball's friendship with the Democratic party paragon and United Nations ambassador was as important as any in his life.

Ironically, Ball's close identification with Stevenson proved at times to be a significant liability. Beyond the old political antagonisms, the Kennedy men considered Stevenson too sentimental and idealistic to be a tough-minded diplomat. By and large, those who came to power in 1961 embraced Acheson's conception of unremitting anticommunism, outlined in his historic 1950 treatise (NSC-68) that effectively institutionalized the Cold War. Acheson's oft-repeated reflection that "Stevenson had no gonads," for example, indicates the dimensions of the considerable rift among the Democratic party leadership, one that has stimulated a quite lively historiographical debate over the interpretation of the Kennedy administration's record in foreign policy.[47]

As William Bundy has astutely noted, in order to fully understand Ball's relationship to the foreign policy Establishment, the broad spectrum of associations he maintained must be appreciated. Ball's views are, Bundy suggests, in many ways a composite of those whose company he kept: a mix of Stevenson's altruism and Acheson's tough-mindedness. "[That Ball and Stevenson] became as close as they did," Bundy adds, "was remarkable." There was little doubt among those acquainted with both men that Ball's was a much tougher mind. "[Ball] was unhappy with the fuzziness of Stevenson and yet," as Bundy has concluded, "there was something in Stevenson that hit some deep Middle Western idealist root in him."[48]

Although as his career developed he would become an author-analyst and speaker in demand, Ball's relationships with the Chicago and New York councils during the 1930s were casual and informal. He was not at all involved in the administration of the council, but "as a friend of Adlai's [he] was quite religious about going to *all* their meetings [emphasis in original]."[49] Although Ball did not keep papers from this early period that might illuminate the record, it is generally understood by his contemporaries that he emphatically supported a policy of assistance to those European states menaced by fascism after 1936. Ball and Stevenson are counted among those activated midwest-erners who, in conjunction with the more traditionally internationalist Eastern foreign policy Establishment headquartered in New York, championed the twin causes of Allied military cooperation and collective security on the eve of the Second World War. As a general proposition, the primary goal of the Establishment in the waning years of the 1930s was to drive isolationism from the field. To most American foreign policy elites, storm-cellar neutrality was no longer tenable. Internationalists such as Ball and Stevenson prided them-selves on seeing the world realistically, which, in 1936, came to mean standing up to Adolf Hitler. Ball's retrospective account is typical of the internationalist position: "After 1936," he wrote, "one could not ignore the mounting evidence that the world was on a pell-mell slide toward a crisis." The future diplomat who would inherit a share of the burden stemming from the American fail-ure to act had wondered aloud how anyone could espouse isolationism, which he regarded as "both cowardly and irresponsible." He had concluded that "[W]estern weakness and myopia were encouraging the destructive dema-goguery to which [Hitler] gave ultimate expression."[50]

By 1940 Ball had cast his lot with the newly formed "William Allen White Committee to Defend America by Aiding the Allies."[51] He became an enthusi-astic spear carrier in the ranks of the committee and a confirmed devotee of global collective security. He believed that America's prolonged flirtation with isolationism in the 1930s had diminished her influence in world affairs to an absurdly low level. Despite his celebrated dovish views on Vietnam, Ball was never, and clearly is not presently, an isolationist, "neo" or otherwise. His critique of prewar isolationism and his direct and immediate (albeit reluctant) support of the Korean intervention refute those who, like his conservative nemesis William F. Buckley, Jr., have come to believe that Ball's Vietnam dissent was an ideological reflex, born of pacifist and isolationist predilec-tions.[52] Ball abhorred the isolationism of the 1930s. We will see that his Vietnam dissent in the 1960s just as explicitly and aggressively inveighed against uncritical globalism—a phenomenon that he regards as merely the other side of the isolationist coin.

With the Japanese attack on Pearl Harbor and the German war declaration, policy options for the United States were precipitously narrowed and clarified. After American entry into the war, Ball briefly considered accepting a commission in the navy, which Stevenson, then an assistant to Secretary of the Navy Frank Knox, could have easily secured. Stevenson, as it became generally known, wielded considerable influence within the Navy Department, and was even once characterized as a "one-man employment agency." But Stevenson insisted that Ball's talents could be best used in Washington and brought him to the attention of Oscar Cox, general counsel of the Lend-Lease Administration. Surrounded by young, energetic, and talented individuals such as Eugene Rostow, Daniel Boorstin, Lloyd Cutler, and Phillip Graham, Ball asserted his creative and administrative energies. "We were determined," he once stated, "not to leave our war to the soldiers."[53] It would appear that, as a group, the young political appointees were determined not to leave the war to their superior civilian managers either. During 1942 and 1943 Ball served as legal adviser to then Lend-Lease administrator Edward R. Stettinius, who, as he writes, "was ill-equipped to cope with the subtle and complex difficulties inherent in supply arrangements."[54] Convinced that the Lend-Lease Administration lacked strong leadership generally, and an intelligent policy for the repayment of lent and leased implements of war specifically, Ball embarked on a scheme for which he has stated he "could have been hanged."[55] Throughout 1942 and 1943 he worked with a staff of lawyers responsible for drafting Lend-Lease reports on behalf of the president for congressional review at ninety-day intervals. When, in August 1943, the Eleventh Lend-Lease Report came due, Ball, Eugene Rostow, and their deputy, Alfred E. Davidson, conceived of a plan which, had it succeeded, would have fundamentally altered the character of the Lend-Lease program.

In December 1939 FDR implored the nation to become "the great arsenal of democracy" with the expressed purpose of fighting a war while at the same time keeping American soldiers far from the battlefronts. As the Congress debated H.R. 1776 (the Lend-Lease Act), the White House remained coyly ambiguous about how the Allies, particularly Britain, would repay their accounts at the conclusion of the war. Recognizing the imperative for Britain to accept the aid without delay and reminded daily of the deeply rooted reluctance in Congress to grant aid and credits, FDR deliberately left American policy vague. It was "Roosevelt's continued policy," according to wartime aid scholar James Dougherty, to deal with Lend-Lease on an "ad-hoc basis." The questions "Should Britain repay?" or "In what medium [should she] repay?" were purposefully left vague in order to give the president leverage in his effort to persuade the British to alter their protectionist trade policies after the war and to move toward multilateral tariff reductions.[56] Aroused by John Maynard Keynes's *The Economic Consequences of the Peace* (which in 1919 had forecast the economic and political instability in the 1920s and 1930s), Ball's "most pressing worry" at the conclusion of the war was to insure that the United States "would not repeat the mistakes of the 1920s [by] draining Europe of resources on the holy principle of the sanctity of debt."[57]

Having unilaterally, and indeed presumptuously, decided that America should forgo exactions from the Allies at the conclusion of the war, Ball directed Davidson to state plainly in the Eleventh Lend-Lease Report that the United States would not jeopardize the war or peace effort by requiring repayment. The passage "victory and a secure peace are the only coin in which we can be repaid"[58] was inconspicuously integrated into the final draft of the report. Unaware of the new language, of which they both emphatically disapproved, Stettinius, now secretary of state, and the president signed the document. When press reaction to Ball's "amendment" surfaced and the presidential oversight became known, the report was expeditiously rescinded and another quickly issued and signed, absent the upsetting sentence.

This not-so-innocent pettifogging in 1943 discloses important aspects of Ball's emerging ideology and bureaucratic personality that reappeared in the 1960s. The integrationist sentiment expressed for reducing Britain's obligations and the extent to which he was willing to risk professional reputation in pursuit of changing a policy with which he emphatically disagreed, contribute to a more complete understanding of Ball's Vietnam dissent. The Lend-Lease chicanery presages Ball's advocacy of an economic and political community for the Western democracies, which was given its fullest expression when, as under secretary, he midwifed Kennedy's plan to liberalize European-American trade policy. But Ball's plan to upset an admittedly ambiguous but settled formula for wartime aid repayment was slippery and reckless. Although his bureaucratic maneuvers would become more subtle and effective during the Vietnam debates twenty years later, in 1943 Ball gained his first experience in what can go wrong when a determined bureaucrat, employing methods just on the windward side of devious, challenges a president and manipulates the instruments of government against the grain of an established policy.

Wanting to be closer to the war, admittedly "more from curiosity than from patriotism,"[59] Ball left the Foreign Economic Administration (the later incarnation of the Lend-Lease Administration) on August 21, 1944.[60] By having made an "exceptionally favorable impression" on the head of the Air Corps Staff, he secured a civilian commission to the Air Force Evaluation Board to study the effects of Allied strategic bombing in the European theater.[61] From his offices in London, Ball quickly found his way into the ranks of the United States Strategic Bombing Survey (USSBS). David MacIsaac's exhaustive, multivolume analysis of the USSBS credits Ball with recruiting into the ranks of the survey team Paul Nitze and John Kenneth Galbraith, who, ultimately, wrote the survey's extremely controversial economic impact report.[62]

Ball was first assigned the directorship of the subgroup charged with determining the impact of bombing on transportation, but his responsibilities rapidly broadened to include analyses of the Royal Air Force's "area attacks," examining the effects of the bombing in the cities, and, as Galbraith's coeditor, drafting the USSBS's final report. Galbraith recalls that as the final assaults against Japan were being contemplated, the USSBS team was being "pressed urgently" to provide the Joint Chiefs with important data they needed to inform their strategic decisions. "While George Ball was not developing unflattering theories about the military administration of the Survey," Galbraith reported in his memoirs, he was diligently working to produce what would be "disturbing conclusions."[63] A representative finding was an alarming conclusion drawn from the study of aerial attacks on industrial Hamburg. Ball's study suggested that the most significant effect of destroying the city's commercial and residential center was to drive the clerks, waiters, shopkeepers, and bank tellers from the burned dwellings to the outlying areas, the ironic consequence of which was to alleviate an acute labor shortage at the defense plants and shipyards outside the city. The USSBS's startling announcement dropped like a bomb itself on the military analysts: German capacity to produce the armaments of war increased through the end of 1944 *despite progressively expanded Allied sorties*.

Ball's bombing survey experience left an indelible imprint on him. His State Department staff counsel Thomas Ehrlich, who worked closely with him on his dissenting memorandums during the Vietnam period, recalls that he "must have mentioned it fifty times" as their arguments against bombing North Vietnam evolved.[64] Ball had also drawn upon the lessons he learned from his World War II experience when, during the Cuban Missile Crisis of 1962, he rebuffed the bold assertions of the air force that surgical strikes could effectively disarm Soviet installations and preempt their capacity to react. While ambling amidst the burned dwellings of postwar Europe, Ball became profoundly skeptical of strategic bombing. He simply doubted that aerial attacks could win wars and believed that they seriously compromised the moral position of the aggressor inasmuch as targets could not be hit without indiscriminate, and hence unacceptable, casualties.[65] In 1964, as we shall see, Ball not only energetically argued against Johnson's conspicuous reliance on bombing North and South Vietnam, he prophetically asserted that it would provoke the enemy to pursue the type of war best suited to its resources, which for the Democratic Republic of Vietnam (DRV) meant virtually unchecked infiltration of forces into the South.

With far less innocence and armed with invaluable experience, Ball returned to private life and his law career after the war. Having experienced firsthand the ravages of wartorn Europe and having assimilated Keynes's admonitions against total economic victory, Ball became an ardent enthusiast of economic reconstruction and, at the same time, an unabashed free trader. Throughout the 1950s this persuasion hardened as he earned profitable retainers as a private attorney from Venezuelan oil and Cuban sugar interests that hoped he could dissuade domestic producers and the Congress from imposing tariffs and quotas on their imports.[66] Germinating in his legal briefs on behalf of foreign clients during the 1950s, a cogent free trade philosophy eventually developed which bore significant political and strategic implications. Ball's was truly "a tradesman's entrance into foreign policy."[67] By the time he had completed his Lend-Lease service and had gained considerably more international experience in private practice after the war, he had come to the conclusion that "it was essential that [America] rid the world economy of its encrusted barnacles of trade and monetary restrictions," and he believed that, as a great commercial power, the United States "had past sins to expiate." What he referred to as America's "mindless protectionism" of the interwar years had, he concluded, "helped precipitate the world's economic collapse and to create the conditions that fostered the rise of Hitler."[68]

By the end of the 1950s, Ball had well formed convictions about America's role within the interdependent global economy. Armed with neoclassical economic doctrines and considerable bureaucratic experience, in 1958 he contributed to the creation of the "Committee for a National Trade Policy," the avowed objective of which was to defeat protectionism. Through this institution Ball was introduced to the country's most powerful businessmen, financiers, and industrialists. While at the apex of his law career, he was invited in January 1960 to address a joint session of the National Industrial Conference and the European Economic Community and European Free Trade Association in New York. His remarks, evidence of his Realist conviction that the security of states begins with a prosperous economic environment, brought him to the attention of then Massachusetts senator John F. Kennedy for the first time. Typical of his later pattern as under secretary of writing historically well-informed speeches, Ball recounted the American economic experience of the 1780s and 1790s, during which time the country was transformed from what he termed a "Balkanized" economy to a vast internal market under a federal constitution. American economic success, he unambiguously declared, is to be understood primarily as a function of its political integration.[69] He believed that Europe had recognized the veracity of this historic example by creating the European Economic Community (EEC) under the auspices of the Rome Treaty of 1958. What Ball then called, and continues to call, "the logic of Europe" was to extend, so far as possible, the integration of the yet politically undefined Continent. In his remarks at New York he lamented the fact that the American posture at the inception of the EEC was merely benign neutrality. In time, as under secretary of state for economic affairs and then under secretary, Ball would enthusiastically champion any and all schemes to more completely integrate Europe and would, as an adjunct policy, continually warn American producers that short-term trading disadvantages and sacrifices would be required to realize the goal of European economic and political consolidation.

Ball worked at the hub of the wheel of European integration throughout the 1950s. Stemming from his public declarations during this period on behalf of integrationist themes generally and the European Community specifically, he was retained by the French Supply Council. In this capacity he befriended Jean Monnet, the prominent French industrial statesman and apostle of European cooperation who was to become the third of Ball's four principal mentors. Ball's close association with Monnet quickly catapulted him into the eye of the storm of French political economy. Monnet's great personal force and ebullient character, as well as the theory and substance of the projects on which they collaborated, made indelible imprints on Ball. Those who worked closely with him during the Vietnam period regard his close association with French industry and politics as crucial to an understanding of his dissent. There is little doubt that his running arguments against the war in Vietnam were greatly informed by his proximity to the French tragedy in Indochina during the 1950s. Few, however, seemed to appreciate the extent and complexity of Ball's Frenchification. He regularly dispensed advice to leaders of an industrial trade association called the French Patronat, edited a journal published to promote transatlantic investment entitled *France Actuelle*, and wrote long papers for the advancement of Franco-American investment enterprises which, as was often noted by his more xenophobic antagonists, were normatively quite advantageous to the French side of the commercial equation. Ultimately, in an age that sanctified 100 percent Americanism, questions about Ball's patriotism surfaced regularly. Though none of the allegations raised ever had the slightest foundation, they illustrate the degree to which Ball had, by 1960, become a citizen of the world. An FBI investigation of Ball's passport record from 1945 to 1960 shows that he spent part of nearly every month in Europe, usually in either Brussels or Paris, where his law firm, now Cleary, Gottlieb, Steen, and Ball, kept offices.[70] In the course of his public career, his close identification with European interests prompted innumerable verbal jibes. For example, in one appearance before a congressional trade committee during his tenure as under secretary, he was asked when he was going to take out American citizenship papers and was impatiently reminded by an American legislator that he was no longer in the pay of the French government.[71]

Ball's close identification with French commercial and political interests was complemented by his role in the creation of, and unwavering involvement in the activities of, the so-called Bilderberg Group. Named after the Hotel Bilderberg in Oosterbeek, Holland, where the first meeting was held in 1954, the annual seminar was tailor-made for the likes of Ball. It has been sarcastically remarked that Bilderberg meetings, normally held in Europe's most picturesque resort towns, are noted as much for their refinements and refreshments as for their reforms.[72] Nonetheless, the objective and success of the group has been to bring thoughtful and influential people from Western Europe and the United States together once a year in a most desirable setting to discuss the West's most pressing trade problems. Missing only one meeting in thirty-two years, Ball has become an acknowledged expert on Western industrial and trade matters.

Delineating Ball's path to this enthusiasm for European integration and a closer European-American cooperation is instructive. Immediately following World War II his interests, professional center of gravity, and the interpretive framework through which he perceived the world were transformed. His first civilian employment was an interim assignment with Monnet in the French Supply Council, which was then charged with planning France's postwar recovery. As council director, Monnet sought Ball's assistance in tailoring French requests to American political sentiments. For the next thirty years Ball and Monnet worked toward the integration of European and American political and economic institutions. The goal then popularly known, and in some quarters derided, as "The Grand Design"[73] became Monnet's, then Ball's, passion. Often working at an extraordinarily rigorous pace under intense and unpredictable political and ideological pressures, Monnet and Ball quickly earned each other's unqualified respect and affection.

The son of a French brandy maker and exporter, Monnet also made a "tradesman's entrance into foreign policy." During World War I he had worked with the Allied Supply Procurement Agency. In 1919 he became France's first delegate to the League of Nations, then deputy secretary general at Geneva. With the outbreak of World War II, he chaired a French/British coordinating committee responsible for organizing war supply in both countries, and after the fall of France in 1940, he became a member of the Free French Resistance and the British Supply Council and worked in the United States to help organize the Lend-Lease program. As head of France's provisional government in 1945, General Charles de Gaulle commissioned Monnet to launch France's modernization program. He conceived and was midwife in the birth of the European Coal and Steel Community and the Action Committee for a United States of Europe. Throughout the 1950s, against stalwart resistance from French nationalists, Monnet worked tirelessly for British entrance into the European Common Market.[74]

In the course of their long and purposeful collaboration, Ball served Monnet in two capacities. As a lawyer, he wrote the technical language required for commercial and legal documents that would inevitably be scrutinized by suspicious American legislators, skeptical economists, and apprehensive representatives of industrial boards. Recalling that "it was a rare paper of any importance that did not go through at least seventeen or eighteen drafts," Ball has accented the severity of work for his French friend by characterizing himself as Monnet's "dialectical punching bag."[75] Working together in close quarters, Ball helped Monnet refine his integrationist message to the Americans in countless conversations, sometimes lasting until dawn, and multiple redraftings of documents. Lessons from work with Monnet were not lost on Ball. When he became under secretary of state he too proved to be a notoriously exacting taskmaster. Schooled on what was commonly becoming known as the "Monnet method," Ball demanded much of himself and required an exceedingly high standard of performance from subordinates throughout his diplomatic career.

Throughout the 1950s Ball also worked for Monnet as a political agent, essentially France's congressional lobby in Washington. His contacts in the Capitol and reputation as an effective attorney were of great value to Monnet in his efforts to prudently frame France's requests for credit and technical assistance. In both capacities, the Frenchman has written, his American partner served France's, and Europe's, cause quite admirably. A bond of shared confidence and mutual respect between Monnet and Ball was sustained for thirty-four years, from 1946 until Monnet's death in 1979. It is perhaps predictable that Monnet's appraisal of Ball's character and intellect is both penetrating and complimentary. A slight man, Monnet was most particularly enchanted with Ball's "striking command of both physical and intellectual resources," as well as his "wisdom," "boldness," "loyalty to friends," and "great capacity to analyze."[76] Their families shared an intimacy that neither man extended to many others. George Ball is "a man of good will," Monnet once wrote; "[he] finds pleasure in helping others" and consistently demonstrates the "very broadest concern for the general interest." Like German chancellor Helmut Schmidt,[77] Monnet found in his friend the rare ability among Americans to comprehend European mentalities: "Often," Monnet once complained, "strong Americans are too simple; they don't see things in their complexity." But Ball "is a spirit who weighs things," a man of "real judgment," a person "remarkably well balanced," not a "divided personality," and "*loyal* [emphasis in original]."[78]

Ball's unquestioned allegiance to French interests permitted his access to the highest level of discussion and to top-secret French government documents bearing upon the building of Europe. Indeed, Ball became intimately acquainted with things French, including economics, politics, language, culture, intellectual processes, and habits of work. As he drew closer to Monnet, to whom he often referred as "the keeper of the conscience of Europe," Ball embraced his mentor's central thesis: If French recovery was to be sustained, it must occur within the context of general European reconstruction, and this required no less than the "creation of Europe" as a cooperative industrial, commercial, and political entity. To this end Monnet devoted the rest of his life, and Ball sacrificed a considerable portion of his energies, influence, and, in not a few instances, effectiveness as an American policy officer.

Ball was utterly transformed by his work and friendship with Jean Monnet. His wife of fifty-six years, Ruth Murdoch Ball, unhesitatingly expresses the private conviction that her husband respected and admired Monnet above anyone.[79] Indeed, Ball's intimates maintain that his many encounters with life at the center of French politics and his studied interest in European economic life are the most salient experiences to have informed his conceptions of foreign affairs. Insights drawn from his work and association with Monnet are, not surprisingly, heavily imprinted on his Vietnam dissent. Before meeting the Frenchman, Ball drew primarily from his middle western origins and professional experience to form impressions of the world. After befriending Monnet, Ball became a consummate Atlanticist, focused almost exclusively on what he perceived to be the complementary objectives of "the building of Europe" and promoting a European-American partnership.

Ball's close identification with European interests did not escape the suspicious observer. A background report assembled by the Federal Bureau of Investigation at the time of his confirmation hearing as under secretary for economic affairs described his law firm (now Cleary, Gottlieb, Friendly, and Ball) as "acting agents" from 1951 to 1961 for the government of France, the European Coal and Steel Community, and the nation of Luxembourg.[80] To his colleagues in the Kennedy and Johnson administrations, Ball's dispositions, prejudices, and loyalties were transparently European. In his official capacities in the Department of State, Ball tirelessly continued the pattern he had established in private life by making the exhausting Atlantic crossing many more times than his associates. To this day, McGeorge Bundy is inexplicably amused that Ball sought, rather than eschewed, travel as a part of his already exceedingly strenuous responsibilities as under secretary.[81] Europe was clearly his bureaucratic calling card, his raison d'être in the executive branch.

As a result of what might be considered overexposure to a single region in an office that demanded a comprehensive view of the world, Ball became fixated on the integrationist "logic of Europe." The concept, it has been observed, came to overwhelm his vision. Beyond the economic component, Monnet, and then Ball, had come to believe that the West's ideological and political survival hinged upon European unity. Their passionate attachments to the North Atlantic Treaty Organization (NATO), the Rome Treaty, the Grand Design, and later the Multilateral Nuclear Force were really functions of their belief that these institutions represented important building blocks toward the political integration of the Continent. Despite the fact that each man realized the limitations of these institutions, they were consumed by the pragmatic calculation that each would serve the larger goal in its own limited way. A "United States of Europe" became their central objective, and both men came to view all world events, as well as their own public lives, through the European prism.

It can be easily demonstrated in any number of cases that Ball's first reaction to a crisis or policy proposal was to calculate its impact upon the European objective. In an examination of his argument against the war in Vietnam this reflex will become patently clear. It was also well illustrated in his and Monnet's shared reaction to the outbreak of the Korean War. On the day the North Koreans swarmed across the border (Sunday, June 25, 1950), Ball was visiting Monnet's thatched-roofed house in the French countryside for a day of work in connection with a plan to pool German and French coal and steel resources. Ball wrote reflectively that "Monnet was quick to see the implications of this" and recalls him stating that "an American intervention would not only jeopardize the so-called Schuman Plan, it would create serious problems for European unity."[82]

Entirely absent from Ball's response and analysis is even a measure of concern for Asian regional security, events on the ground in Korea, or domestic political ramifications stemming from the crisis. As William Bundy once deduced, for those who knew him this was not surprising: Asian matters were peripheral. "He put just about zero on China," for example, as an issue with which the United States needed to be overly concerned.[83] Europe was the conceptual and practical center of Ball's world, and he would not easily generate interest in, or enthusiasm for, enterprises not tangibly connected to the objective of "building Europe."

Sharing Ball's conceptualizations of the world order was his good friend and Washington neighbor Walter Lippmann—the last of his four mentors. For more than twenty years Ball sharpened his strategic and political convictions on the whetstone of Lippmann's penetrating intellect. Returning from Europe in 1945 for one of their intermittent stays in the United States, the Balls moved into a home on Woodley Road in Washington and soon discovered to their surprise that Walter and Helen Lippmann lived at the opposite end of the block. *New York Times* columnist James "Scotty" Reston, who lived in the middle of the block, regards it as quite fortunate that all three men were able to delight in each other's company and intellectual acumen.[84] Though Ball affectionately chided Helen Lippmann's "undistinguished kitchen" and the "poor quality of liquor served" at the residence, the two couples dined together regularly, and Ball and Lippmann saw each other at frequent intervals for "an afternoon drink."[85]

Ball found Lippmann compelling but did not uncritically embrace what scholars generally refer to as Lippmann's Realist theory of international relations. In the course of his long career the influential journalist evolved as a strategic thinker and was constantly reexamining his assumptions about international relations. In fact, Ball complains, "Lippmann had a dozen [theories] and was all over the map on so many points." But he was soundly persuaded by one of Lippmann's fundamental theses, and it immeasurably influenced his thinking. At a Harvard commemoration of Lippmann in 1979 Ball eulogistically praised his friend by recalling that "if there was one theme Walter Lippmann most consistently emphasized, it was the need to keep our commitments in harmony with our resources. That meant avoiding adventures in areas only marginal to our interests."[86]

Ball's initial fascination with "Mr. Lippmann," as he respectfully referred to him in their earliest encounters, originally emanated from his admiration for a celebrated American pundit twenty years his senior. In time the relationship became a reciprocal intellectual nourishment. The friendship was sustained through crises, extended absences, and disagreeable personal events. As it would for so many others, Vietnam significantly changed their friendship. A serious and lasting strain on the relationship resulted from Ball's failure to noisily resign in protest of Lyndon Johnson's July 1965 decision to Americanize the war. Though Ball privately applauded—and even covertly informed—Lippmann's mortifying editorial attacks on Johnson and his war policy, his continued presence in the administration involved a complex of considerations that Lippmann could not, or would not, understand. In the summer of 1965 their once warm rapport cooled. Despite this cleaving of their close intellectual collaboration, Lippmann's political axioms and broadbrush theories of international relations contributed to the development of Ball's world view, and he generously credits Lippmann with "clarifying his muddled thinking" at a time in his life when his own diplomatic and political principles were becoming galvanized.[87]

As the remainder of this study illustrates, Ball's Vietnam dissent was a complex whole, but one forged from disarmingly simple parts. That Ball eventually interpreted events in Southeast Asia as he did was a consequence of his homespun Middle American skepticism about esoteric operational hypotheses ("nation building"), a nascent personal aversion to war (particularly strategic bombing), a populist belief in the principle of self-determination (that allowed him to abide a Communist Vietnam governed bu Hanoi), and his frustration and impatience (stemming from his work with Monnet and ringside seat to the French debacle in Indochina in the 1950s) with so many diversions from what he considered to be the grand European objectives of American foreign policy. The manner in which Ball acted upon his convictions while arguing his case against American intervention in Vietnam and the manner in which his actions were conditioned by ideological and bureaucratic forces within the Kennedy and Johnson administrations are the crucial elements in his dissent to which we now turn.

Chapter 2

At the Margin of Power

I could, I think, be a reasonably effective under secretary for economic affairs. . . . I think it vitally necessary that the whole structure of our foreign economic policy be redesigned.
—George Ball

BY NOVEMBER 1960 Ball was well placed to make meaningful contributions to the national political and foreign policy agendas. A respected Washington lawyer,[1] a Democratic party activist with a proven political track record as chairman of "Volunteers for Stevenson" in 1952 and 1956, at the apex of his career at the age of fifty-one, and with broad experience in European political and economic affairs, he could be quite useful to the new president. Though to Kennedy the association was fraught with conspicuous political impairments, as Stevenson's intimate, Ball was well connected at Camelot. Notwithstanding the fact that Stevenson had indulged himself in the fantasy of a draft movement and seriously complicated Kennedy's bid for the nomination in 1960—and in the process nearly destroyed their already tenuous personal relationship—the candidate and the party owed Stevenson a debt of gratitude. "In a sense," Kennedy assistant Arthur M. Schlesinger, Jr., recalled, because he had resuscitated New Deal liberalism in the campaigns against Eisenhower, "Stevenson had made Kennedy's rise possible," and Kennedy knew it. In the 1960s the Democrats were "talking in the Stevenson idiom," emphasizing economic democracy and shared purpose. Discerning members of Kennedy's entourage knew their boss was "heir and executor of the *'Stevenson Revolution'* [emphasis added]."[2]

With the narrow Democratic victory over Richard Nixon in November 1960, Ball's intimacy with Stevenson positioned him on the outskirts of the New Frontier. Further, his close personal friendships with Cambridge insiders, including Schlesinger and John Kenneth Galbraith, insured that Ball's name

31

would surface in the nationwide talent search about to ensue.[3] However, not one to leave career plans to Providence, or even to the designs of his two well-placed friends, Ball deftly solicited additional support from Walter Lippmann, who ultimately proved to be one of Kennedy's most influential transition advisers. Lippmann was, in fact, instrumental in the decisions to fill major foreign policy and White House staff positions. Shortly after one of Kennedy's occasional visits to Woodley Road to see the sage and respected Washington columnist,[4] Ball entreated Lippmann in a carefully phrased, handwritten letter that elucidates Ball's professional aspirations and unbounded self-confidence:

> If in the course of your visit with Jack Kennedy tomorrow he wishes to discuss personnel and you feel you can do so without perjury, I should greatly appreciate it if you would mention that I have some small competence in the field of foreign economic policy. I could, I think, be a reasonably effective under secretary for economic affairs. My personal relations with Bill Fulbright and the other majority members of the Senate Foreign Relations Committee are excellent. I doubt very much that Jack is thinking of me for that slot since I suspect he has already decided to give it to Chet Bowles. But I could not consider withdrawing from my law firm for any lesser assignment. I put this suggestion forward with diffidence as I hate to be an advocate for my own cause. Please don't feel any need to bring the question up unless it arises naturally in your conversation. PS: I think it vitally necessary that the whole structure of our foreign economic policy be redesigned.[5]

Even before Ball wrote Lippmann he could justifiably believe that he had earned a position of considerable importance within the new administration. Indeed, by the time the transition period was winding down, he had completed much work for the president-elect of which Kennedy was not the least aware. With unashamed calculation, Ball concluded that his close identification with Stevenson was potentially poisonous, and he did not openly trumpet his intimacy with the former Illinois governor. It was then common knowledge that Kennedy would be slow to forgive Stevenson's failure to readily endorse him at the 1960 Democratic convention. Obvious mutual misgivings lingered in their relationship. Aware of the manner in which political footballs were being tossed about as top positions in the new administration were being filled—and that his relationship with Stevenson was a two-edged sword, able to cut for him or against him—Ball craved temporary anonymity during the transition.

Earlier in the campaign Ball had sagely predicted events that unfolded immediately after the election. He had correctly concluded from his conversa-

Ball, *right*, with Secretary of State Dean Rusk, *center*, and State Department
protocol officer. Although a somewhat diffident New Frontiersman in 1961,
the new under secretary of state for economic affairs was nevertheless determined
to make wholesale changes in the country's foreign economic policy. (Photograph
courtesy of George W. Ball)

tions with Lippmann about transition politics that if Kennedy were elected,
Stevenson would be offered the only marginally desirable post of United
Nations ambassador. On July 26 Ball wrote Stevenson to tell him that he
should immediately declare his intentions to serve in a "post of major responsibility," implying the office of secretary of state. As a well-traveled student of
foreign affairs and as the recognized leader of the party in the 1950s, Stevenson would be an indispensable asset in the general election campaign. Recognizing these political realities, and perhaps with an eye on his own political
future as well, in the summer of 1960 Ball implored Stevenson to prepare a
"blueprint" for foreign affairs which, in addition to no less a task than charting
a course for the Free World, would make it difficult for Kennedy to deny
Stevenson the State Department.[6] Acknowledging the need for such a document, and realizing the political advantages if the project were undertaken by

Stevenson, the ever pragmatic Kennedy accepted the offer and commissioned the report—but clearly *without* conceding the State Department to Stevenson.

After the convention in Los Angeles, Stevenson stumped tirelessly for the Kennedy-Johnson ticket, making no fewer than eighty-four campaign appearances.[7] As a consequence of his campaign junkets, as well as his idiosyncratic inattention to detail, the lion's share of work on the foreign policy task force report was delegated to a cluster of Stevenson lieutenants. Having long before won the governor's unbounded confidence with his task-oriented style and notorious capacity for labor, Ball was asked to staff committees, assign them issues and geographic regions to be discussed in the document, and to generally orchestrate the creation of the prodigious "Report to the Honorable John F. Kennedy from Adlai E. Stevenson."[8]

As he was temperamentally, and perhaps compulsively, prone to do, Ball took the bull by the horns. In addition to looking after his legal clients, he worked mornings and evenings on the foreign policy blueprint throughout November and December. J. Robert Schaetzel, Ball's senior special assistant and State Department staff chief from 1961 to 1963 (and later American ambassador to the European Community), worked closely with him on the task force report in the fall of 1960, applying his special aptitude for conjoining information and insight. Schaetzel recalls feverishly chasing around Washington and working long lunches, nights, and weekends at his home in Bethesda on what was "sort of a clandestine operation."[9] While Kennedy was meandering about the country blowing wind into the sails of his political campaign, a cabal of Washington insiders, all of them Stevenson men, were writing a foreign policy agenda for the 1960s.

It has been generally, and quite mistakenly, believed that Stevenson himself played an integral role in the evolution of the 1960 foreign policy task force report. Schlesinger writes in his Pulitzer Prize–winning account, *A Thousand Days*, for example, that after the document was assembled it was taken to the governor's home in Libertyville, Illinois, and "Stevenson put it into final shape."[10] Ball demurs from this interpretation and even asserts that "Adlai probably never even read the damned thing." Ball maintains that he actually "did *all* the work [emphasis in original]."[11] With his characteristic candor, Schaetzel recounts that as the report was being written and redrafted, "it was difficult to get Stevenson's attention," and that his involvement probably did as much to retard as to advance the operation. Schaetzel found the four meetings in which Stevenson did actually participate to be "unnerving" and, while admitting to being "filled with admiration" for Stevenson, was "startled by the way his mind worked," particularly his inability to reach settled conclusions.[12]

Confirming the impression that Stevenson was woefully distracted, Ball is unambiguous about his claim to authorship of the report and shamelessly invokes the first person pronoun in describing the development of the document: "I immediately set about mobilizing knowledgeable friends," he writes; "I would have to take the laboring oar of drafting the report"; "I completed the task force reports just after Christmas Day."[13] Further, Ball's preeminent contribution to the document, which may properly be regarded as a blueprint for Kennedy's European and foreign economic policies, is corroborated by the task force's principal committee members.[14]

But the most compelling evidence of Ball's signal contribution to "Stevenson's" recommendations, and thus to President Kennedy's initial foreign policy initiatives, are the integrationist and Open Door themes distinctively underscored throughout the document. Just as predictably, Ball's Eurocentrist conceptions of American foreign policy were manifest throughout the white paper. The task force made particularly "urgent" proposals for a coordinated NATO nuclear force;[15] it warned of "the dangerous trend on the part of the NATO Allies toward the development of independent national nuclear deterrents";[16] and it included a twenty-page support paper developing a plan for "Partnership between a United Europe and America within a Strong Atlantic Community" which, not surprisingly, paralleled the integrationist principles espoused by Jean Monnet's "Action Committee for a United States of Europe."[17]

Ball's economic liberalism and free trade advocacy were also abundantly evident in the document. In a section entitled "A Comprehensive Program for the Economic Progress of the Free World," the report lamented the "parochial attitude of the Treasury Department" under Eisenhower. Further, Ball faulted the previous administration for failing to extend adequate credits and markets to developing nations (particularly in Latin America), recommended that the executive branch be endowed with new and greater power to effect trade policy, and proposed a 50 percent across-the-board tariff reduction within five years.[18] Also with reference to the Third World economic malaise, and under the heading "Special Urgency," Ball analyzed the collateral problems of nationalism and decolonization. Though he generally lacked fervor for the many Third World development strategies then circulating, he instinctively felt, as a general proposition, that classical European colonialism was both morally and economically iniquitous. With few decided opinions on what the emerging nations were to do with their independence, Ball was driven by the populist instinct that self-determination was an inalienable right. The task force report specifically recommended to Kennedy, for example, that a "high level approach to de Gaulle [be initiated immediately] to indicate the importance which the new Administration attaches to an early settlement of the Algerian conflict."[19] Also predictably, given Ball's unique taxonomy of world problems, much smaller support papers on China, Subsaharan Africa, and Latin America were relegated to appendixes.[20] In a particularly elucidating passage from a section entitled "The World in Revolution," with direct bearing on Ball's views on Southeast Asia that would emerge within the year, the report declared that "it is important that we not try to impose our own political or economic ideas" on Third World nations receiving American assistance. As his arguments against military intervention in Vietnam evolved, Ball would repeatedly return to this principle.[21]

Not wanting to "upstage Adlai by advertising [his] own role,"[22] upon completion of the report Ball preserved a degree of anonymity by assigning a young assistant from his law firm, John Sharon, the task of delivering the 120-page document to Kennedy in Palm Beach, Florida.[23] It might also be true, and perhaps too painful or embarrassing for Ball to admit, that he strategically chose not to identify himself too closely with Stevenson at this critical moment. As his remarks to Lippmann reveal, Ball considered his chances of being offered an acceptable post within the new administration slim, and he probably felt that he needed to play his cards carefully in order to enhance his stock. Not an once of wool was pulled over anyone's eyes, however. Despite this thinly veiled deception, Kennedy's Senate staff—who, after the election, exercised considerable leverage on personnel matters relating to the most attractive positions within the executive branch and White House staff— "regarded the Ball-Sharon operation with particular mistrust," and as a "device to gain Stevenson a bridgehead in the midst of the Kennedy camp."[24] Despite these political suspicions, Kennedy expressed his emphatic approval of Ball's work immediately upon receipt of the report: "Very good. Terrific. This is excellent. Just what I needed."[25] Conscious of his political vulnerability as the youngest president-elect succeeding the oldest sitting chief executive, Kennedy was delighted to have a systematic exposition of a progressive foreign policy in hand. As it turned out, the task force report "helped Kennedy dazzle Eisenhower during their December [transition] meeting."[26]

As President-elect Kennedy familiarized himself with the report, he became more aware of Ball's vital contributions to the work of the foreign policy committee; indeed, the work proved to be his ticket to Camelot. Schlesinger has correctly observed that Ball "might not have come to his [Kennedy's] favorable attention if it had not been for the task forces."[27] Ball's work on the foreign policy report provided an opening that his conduits to Kennedy, including Lippmann, Schlesinger, and Galbraith, were able to successfully exploit. More baldly assessing Schlesinger's personal intervention in the process of Ball's eventual appointment to the State Department, Schaetzel recalls that "because he was obviously in the alien [Stevenson] camp, Arthur [Schlesinger] in particular played a crucial role in getting Kennedy to give George the job [as economic under secretary]."[28]

Ball's appointment, however, was not without perilous complications. Kennedy's personal interest and involvement in foreign affairs was widely known, as was his direct personal role in staffing many junior positions in the State Department during the transition. Much has been written of Kennedy's decision to appoint the "Buddha-like" and laconic Dean Rusk to facilitate the new president's de facto maneuvers as his own secretary of state.[29] Equally well documented is Kennedy's politically pragmatic tactic of generously sharing cabinet and subcabinet positions with Republicans in order to broaden bipartisan support for his agenda *and* deflect political heat for possible policy misfires.[30]

In filling the post of under secretary for economic affairs, Kennedy had exercised this politically inspired spoils strategy and initially selected William C. Foster, a liberal Republican formerly in the Truman administration. Foster was not without credentials, though it was widely believed that equally skilled Democrats were abundantly available. According to Schaetzel, who worked as a talent scout preparing lists of qualified appointees from around the country, Foster was an "able," "amiable," and "good man," but "with about an eighth of Ball's talent." In a political drama common to the Kennedy administration, Foster, Schaetzel tartly recalls, was "skewered." Using Schlesinger as his "stalking horse," Ball "set himself to the task of upsetting the quasi-decision [to appoint Foster], and obviously pulled it off." It was a decidedly bold political machination. At the outset Schaetzel had been "startled" when Ball declared the specific intention to become economic under secretary. "For a guy who came out of the bushes, and nobody was even thinking about him at all, that seemed to be outlandishly ambitious, and shooting very high indeed."[31]

Perhaps not. Even to those most sympathetic with Kennedy's style of dispensing patronage, placing so many high ranking Republicans in the administration seemed "excessive."[32] Defense secretary Robert S. McNamara and Treasury secretary C. Douglas Dillon, both Republicans, had already been named, and expectant Democrats had expressed their dismay with what they considered to be Kennedy's exorbitantly generous treatment of the defeated opposition. Therefore, in a somewhat elaborate circuit, Stevenson was alerted to Foster's appointment and, ever cognizant of his own liabilities with the president-elect, sagely petitioned Arkansas senator J. William Fulbright "to take the matter up with Kennedy."[33] Stevenson's plan worked. Kennedy rescinded Foster's appointment and on January 10, 1961, sent Ball's nomination as under secretary of state for economic affairs to the Senate.[34]

A man of considerable pride and ego, as his December letter to Lippmann attests, Ball had, by that point in his career, developed an almost imperious faith in his own abilities. As events retold above demonstrated, his instinct was to be close to the center of national political action at the highest possible level. Getting close to the center occasionally required a degree of bureaucratic gamesmanship. What might be described as a tendency to crass career opportunism over the years is ill concealed. From the more objective vantage point of semiretirement, he is not the least bit apologetic about a single career ploy. In his New Deal and Lend-Lease work, within the ranks of the Bombing Survey, and, in the winter of 1960, his solicitation of friends who brought him to the attention of a youthful and ambitious president, Ball soundly demonstrated his audacity and toughness as an aggressive and self-starting bureaucratic infighter.

Notwithstanding his own talents for bureaucratic maneuver, it is abundantly clear that Ball's career evolved as it did predominantly because of his affiliation with Adlai Stevenson. Indeed, his public service experience is really a function of his professional relationship and close personal friendship with the Illinois governor. Ball grants this point. "More than anyone else," he concedes, Stevenson was "responsible for [his] six years in the State Department." He also freely admits that they were "the most rewarding years of [his] life."[35] But paradoxically and, from a political perspective, quite wisely, Ball was mindful of the fact that his close affinity with Stevenson had to be carefully understated if his role within the Kennedy administration were to be enhanced.

This would come quite naturally. There was an unmistakable breach between the personal affections and political accord Ball maintained with Stevenson and the degree to which he shared Stevenson's analyses of America's role in world affairs. Their intellectual processes were conspicuously dissimilar as well. Both successful lawyers, Stevenson was generally considered to be indecisive, inattentive, and at times even "comediodic"[36] in the way he worked, while Ball, on the other hand, had established a reputation as a deliberate thinker and a tough-minded advocate possessed of a disciplined and incisive intellect. Ball's posture on the outskirts of the New Frontier in 1960 is testimony to his political savvy as well as his intellectual gifts. When the Kennedy administration was fully airborne and he had assumed a progressively greater degree of responsibility for policy, he never forgot that his voice could quickly lose resonance by too close an association with Ambassador Stevenson.

As Ball sought to enhance his role within the Kennedy and Johnson administrations, he nimbly distanced himself from his former benefactor. It is plausible that he consciously discounted his relationship with Stevenson in order to increase his influence within the executive branch, although he would never openly admit to this sort of crude bureaucratic subterfuge involving his good friend. Just as easily, it may have been that the relationship between once close companions was strained by honest policy disagreements and by the physical and intellectual distance between the decidedly internationalist forum at New York and the decidedly nationalist mentality in Washington. Indeed, during Stevenson's tenure as U.N. ambassador, Schaetzel observes, "there was no real intimacy between the two at all," and he recalls a number of "very substantial policy disagreements between them." It was the prevailing view that there was a "softness about Stevenson's approach" that alienated him from the more aggressive types within and around the Kennedy White House.[37] Further, Adlai Stevenson believed in the United Nations system. Although Ball's ungenerous views of the organization have mellowed appreciably in recent years,[38] in the 1960s, in stark contrast to Stevenson, he thought the United Nations to be irrevocably prejudiced against American interests and serviceable as little more than a debating society. Ball's firsthand observation of Stevenson's tribulations in New York merely confirmed what his staff chief called "his latent contempt for the organization."[39]

After Foster's appointment was unceremoniously rescinded and Ball's nomination was sent by Kennedy to the Senate in January 1961, the single remaining obstacle to his appointment was what became a rather perfunctory confirmation hearing. Close inspection of the transcript in the *Congressional Record*, however, contributes to a greater understanding of Ball's Vietnam dissent and reclarifies the rationale for his selection to the Kennedy team. Appearing before the Senate Foreign Relations Committee on January 24, 1961, Ball was unerringly introduced by Chairman J. William Fulbright as a man with "a great deal of experience in international law matters." In the course of his own preliminary remarks, Ball testified that "during the last fourteen years, the nature of [his] law practice required [him] to spend a considerable part of [his] time abroad, mostly in Europe." When asked by Iowa senator Bourke B. Hickenlooper about the extent of his experience outside Europe, Ball replied that he had "traveled and done business . . . as a private lawyer in almost all the countries of Western Europe," but he conceded that his travels to other parts of the world "were not extensive." In speaking about

Latin America, Ball admitted that he had "a great deal to learn," and within the context of specific remarks about Asia, he reported that he had "very little professional experience."[40]

Quizzed on the particular subject of foreign economic assistance, for which the under secretary for economic affairs has direct managerial responsibility, Ball disclosed a nascent cynicism about foreign aid generally and developmental economics specifically. He told the committee that "the thrust of these programs, *so far as possible*, should be to assist the underdeveloped countries of the world to resist the pressures brought to bear on them [by the Communist world]," adding that the thrust of foreign assistance, "*so far as possible*," should be in the direction of "long term development rather than short term emergency aid [emphasis added]."[41]

Simply stated, and as it became quite obvious to his Senate interrogators, Ball lacked genuine enthusiasm for massive unilateral foreign aid programs (and had even less enthusiasm for their originators), believing that they raised unrealizable expectations of industrial, cultural, and social progress. While at times as an administrator he would by necessity be identified with policies he did not personally endorse, since leaving government he has been a good deal more candid on the subject. A passage from his first book, written after he left public service for the last time in 1968, is particularly disdainful of what he has called "the esoteric cult of academics" who "think they know a lot, but don't know anything." Ball reduces the entire lot of developmental economists within the ranks of Kennedy's New Frontier to "a few high priests, who talked a strange, sacerdotal language" and who were annoyingly predisposed to flamboyant neologisms with a "quaintly Madison Avenue ring" such as "take-off," "the big push," and "the great ascent."[42]

The dissimilarity between the manner and metaphor employed by a nominee before a Senate committee addressing the topic of foreign assistance and the literary license enjoyed by a retired diplomat is inescapably amusing. In composing his memoirs, elder statesman Ball, now impatient with much in life, endeavored and failed to find generous terms with which to describe those bent on leading the Third and Fourth Worlds into the twenty-first century. Derogating the then fashionable political and economic theories, collectively known as "nation building," as "a most presumptuous undertaking," Ball openly questioned whether it was ever realistic to expect that "American professors could make bricks without the straw of experience and with indifferent and infinitely various kinds of clay."[43] As a policy officer in the Kennedy administration, he would leave little doubt as to his fundamental orientation to the developing world or his decidedly qualified eagerness to administer the many foreign assistance programs he oversaw. And his skepticism about developmental economics as a science did not bypass individual practitioners. Sarcastically regretting that he even owns the numerous books by Walt Rostow (who is widely regarded to be an influential force behind the New Frontier's Third World development schemes and a dissonant hawk on Vietnam), Ball was then, and remains, intellectually contemptuous of the clique of nation builders from the Kennedy-Johnson era, and, quite frankly, they of him.[44]

In even more piercing rhetoric from a section of his memoirs most appropriately entitled "Assisting and Resisting the Third World," Ball sardonically deflates Kennedy's developmental academics and, in the process, an integral element in the New Frontier mentality. It was what he called the "theological aspect" of foreign assistance that most distressed him. Brimming with what he terms an "overblown nomenclature," all manner of experts during the Kennedy and Johnson administrations, including economists, sociologists, psychologists, city planners, political scientists, "and experts in chicken diseases," embarked for the distant corners of the globe to construct all manner of "new Jerusalems."[45] With little meaningful impact on the developing nations, Ball has concluded, so many Harvard and MIT economists only succeeded in straining America's primary diplomatic relationships by their constant din of requests from European governments for more aid for America's daring projects in the emerging nations. Rostow, in particular, regularly telephoned him in the State Department urging him to entreat his European friends for more marks, francs, and lire to be spent on projects emanating from his Third World think tank.

Having made well known his more conventional views of foreign assistance, Ball was generally perceived as a somewhat aloof and independent man in the Kennedy administration—"too independent," according to national security adviser McGeorge Bundy.[46] In Galbraith's words, Ball was clearly "not one to accept fashionable intellectual trends or the popular answer."[47] He admits that he never fully harmonized with the intellectual style of the Kennedy clique and has conceded that he "could not avoid feeling somewhat detached from the new team's exuberance and its confidence in the bright new plans and brilliant insights" that swarmed around the room during policy planning meetings.[48] Simply put, as a Stevenson man and as a middle westerner, Ball was an outlander at Camelot.

Augmenting his alienation was, as he somewhat sarcastically acknowledges, the fact that he "had not taught or studied on the Charles River."[49] In contrast to the elite preparatory academies and universities attended by his colleagues, Evanston Township High School and Northwestern University were considered, at least by Ball, to be second-class institutions. He also considers his age to have been a factor in his relationship with most senior bureaucrats and White House staff in the Kennedy administration; he was simply older than his boss and most of his new colleagues, and he had lived through and participated in events they had only read about (or written about) in books. A Europeanist, he was surrounded by younger men who saw Africa and Asia as the first orders of business on America's new global agenda. "The young movers and shakers of the Kennedy Administration," he once wrote, "thought of themselves as pragmatists, well equipped to resolve America's emergent international problems with flair and imagination," and generated a "surfeit of theories regarding the economic development of the Third World." However, as he caustically adds, "they had fewer settled views on the structure of relations among the Western industrialized democracies," which he believed then and continues to believe today were the principal building blocks of a successful American foreign policy.[50]

Ball's candid observations shed light on the larger dichotomy of the Kennedy State Department and, indeed, the composition of the foreign policy Establishment during the 1960s. Two contending schools of thought competed for control of the American foreign policy agenda. One may be termed the Dean Acheson–John McCloy–Ball group,[51] whose members, to varying degrees, shared a Eurocentrist conception of American foreign policy. Acheson and McCloy accepted and even encouraged the mentality of the Cold War as a reliable strategic paradigm as well as a useful political instrument. Indeed, as biographer Gaddis Smith wrote, "the Soviet menace made it easier for Acheson to persuade Congress and people to do the things *he* deemed necessary for security [emphasis in original]."[52] These individuals tended to view the Cold War exclusively in terms of power realities; the correlation of political, economic, and military forces in Europe loomed as the controlling problems in American foreign policy. At the Acheson end of the spectrum they were the tough-minded adherents to the National Security Council white paper (NSC-68) which in 1950 had made sweeping assumptions about Soviet behavior and capabilities and called for greater institutionalized strategic and political efforts to meet the Communist challenge.

The Eurocentric hard-liners were opposed by what may be called the Averell Harriman–Chester Bowles–Stevenson school.[53] This group gravitated toward diplomatic rather than military initiatives and, in viewing the Cold War more in terms of its Third World arena, emphasized the importance of the emerging postcolonial nation states of Africa and Asia in the advancement of global free enterprise. They saw the Cold War more as an ideological contest;

the goal of winning the allegiances of the developing nations governed their responses to international relations. Stevenson particularly, caught up as he was in what was then fashionably termed the "revolution of rising expectations,"[54] endorsed, far more passionately than Ball, proposals for the economic, technological, and even cultural development of the emerging nations.

As a general proposition, the administration inaugurated in January 1961 drew its basic assumptions about the world generally, and the Soviet-American confrontation particularly, from the former group—but to a very considerable degree was intellectually stimulated by the latter group. This duality has been insightfully illustrated by Schlesinger, who reminds us that while Kennedy was, in terms of training, experience, and instinct, an Atlanticist, he also became the first American president to exhibit an active interest in the Third World. JFK counted African and Asian heads of state among his close personal friends and was himself periodically preoccupied with the sweeping theories of the developmental economists he brought to Washington from the academic climes of Massachusetts.[55]

Understanding this dichotomy of personnel within the administration is critical to understanding the American experience in Vietnam. Admittedly, it is impossible to precisely define the ideological formulation or identify the ranks of either camp. Convenient labels such as "Europeanist," "Third Worlder," "hawk," or "dove" quickly loose their descriptive power when employed to describe the policy recommendations an individual might make on more than a few issues. But it is also true that the manner in which the bureaucracies were initially activated on Vietnam—and which camp prevailed when the initial decisions were framed—proved to have profound implications. A tone was set and courses of action were predetermined as a function of specifically who was in charge of specifically what problem. Kennedy listened intently to advice he received on Vietnam from old Establishment hard-liners outside the administration such as Acheson and McCloy. Inside the government he gravitated toward the rather doctrinal antiappeasement mentality to which McNamara, Rusk, and Rostow were inured.

Thomas L. Hughes, former director of the State Department Bureau of Intelligence and Research, recalls with great perspicacity that "there was an implied trade-off within the Kennedy administration on Southeast Asia, as there was on almost everything else." With considerable firsthand knowledge of the alignment of ideological forces within the Kennedy State Department, Hughes describes the conflict between the two rival camps vis-à-vis Vietnam—and its telling political and bureaucratic resolution: "This trade-off was, crudely translated, to give Laos to the doves and Vietnam to the hawks." As a

Southeast Asian strategy developed within the administration, Harriman "was instructed to pursue a peace policy in Laos," and, in order to strike a political balance between the two camps, "the more forceful types [meaning in this case Walt Rostow] were encouraged to concentrate on Vietnam."[56]

In order to evaluate Ball's impact on the administration's emerging Vietnam policy between 1961 and 1963, it is essential to determine his relationship to the center of gravity and bureaucratic power within the administration, to identify upon what side of the fence he sat at the earliest stages of the conflict, and to recognize how clear his view of the field and the actors on the other side actually was. As the record shows, Ball kept relatively quiet about Southeast Asia during the Kennedy presidency. Unless one specialized in East Asian affairs, one would not have had cause for too great an involvement in 1961 or 1962. But to assert that his opposition to military involvement in Vietnam was less pronounced under Kennedy than it would become under Johnson simply because Vietnam was less critical an issue until after 1963 is insufficient. Students of the war have, to date, uncritically accepted the glib assertion that Vietnam was a "back burner" issue before the Gulf of Tonkin incident in August 1964.

An examination of the National Security File from 1961 to 1963 clearly shows that the State Department bureaucracy—which, as under secretary, Ball oversaw—was quite active on the problem, and the extensive papers produced by various agencies within the department anticipate the struggle that lay ahead with great discernment. Vietnam did not lack urgency or clarity on Kennedy's watch. While it is true that Kennedy did not accede to the specific magnitude and type of buildup called for by General Maxwell D. Taylor and Walt Rostow in October 1961, the deployment of 16,000 "advisory troops" and expenditure of a half-million dollars a day by the end of 1962 indicate a deepening commitment to the Saigon regime. Though in time Vietnam obviously became a qualitatively different and more compelling foreign policy challenge, examination of the record and an assessment of the sheer volume of studies and reports that were prepared belie the "back burner" hypothesis as applied to the Kennedy administration.[57] By 1963 the contours of an expansive American commitment had clearly evolved under Kennedy, but Ball was noticeably less disposed to voice a sustained opposition than he would become under Johnson.

Indeed, the under secretary's relative silence on Vietnam must have appeared to be quite odd. Eschewing the development theory and nation-building bandwagons and never persuaded that Indochina possessed any substantive strategic, economic, or political importance to American interests, Ball perceived Vietnam from the start primarily as a political nuisance and a diversion of diplomatic energies from the development of the Atlantic Partnership. As has been noted, the antecedents of his Vietnam dissent are found in his regional identification, education, experience in international law, and government service before 1961. He was well placed to offer the countervailing argument against a deepening involvement and was inured with the strategic rationale suggesting why the United States should forgo open-ended commitments to areas of the world with only marginal strategic significance.

Why did he keep quiet? Investigation of the political tides at Camelot shows that Ball's reticence during the period 1961 to 1963 stems first from his qualified relationship with Kennedy. As economic under secretary he had been a principal actor in a bureaucratic realignment initiated by the president which would significantly condition his dissent. Near the end of his first year as president, frustration with foreign policy setbacks in Cuba, Vienna, Berlin, and Laos prompted Kennedy to reorganize the State Department. What JFK considered to be indecision, inertia, and lack of management at Foggy Bottom led to, among other things, the "sacrifice"[58] of Under Secretary of State Chester Bowles and Ball's elevation to the number two position in the State Department.

Former Connecticut governor Bowles had from the beginning been a thoroughly political appointment. With Stevenson "playing Hamlet"[59] in trying for a third consecutive nomination in 1960, Kennedy could not count on his unconditional support and was compelled to look elsewhere for liberal endorsements within the Democratic party. Almost by political necessity, Kennedy was forced to court the favor of "the liberal icon"[60] Bowles to bolster his left flank. The liberal wing of the party, the "New Republic Democrats,"[61] were in fact openly dubious about Kennedy. He was thought to be too pragmatic, to have "made too many accommodations in deference to the Cold War climate," and to be unwilling to "risk political defeat on behalf of a great moral issue."[62] To counter such perceptions, and unable to enlist the unconditional support of the leader of the liberal wing of the party throughout the 1950s, Kennedy embraced Bowles.

Both liberal New Englanders, the Massachusetts senator and Connecticut governor did share a genuine mutual respect and even sincere affection. There was an affinity, though decidedly not in their approach to specific problems, which sprang from their sensitivities as politicians and complementary interests in international relations. Both Kennedy and Bowles were aroused by the plight of the developing nations and held an expansive view of American obligations to them. And Bowles was politically useful to Kennedy; it was a generally held view that he had "unusual gifts for public persuasion" and "personal idealism," was identified with "affirmative impulses of American foreign policy," and had "a strong following in the liberal community."[63]

But Bowles's considerable assets were compromised by significant liabilities. The Kennedy team "put a premium on quick, tough, decided people" and was "easily exasperated by more meditative types,"[64] whom Bowles epitomized. Even Ball, who admired and liked Chet Bowles and even maintained a warm relationship with him after he unceremoniously left government, remembers him as a "generalist," "contemplative," an "idealist," and "voluble." He found that Bowles "favored the romantic clichés to which Stevenson was addicted" and too "frivolously discounted the Soviet Threat."[65] There existed "a fatal difference in tempo between Bowles and the New Frontier."[66] Bowles himself clearly recognized the chasm. "I think the President shared my views on Asia, Africa and Latin America, the importance of the areas and the need for dealing with them sensitively," he once told a Kennedy confidant. But he added that by the end of what was a frustrating first year, Kennedy succumbed to a kind of "crisis philosophy" and noted that the administration was merely "responding to crises, rather than, as [Bowles] was desperately trying to do, foreseeing some of the situations and attempting to forestall them before they became crises."[67]

Blackest in the pantheon of Bowles's sins, however, were, first, his open disagreement with Kennedy on the type of assistance contemplated for the Diem regime in Vietnam and, second, his verbose public announcement of his opposition to the Bay of Pigs invasion. Inasmuch as the Kennedys were notorious for demanding "Irish-style loyalty"[68] within the bureaucratic ranks, his dissents were considered to be unpardonable offenses. With public disclosure of his opposition to the failed Cuban incursion, Robert Kennedy, in a crude effort to minimize breakage by insisting that Bowles publicly recant, "jammed his fingers into Bowles's stomach" and said "look, you son-of-a-bitch, you were *for* the invasion [emphasis in original]."[69] But it was, of course, too late. Despite his usefulness to the administration, he had committed too grievous a transgression and was "re-assigned" as "roving Ambassador,"[70] a sort of diplomatic purgatory. Bowles, who had written the Democratic party platform on which the president was elected and who had "delivered Connecticut to Kennedy,"[71] was rudely castigated by the president's brother and, "partly owing to the machinations of [National Security Adviser] McGeorge Bundy, ignominiously dismissed."[72]

From his vantage point at the margin of power as economic under secretary, Ball had learned a Kennedy-style bureaucratic lesson: contemplative and disagreeable under secretaries were not to be patiently suffered and were certainly expendable. This episode clearly changed the character and mood of the Kennedy State Department and reasserted the president's preeminence in the conduct of foreign policy. A new climate of single-mindedness was established which gave rise to an important question: How freely could a single bureaucrat maneuver in Kennedy's foreign policy machinery? The Bay of Pigs fiasco was both a strategic and political lesson to the New Frontiersmen. From November 1961 to the tragic end in November 1963, the advisory process at Camelot was suddenly less open than many imagined it would be. As an illustration, Ball himself admits that, because of his unfamiliarity with the president, had he been privy to the secret planning of the Bay of Pigs affair, he might not have expressed his opposition to the implausible operation.[73]

As insurance against a repeat of the embarrassing Bowles affair, Kennedy would get people more loyal to *himself* than to ideals or the department. "Ball could be depended on. He is loyal to *you*," Schlesinger wrote Kennedy in 1961; "he believes in your policies [emphasis in original]." By the end of 1961, Schlesinger thought that too many Republicans, and indeed conservatives of either party, had found prominent places within the administration. "It would be a great error," he told Kennedy, "to replace Bowles with someone who is neutral or Republican in his political orientation. We cannot afford a conservative New York lawyer, however competent, in this spot, unless we want to end up with an intelligent updating of Eisenhowerism. Ball is imaginative, practical, and able."[74]

Even well before Bowles's departure, it was generally understood that Ball, who as economic under secretary had technically ranked third in the State Department hierarchy, had "risen gradually to become the [de facto] No. 2 policy maker in day-to-day political operations." Very early in the administration Ball "moved significantly into day-by-day political affairs," where Bowles was "never especially active." There was, in the first months of the Kennedy presidency, a "general understanding at the assistant secretary level that the rest of the department is to check all immediate political matters either with Mr. Ball or Secretary Rusk."[75] Ball's elevation to under secretary officially confirmed that which had been, for the past year, implied. However, in terms of the practical administration of the State Department, it is not clear that Ball was an improvement upon Bowles. "Under George Ball," as Bowles protégé James C. Thomson complained early in 1962, "the under secretary has been less of an 'administrator' in the housekeeping sense, showing no interest whatsoever in this side of the job."[76]

Ball has also been roundly criticized for the manner in which he managed his personal office staff. A characteristic fickleness was commonly cited as a "constant problem" by those closest to him. Likened to a "woman chaser" who became easily infatuated, then just as quickly disenchanted, with people he brought in, he was quick to add personnel and slow to rid the department of dead weight, usually leaving the messy chore of firing to his staff chiefs. Among Schaetzel's most prominent recollections of work on the seventh floor was that "he would get people he'd like and then fire them because they weren't as good as he thought they were." The under secretary's special assistants were particularly frustrated by his tendency to measure people's talents, dedication, and energies against his own. Many of those Ball hired, Schaetzel has remarked, "weren't as good as he was, and of course there [were] very few people as good as he was." George S. Springsteen, Schaetzel's successor as Ball's staff chief, also considers the problem of personnel as among the most frustrating factors in working for the under secretary. Both of his top assistants found his softheartedness "really curious in a way, because of [the] macho image that [he] likes to present." Springsteen recalls that "when it [came] to getting rid of someone, he [Ball] really didn't have the guts to do it."[77]

Like Bowles, Ball was not inclined to busy himself with the more monotonous aspects of the daily routine. He much preferred to look after Europe, advance causes in which he had a studied interest, and write. An oft-repeated anecdote among those who affectionately regret "the misfortune of working for him"[78] was that Ball's passion for the graceful expression of the written and spoken word greatly complicated life in the outer office of the under secretary of state. Nurtured by his undergraduate training in literature and English at Northwestern, Ball maintained high personal standards of precision, clarity, and grace in both his written and oral communication. As one of the last of a vanishing breed of senior bureaucrats to write his own speeches, Ball penned elegant, even "brilliant prose,"[79] often laced with subtle and sometimes biting humor. To many of his colleagues, Ball epitomized the literate, cosmopolitan, Establishment paragon.[80] Moreover, he was evangelical about it, constantly insisting upon better writing from the bureaucracy. Only half-jokingly, State Department legal affairs adviser Abram Chayes counts being instructed in the "which/that rule" as a curiously memorable episode in his long and close association with Ball.[81] Too often to the exclusion of important diplomatic and administrative business, the under secretary would incessantly revise his speeches, memorandums, and occasional opinion-page articles for the *New York Times* or *Washington Post*. Admitting that "it got exasperating at times,"[82] Springsteen, who for the past twenty-seven years has exhibited what Ball himself has characterized as "Kamikaze-like personal loyalty,"[83] roundly criticized his boss for his imprudent preoccupation with style.

Otherwise admiring, Springsteen faults Ball for his compulsions with rhetorical technique and for his "sense of perfectionism," which he maintains was of "marginal" importance to the operation of the department and "not worth the time and the effort for the results that were produced."[84] Somewhat less generously, but also from a context equally admiring of Ball's political talents and intellectual gifts, Schaetzel asserts that the under secretary's proclivities as a wordsmith seriously detracted from his performance as an administrator. Particularly with regard to the delegation of authority, Schaetzel sees a significant foible in Ball as a bureaucratic manager, noting that he did not take the time to cultivate confidence in his subordinates and was loath to delegate tasks. "It had to be his own piece of work," Schaetzel adds, "whether it was a speech or an article or what. He'd work his tail off on those things. Frequently, because he was giving some speech, he would cancel all appointments, upsetting the whole routine. He had his priorities wrong."[85]

In addition to disclosing fundamental lessons about bureaucratic loyalty, Bowles's departure also signaled an ideological watershed in the Kennedy presidency. Replacing Bowles was problematic from the standpoint of the larger struggle between the State Department's liberal and conservative camps. Because Ball was essentially inoffensive to either group, his elevation was hailed as a pragmatic compromise, both by Department of State and White House insiders.[86] Because he was solid on Europe, enthusiastically supported NATO, and (then) embraced fairly conventional Cold War positions concerning the correlation of forces between the superpowers, he was acceptable to hard-liners. At the same time, however, Ball was known not to be overly exercised about "the Communist menace" and, since he was closely identified with Stevenson, had solid liberal credentials. He was also considered to be courageous: in 1951, at considerable risk to his political career, he had appeared before the Senate Subcommittee on Internal Security as a *pro bono* counsel to former vice-president Henry Wallace.[87] Unlike so many of his contemporaries, Ball was "optimistic on Red Countries," and held what was then an advanced position that there was "a discernable movement" toward normalized relations between East and West. He shared the liberal assumption that the Soviets could be dealt with and that the Socialist bloc could not indefinitely "maintain a hermetically sealed society."[88]

Although he was ultimately checked by a president active in foreign affairs, an able secretary of state for whom he had unqualified respect, and exceedingly influential defense and national security chiefs, Ball enjoyed considerable license in the development of European policy and economic initiatives. Rusk preserved as his own policy domain the particular European problem of Berlin and the whole of Asia. This was an inherently logical, if, as it turned out, unfortunate, division of labor. To the same extent that Ball was Eurocentrist, Rusk was Asia-centrist. A veteran of the China-Burma-India theater in World War II and assistant secretary for Far Eastern affairs during the Korean conflict, Rusk was well equipped to take a leading role in developing initiatives for America's new and growing presence in the Far East.

And Rusk was not a self-deluded man. He seems to have clearly understood the ideological and political forces working in the undercurrents of the Kennedy administration. Throughout his eight years as secretary of state he was painfully aware of the intrigues engineered against him by Bobby Kennedy and the White House staff. Rusk once openly declared: "I knew there were a dozen people who wanted my job."[89] In the tradition of his mentor, George C. Marshall, he was passionately dedicated to the service of his country and his president. He had neither the time nor the energy for political self-aggrandizement and very little patience for bureaucratic infighting. If uneasy at the White House, the secretary was eminently confident in his relations with Congress, and his unpretentious and earthy style helped him maintain warm relations on the Hill. Because Rusk enjoyed a credible political base—and was widely regarded as a potential national political candidate from Georgia—he spoke with a larger voice than he might otherwise have.[90] The secretary's intelligence, reserve, and humility made him, until Vietnam snarled him in its net at any rate, a popular witness at hearings.

Despite Rusk's initially solid relations with Congress, no love was lost between the Kennedy State Department and the House of Representatives, and if Ball was not part of the problem, he was certainly not part of the solution either. On more than one occasion the under secretary's ardor for the global Open Door excited suspicions among the more parochial congressmen whose main business was to protect regional economic interests, which frequently meant textiles. In one especially notable episode that would have delighted Adam Smith, Ball's classical economic liberalism produced a state of open war between himself and Congress. Early in 1961, having boldly declared to a congressional trade committee that the American economy was "in transition" and that certain manufacturing interests would inevitably give way to world competition, he found that he had provoked the powerful textile lobby into action when he explicitly denounced tariffs and quotas on imported clothing. Wasting little time, the Amalgamated Clothing Workers of America, joined by a cohesive gaggle of outraged New England legislators, roundly attacked the under secretary. Mail poured into the White House and newspapers carried accounts of the Hill's disaffection with Ball's brand of economic international-ism. In the wake of his testimony, Kennedy's special counsel Meyer Feldman was dispatched to disclaim the under secretary's intransigence against any and all barriers to foreign imports.[91]

Ball never personally endeared himself to Congress the way Rusk could. He deplored the trite political clichés and demagogic politics that were some-times necessary in persuading legislators who were only marginally interested in, or informed about, matters dear to him. In his personal manner he could be stiffly pretentious, and he was just as apt to deliver "instructional" as "infor-mational" testimony to inquirers. He was generally less patient with the pro-cess of congressional appearances than Rusk, and as one scholar of European-American relations, Alfred Grosser, has noted, his loyalties were widely considered to be divided. "On Capitol Hill," Grosser writes, "Ball's foreign ties were not forgotten." In one extraordinary encounter with the legislative branch when he was advancing a transparently European perspective on trade, an impatient senator caustically reminded him "that he was in the pay, not of M. Monnet, but of the United States."[92] Perhaps too much the urbane "One Worlder" for congressmen with primarily regional identifications and nar-rowly focused constituencies, he was widely considered to be too cosmopoli-tan and too complex. Although he maintained excellent personal relations with a few key members such as Fulbright, those not more than casually acquainted with him, as we will see below, chided his vision of an interdependent world economy.

Throughout his government tenure, Ball was primarily interested in build-ing the requisite political instruments for a new world trading structure. It is really quite ironic that, among the general public, his reputation sprang mostly from his position on the war in Southeast Asia. Vietnam was, for him, a painful annoyance. Somewhat capriciously believing that there were "much more interesting and important matters" to which his energies should be devoted, he has estimated that Asian issues consumed less than 5 percent of his working time during the Kennedy administration. Close examination of his appointment books in the period from 1961 to 1963 suggests that even this is a generous estimate.[93] Although Indochina did not then generate an atmosphere of military and political crisis in the government in the way it did after the Tonkin Gulf incident in August 1964, he nevertheless paid close attention to the manner in which the president and the bureaucracy were engaged on Southeast Asia and closely monitored who was saying what to whom about Vietnam. If he was not initially in the forefront of policy development, "Ball became," as Thomas Hughes confirms, "a consumer of INR [State Department Bureau of Intelligence and Research] briefings," particularly after the seminal Taylor-Rostow "fact finding" mission in the fall of 1961.[94]

Quite frankly, Ball was suspicious of the new president's foreign policy conceptions. (He admits that there was a history to his mistrust of the family stemming from a quite different issue and era, as he had utterly deplored the economic isolationism to which Joseph P. Kennedy had given ultimate expression by undercutting FDR's fight for Lend-Lease legislation.) He feared that JFK would be too willing to make a test case out of resisting communism on what he thought was the untenable physical and political terrain of Southeast Asia. In his first two years as president, Kennedy did very little to allay his fears. Inspired by his own visit to Indochina a decade earlier, in the fall of 1961 Kennedy commissioned Walt W. Rostow, then head of the State Department Policy Planning Bureau, and his top military adviser, General Maxwell D. Taylor, to calibrate the pulse of Vietnamese nationalism and speculate about how the United States might succeed where the French had failed in checking the territorial and political expansion of North Vietnamese communism. After a fact-finding and advisory mission, Taylor and Rostow reported a "deep and pervasive crisis of confidence and a serious loss of national morale" due to the intensification of Vietcong military and political activity. They recommended "the dispatch of an 8,000-man logistic task force comprised of engineers, medical groups *and the infantry to support them* [emphasis added]." Their report emphasized that these were "minimal steps" and that more may be required later.[95]

The precise composition of the Taylor-Rostow mission certainly compounded the great difficulty that Ball, or any potential dissenter within the State Department, might have had in rebutting the report from inside the diplomatic corps. The fact that Taylor was a general, according to Schlesinger, "expressed a conscious decision by the Secretary of State to turn the Vietnam problem over to the Secretary of Defense." And, in 1962, the absence of a high-ranking State Department officer engaged full-time on the Vietnam problem by default illustrated Rusk's belief that military problems in Vietnam were more pressing than the political or diplomatic concerns. "Kennedy acquiesced," Schlesinger notes, "because he had more confidence in McNamara and Taylor than in State." Following directly from the manner in which the bureaucracies were initially engaged, Vietnam became "primarily a military rather than political problem."[96]

Immediately after the Taylor-Rostow report was delivered to the president, Ball became openly, if only temporarily, exercised about Vietnam. "In due course," Hughes remembers, "there were private meetings at his [Ball's] home and office."[97] The stream of intelligence reports he now digested from INR and his contacts at the Central Intelligence Agency (CIA) merely confirmed a view of Indochina which he had synthesized prior to the fall of 1961: Vietnam was a trap. Ball had long been impressed with the virtuoso performance of Pierre Mendès-France, who had liquidated France's involvement in Indochina within ninety days after his election as prime minister in 1954. Ball never believed that Americans would fare better than the French and regularly referred to the wisdom Mendès-France had displayed in "cutting French losses."[98] He privately hoped that Kennedy would heed the painful French lesson.

On November 4, 1961, Ball met with Taylor and Rostow to review the findings they gathered from their mission.[99] In that fateful meeting he laid out what would become familiar themes: "The Viet Cong were mean and tough, as the French learned to their sorrow . . . there was the danger of Chinese intervention as we learned in Korea . . . [and the United States would be] mixing [herself] up in a revolutionary situation with strong anti-colonialist overtones."[100] But he was hemmed in. The president's senior staff was, at that time, not asking *whether* to commit American resources to South Vietnam but *how* the United States could deny the Communists a victory in Indochina. Three immovable obstacles blocked Ball's remonstrations and, as he was ever mindful of the Bowles affair, qualified his dissent: their names were McNamara, Rusk, and Kennedy.

Defense secretary Robert S. McNamara, the panjandrum of Kennedy's cabinet, believed in 1961 that with the proper application of an overwhelming force the United States could ultimately produce an important victory for the Free World forces in Vietnam. To him the problem was operational: the principal variables were how to best organize resources and to develop a strategy which would deny the Communists the country—or, as it was euphemistically stated, "to arrange for the capitulation of the North Vietnamese."[101] Of innumerable McNamara memorandums on Vietnam in the early stages of U.S. involvement, one illuminates his operational and statistical orientation to the Vietnamese crisis particularly well: "It seems, on the face of it," the secretary of defense told the president on November 11, 1961, "absurd to think that a nation of 20 million people can be subverted by 15-20 thousand active guerrillas if the government and the people of that country do not wish to be subverted." McNamara then linked American credibility to the arms equation by stating that "the United States should commit itself to the clear objective of preventing the fall of South Vietnam to communism." Moreover, as the same document demonstrates, McNamara was committed to Saigon's defense, even if it was necessary to fight alone. As he put it to Kennedy, the introduction of American forces "should not be contingent upon unanimous SEATO agreement thereto."[102]

Two months later the secretary of state, on track with the essential thrust of the defense chief's analysis, wrote a similar memorandum stating that the "United States regards the Communist attempt to conquer South Viet-Nam as a threat to our own security" and that America should be "heavily committed to the defense of South Viet-Nam." Rusk took very seriously the potential injury to American credibility in Asia that the "loss" of Vietnam would represent. Worse, according to Rusk, failure to uphold what he emphatically considered to be America's South East Asia Treaty Organization (SEATO) obligations would tear at the fiber of American credibility around the world. Arguing that Asians "on the fence" would construe a Communist takeover of South Viet- nam as "the wave of the future," he echoed McNamara's frank recommenda- tion to deploy U.S. forces should they become necessary. In a comprehensive strategic evaluation, the secretary of state emphasized that conquest of South Vietnam's rice surplus (350,000 metric tons) would solve the pressing food problem of the Democratic Republic of Vietnam (DRV) and that with this barrier to industrial expansion removed, North Vietnam could become one of the "most formidable members of the Bloc." Finally, Rusk maintained that the fall of South Vietnam would grant the Communists a vital strategic base and "seriously increase the difficulty of defending the rest of South East Asia."[103] With this terse exposition of his views, he essentially "signed-on" to the Taylor-Rostow finding.

John F. Kennedy had long been interested in Indochina. In June 1956 he had invoked what became representative (if now much maligned) symbols which illustrate the depth of his interest in, and commitment to, the region: Vietnam, he declared, was the "cornerstone of the Free World," "the keystone of the arch," and "the finger in the dike." Extending this string of mixed and excited metaphors before the American Friends of Vietnam, Kennedy alleged that "Vietnam represents a proving ground for democracy—a test of American responsibility and determination in Asia." Kennedy's manifest paternalism— an ingredient of U.S. diplomacy that would be deeply resented by Ngo Dinh Diem and his successors—was transparent. "If we are not the parents of Vietnam," he added, "then surely we are the godparents. We presided at its birth, we gave assistance to its life, we have helped to shape its future. . . . This is our offspring—we cannot abandon it, we cannot ignore its needs." When Kennedy became president he, like McNamara and Rusk, also considered American credibility to be at risk. "If it [South Vietnam] falls," he concluded, "the United States, with some justification, will be held responsible; and our prestige in Asia will sink to a new low."[104] Although as the junior Massachusetts senator Kennedy may have irresponsibly exaggerated the importance of Vietnam to real American security interests, as commander-in-chief of the United States armed services he was determined to contain the advance of what he called "the red tide of communism"[105] in Asia as part of a grand Cold War strategy to which he was passionately pledged.

Toward that end, President Kennedy sought to distance himself from his predecessor in foreign affairs. Boldly declaring in his inaugural address that "the torch has been passed to a new generation,"[106] he set about to reassert America's ideological leadership under the containment doctrine by endorsing initiatives across a broad front to bolster America's Free World leadership. The young chief executive was notably less reluctant than Eisenhower to take risks and to provide the means by which developing countries "on the fence" could modernize and democratize in America's image. Kennedy rejected the Eisenhower-Dulles strategic doctrine of massive retaliation, which he believed utterly lacked credibility, and embraced the more subtle strategy of "flexible response"[107] to meet the Communist challenge in the increasingly volatile Third World arena. The new president ambitiously proposed to "deter all wars, general or limited, nuclear or conventional, large or small."[108] Part of the strategy was psychological: America must demonstrate the will to take up arms in a nuclear age. As a "small war," Vietnam came to be considered a test case for what was then popularly known as "limited war strategy."[109] Brought to Kennedy's attention through General Taylor's 1960 publication, *The Uncertain Trumpet*,[110] the "limited war" concept provided the United States "a chance to make demonstrations of its will to use force in the world"; it offered America the opportunity "to demonstrate its credibility."[111] By the time of Kennedy's inauguration Taylor, Harvard political scientist Henry Kissinger, and others had independently developed the political and operational codes for fighting limited wars in a nuclear age. The United States would respond in kind to Soviet general secretary Nikita Khrushchev's pledge to support "wars of national liberation."

As *New York Magazine* reporter Jonathan Schell observed, "rarely has such a large body of military theory been developed in advance of an outbreak of hostilities." Vietnam, then, was seen as a laboratory experiment, a "theorists' war par excellence." It was ironic that the theorists were "only slightly interested" in where the war might occur.[112] Kennedy, having inherited messy Cold War crises in Laos and Cuba, would get out in front and stay ahead of the

Vietnam problem. He became one of the limited war theory's most passionate devotees, focused the energies of his administration on restoring American credibility in Vietnam, and gathered around him those who would provide the operational plan. Though the president was sobered by Taylor and Rostow's findings in the fall of 1961, his foreign policy vision, laced as it was with "a touch of machismo,"[113] complemented the views of McNamara and Rusk: the United States must accept the Free World challenge in Southeast Asia.

On November 7, 1961, at 4:30 P.M., Ball went to the White House for an "off the record" meeting.[114] The principal object of the small gathering was for the under secretary to introduce the president to Clarence Randall, a diplomat who was then about to be sent on a mission to the Congo. After a twenty-five minute interview, Ball excused Randall, telling him that there was something about which he needed to speak privately with Kennedy. In the brief exchange that followed, he told the president that he believed the Taylor-Rostow plan would produce "the most tragic consequences." He asserted that the Vietnamese topography was "totally unsuitable for the commitment of American forces" and argued that from the standpoint of American credibility "it was very dangerous" for the United States to become too deeply committed.[115] Speaking with specific reference to the Taylor-Rostow recommendations, Ball added prophetically: "If we go down that road we might have, within five years, 300,000 men in the rice paddies of the jungles of Viet-Nam and never be able to find them." He surmised that "it would have been one thing if we were just maintaining 600 observers," which had been agreed at the Geneva Conference in 1954, but considered the Taylor-Rostow report "an open ended commitment of people" and told the president that he thought their proposals were "absurd." In the fall of 1961, to employ Ball's metaphor, "the balloon was going up." The president "had better be damned careful."[116]

Kennedy was unmoved. In fact, after the under secretary had expressed his misgivings, the president shot back: "George, you're just crazier than Hell." Ball was taken aback. This was not the opening he hoped for. Kennedy continued the brief but pointed diatribe: "I always thought you were the one of the brightest guys in town, but you're crazy. That just isn't going to happen."[117] Not a little surprised by his response, Ball recalls thinking that he had "rather annoyed the President."[118] Formerly, his relationship with Kennedy had been, from his viewpoint at any rate, quite solid. They had never had a strained or disagreeable encounter. The November 7 exchange, Ball admitted later, was the "only time Kennedy was a little acerbic with [him]."[119] It was patently clear that Kennedy neither agreed with his analysis nor encouraged him to expound upon his thesis. Recognizing this fact and wishing to preserve a good working relationship now strained by a stern rebuff, he did not pursue the matter.[120]

During the Kennedy administration Ball would meet with the president ninety-four times in scheduled, "on the record" appointments, twenty-five of which were on the subject of Vietnam.[121] Additionally, as evidenced by the logged summaries of his incoming and outgoing calls transcribed by his secretaries (TELCONS), he had substantive telephone conversations with Kennedy on the subject of Vietnam at least a dozen times.[122] On none of these occasions did he seize upon the opportunity to advance his central thesis a second time with the president. Nor did he write a single memorandum to Kennedy on Vietnam. "I talked with him the one time [the November 7 meeting]," Ball confesses, "and got no expression of sympathy" and "no encouragement." He never bothered to give Kennedy a sustained exposition of his views regarding Southeast Asia.[123] In a noticeably defensive tone, he claims he had "a thousand things to do which were far more interesting to [him], and decided the Hell with it."[124] Though a serious student of INR reports that, by 1962, had dispelled any optimism about the likelihood of America prevailing in Vietnam, he kept curiously quiet. "As the crisis in South Vietnam grew," however, Hughes notes that Ball "became a focal point in the State Department for those who, like him, had doubts."[125] But he did not reassert his advocacy with the president, or any senior member of the White House staff, during the Kennedy administration. Reconstructing the mind-set of the fall of 1961, Ball flatly stated: "If he [Kennedy] didn't want to hear my views, I wasn't going to press him on it. He showed no inclination to want to examine the issue or pursue it—at least with me."[126]

Though after the November encounter Ball's growing pessimism was withheld from Kennedy, their many exchanges about Vietnam are nonetheless instructive. Despite the fact that the under secretary loyally resigned himself to servicing the president's policy of economic, political, and military assistance to South Vietnam, the subtle imprint of his concern is seen in the way he steered conversations with Kennedy. Equally importantly, clues can be gleaned from the examination of the Ball-Kennedy correspondence as to how the president might have proceeded had his administration not been tragically truncated. It is at best a paradoxical record. At times presidential advisers, including Ball himself, simply deferred to Kennedy's impatience with suggested departures from the declared commitment to South Vietnam. This can be noted in any number of transcribed conversations. For example, on September 23, 1963, Ball took a call from State Department intelligence analyst Roger Hilsman concerning South Vietnam's deteriorating political condition.

In the course of their conversation the under secretary remarked that he "wouldn't think that the president would want any indication that we [Hilsman and Ball] have any grave doubts about the situation." Hilsman concurred.[127] Although both men had serious reservations with the adventure in "nation building" as it was then unfolding and in time became open opponents of further military involvement, they decided not to express their collective misgivings to Kennedy.

At other times, however, Ball and others actively participated in Kennedy's frustrated search for alternatives to military intervention. Four TELCONS stand out as important benchmarks in the discussions between the under secretary of state and the president after November 7, 1961. They are for the most part concerned with South Vietnam's internal political problems. As is well chronicled, South Vietnamese president Ngo Dinh Diem's persecution of Buddhist political dissenters, his flagrant nepotism, and the rampant political corruption in his regime were central factors in bringing Vietnam to the foreground of American foreign policy during the summer of 1963. Diem, though once hailed by Vice-President Johnson as the "George Washington of South East Asia,"[128] was by then widely considered a positive menace to the American effort to restore political stability and security to South Vietnam. When the North Vietnamese demonstrated their ability to capitalize on his ineptitude and continually foment insurgency in the South, Diem adopted a siege mentality. Repression was the order of the day; political demonstrations were brutally crushed. The corruption and rigidity of his brother, Ngo Diem Nhu, the confrontational demeanor of his sister-in-law, Madame Nhu ("The Dragon Lady"), and Diem's own intransigent refusal to rid his government of them despite repeated American insistence rendered political stability in South Vietnam impossible.

The first significant Kennedy-Ball conversation after November 7 occurred on the morning of January 28, 1962, and was followed by two additional talks during the course of the day.[129] On this occasion Ball earnestly advised the president to study Hilsman's recently submitted "Saigon Report." As a practice, Ball inconspicuously fed Kennedy intelligence from a range of sources which tended to corroborate his own views, and in Hilsman he found an ally who was working hard to develop intelligence data to support a policy of diminished involvement. In that winter Hilsman had become convinced that North Vietnam's aggression was less a function of world communism than of Vietnamese nationalism and called for a much greater political effort on the ground in South Vietnam. Ho Chi Minh and the North Vietnamese Communist party, Hilsman and Ball had earlier concluded, had become converts to communism more from Lenin's anticolonialism and less from Marx's scientific treatises on political economy. South Vietnam's nationalist movement and revolution were, in other words, endogenous phenomena. A massive influx of American personnel or aid would do little to alleviate the colonialist overtones of the assistance policy. Ball was quick to realize that whatever Vietnamese leader the Americans might install and buttress with aid, credits, and bayonets would be stigmatized as an American puppet and become a ripe target for Communist propaganda. Speaking for a group of cautious critics of the president's policy that included Hilsman, Far East secretary Averell Harriman, and White House aide Michael Forrestal, Ball indicated to Kennedy that all of them were allied in their concern about the implications of the Taylor-Rostow report and pessimistic about the political viability of the Diem regime. Though he made no specific recommendation for a change in policy, by confederating with Harriman, Hilsman, and Forrestal, Ball identified himself as an "anti-Diem activist" within the administration.[130] In time this group played a crucial role at a critical juncture in the "limited partnership" that Kennedy had developed with Diem.

The second telling exchange that Ball had with Kennedy occurred on February 14, at which time the president asked the under secretary to develop a brief on the history of the Eisenhower policy regarding the organization of SEATO.[131] Given their interests, expertise, and experience, it is curious indeed that the president sought Ball and not Rusk for this assignment. He must have known that Ball did not share the secretary's conviction that the United States had an explicit obligation under SEATO to defend South Vietnam. (Ball ultimately wrote an extended memorandum to President Johnson detailing his conviction that the United States was not "militarily" obligated to defend South Vietnam.) Perhaps Kennedy, by employing Ball's talents as a lawyer—and more importantly, his insights as a skeptic—believed he might find legal loopholes in the SEATO arrangement which could increase his diplomatic and political maneuverability. It is quite possible that Kennedy, notwithstanding the fact that his rhetoric and his actions to date had given the impression of a rock-solid commitment, sought to map out a return trail of diplomatic extrication should military advice and political assistance fail. This certainly reinforces the views of those Kennedy confidants who, like Hilsman, emphatically declare that "never in a thousand years"[132] would he have bombed North Vietnam or deployed a regular force command in South Vietnam.

Included in the admittedly conjectural evidence that Kennedy would not have significantly broadened America's military commitment in Vietnam is a heretofore unexamined TELCON between Ball and the president dated August 21, 1963.[133] Reacting to a rather spectacular incident of governmental repression of the Buddhists during the evening of August 20, Ball had called the president at 8:40 A.M. to brief him and to clear an outgoing State Department cable, the operative part of which read: "The Republic of Viet-Nam has instituted serious repressive measures against Vietnamese Buddhists . . . in direct violation of assurances by the Vietnamese Government that it was beside the policy of reconciliation with the Buddhists. The United States deplores the repressive actions of this nature." What was intended as a reprimand concluded with the curious sentence, "We shall continue to assist Viet Nam to resist communist aggression and maintain its independence."[134] After Ball read the cable to the president over the phone, Kennedy asked if it had already been transmitted. It had not. The president then declared, "I don't know about the last sentence," and continued, "Why don't you leave the last sentence out?" Ball agreed that it took the teeth out of what was supposed to be a stern admonishment and lined it out.[135] Whether Kennedy simply thought the sentence a non sequitur or was consciously attempting to downscale the American commitment may not be conclusively determinable. But the conversation does show that President Kennedy was, at that moment at any rate, less inclined than he was as a senator to avail himself of every opportunity to declare the United States's unequivocal support to South Vietnam.

A fourth representative sample of Ball's less formal discussions with Kennedy on Vietnam focuses on the disposition of Diem. Long before the generals' rebellion which finally overthrew him in the first week of November 1963, it was believed by the so-called anti-Diem activists in the State Department (a belief shared and communicated by Ball's good friend Ambassador Galbraith in Delhi)[136] that Diem had simply become part of the problem and not the solution in South Vietnam. For a full two years there had been talk of a coup d'état in Saigon. Indeed, newly appointed assistant secretary of state for Far Eastern affairs Hilsman had reported to Rusk on November 28, 1961, that "two reliable reports" indicated a coup was being plotted against Diem and Nhu.[137] Hilsman, Forrestal, and Harriman were resigned to Diem's departure. Hilsman recalls that Ball had shared their sentiments but laments the fact that at this stage the under secretary failed to adopt a very high profile on the matter.[138] But Ball's anti-Diem activism subsequently materialized in the infamous "August Telegram" or "coup cable," known in the State Department archives as DEPTAL #243.[139] The cable was drafted jointly by Hilsman and Harriman, who, continually frustrated and outraged by Nhu's raids on the Buddhist pagodas, hoped to prepare a new operating policy for the ambassador soon to be arriving in Saigon.[140] On Sunday, August 24, 1963, recently appointed ambassador to South Vietnam Henry Cabot Lodge was informed that "the US Government cannot tolerate situation in which power lies in Nhu's hands." The cable continued that "if, in spite of all your [Lodge's] efforts, Diem remains obdurate . . . we must face the possibility that [he] cannot be preserved."[141] This was interpreted on the ground in South Vietnam to mean that the generals then plotting against Diem would not meet with American resistance in their efforts to bring him down.

The cable seemed doubly fated. Due to the coincidental absences of senior government officials on a Sunday afternoon, at that time Ball was acting secretary of state and was charged with the responsibility of clearing or killing the telegram. Ball hastily telephoned the president in Hyannis Port. Kennedy concurred with the thrust of the message *pending Rusk's approval*. Ball then telephoned Rusk in New York. Rusk concurred *pending Kennedy's and Harriman's approval*. Recognizing the pace and complexity with which events were unfolding, but passionate in his belief that "the Nhus were destroying what little moral justification remained for [the American] position in Vietnam,"[142] Ball ordered the cable to be sent. In this somewhat haphazard manner, what proved to be a pivotal intrusion into the internal affairs of South Vietnam was initiated without sustained and careful analysis provided by a patient review and a face-to-face meeting of the president's senior advisers.

Had Ball acted capriciously? Had Kennedy and Rusk? For two years there had been a heated debate within the administration about the disposition of Diem. It was then believed, principally by the military, that a viable alternative to him did not exist,[143] and the subsequent rapid succession of failed governments in Saigon certainly gives credence to that view. Ball concedes in retrospect that "we should have waited until the question could have been fully discussed in a well-prepared meeting."[144] However, concluding that the importance of the August 24 telegram has been overstated and that the coup which lead to Diem's ouster and killing on November 2 was distinctly Vietnamese in origin and execution, Ball has second-guessed himself surprisingly little on the matter.[145]

With President Kennedy's murder in Dallas on November 22, 1963, Ball's engagement with Vietnam was profoundly altered. Lyndon Johnson inherited a complex policy for Indochina to which he had given surprisingly little attention as vice-president. As an outsider to the problem—and with decidedly less comprehension than Kennedy of the subtle contours of America's complex foreign policy machinery—Johnson enthusiastically sought information and advice where Kennedy had often been impatient with briefings. This proved to be an opening. Ball never developed the relationship with Kennedy that he would with Johnson and never established an independent reputation within the Kennedy subcabinet as he would under LBJ. His working relationship with Kennedy was incomplete and did not include the propinquity or confidence required to express excited opposition to an already decided course of action.

Ball's circumscribed political relationship with Kennedy resulted primarily from his association with Stevenson, the trade tangles in which he found himself on Capitol Hill, and the aborted Multilateral Nuclear Force scheme (discussed in Chapter 4) which he championed. Attorney General Robert Kennedy's evaluation of his brother's senior advisers illuminates the more personal aspects of the qualified relationship that Ball had with Kennedy. When asked in February 1964 to recall the selection process of his brother's cabinet and senior advisory staff, he said of Ball that he "[didn't] think the President knew him particularly well." Bobby Kennedy could not recall who had initially recommended Ball for the job. "Of course," Kennedy continued, "he had that relationship with Adlai Stevenson." Additionally, Bobby felt that the president was "impatient" with Ball and that "he felt that several assignments that he gave him were not well handled." Bobby Kennedy personally "always thought that George Ball never focused attention sufficiently on some of these matters [including foreign policy for the Third World]" and has stated that his "advice to the president on certain matters [including] South East Asia, was bad. The President felt it was bad." Apparently, according to the attorney general, the president "didn't feel good about him the last year as he had before."[146]

It also appears to be abundantly clear that during the episodic "Get Rusk" exercises conducted by the White House staff, Bobby Kennedy never considered Ball as a viable successor to the secretary. If an index of one's persuasiveness with a president is measured by the extent to which he is considered for higher position, Ball was, according to the president's brother at any rate, hardly a factor. Kennedy has stated that as alternatives to Rusk were considered, Ball "was never mentioned."[147] The president apparently doubted Ball's "organizational ability." It is clearly evident that on European and economic matters the president had a degree of confidence in Ball, but, at least from Bobby Kennedy's vantage point, "[he] didn't have any rapport with him."[148]

Chester Bowles's expulsion in the "Thanksgiving Day Massacre" conditioned Ball's Vietnam advocacy during the Kennedy administration. Hughes has noted that "[Ball] had before him the warning lesson from what Bowles had done on the Bay of Pigs and Vietnam, and it was very clear that loyalty to the Kennedy administration was a prime requirement." Hughes has no doubt that "if there had been leaks attributable to him [Ball] about his opposition . . . the retribution would be the same [as Bowles's]."[149] On Kennedy's watch, Ball's Vietnam dissent, emanating as it was from only the margin of power, had lain dormant on the seventh floor of the State Department. After the tragedy in Dallas a new context for dissent was created. With a new chief of state ravenous for insights into the complex world of foreign policy about which, by his own admission, he was inadequately informed, the under secretary availed himself of every opportunity to put his views forward. Indeed, during the Johnson administration Ball embarked on nothing less than a systematic effort to persuade Johnson not to fight in Vietnam.

Chapter 3

Chess, Not Dominoes

What was the point, [Ball] asked, of massive forces in Vietnam,
if Southeast Asia was about to be taken over from the rear by
Chinese oriented Indonesia?
—William P. Bundy

IN THE SPRING OF 1964 the under secretary of state underwent a tortured ideological and bureaucratic metamorphosis. Formerly identified with grand political structures (such as the European confederation) and busied with the advancement of progressive initiatives (like the "Kennedy Round" tariff revisions), with the advent of the Johnson administration Ball became somewhat of an iconoclast, arguing for a searching reexamination of the containment doctrine and its corollaries. A consummate Europeanist, without a conspicuous bureaucratic portfolio that would suggest a prominent role in making or managing America's Vietnam policy, in the aftermath of the Kennedy assassination the Atlantic-oriented diplomat was elevated to an intimate circle of men who advised Lyndon Johnson on the deteriorating political and military situation in Southeast Asia.

Ball once wrote that "the great captains of history drew their lessons from complex chess, not simple dominoes."[1] Though to the postwar generation the falling dominoes metaphor possessed a compelling logic and an attractive political simplicity, Ball argued that it had become a specious substitute for systematic analysis of individual Cold War crises. It had caused American leaders to become reactive rather than deliberative. He had never been hysterical about the advance of communism into areas of the world not considered vital to America's strategic interests and had long felt that Vietnam was peripheral to the transcending objectives of American foreign policy, which in his mind included maintaining peace among the major industrial states, advancing the principle of free trade, and securing a modus vivendi with the

Soviet Union. In 1964, through his incessant assertions that America possessed a finite capacity to influence world events, Ball began to make these general Realist perspectives on international relations more explicit. Imploring his colleagues to judiciously select the terrain upon which to take stands against perceived Communist threats to the national security, the under secretary embarked on a lonely and at times quite contrary enterprise at the top level of government to reverse the course of American policy in Indochina.

During his final twenty-four months as the nation's second-ranked foreign policy officer, the rhythm of life at Ball's Woodley Road residence changed precipitously. Rumors of war, and then war, came to dominate family discussions.[2] Though his visceral and at times emotional response to the siren song of escalation was wisely absent from the dissenting case he would tender within government councils, in the sheltered sphere of his own family, and particularly with his historian son Douglas, Ball continuously expressed his moral indignation at the incongruence of the United States making war in Vietnam.[3] It was a David and Goliath epic rewritten, and the world, Ball feared, was cheering for David. Appending sleepless nights to fourteen-hour workdays, he would habitually awaken, with a yellow legal pad at his bedside, to scrawl impassioned fulminations in a private effort to arrest what he considered the irresponsible and reckless Americanization of Vietnam's civil war. Ruth Murdoch Ball recalls that at frequent intervals from the date of his first extended memorandum (to Dean Rusk on May 31, 1964) to his last (to Johnson on April 21, 1966), her husband would leave the bed at odd hours to noisily dictate arguments he would later use in prodigious briefs against the war into a tape recorder, only to return to an intermittent sleep encumbered by dire predictions of tragedy and a brooding sense of powerlessness about how to forestall it.[4]

Although it was initially known only to a select few among his personal staff and the small circle of senior cabinet architects of the war policy, Ball developed a comprehensive rebuttal to Johnson's escalatory course at every critical decision-making juncture. In contrast to the manner in which Kennedy had perceptibly muted Ball's dissent, Johnson encouraged it and in point of fact, as we will see below, commissioned it. Not only did Ball advance his views without trepidation or fear of political retribution, he considered Johnson his best ally. With a solid presidential blessing, Ball wrote eighteen memorandums and talking papers against the war, comprising an advocacy distinguished by its singularity at the highest level of government. Save for his prediction of massive Chinese intervention in the earliest stages of American involvement, Ball predicted the course, character, and consequences of the

Vietnam conflict with extraordinary prescience. Indeed, after examining his dissenting memorandums one would suspect that they were written after, and not before, the American agony in Southeast Asia.

A small portion of the total body of Ball's papers, excerpts of four presidential memorandums, have been known to students of the Vietnam War since the publication of the *Pentagon Papers* in 1971. Since then he has been universally venerated in the predominantly liberal scholarship on the war as the single top-ranking presidential adviser to challenge Johnson's assumptions before and during each increment of escalation. Examination of the complement of those papers provides insights into how the momentous questions of war and peace were framed within Johnson's war councils and illuminate aspects of what appears to have been a seriously flawed policy process. The papers systematically argue against the Americanization of the war and embody Ball's profound private misgivings about a policy he has come to regard as "the greatest single error that America has made in its national history."[5]

The corpus of Ball's Vietnam materials (including outgoing Department of State telegrams, limited distribution memorandums, TELCONS, talking papers, and personal notes) may be understood as the exposition and development of four assertions: (1) that his senior colleagues were exaggerating the strategic importance of the Vietnam conflict by misinterpreting it as a Free World struggle against monolithic world communism; (2) that the potential gains from military intervention in Southeast Asia were incommensurate with the hazards; (3) that the United States was pursuing a flawed negotiating strategy throughout 1965 and 1966; and (4) that South Vietnamese and American military forces would ultimately be defeated by the Vietcong and North Vietnamese.

In the summer of 1964 Kennedy's policy of "limited partnership" with South Vietnam was profoundly altered. Ironically, what had been the rationale for staying out—the inability of the Saigon regime to stabilize itself and effectively take the war to the Vietcong—in time became the rationale for increased American involvement. Employing one of the more memorable allegories of the Vietnam War period, Ball alluded to the perilous prospect of encountering the most tenacious beast of ancient Tonkinese folklore on his own terrain when he wrote, "Once on the tiger's back we cannot be sure of picking the place to dismount."[6] In the aftermath of the Tonkin Gulf resolution which had given Johnson carte blanche to prosecute the war in Southeast Asia, Ball remained unpersuaded that American policymakers could control the rhythms and risks of an expanded and Americanized war. He vehemently argued that a thorough evaluation of the assumptions on which policymakers were operating should *precede* an upgraded U.S. commitment. Doubting that the "action intellectuals"[7] of the Kennedy-Johnson administration could with certainty control the battle on the ground in Vietnam or anticipate the responses of America's allies or adversaries, he quickly became an apostle of restraint. Within a few short months after the Tonkin Gulf incident of August 1964, Ball became intellectually alienated from his colleagues on the subject of Southeast Asia and for two more years would fight a solitary and dispiriting battle of persuasion.

At the outset of the debates over escalation, Ball frantically declared that the United States was not (as Rusk and McNamara asserted and Kennedy and Johnson had both tacitly accepted) *legally* committed to military intervention in the defense of South Vietnam. As early as February 1962, he had tried to convince Kennedy that America's legal obligation to Saigon was wholly ambiguous and that a self-interested interpretation of the 1954 SEATO accords provided the United States with considerable political maneuverability.[8] At the very moment the Johnson administration was debating the precise size and mission of the force about to be sent to aggressively defend Da Nang Air Base, Ball submitted, at Johnson's request, a formal legal interpretation of the SEATO pact. He correctly noted in a June 1965 memorandum that the South East Asia Treaty (signed in 1954 by the United States, France, Great Britain, Australia, New Zealand, Thailand, Pakistan, and the Philippines) "provide[d] that in the event of aggression by means of armed attack against South Vietnam *each party* would act to meet the common danger [emphasis added]." Observing that the United States was the only nation to have mistakenly made the determination that South Vietnam confronted armed aggression from a foreign power, Ball reminded the president that there had been no decision by the SEATO members to "*act collectively* [emphasis added]." Further, pursuant to the Geneva accords of 1954, South Vietnam was not a signatory to the South East Asia Treaty but was merely a protocol state. From this, Ball concluded, America's "obligation under the treaty [did] not run directly to South Vietnam." In a most aggressive manner of reasoning and persuasion the under secretary of state submitted that scholars of international law generally acknowledged that "only parties, and not third party beneficiaries, acquire rights under a treaty."[9] The United States was not bound by treaty commitments to fight in Vietnam.

If not an obligation under SEATO, the legal pretext for an American intervention did exist. Ball conceded that an American military role in Vietnam's civil war was certainly legitimized by Article 51 of the United Nations Charter, which recognized the inherent right of individual and collective self-defense. But when the Soviet Union would inevitably block a United Nations intervention in Vietnam through the exercise of their Security Council veto (having learned their lesson in Korea), any legal obligation to the defense of South Vietnam would be erased. Ball's case was formidable, but in the aftermath of the controversial Tonkin Gulf affair, Johnson was persuaded that increased military action was called for. Ball's brief was one year too late. As would occur and reoccur time and again in Vietnam, events seemed to race out ahead of cerebration. One may only speculate what may have happened if the president had been positively persuaded that the United States was not legally bound to the defense of South Vietnam. It may well have been that, with the strategic and political premium Johnson gave to the region, he would not have been detained.

Believing that he had made the strongest case he could against a war thought to be waged to uphold treaty commitments, Ball recognized that an American political obligation to South Vietnam had *informally* commenced in October 1954. President Eisenhower had indeed "promised to aid the government [of South Vietnam] in developing and maintaining a strong and viable state capable of resisting attempted subversion and aggression through military means." Because the United States was ostensibly bound by the moral responsibility to assist those in South Vietnam who had been encouraged by an American president to resist Communist insurgency—as well as a manifest concern for its own credibility—Kennedy and Johnson had accepted the somewhat paternal view that South Vietnam was America's offspring and this country was pledged to its survival. In a failed attempt to dispense with this view, the under secretary simply reiterated the "implied and frequently expressed conditions" to the provision of U.S. assistance promised by the Eisenhower administration. Citing the Eisenhower communiqué of 1954, Ball reminded Johnson of his predecessor's stipulation that aid would be forthcoming pending the "continuing request" of the South Vietnamese government and *"its will and ability to use [the] assistance effectively* [emphasis added]."[10] In Ball's judgment, and indeed in the judgment of many others, South Vietnam had not lived up to its end of the bargain. For the first time the full implications of what he had been arguing became clear. Ball was willing to accept the consequences of giving the country over to the Communists and the advocates of escalation were not.

While denying that the United States had a legal obligation to maintain South Vietnam's sovereignty through armed intervention, in the summer of 1965 Ball unilaterally advanced a formula to end the war through a multiparty political settlement and negotiated withdrawal. In doing this he harbored no illusions about South Vietnam's ability to maintain its independence. Quite willing to argue his case on legal, political, and psychological grounds, Ball contended that his suggested course of action should "not be judged in juridical terms but in terms of its effect on the credibility of our commitments throughout the world."[11] In other words, he engaged Rusk, McNamara, Bundy, and the president on their own terms, the sanctity of American credibility. He recommended that the United States accept short-term losses in prestige for what he calculated would be longer-term gains in other nations' estimations of American judgment and wisdom as a great power, with concomitant great power responsibilities.

Predictably, Ball declared in a memorandum that America's obligations under the North Atlantic Treaty, which ran "*directly* to each of the NATO partners [emphasis in original]," were "quite different" from American responsibilities for Vietnam under SEATO.[12] The United States had an explicit legal obligation (and significantly, Ball would add, a primary strategic interest) to defend Europe, and it was incumbent upon the American leadership to insure the survivability of its capacity to meet that commitment under any exigency. In part, Ball reasoned, this capacity could only be maintained if the United States prudently preserved tactical, fiscal, and political capabilities. Empowered by his direct personal encounters with Walter Lippmann and his passionate embrace of Lippmann's Realist dispositions, Ball cautioned the president not to undermine American power in what he believed would surely be a failed attempt to defend an area in which the nation did not have an explicit legal responsibility or a compelling security interest.

In diametric opposition, by the spring of 1964 Ball's senior administration colleagues had begun to harden their collective assumption that inattention to Vietnam would cause America's allies to doubt U.S. resolve to fulfill its Free World security promises. If the United States would not defend Vietnam, the logic went, how could it be depended upon to make good its treaty obligations elsewhere? This view was epitomized by Attorney General Robert Kennedy's emotional declaration while in Germany on a political junket: "If Americans did not stop communism in South Vietnam, how could people believe that they would stop it in Berlin?"[13] Ball systematically challenged such views with a genuine sense of urgency. In a top secret memorandum to Secretary Rusk dated May 31, 1964, he registered his alarm that the plans to extend the commitment to the government of South Vietnam (GVN) "were going forward too precipitously," and he asserted that "the world would not, either from a self-interested perspective, or altruistic reasoning, support an Americanized war in Vietnam."[14] Ever cognizant of the domestic political implications and

Ball, *right*, and "roving ambassador" Averell Harriman in 1962. Harriman's "neutralist solution" to the Laotian crisis inspired Ball's thinking on Vietnam. (Photograph courtesy of George W. Ball)

potential damage to American prestige resulting from military failure or negotiated withdrawal, Ball tried to impress upon Rusk what he considered to be the much greater domestic political hazards of waging a land war in Asia.

As an active member of the Committee to Defend America by Aiding the Allies before World War II, Ball was intimately acquainted with the arguments *against* appeasement and *for* a vigilant collective security system. However, "against these concerns," he argued in the 1960s, "one must balance the view of many of our allies that we are engaged in a fruitless struggle we are bound to lose." Noting the "erosive effect on [America's] alliances of direct U.S. intervention," Ball challenged the conclusions of those who had indiscriminately embraced the doctrine of credibility. He argued that America's European partners believed that if the Americans became too committed on the Asian mainland, they would "lose interest in their problems" and declared that "what [the United States] might gain by establishing the steadfastness of [its] commitments, [it] would lose by an erosion of confidence in [its] judgment."[15]

During this period the Europe-focused under secretary maintained a personal file of clippings from European periodicals tracking the responses of Western Europe's parliaments and heads of state to America's Vietnam policy. Believing that he very well understood the mind-set on the old Continent, he baldly told Rusk in May 1964 that the United States simply "cannot assume that escalation would be universally applauded by our [European] friends."[16]

The under secretary of state had done nothing less than invert the logic of his senior cabinet colleagues who held that the United States must follow through on the commitment to South Vietnam in order to maintain credibility with its principal allies. Ball's controlling fear was that a war in Vietnam would rapidly consume the diplomatic energies directed toward the realization of the grand economic and political objectives under the umbrella of the European partnership. Worse, an American war in Vietnam would most certainly have a corrosive and divisive effect on the Atlantic Alliance. On March 17, 1965, he told J. Robert Schaetzel, then at the State Department European Bureau, that "there is really a great tendency for [the president] to forget Europe at the moment unless it is made clear that a continued American interest is essential."[17] In the spring of 1965 Ball set out to counterbalance Lyndon Johnson's progressive preoccupation with Southeast Asia. Fearful of any "further disruption of Western solidarity,"[18] he asserted that in order for the United States to maintain its Free World leadership, it needed to maintain the integrity of its defenses in those areas vital to the defense of the Free World and not dissipate its resources in marginal activities. While reaffirming America's conspicuous commitments to Europe under the North Atlantic Treaty and to Latin America under the Rio Pact, Ball argued that the United States would be wise not to become mired down in an area of the world with little importance to the total United States strategic equation.[19]

Furthermore, Ball asserted categorically that, save for the Thais and the Republic of China, America's Asian allies would be quite cool to an Americanization of the war in Vietnam. Indeed, America's Asian friends blanched at any scenario that included even the remote possibility of war with Red China to promote American credibility. The Japanese, he wrote, "would prefer wisdom to valor," and he noted that Tokyo was satisfied that America was serious about preserving the regional balance of power: "The U.S. record in Korea shows the credibility of [the American] commitment."[20] Identifying a theme for the first time to which he would return on innumerable occasions, Ball cited obvious cultural and racial dimensions to the problem of an American war in Asia. In his May 31, 1964, memorandum to Rusk, he likened the U.S position to the French and British predicament at Suez in 1956 and asserted that "world opinion would be against [the United States] and opposition would be heightened by the racial implications of a white attack upon Asian people." Alluding to "the old colonial bogey" and the public relations difficulties the specter of a resurgent American imperialism would pose in an American effort to generate multilateral support, he quite prophetically argued that "America's Asian friends could not be counted on to stay with [her] far down this track."[21]

In this assertion, Ball was remarkably prescient. Johnson's "more flags" drive in April 1964 was an unqualified public relations failure. The administration did not generate additional enthusiasm among America's Southeast Asian allies for the bloodletting in Indochina. Worse, from the perspective of Johnson's advisers, it revealed the depths of Asia's ambivalence about an American war against communism in Vietnam. To the degree that an Asian-American partnership existed, it was a flagrantly lopsided affair. None of the Asian allies were invited to National Security Council (NSC) meetings to contribute in any way whatever to the development of policy, and the domestic political winds in each of the countries blew decidedly against participation in the American war. On a political trip to New Zealand, for example, Vice-President Hubert Humphrey was dismayed when his greeting from the country included an antiwar demonstration. The offense was compounded by the irony that the protest was led by an American schoolteacher on a U.S. government scholarship. Marchers against the American war in Japan carried placards asserting that the United States was no longer the model of behavior. In time however, Australia sent what has been described as a "token force," and the Philippines, a troop of 1,120. Korea, by comparison, sent 48,000 men to fight outside their borders for the first time in their history, a contingent that was, expressed as a percent of population, as large as the American force. But even this was not without its liabilities. In persuading the Koreans that it was in their best interests to fight, the United States transferred billions of dollars in credits and may have indeed lost in politics more than it gained in battlefield capacity by the conspicuously mercenary overtones of the arrangement.[22]

In the last week of August 1964, newly appointed assistant secretary of state for Far Eastern affairs William Bundy (Johnson had unceremoniously fired Roger Hilsman for what he considered unforgivable and disloyal criticism of his policies) began to seriously take account of Ball's arguments against deeper military involvement in Vietnam. Assessing Ball's views at this early stage in the war, Bundy vividly reconstructed the contours of a meeting in his office at which the under secretary pressed the view that Vietnam was a comparatively insignificant element of the total Southeast Asia security problem. "With his usual sense of the big picture," Bundy recalls, "George poked and probed about Indonesia. What was the point, he asked, of massive [American] forces in Vietnam, if Southeast Asia was about to be taken over from the rear by Chinese oriented Indonesia?"[23] Later Ball also advanced "the big picture argument" with NSC director McGeorge Bundy. After a meeting with heads of western oil companies doing business in Indonesia, he telephoned Bundy to report that he was "very worried about being pushed clear out [of the country]" and reminded him of the seriousness of losing to the Communists the fifth largest country in the world in a location of vital strategic importance to the United States.[24] Because of its size and resources, Indonesia was a problem of far greater consequence to America. If the United States was to have an ambitious anticommunism policy in Southeast Asia, he reasoned, it was implementing that policy in the wrong place.

As an extension of his comprehensive and confrontational examination of the assumptions upon which Johnson and the proponents of escalation formulated policy, the under secretary roundly attacked what was then popularly known in diplomatic and strategic councils as the "Korea analogy." Since the messy but vindicative conclusion of the struggle in 1953, comparison of the two "Free World challenges" had provided the proponents of escalation in the top echelon of the government with a powerful rationale for a more aggressive anti-Communist policy in Indochina. Ball, however, instinctively felt that drawing too close a comparison between what, in his mind, were only faintly analogous problems perverted an understanding of the Vietnam question and ignored what he felt were manifest dissimilarities between the two settings. Emphatically stating that "Viet Nam is not Korea," he enumerated the ways in which he felt his superior officers had recklessly misconstrued history in their analyses of the Vietnam predicament. The United States, he asserted, had enjoyed a "clear UN mandate" during the Korean War which sanctioned its military intervention in the court of world opinion. At the apex of the Korean intervention, 53,000 infantry and 1,000 additional troops were provided by no fewer than fifty-three nations. In Vietnam, by contrast, America was "going it alone." Without U.N. sponsorship the United States's position depended upon what he considered to be the highly uncertain SEATO protocols and the continuing requests for assistance from a series of tremulous South Vietnamese governments.[25]

Furthermore, Ball continued, Korea was a "classical type of invasion across an established border," providing the United States and the U.N. with an "unassailable political and legal base for counteraction." South Vietnam was experiencing no similar invasion but rather a "slow infiltration" which "by its nature [was] ambiguous" and which also enjoyed "substantial indigenous support." Much of the world, he pointed out, "remained unpersuaded that Hanoi [was] the principal source of the revolt." At the time of the Korean intervention in June 1950, the South Korean government of Syngman Rhee was stable and had enjoyed the "general support of the principal elements in the country." By contrast, Ball's piercing memorandum characterized the political situation in Saigon as "governmental chaos." The Koreans, he reminded his colleagues, were fresh for the fight in 1950, defending their sovereignty just two years after its inception. The South Vietnamese were, on the other hand, in the midst of a bloody quarter-century struggle, first against the French, then against Ho Chi Minh's Democratic Republic of Vietnam (DRV).[26] In stark contrast to Korea, not a single Chinese or Russian soldier or even a technician from either country had (to date) entered the conflict. Vietnam was in the throes of an anticolonial revolution; in lending support to South Vietnam, the United States was, in the eyes of the world, identifying with the less than wholesome remnants of French imperialism.

Saigon in 1964 utterly lacked the political solidarity enjoyed by Seoul fourteen years earlier. Indeed, Ball was entirely convinced that the generalized and popular support for the November 1963 coup which had toppled Diem was a manifestation of a deeply rooted pessimism felt by the South Vietnamese concerning the future independence of their country. In his analysis, neutralist elements eager to make an accommodation with the Vietcong and Hanoi were a most potent and dynamic force in South Vietnam's political structure, and he consistently maintained that, even with massive American assistance, Saigon lacked the political and moral resources to sustain its independence. Accepting the inevitable consequence of his interpretation, Ball simply did not give great weight to the advance of communism into South Vietnam, nor was he persuaded that a unified and socialist Vietnam necessarily represented a significant extension of Chinese or Soviet hegemony in Southeast Asia. His papers frequently assert the thesis that, though the Chinese and/or Soviets might find it politically useful to assist the DRV, nascent Vietnamese nationalism would repel attempted subjugation by either imperial power. Arguing that the insurgency directed against the Saigon government sprang primarily from endogenous sources, Ball frequently postulated that North Vietnam sought outside resources only to the extent that it required them as a counter to American assistance given to South Vietnam.[27]

There were other more subtle reasons that Ball came to the conclusion that an American war in Vietnam would not wash. There were, he felt, distinct and significant differences between the purposes of the South Vietnamese and their American patrons. The reunification of the two Vietnams was decidedly *not* an

American objective, and he forcefully argued that the United States incorrectly assumed that a majority of South Vietnamese people desired a permanent partition of their country. In pressing this point he cited a speech delivered on July 19, 1964, by South Vietnamese general Khanh (who had begun a fated year-long term as prime minister in January) declaring that the ultimate objective of the Southern-based "Vietnamese National Liberation Revolution" was *"reunification* of the fatherland [emphasis added]." Consideration of this powerful nationalist sentiment suggested one of three scenarios: the South's military and political conquest of the North, which seemed wholly unlikely; the North's military and political domination of the South, which Ball predicted; or the advent of a neutralist regime in the South that would advance the peaceful integration of the two sections of the country, which was the only outcome, in Ball's mind, that the United States could help bring about. Further, as evidence of the affinity for North Vietnam felt by the majority of the Southern population, Ball cited a Central Intelligence Agency (CIA) finding that *only one in twenty-five* South Vietnamese registered unequivocal support for American air strikes above the 17th parallel, and he insisted that there was "little evidence to suggest that the South Vietnamese would have their hearts lifted by watching the North suffer a sustained aerial bombardment."[28] It was clear to the under secretary of state that the political and strategic objectives of the United States and its Asian client did not correspond. In time, Ball feared, this incongruence would cause the American policy to unhinge.

When he was not busy attempting to shatter the political and cultural assumptions which he believed imprisoned the thinking of his colleagues, Ball appealed to their sense of strategic equilibrium. For months he had been stating that in recommending a policy of potentially limitless graduated responses (described as "reprisals" for North Vietnamese "aggression" in the Tonkin Gulf) his colleagues had egregiously exaggerated the importance of Indochina as a factor in America's total security equation. He further believed that they had uncritically invoked a specious doctrine of credibility with dangerous implications. To these familiar points, however, Ball now added a sober prediction. On July 1, 1965, the under secretary of state declared rather flatly that the United States would be defeated in Vietnam. From this point forward he systematically attacked the generally held assumption that the United States could not lose a war to North Vietnam. Ball believed that this assumption was rooted in a nearly unbounded faith in America's overwhelming technological superiority and the naive hope that at some future point South Vietnam's political factions would coalesce around an able leader.

Writing on the eve of the ominous July 21, 1965, decision to significantly increase troop levels and expand American combat operations, Ball plainly told his cabinet colleagues that Vietnam was "a losing war . . . no matter how many hundred thousand white, foreign troops [America] might deploy."[29]

Ball would simply not allow himself to be seduced by America's superior firepower and instinctively believed that there were intangibles which were difficult to evaluate statistically: the élan of the Vietcong and North Vietnamese troops, the oppressive terrain, the Indochinese climate, and the moral ambiguities of the American position which were constantly noted throughout the world. These were subtle elements of the problem to which the cosmopolitan under secretary was highly sensitized. But Ball did not simply take his cues on Vietnam from his European contacts. Throughout 1965 he was impressed by the hard-boiled data which was funneled to him by his contacts in INR. "The enemy," he asserted, "possessed an insurmountable intelligence advantage" that would make it difficult to engage him at times and places advantageous to the American style of war. To illustrate, Ball cited three recent and representative anecdotes from the summer of 1965: A search-and-destroy mission conducted by the 173d Airborne regiment spent three days looking for the enemy, suffered twenty-three casualties, and never even saw a single Vietcong; a penetration of the Da Nang Air Base was discovered to have been made possible only through the cooperation of the local population; and a B-52 raid had failed to kill a single enemy soldier because they had previously been informed of the precise coordinates and timing of the attack.[30] Again, Ball proved to be prophetic. As the military history of the Vietnam conflict would ultimately confirm, the Vietcong and North Vietnamese army (NVA) exercised nearly complete control over the timing and positioning of battles. National Security Memorandum 1 on "The Situation in Vietnam" (circulated in December 1968) found that "three-fourths of the battles are at the enemy's choice of time, place, type, and duration." The report also noted a CIA study which stated that "*less than one percent* of the nearly two million Allied small unit operations conducted in the last two years resulted in contact with the enemy and, when ARVN [Army of the Republic of South Vietnam] is surveyed, the percentage drops to one-tenth of one percent [emphasis in original]."[31]

Throughout the fall of 1964 Ball had incessantly argued that because the conflict was "a civil war between Asians in jungle terrain in the midst of a population that refuses cooperation with white forces,"[32] there were no assurances that American and South Vietnamese forces could defeat the Vietcong. He seems almost to have instinctively understood the liabilities of the South

Vietnamese military and political structure dating back to the Diem regime. The Diem clan, for example, had been unwilling to fully and aggressively commit the ARVN forces to a war because, as *New York Times* correspondent Neil Sheehan has written, "the army was the mainstay of their rule." American war planners perceived the ARVN as an instrument with which to kill Vietcong. "The Ngo Dinhs, on the other hand, saw the ARVN primarily as a force-in-being to safeguard their regime." Diem and his successors thought mostly of political survival; their first priority was the preservation of their political life. "To hazard the ARVN in a war was to hazard their regime, and that was unthinkable." Even if most of the territory of South Vietnam was lost to Ho Chi Minh, whoever might be in control in Saigon could, with a viable army and unflagging American assistance, preserve their power in the South's major population centers.[33] In the face of this untenable political/military arrangement, Ball remained unpersuaded by those who argued that a combination of severe military and diplomatic pressure against Hanoi could greatly improve the chances of negotiating a political resolution to the conflict. For the sake of argument (even today he is not entirely persuaded of the thesis he advanced in the 1960s),[34] Ball forcefully asserted that the Vietcong operating in the South were semi-independent and quite capable of carrying the war to the South Vietnamese regime despite dislocation and disruption of supply lines from the North. "Even with the DRV [and NVA regular army units] out of it," the under secretary proclaimed, "the struggle in the South would be protracted."[35]

But Ball's earliest, most cogent, most earnest, and most persistent remonstrations in 1964 were directed against the American policy of strategic bombing. He instinctively felt that the emerging bombing policy was rooted in an anachronistic and failed doctrine of warfare wholly inappropriate to the Indochinese setting. In the wake of the August 1964 Tonkin Gulf resolution and the initiation of large-scale aerial attacks against the North, he put forth the view that bombing would not achieve desired results—and would in fact create hazards that were incommensurate with the highly equivocal gains that could reasonably be anticipated. There had been a lively administration debate during the fall of 1964 over the political desirability and military efficacy of what was dubbed "Operation Rolling Thunder." Ostensibly secret, the arguments and actors on each side of the issue were fairly well known to Washington insiders and the establishment press, and Ball was very early recognized and lauded as a spokesman for restraint. It was Johnson's decided policy to liberally employ strategic and tactical bombers in Vietnam while parsimoniously employing combat troops in what, in 1964 at any rate, were very limited ground operations. Johnson would wage "techno-war," and while he wielded sticks—bombing missions—in one hand, he repeatedly brandished carrots—offers to suspend the bombing—in the other. Despite Johnson's fervent desire "to keep the factors that entered into his decisions a closely held secret," Tom Wicker of the *New York Times* had accurately identified the advocates on each side of the issue, as well as the intelligence data that was being processed. Much to Johnson's lament, the identities of the players in the December 1964 drama of whether and when North Vietnam was to be bombed—and who did and did not accept the much-ballyhooed strategy of bombing pauses as a diplomatic incentive—became public information.[36]

Johnson's "hitting back" policy had been sustained throughout the fall and into the winter. In the first "pause debate" of January 1965, those who favored an aggressive resumption of the bombing campaign that had ensued since the Tonkin Gulf incident in August 1964, and which had been interrupted during the Christmas season to test the diplomatic waters, included General Taylor, Under Secretary of State for Political Affairs U. Alexis Johnson, Ambassador Henry Cabot Lodge, Rusk, McNamara, and, as a group, the Joint Chiefs of Staff. Those favoring prolonging the pause included the under secretary of state.[37] Indeed, it was the first of many encounters in which Ball would find himself pitted against virtually all of the president's senior advisers on a seminal question. To his credit, Ball maintained his position—and the dubious distinction of being a minority of one. From the vantage point of retirement, President Johnson recalled that "Ball was pretty consistent all along in minimizing the results that could be obtained from bombing. [He] generally felt that [the United States] incurred greater risks than results from bombing." And Johnson accurately added, "I don't think anybody else felt that way."[38]

The arguments advanced by his advisers in January 1965 *for* resumption and extension of the bombing campaign were compelling to Johnson. The advocates of air war advanced the view that extended pauses would allow Hanoi time to resupply Vietcong guerrillas and build new infiltration routes to the South. In addition, the president was painfully aware that any attack on a large American military installation might be directly attributable to a pause.[39] Finding himself once again in diametric opposition to his colleagues—and operating from a theoretically different framework—Ball frontally challenged their analyses. While everyone else was thinking primarily in terms of the war on the ground in Vietnam, Ball thought nearly exclusively in terms of world reaction to bombing, particularly the likely Soviet and Chinese responses. According to notes written by presidential assistant Jack Valenti, in a meeting with Rusk, McNamara, Bundy, Clark Clifford, Abe Fortas, and the president on December 18, 1964, Ball had argued that a pause "would relieve [the North

Vietnamese and their Soviet and Chinese allies] of the intense pressure to respond to our actions." Though he would later reverse his calculation and argue that Chinese intervention was more likely, at this point in 1964 Ball told his colleagues that "we must not push them [the Russians] into a corner."[40]

As would so often occur, Ball's colleagues were impressed but not persuaded by his diplomatic perspective. His response was to try another line this time, a political argument: At best, as he first stated in October 1964 and would continuously repeat, bombing would produce a "Pyrrhic victory." Even if the capability of the DRV to supply the Vietcong was appreciably diminished—and Ball held that in relying primarily on bombing it would not be—"a disorganized South Vietnamese Government would be unable to eliminate the insurgency."[41] Additionally, whereas some of his colleagues asserted that the United States should bomb primarily to bolster the confidence of the South Vietnamese allies,[42] he had consistently felt that if "air bombardment is not followed by the fact—or even the promise—of a military invasion of North Viet-Nam, there is no assurance that it would improve South Vietnamese morale."[43] Moreover, Ball had expressed the private view to Rusk months earlier (May 1964) that the Vietcong possessed "self-sufficient tactical centers in the South adequate to enable the carrying-on of their campaign with only marginally diminished effectiveness," underscoring the Vietcong's "history of carrying on underground when necessary." Events seemed to corroborate his pessimistic views. Bombing would not be conclusive because Johnson at no time seriously contemplated a military invasion or occupation of North Vietnam.[44]

Not only would bombing be strategically inconclusive, Ball contended, it would rapidly transform the war into a struggle of the type that the United States was least eager and least prepared to wage. Citing a Joint War Games Agency exercise (code-named Sigma II) held in September 1964, the under secretary concluded that the "presently proposed air strikes would not cripple Hanoi's capability for increasing its support of the Viet Cong" and would in fact prove to be counterproductive. Believing that each party would "choose to fight the kind of war best adapted to its resources," he was convinced that the North Vietnamese would "retaliate by using ground forces which they possess[ed] in overwhelming numbers," and he predicted the number might be "six divisions or 60,000 men." And worse, Ball believed, the counteroffensive by the North Vietnamese would come at a time in 1965 when there was "no current estimate of what US response would be needed to stop this action."[45]

From his perspective as a "European-American" and an ardent student of Allied strategic bombing during World War II, the under secretary of state simply felt that the Pentagon war planners had not thoroughly examined the implications of their actions. The advent of Operation Rolling Thunder in February 1965 with its sustained and graduated air strikes against targets in the North and South gravely worried him and destroyed any remaining hope he harbored that his recommendations might be heeded. However, having lost the battle over *whether* the United States should bomb targets in North Vietnam, Ball began to argue more forcefully for pauses, reductions, and delays. Months went by before he came at the problem again. At an NSC meeting on December 14, 1965—in yet another despairing effort to persuade his senior colleagues to reverse their decisions—Ball reviewed the original rationale for air war advanced by his colleagues a year earlier and offered an unsolicited and quite negative evaluation of naval and air force operations in Vietnam up to that time. He reminded the war managers of the bombing campaign's three original objectives: to "improve morale in the South," to "interdict the movement of supplies," and to "persuade Hanoi to come to the conference table."[46]

By late 1965 Ball argued that the first objective could be said to have been met as the result of the bombing and the massive deployment of American troops that summer. With regard to the second objective, he argued persuasively from intelligence reports that though it significantly imperiled NVA and Vietcong supply lines, bombing had a very negligible effect on the aggregate flow of men and supplies to the South.[47] As to the third objective, Ball was convinced that bombing had had the negative effect of driving the Soviets and Chinese closer together in a cooperative effort to help the DRV defend itself against air strikes. The bombing seemed to the under secretary to have hardened Hanoi's negotiating position.[48]

As the war exponentially expanded throughout 1965, Ball became progressively more concerned about the seemingly boundless capacity of the DRV regular army units to upgrade their effort in the South. He was particularly alarmed by what he termed "signs of creeping involvement" from both the Chinese and Russians.[49] If the United States "hit targets in or approaching the Hanoi-Haiphong area," he wrote in February 1965, it would be likely "at some point to trigger a DRV ground force move South."[50] The under secretary's position was that the DRV could support a movement of 125,000 troops through the demilitarized zone and Laos at a time when there was no estimate of what would be required by the United States to stop the action. Drawing upon the recommendation of what he quite presumptiously claimed was the collective conclusion of "the entire intelligence community," he argued that the 19th parallel was the critical coordinate; attacks above that line, he said, would quite likely precipitate Chinese intervention. This, in his judgment, would include Chinese ground forces moved into North Vietnam, South Vietnam, Laos, and possibly Thailand, as well as fighter aircraft "operating from the sanctuary of Chinese territory."[51] Ball pressed the point that 350 Chinese jet fighters deployed in the Hainan area of South China (within striking distance of North Vietnam) portended the wider war that Johnson so desperately sought to avoid. Stimulated by fear of uncontrolled escalation, he cautioned the president that in the event Chinese fighters attacked American aircraft, he would be under "considerable pressure" to order U.S. forces to knock out the offending Chinese bases—"and even to strike at Chinese nuclear production installations."[52]

Ball thus played a very hard "China card." Allen Whiting, a State Department expert on Asia from whom Ball solicited intelligence data and political analysis, recalls that "the information that [he and the under secretary] had been monitoring showed that the Chinese were quite willing to put themselves into North Vietnam to deter, or, if necessary, to engage [the United States]."[53] Painfully aware of the implications of a war with China, the two advocates of restraint presented worst-case scenarios in an effort to demonstrate the gravity of the situation but, in so doing, were careful not to overestimate the Chinese threat to the point of risking their credibility. For example, though they were both quite sanguine about the prospect of a land war with the People's Republic of China (PRC), they did not anticipate that the Chinese would unnecessarily risk intervening too far south of the North Vietnamese border. Intelligence officers in the State Department surmised Chinese intervention to be unnecessary, and Whiting in particular calculated that China's participation would likely "kill the Viet Cong's appeal as an indigenous national unification movement." The Chinese, Ball felt, were not looking for "that kind" of involvement.[54]

Notwithstanding these moderating considerations, Whiting and Ball were awakened and alarmed by the fact that the Chinese had constructed new airfields in the province of Hainan, suspiciously close to the Hanoi-Haiphong area. They were both convinced that the bases, even though they were built on Chinese soil, were not designed for mainland protection but existed primarily to defend North Vietnam in the event of an extension of the battle line too far northward as had occurred during the Korean conflict. Believing that the Chinese would not build bases so close to the border for defense of their own territory, Whiting and Ball felt that the only conceivable use they could have would be to provide cover for North Vietnamese aircraft which might be pursued by American fighters. The installations, Whiting noted, had a "separate language command," and "the North Vietnamese radar network was set up to lock into the grid for South China." Finally, if by inference the purpose of the bases was not clear, in May 1965 the Chinese minister of defense gave what Whiting assayed to be an "astonishingly graphic speech about a strategy of deterrence and advanced defense lines" which specifically and ominously included North Vietnam within China's defense perimeter. Ball and Whiting "took that as proof of the [Chinese] commitment, and argued that if [the United States] was going to bomb the North [it] would have to have cut-off lines." The 19th parallel, they repeatedly argued, was the critical coordinate. With attacks above that line, American air forces risked engagement with China's newly assembled border squadrons.[55]

There were other manifest risks attendant to further escalation. In July 1965 Ball repeated to the president and the war cabinet what was by then his familiar "investment trap warning": With increased troop deployments in Vietnam and an expanded bombing program, the United States would be inexorably compelled to commit progressively greater resources to achieve its military and political objectives. Mounting casualties would "produce increasing pressures on the president to escalate the war beyond prudent levels, and would cause a fall-off in public support."[56] Departing from his characteristically broadbrush political style of argumentation, at a July 21 NSC meeting Ball confronted McNamara on his own terms by circulating a statistical analysis of the Korean War prepared for him by Whiting. Hoping that he would be able to persuade the secretary of defense in the quantitative terms he would appreciate that Vietnam was a loser, Ball launched what was to be a failed effort. He attempted to demonstrate that the American public would not support a war in Vietnam long enough for the military to prevail with the means envisioned. Popular support for the Korean War, he argued, could be measured in inverse proportion to rising casualties.[57] There would be, Ball prophetically warned, a point at which the president would face pressures to decisively end the war in Vietnam. In the recesses of his mind lay the ominous specters of massive invasion and/or the nuclear option to which he had alluded in an earlier memorandum.[58]

McNamara was unimpressed. The secretary of defense had not yet allowed himself to even consider (as he would during the final months of 1967) that the North Vietnamese and Vietcong might prevail. Escalation continued virtually unabated. For six months after General William Westmoreland's request for forty-four additional combat battalions had been granted on July 28, 1965, Ball withdrew from the front lines of dissent. By his own admission he was, "as a professional,"[59] committed to the service of the president and his policies. Willingly, even enthusiastically, Ball performed various functions (discussed in Chapter 5) to advance the administration policy. Like most Americans, Ball "rallied-round-the-flag." It remains a curiosity of public opinion polling on the war that for many, initial disagreement with the commitment gave way to a "get on board" response and demonstration of support for Lyndon Johnson.[60] For Ball, the enthusiasm would be short-lived.

Throughout December and January his doubts about policy were activated once again as a result of the perennial debate over whether, and how long, to extend the 1965 version of the president's Christmas bombing pause. With what his colleagues must have come to regard as habitual apprehension, Ball drafted a memorandum to Johnson in January 1966 entitled "The Resumption of Bombing Poses Grave Danger of Precipitating a War with China" in which he recast and reiterated his antibombing arguments.[61] In a noticeably apologetic tone, stating that he did "not wish to add to [the President's] burdens," he wrote that he felt "an obligation to amplify and document [his] strong conviction that sustained bombing [would] more than likely lead [the United States] into war with Red China in six to nine months," a war that would also precipitate "at least a limited war with the Soviet Union." Citing "forces at work on both sides of the conflict" which could affect this dire outcome, Ball challenged the administration's "philosophy of bombing." Attacking the "inarticulate major premise" held by his senior colleagues that graduated air strikes would eventually convince Hanoi to stop the war, Ball asserted that the DRV was in no measurable way closer to the negotiating table in January of 1966 than it had been in January of 1965. The bombing campaign was not working.[62]

At a meeting with Johnson's narrowing Vietnam Advisory Group on January 25, 1966, Ball spoke from a flowchart prepared by Whiting to illustrate a foreboding reality: Even as the selection of targets had inched northward toward the prohibitive "Hanoi-Haiphong circle" throughout 1965—and "steadily constricted the geographical scope of immunity"—very little movement on the political and diplomatic fronts could be demonstrated. As American casualties on the ground continued to mount in 1965 and into 1966, Ball argued that the United States was being led "by frustration to hit increasingly more sensitive targets," including Haiphong Harbor, the DRV's petroleum, oil, and lubricant (POL) depots, power stations, airfields, and surface-to-air missile (SAM) installations. With explicit reference to the Cuban Missile Crisis experience of October 1962, Ball hypothesized that the consequences of attacks against important industrial targets would be to "impose a major decision" on the Soviet Union to respond by sending increased assistance or by "squeezing the United States at some other vital point, such as Berlin." Believing the benefits from the enterprise would be "marginal and speculative" while the dangers would continue to be "substantial and the costs considerable," Ball argued against the proposed policy of graduated bombing primarily as "a bad business risk."[63]

In measured words, carefully selected for the edification of his respected senior colleagues who had advocated a considerably upgraded bombing program, Ball decried the proposed aerial assaults against North Vietnam. Making only a brief reference to his own private view that it was morally outrageous for the United States to unleash a generalized bombing campaign in North Vietnam, he suggested that *not* striking the "Hanoi-Haiphong circle" had become a symbol of American restraint and that attacks in the area would involve "a new magnitude of industrial destruction and civilian casualties." Further, as he specifically pointed out to Rusk, McNamara, and Johnson, as aircraft were lost, demands to increase aerial attacks on the offending SAM sites and airfields would most surely mount. The psychology was ominous: "Yielding at one point," Ball wrote, "gives away the logic for resisting at another." Declaring that the United States lacked a coherent and systemic plan for the strategic bombing of industrial targets in North Vietnam, the under secretary maintained that attacking Haiphong was "pragmatism at its worst and most dangerous."[64]

Ball reminded his associates that in strategy discussions during the 1962 Cuban crisis, the air force, when pressed, had speedily retreated from a blanket guarantee that any target could be destroyed in a single attack. As well, his survey of Allied strategic bombing after World War II contributed to his already considerable skepticism about reliance on bombing as a monolithic strategy. As requisite second- and third-wave assaults would meet "heavy aircraft resistance" (Ball cited ten MIG engagements that month as evidence of the DRV's capability of defending the skies over Hanoi and Haiphong), targeting would, by military necessity, become incrementally less discriminating. Ball calculated that once urban and industrial targets were hit, the enemy would assume that a general air assault was under way, and the already significant pressure of the DRV "to request use of Chinese air bases North of the border for the basing of North Vietnamese planes" would be intensified.[65]

Worse, Ball argued, the effect of the strikes would be felt mostly by North Vietnam's primary supplier nation, the Soviet Union. He predicted that with a graduated air war and attacks on North Vietnam's major harbors, the Russians would be tempted to off-load cargoes in China for transshipment by rail to the DRV, the consequence of which would be to drive the Chinese and the Soviets more closely into each other's arms in a cooperative enterprise. On the diplomatic front, which always factored most prominently into his analysis, the Soviets would construe the air strikes "as a major attack on their independent leverage *vis-à-vis* the Chinese with the DRV." Moreover, an attack on Haiphong Harbor, with an "almost constant presence of foreign [particularly Russian] shipping," would create hazards which would be difficult to overstate. This, as Ball well knew, greatly worried Johnson. The president's worse nightmare was that an American pilot from Johnson City, Texas, would drop a bomb down the smokestack of a Russian freighter with a Russian diplomat on board and ignite World War III.[66]

In a final persuasive effort, Under Secretary Ball attacked what he felt were "illusory tactical advantages" of bombing POL targets in and around Haiphong and Hanoi. In a comprehensive and exceedingly complex analysis of North Vietnam's POL imports and storage capability, he aggressively set about to undermine the enthusiasm of those who believed that Ho Chi Minh could either be bombed into submission or persuaded to negotiate a settlement that fell short of guaranteeing his ultimate conquest. During the preparation of this particular memorandum in May 1966, Ball became consumed with the argument, taking valuable time away from other obligations to which he was more fully committed. It is obvious from an examination of the memorandum that Ball had painstakingly mastered an extraordinary amount of raw intelligence and carefully condensed it into a cogent argumentative brief: The ability of the DRV to develop alternative supply routes, together with their frugal use of industrial materials, decidedly minimized the adverse impact of American bombs on the war effort. He soon reached the distressing conclusion that even "optimum destruction" of the Hanoi and Haiphong POL would have "*no appreciable effect*" on the supply of POL" required for the movement of men and supplies into Laos and on into South Vietnam. Citing a Special National Intelligence Estimates (SNIE) study of February 4, 1966, Ball prophetically argued that "even if *all* POL were destroyed, and *all* ports closed, sufficient supplies for [infiltration] could be brought in by alternatives means [emphasis added]."[67]

Once again, as the record shows, Ball lost his argument. POL depots in the North—and in their wake, commercial and urban areas—were targeted for American bombs on June 29, 1966. Once again, history validated Ball's predictions. Admittedly miscalculating the scope of Chinese intervention, he proved to be extraordinarily accurate in his before-the-fact bombing prognosis. With all dispatch, as American aircraft flew 8,100 sorties over North Vietnam between June 29 and July 29, at least 80 percent of the POL targets in and around the Hanoi-Haiphong area were destroyed. Indeed, the American "strangulation program" hit every known storage depot. By December 1966, the Defense Department boasted that the air war had obliterated nearly 4,000 POL areas while partially wrecking at least that number. American bombs had also razed dozens of thousands of boats, railroad vehicles, trucks, more than 100 ports, 8,000 buildings, and literally thousands of other targets.[68]

Told in bare bones statistics, the bombing campaign in Vietnam can be said to have been a spectacular success. But as so often would be the case during the course of the complex war, the numbers belied stark realities. Numerical indices of progress were counterbalanced by paradoxical indices of failure. Despite so many American bombs, at the end of 1966 North Vietnam still managed to maintain between 30,000 and 40,000 tons of POL storage capacity in medium-sized sites distributed throughout the countryside and approximately 28,000 tons of capacity in smaller tank and drum farms. The incongruous punch line to the cold statistical analyses was that the DRV needed just 32,000 tons of POL to carry on the war at the 1965–66 level of engagement. The CIA—consistently more pessimistic in its forecasts than the Defense Department—confronted the essential problem: notwithstanding the fact that more than 50 percent of North Vietnam's POL bulk storage capacity had been destroyed, "substantial stocks" survived, enabling them to "keep at least essential military and economic traffic moving."[69]

With the revelations of the CIA report, McNamara commissioned a panel of war scientists to study the bombing campaign. The Jason Group, as it came to be called, spent the summer of 1966 sifting through data gathered from aerial reconnaissance and battlefield reports. Not unlike the impact report Ball and Galbraith wrote after their survey of Germany after World War II, the Jason Group came to a number of disturbing conclusions which challenged McNamara's "Technowar" doctrines: "In view of the nature of the North Vietnamese POL system . . . and the options available for overcoming the effects of U.S. air strikes . . . it seems doubtful that any critical denial of essential POL has resulted." The Jason Group report emphasized the point that North Vietnam distinctly was *not*, like Germany in 1945, an industrial economy and concluded that after more than 8,000 missions, American bombs had produced "no measurable effect" on North Vietnam's capability to initiate and maintain offensive operations against South Vietnam.

Resigned to the fact that his repeated contraventions about bombing and dire predictions of defeat were rendered hollow without a viable plan for withdrawal, throughout the spring and summer of 1965 Ball began to develop a "peace strategy." He passionately hoped, without deluding himself, that he could lead his president out of a mess. If Johnson was going to get out of Vietnam, he believed, someone would have to tell him how. The story of Ball's role in the search for peace in Southeast Asia is marked with starts and stops and, in the end, disappointment and discouragement. Johnson's clarion call for "unconditional discussions" in his address at Johns Hopkins University on April 7, 1965, had proven to be a good deal less than a springboard to substantive, high level "negotiations" toward peace. Nevertheless, the president's unquestionably sincere desire to stop the killing fostered an atmosphere in which numberless schemes—both official and unofficial, foreign and domestic—were considered.

Observers of Vietnam-era diplomacy generally give poor marks to Johnson, to the State Department, and to the White House staff for their failure to seriously and systematically cultivate any one of the many opportunities for meaningful negotiations that regularly surfaced during the course of the war. Though not a recognized expert on the diplomatic history of the war, journalist Stanley Karnow is representative of the lot when he writes that "the Johnson administration's handling of the peace contacts was as confused, disorganized, and aimless as the war itself." Intermediaries, Karnow adds, not only "lacked clear concepts of the issues at stake, but, in many cases were striving to promote their own interests."[70] In more exculpatory terms, diplomatic historian George C. Herring has concluded that peace may have been wholly unattainable and that "the utter irreconcilability of the negotiating positions staked out by both sides rendered a settlement impossible."[71] Despite the fact that international and domestic political pressure prompted Johnson to incrementally liberalize the terms on which Washington would seek peace with Hanoi, in the end it was the military stalemate that gave rise to the diplomatic impasse. Both sides resolved not to concede at the conference table that which they believed could be won on the battlefield.

As a professional diplomat who struggled firsthand with the peace process, Ball keenly anticipated the cynicism of the academics; twenty years of reflection has merely corroborated his analysis of events as they unfolded in the late 1960s. Reflecting on the omnipresence of new "peace plans," "peace offensives," and "peace feelers," he curtly recalls that "we got ten a week, and not one of them amounted to a damned thing."[72] Though there may have been as many as 2,000 attempts to initiate peace talks between 1965 and 1967,[73] Ball believes that "[the United States was] not actually negotiating because [it] wasn't offering anything"—at any rate, not anything Hanoi did not think it could ultimately achieve militarily with patience and endurance. Ball dismisses the entire peace process during his tenure as under secretary of state as a political formality, simply "keeping the lines of communication open for symbolic reasons."[74]

The fundamental elements of the diplomatic impasse were painfully obvious to America's policy officers. Throughout the Johnson administration, Ho Chi Minh had declared regularly, with only minor variations, that the American presence in South Vietnam was an egregious violation of the 1954 Geneva accords and that, as fundamental preconditions to negotiations, the DRV required that the United States cease bombing and withdraw its military forces and political agents from the South. Subsequent to these actions, Hanoi would negotiate with Saigon on the subject of the political unification of Vietnam through the National Liberation Front (NLF) representatives. During the Johnson presidency the American preconditions for peace included that North Vietnam cease its attacks on the South, withdraw its paramilitary and military forces across the 17th parallel, and respect the sovereignty of the Saigon regime.

Ball's private efforts to recast Washington's negotiating strategy antedate the first comprehensive official attempts to break the diplomatic impasse. Throughout 1965 and 1966 Johnson was obviously attracted to what he referred to as "the Ball Plan," and he regularly called upon his under secretary of state to test the diplomatic waters for options—in the president's words, to "raise red flags."[75] Johnson gave Ball carte blanche to deploy personnel, to develop channels of communication with foreign governments, and to draft blueprints for a negotiated settlement. White House aide Bill Moyers has graphically conveyed Johnson's perception of Ball's role as peacemaker: Demonstrating how the president's long arms would be stretched out far to each side of his imposing frame, his eyes alternately fixed on each of his clenched fists as he spoke, Moyers recounts how Johnson kept saying, "I've got the best minds and the best brains in the country working on this. I've got Bob McNamara over here thinking about just how to turn that military tourniquet enough to make the other guy cry ouch, and I've got George Ball over here working to make sure that when he cries ouch we will be ready to act."[76] From Johnson's perspective, however, there was regrettably little to act upon. The enemy did not cry ouch. The North Vietnamese seemed intransigent.

From the beginning of escalation, Ball had been in the patently unenviable position of having his recommendations for a negotiated settlement held hostage to any one, or combination, of three phenomena: (1) precipitous South Vietnamese or American military reverses which might prompt withdrawal (which he predicted); (2) conspicuous American and South Vietnamese military successes (which he thought highly unlikely); and (3) a timely reexamination of America's basic foreign policy doctrines (of which he thought his colleagues incapable). Leaving no doubt as to which of the three events he thought most likely to occur, the under secretary took it upon himself to develop a negotiating strategy in the event that the fall of the Saigon regime became imminent.

Ball operated from the view that McNamara and Rusk "tended to exaggerate the losses involved in a compromise settlement in South Vietnam."[77] Believing that each side would constantly "be led to accept more dangerous and onerous expedients in an effort to achieve its objectives,"[78] he endeavored to move the lagging diplomatic side of the struggle ahead. Seeking to enhance his credibility, Ball dexterously conscripted Dean Acheson and presidential counsel Lloyd Cutler into his small army of dissenters; together they developed a blueprint for diplomacy.[79]

Though Acheson had originally taken a stereotypically cold warrior position on Vietnam, events—and his close collaboration with Ball—prompted him to consider alternative ways of looking at the problem. Working with Ball, Acheson began his personal metamorphosis from hawk to advocate of withdrawal. This collaboration with a former secretary of state and Establishment luminary is a most remarkable part of the story of Ball's dissent. The fact that he was able to persuade Acheson to identify with a formula for a negotiated settlement— which was, in the spring of 1965, a somewhat impertinent position—testifies to Ball's political skill and personal influence with the elder statesman. During the month of May 1965, Ball, Acheson, and Cutler wrote five papers outlining a theory of negotiation and the procedural mechanics to implement their new approach to achieve a political resolution.

With the risks of continued bombing uppermost in their minds, the three lawyer-diplomats told President Johnson that they saw great advantage for the United States in moving the struggle "from the military to the political arena." Their reasoning was simple and direct: The North Vietnamese were going to defeat the South and their formula proposed to let them do it in politics rather than war. The plan was also based on their shared contention that for too long the United States had been in the embarrassing and confounding predicament of behaving like "a puppet of its puppet."[80] With the present commitment, directed as it was to a specific regime in Saigon, the United States could perform no better in war or diplomacy than its Vietnamese ally. That relationship, they held, must change. They asserted that the United States had never meaningfully invoked Eisenhower's contingent requirement of a standard of political and military performance on the part of South Vietnam.[81] Indeed, the United States had violated its own prearranged criterion by sending greater amounts of aid and military support to a continually deteriorating government. To remedy this, the Ball-Acheson-Cutler plan established a negotiating position for the United States which was independent of the government of South

Genial but forceful, Under Secretary Ball amplifies an argument at a cabinet room encounter on Vietnam in the spring of 1965. (Photograph courtesy of George W. Ball)

Vietnam. In fact, their plan "did *not* require South Viet-Nam to enter into negotiations," and it declared a U.S. "posture of willingness to hold discussions with any government concerned [emphasis in original]."[82]

Somewhat speciously asserting that they had developed a plan that would "enable each side to conclude that it [had] substantially as good a chance of achieving its long-range goals in the political arena as by continuing military action" (in fact Ball shared Ho's belief that Vietnam's unification under communism was inevitable), the Ball-Acheson-Cutler plan proposed that the United States offer, through the government of South Vietnam if possible but independently of Saigon if necessary: (1) amnesty to "all Viet Cong adherents who cease fighting"; (2) a program for the development of constitutional government based upon an electoral process in which the former Vietcong and NLF cadres would vote and stand for election; (3) the continuation, at the local administrative level, of GVN apparatus; (4) economic and social reconstruction programs; and (5) a pause in military operations and phased withdrawal of American military forces. The major distinction and, from a domestic political perspective, the ultimate liability of the plan was that it invited "the peaceful participation of Viet Cong adherents in the National life of South Viet-Nam."[83]

For its part, Hanoi would need to render explicit guarantees that it had ceased any new infiltration of men and supplies into the South and had halted its aggressive activity against the Saigon regime. Facing up to the fact that the North Vietnamese would never accede to giving back territory they had paid such a high price in blood to achieve, the demand that North Vietnamese forces withdraw from the South was conspicuously absent from the Ball-Acheson-Cutler proposals.

During the spring of 1965 the three peace advocates tried to align their plan with the deteriorating political situation in Saigon. Working independently with his personal State Department staff, Ball was prepared to confront the major question on the American side: Could the U.S. mission in Saigon persuade the South Vietnamese to negotiate on the five points? In May Ball sent his personal assistant, Thomas Ehrlich (an able young lawyer who had helped him prepare his dissenting memorandums), to Saigon to lobby Ambassador Maxwell Taylor and deputy of mission U. Alexis Johnson on the merits of the plan and to record their reservations and questions. It was from the beginning an ill-fated attempt. Ehrlich, somewhat cynical about the assignment anyway (and racked with fever on the trip to Saigon), came back bewildered and pessimistic.[84] Taylor was unmoved. He had no reason to trust Ball's instincts or methods, believing that he had acted capriciously and wholly improperly by clearing the cable that led to Diem's downfall, and had always considered Ball devious.[85] Ambassador Taylor made it abundantly clear to Ehrlich that he would have none of it and later sneeringly referred to the Ball-Acheson-Cutler initiatives as "a giveaway policy."[86] In a second attempt that same month, Ball telegrammed Taylor with hopes of ameliorating his principal objection to Vietcong power sharing. But the argument was transparent. Taylor saw it for what it was—a spurious plan for the United States to back away from a fifteen-year commitment to South Vietnam. Taylor was not yet ready to make that move and was quite disagreeable to the notion, which Ball had made explicit in the correspondence, that the attraction of the plan for the North Vietnamese would be that it "offered them an adequate chance to achieve their long standing objectives." The desirability of the plan to the North Vietnamese would be sustained, Ball said, by their conviction that "the United States would lose interest in South Vietnam."[87] This was not Maxwell Taylor's style. He used his considerable influence with Rusk, McNamara, and the president to extinguish movement toward a negotiated statement, and Ball's peace initiative was finished.

On the momentous question of whether the United States should fight in Vietnam, on the problem of how war, once decided upon, should be waged, and with regard to when the United States should uncouple itself from an increasingly untenable political and military situation, Ball found himself in diametric opposition to his senior colleagues. His arguments had been openly received, circulated, analyzed, and then unceremoniously rejected by the president and his senior war counselors. But set against this pattern of failure, it is also true that Ball inspired and cajoled his associates to contemplate new approaches in dealing with the Vietnam nightmare and, indeed, to reexamine the entire theoretical structure of American foreign policy.

Even in failure, Ball's articulate voice and dogged persistence insured that a sense of proportion and balance would be injected into the rapidly expanding war plans. His unremitting challenges to the assumptions upon which his colleagues were operating proved, in the end, to be at least marginally fruitful. Though he initially lost the bureaucratic battle on the big questions of war and peace, Ball's advocacy and analytical framework were nevertheless compelling. History records that, save for Dean Rusk, each of the architects of escalation ultimately experienced painful metamorphoses. Though Ball himself would be the last to claim credit for their conversions (certainly South Vietnam's tendency to political corruption and the disintegrating war effort baptized many to the new religion of extrication), in waging a war for the hearts and minds of his colleagues, he set in motion a train of events that aroused key individuals to a reconsideration of their views. History shows that Ball's counsel on Vietnam was conspicuously astute. In retrospect, it appears that the manner in which his colleagues received his arguments—and how they perceived him—prejudiced and discounted his advocacy. The dissident under secretary's personal and professional relations with his administration colleagues thus becomes one of the most problematic and pivotal aspects of the agony called Vietnam.

Chapter 4

Antagonists and Allies

I admired George for his courage. He was doing everything he could within the limitations that a president extends to you when he disagrees with you. George just saw it more accurately than the rest of us, and I think he was very gratified when I came around.
—Clark Clifford

BALL FAILED in his efforts to prompt the architects of escalation into revising their fundamental strategic and political assumptions regarding Vietnam's civil war. As the small, seemingly innocuous, incremental escalations were rapidly becoming tyrannical captors of Lyndon Johnson's presidency, few in government, and indeed no one else in the executive branch, so openly expressed the view that the United States was sliding pell-mell toward an unmitigated disaster. But from the date of his first dissenting paper in May 1964 to his departure from government in September 1966, Ball's memos and oral arguments competed unsuccessfully with the forceful advocacy from the president's principal Vietnam proconsuls—the secretary of state, the secretary of defense, and the national security adviser. Had any one among these three individuals been persuaded by Ball's appeals, the course of history could have been profoundly altered. Indeed, as presidential aide Jack Valenti confidently declared, "Had George been able to find *any* ally within the government to confirm his judgment, his opinions would have been extraordinarily effective [emphasis in original]."[1] The ally to which Valenti referred proved to be distressingly elusive.

In evaluating the efficacy of Ball's dissent it is important to recall the chronology of decision making, as well as the political and, indeed, emotional context within which Vietnam policy determinations were made. As noted, Ball registered explicit opposition to any and all American military commitments to Saigon as early as November 7, 1961, only to have Kennedy acerbically brush aside his concerns. Soon afterward, as Kennedy responded positively to the Taylor-Rostow recommendations, while the experimental Strategic Hamlet program was initiated, and while the State Department benignly oversaw the continuous decay of the Diem regime, Ball made a tactical retreat from the front lines of dissent. It was not until the spurious Tonkin Gulf incident and the debates over bombing in the summer and fall of 1964 that Ball again confronted his superiors on the subject of Southeast Asia. During the cabinet-level talks concerning the origination and acceleration of the bombing campaign, Ball spoke up once again, challenged the strategic doctrines of the war managers, and passionately argued against the introduction of American ground forces. On March 8, 1965, events completely overran Ball's position when two Marine battalions landed to defend Da Nang Air Base. Though continuously recommending that the United States should withdraw and seek a negotiated settlement, Ball's realistic objectives after the spring of 1965 included little more than slowing the buildup that had been set in motion between August 1964 and March 1965. During those critical months when the defense of South Vietnam was effectively assumed by the United States, Ball retreated to piecemeal attacks on the increments of escalation, arguing for bombing pauses, reductions in troop level requests, and other modes of restraint when and where he could. The record shows, however, that throughout his entire tenure as under secretary he was without a counterfigure of sufficient rank within the government to substantiate his opposition to the Americanization of Vietnam's civil conflict.

Ball's inability to convert those men at the top ranks of a government determined to wage a limited war in the nuclear age was the consequence of four disarmingly simple factors. First, there were the granitelike convictions of Johnson's closest strategic and military advisers. Rusk, McNamara, Bundy, and the president axiomatically accepted that the United States was legally and morally obligated to maintain South Vietnam's independence and believed that the political, psychological, and strategic implications of withdrawal were unacceptable. Though they did not desire war, they would accept it. With so much written about the period that is flagrantly antiheroic, it must be said that Johnson's war cabinet was not a rogues' gallery but a clique of self-confident, patriotic, and action-oriented liberals who took their responsibilities for the preservation of global security arrangements—and what they mistakenly perceived to be American interests—quite seriously. Secondly, despite the fact that Johnson encouraged Ball to develop contrary arguments, certain organic limitations imposed upon a dissenter in a presidential system became evident. Simply stated here (and developed in Chapter 5), Ball served at the pleasure of the executive and did not enjoy an independent political base from which he could organize a campaign within—or outside—the government to undermine the administration's policy. He was, quite simply, politically and bureaucratically hemmed in by those with whom he disagreed. Thirdly, following from the boundaries imposed upon him as a subcabinet officer, Ball could not make extravagant demands upon the resources of the bureaucracies over which he ostensibly exercised control; his dissent was by definition secretive, and his responsibilities and loyalties were unquestionably divided. Fourthly, Ball's professional preoccupations kept him from devoting an exorbitant amount of time to the persistent stream of political and military crises in Vietnam. Despite the gravity of the unfolding situation in Southeast Asia, Vietnam remained, by his own admission, the least interesting of his concerns as under secretary of state. As we will see, his career-defining focus on the European-American entente seriously compromised the value of his analysis of a guerrilla war in an Asian jungle.

Ball was working against a formidable consensus at the top. Secretary of State Dean Rusk, the most experienced of Johnson's war counselors, was unwavering, even rigid, in his commitment to South Vietnam and proved to be an insurmountable obstacle. Notwithstanding the fact that the secretary and the under secretary were locked in diametric disagreement on the preeminent issue of their day, Rusk and Ball enjoyed a most congenial professional and personal relationship. Openly and sincerely expressing "unlimited admiration"[2] for his under secretary, Rusk regularly endorsed Ball's judgments on a great many subjects. This was particularly true on economic matters, which Rusk "shunned like the plague."[3] Indeed, as Rusk's biographers have found, the secretary of state was "bored by economic issues [and] was delighted to allow Ball to relieve him of such worries."[4] Beyond economic policy, the well-traveled secretary of state admits that he "was always entirely comfortable about having George act as [his] alter-ego when [he] was away on foreign trips." The two men were quite comfortable with each other, admired each other's convictions, and operated "on a kind of interchangeable basis."[5]

To a close observer of both men, the overriding fact that shaped their partnership during the trials of the turbulent 1960s was that "Rusk trusted Ball, and Ball *never once* violated that trust [emphasis in original]."[6] Their warm relationship was built in part upon an end-of-the-day ritual which they regularly shared. It is common knowledge among observers of the State Department during the 1960s that the secretary and under secretary both had a well-deserved reputation for being able to imbibe a considerable volume of Scotch on the rocks.[7] At the end of most working days when they were not away on foreign trips, Rusk and Ball rendezvoused in the secretary's seventh-floor office for "four or five drinks"[8] and a "little bull-session." In "countless conversations about Vietnam" in this decidedly informal setting, Rusk "took notice" of the concerns Ball raised.[9]

But while expressing his admiration for Ball as a statesman and a friend, Rusk is transparently condescending in his evaluation of his under secretary's advice on Southeast Asia: "I had respect for George Ball's views and respect for George Ball as a person," Rusk generously admits, "and I thought that the considerations he brought to bear were not silly; they were real and had to be taken into account." Rusk continues to believe that "it was a value to the government to have George Ball's views." That said, the impression is left that the secretary regarded the under secretary's views on Vietnam as singularly offensive to the orthodox strategic wisdom of the postwar era which he so ardently embraced. Imparting a cryptic assumption that worked against Ball's views, Rusk gives account of the weight given to Ball's judgments on Vietnam by Johnson's unyielding senior advisers: "*We* [ostensibly those counselors who took seriously American responsibilities in South Vietnam as opposed to those who did not] never thought that George Ball was foolish or lacked understanding when he presented his views, *we* simply disagreed [emphasis added]." Rusk has further qualified his assessment of Ball's judgments on Vietnam by emphasizing the depth of his European experience. "George had friendships with many of the European leaders, with many of them on a first name basis." Because of this exposure, the under secretary's views on Southeast Asia were seriously compromised. "George's long exposure to Europe," Rusk admits, jaded his vision on Southeast Asia. Despite his abiding respect for him, Rusk still believes that "Ball lacked a comprehensive view of the world" of the type he claims his own mentor, George C. Marshall (and, by extension, Rusk himself), possessed.[10]

Agreement on most foreign policy issues, open—and well-oiled—exchanges in Rusk's office at the end of long days at the Department of State, and the happy arrangement that their wives became close personal friends substantially neutralized their conceptual and experiential differences and contributed to a most positive and harmonious working relationship.[11] At Foggy Bottom during the 1960s it was quite fashionable to mock the secretary of state for his reticence and perceived lack of creativity. But Ball, it has been repeatedly observed, never once uttered an unflattering remark about the taciturn Rusk,[12] and even within the candid contemplations of his memoirs, he generously characterizes Rusk as his "self-contained leader."[13] Consequently, their association "was one of the most solid relationships that Rusk had."[14]

Indeed, Rusk "loved Ball as a brother, and had enormous respect for his competence and judgment." Years after they had both finished their long public careers, Rusk would say that "Ball was the closest associate he ever had in government" and regret that he never became his successor. Rusk felt that "George was fully qualified to be secretary of state."[15] This bond is also evidenced by the epistles that they exchanged for years after they left government. Though not frequent in the past decade (Ball in particular is wearied by what he considers the burdens of personal correspondence), the letters they exchanged throughout the 1970s demonstrate their continued warm relations and reveal surprisingly parallel philosophies on a wide range of strategic, diplomatic, and domestic political issues.[16]

Curiously, the mutual affection and respect so openly expressed by the two professional diplomats made Ball's Vietnam dissent possible. Without being bound by law or convention to do so, and with a profusion of tradition and precedent to suggest otherwise, Rusk graciously granted Ball the license of in-house disagreement. Ball's staff chief George Springsteen is unalterably persuaded, and Ball himself admits, that if their roles had been reversed, "if Ball had been secretary of state and Rusk under secretary, Ball would have told him to knock it off, and, if you don't like it, quit!"[17] Ball has always believed that he was allowed to buck the tide of escalation because Dean Rusk was "a man of integrity and extraordinary selflessness"[18] and is "by no means sure that under similar circumstances [he] would have been so tolerant or generous" of a naysaying subordinate.[19]

But Rusk was immovable on Indochina. To the extent that Ball was Eurocentric, Rusk was Asia-centric. Never forgetting about the perilous strategic challenges in Europe and what he admitted was the "main area of our concerns,"[20] the secretary's World War II experience and diplomatic training were, in contrast to the under secretary's, rooted in Asia. Colonel Dean Rusk had served as deputy chief of staff to General "Vinegar Joe" Stillwell in the China-Burma-India theater during World War II. At the personal invitation of Secretary of State George C. Marshall he became assistant secretary of state for Far Eastern affairs in 1949 and later, as deputy under secretary of state to Dean Acheson, had accompanied President Truman to Wake Island to confer with General MacArthur during the Korean War—an enterprise which he considered a noteworthy success and which profoundly influenced his analysis of the American mission in Vietnam. Rusk ardently embraced the all points containment doctrine of John Foster Dulles, for whom, in stark contrast to Ball, he had great affection and great admiration.

So it was Ball's Atlanticism versus Rusk's Universalism. Because Rusk's analysis of the Indochinese problem sprang from the geopolitical assumption that the United States could not turn its back on SEATO, he "mistrusted Ball's premises on Vietnam"[21] and thought Ball "too inclined to look at problems in other parts of the world as peripheral to the main area [of Europe]."[22] Rusk and Ball found little common ground between them on the subject of Vietnam. Indeed, their general views were irrevocably antithetical, and with specific regard to the question of an American commitment under SEATO, their views were equally irreconcilable. To the credit of both men, profound disagreements over the American policy in Southeast Asia never tainted their good friendship, and they remain quite charitable in discussing each other's role in the Vietnam agony. In an act of graceful understatement with reference to the U.S. obligation pursuant to the SEATO pact, Rusk concluded, "I think George and I may have had some different evaluation of that."[23]

In truth, the record shows that Rusk aggressively challenged Ball's memo of June 23, 1965 (entitled "United States Commitments Regarding the Defense of South Vietnam"), which had denied that the United States was explicitly bound to the military defense of the Saigon regime. The secretary forcefully attacked all the under secretary's major legal premises as well as his general conclusions regarding the diplomatic arrangements under SEATO. "There can be no serious debate about the fact that we have a commitment," Rusk wrote, and he concluded that "the integrity of the US commitment is the principal pillar of peace throughout the world."[24] Inverting Ball's argument about the Europe-first hierarchy of America's strategic commitments, Rusk asserted that "[the SEATO accords] automatically connected that treaty with the entire structure of collective security in the rest of the world." The secretary presumed then, and continues to presume today, that the American signature on the SEATO document "related our conduct under the South East Asia Treaty to the Rio Pact and NATO." Rusk asserted that "in a real sense, how we acted in Vietnam had a direct bearing upon [what was admittedly] the main relationship we had in Western Europe."[25] Thus, in Rusk's view, the United States had to be both a European and an Asian power. He believed that the United States was "inevitably a two ocean nation" and once told a NATO conference that the Europeans "should not expect us to be a virgin in the Atlantic and a whore in the Pacific." To Rusk, American pledges in Southeast Asia reflected "the fidelity of the United States toward security treaties, and that point was a very important one for NATO itself."[26]

Though Ball concurred that the United States had interests and obligations in Asia, he disagreed with Rusk about the specific zones of obligation and the specific applications of power appropriate to fulfilling them. Ball had, for

Ball, *left*, and Secretary of State Rusk at 1965 discussion of Vietnam policy. Rusk listened intently in the spring of 1965 but felt that the United States was obliged to honor its commitment to South Vietnam. (Photograph courtesy of George W. Ball)

example, supported (albeit reluctantly) the Korean intervention and had even proposed the limited deployment of American military forces in Indonesia and Thailand—as a more plausible alternative to planting the flag in Saigon—to satisfy those bent on "checking the spread of monolithic communism." But, unlike Rusk, Ball does not so casually discount the depth of his disagreement with his superior over Vietnam. In their many unguarded exchanges about Vietnam Ball would instruct Rusk: "Look, you've got no government [in Saigon]; it's impossible to win in a situation where you've got this totally fragile political base. These people [South Vietnam's leadership] are clowns." Rusk would typically respond, "Don't give me that stuff," and was not above lecturing Ball: "You don't understand that at the time of Korea that we had to go out and dig Syngman Rhee out of the bush where he was hiding. There was no government in Korea either. We're going to get some breaks and *this thing is going to work* [emphasis in original]."[27] Rusk would also remind Ball of the dire events in 1942 when Hitler was overrunning Western Europe and the Japanese were menacing all of Asia. "What if Roosevelt," he asked Ball, "had gone on nationwide radio and said, 'My fellow Americans, the jig is up'?" In

Europe and again in Korea, Rusk tirelessly repeated to Ball, the Americans "stuck it out and prevailed."[28]

With his energies often sorely depleted by the excited diplomatic environment of the 1960s, Rusk could instinctively articulate a handful of antiappeasement and Cold War clichés. It is commonly understood that Rusk battled with physical and emotional fatigue. Throughout his tenure as secretary of state, he kept what has been described as "a killing schedule." Most of his associates recognize that his work habits—"keeping twenty or thirty appointments a day," the constant travel, seemingly endless negotiations—all took a toll on his psychological and physical health. Throughout 1965 there were repeated appeals to Johnson to get him to slow down, but Rusk maintained an exceedingly rigorous and debilitating pace. To his closest associates, "he seemed to live on cigarettes, scotch, and aspirin." During frequent bouts with fatigue, it has been observed, "his vision seemed to narrow, and he reverted increasingly to the old, tested themes of his experience [including] the absolute necessity of collective security to keep peace in the nuclear age, and the deterrence of aggression by Communist states preaching subversion against the free world."[29] As the war in Vietnam went badly, Rusk's general health continued to deteriorate.

Given this collision of opinion conjoined with the emotional stresses of steering a course for American policy in an increasingly dangerous world, it was predictable that Ball would become embroiled in "very hot arguments" with his senior colleagues over Vietnam. This was particularly true in his encounters with Robert S. McNamara. Ball maintains that though the normally cool and rational secretary of defense at times got "very angry" at him during their many disputes over Vietnam, the disagreements "never affected [his] relations with Dean or Bob."[30] The impressions of other principals—and the record—suggest otherwise, however. Unlike Rusk, McNamara never developed a close friendship with Ball and was decidedly less patient with what he considered to be the under secretary's schismatic, and even disloyal, conception of America's role in Southeast Asia. According to then assistant secretary of defense Cyrus Vance, who considers himself to have been "close to both men" during the mid-1960s, "McNamara admired George's mind and considered him a powerful intellect," but Vance adds that "the chemistry between the two was never particularly good." An admirer of Ball's position on the war, Vance in retrospect continues to lament McNamara's inability to see past the exterior of Ball's advocacy, and he regrets that "George's [Vietnam] position never had much effect on Bob."[31]

In contrast to the laconic Rusk, who was in clinical terms a "passive

Ball, *left*, with Rusk, *center*, and President Lyndon B. Johnson. Confidently poised between Ball and Johnson, Rusk was unwavering in his opposition to the under secretary's counsel to withdraw from Vietnam throughout the intense deliberations of July 1965. (Photograph courtesy of George W. Ball)

aggressive" in the bureaucratic debates over Vietnam (and who usually made his views known to the president only in private), McNamara was an "obsessive compulsive," responding quickly and sharply to challenges of his computations in general meetings with the president's advisory staff. With most working memorandums on Vietnam written for presidential discussion predicated by McNamara's basic formulations—and no other systematic and sustained dissent on the table for discussion—Ball was the lone counterpuncher. McNamara did not quietly tolerate the blows from a subcabinet officer. To put it mildly, Ball got under McNamara's skin, and their exchanges could be quite heated indeed.[32]

One factor contributing to what at times was their easily irritable relationship was that they thought and communicated in wholly dissimilar modes. Ball believed that McNamara was too stiffly quantitative and did not immediately grasp or give weight to the political or psychological implications of what he was proposing to do in Vietnam. "America," it has been shrewdly observed, "was not McNamara's business. Managing the machinery of war was his business."[33] The secretary of defense busied himself only with the question of how, not whether, to deter the Communists in Vietnam. Further, McNamara felt that Ball was out of his element when it came to planning a counter-insurgency war in Indochina; worse, he believed that the under secretary was prone to reckless exaggeration in his dissenting arguments. In McNamara's presence, Ball would tell the president of his experience with French clients during their 1954 retreat from Southeast Asia and "it would just drive him [McNamara] up the wall." Ball noted sarcastically that, with the French, "there was always a new plan—the Navarre Plan, the DeLattre Plan, de Tassigny Plan"—which produced only disillusionment and, in the end, defeat.[34] McNamara could not, or would not, see the relevance of Ball's analogies to the French debacle. He simply refused to concede that it was even possible for the North Vietnamese to prevail on the battlefield. When it came to the subject of Vietnam, their dialogue followed a set pattern. McNamara would propose and Ball would oppose, often saying, "Well, I don't think it's demonstrated that this is going to achieve the purpose at all, and I don't think the argument has been made in any convincing form that this can succeed or that it's going to do any good." McNamara was always quick to counter what he considered to be Ball's meddling in the conduct of tactical military operations. "All right George, what do you propose to do?" McNamara would bite back. Of course Ball's set answer was to seek an immediate negotiated withdrawal by making huge political concessions, a formulation which remained patently unacceptable to Johnson and his principal advisers.[35]

To appreciate the intensity of their discord during the in-house Vietnam debates, it is important to note that they also harbored fundamental disagreements about the nature of dissent within the advisory system. Both Rusk and McNamara put a premium on consensus among cabinet and subcabinet officers; intramural disputes, they believed, should be carefully "managed" and "contained." Rusk took great care to establish an excellent working relationship with the secretary of defense. His memories of the destructive feud between Secretary of Defense Louis Johnson and Secretary of State Dean Acheson in the Truman administration had convinced him that harmony between State and Defense was absolutely essential to the smooth conduct of foreign policy. Rusk established regular meetings with McNamara, usually on Saturday mornings, when interruptions would be minimal and they could talk at length. Rusk thought it was important that they resolve their differences by themselves, in order to present a common viewpoint to the president.

More lawyerly, and personally stimulated by dialectical debate, Ball thought the relationship between the two department chiefs was a little too harmonious and felt that the president and the country would benefit from open exchanges on the issues at the senior cabinet level. Further, he thought Rusk deferred too quickly and too often to McNamara on strategic and tactical concerns. But Rusk and McNamara both consistently operated on the premise that disagreements should be thrashed out in small groups before a policy recommendation—based upon an evolved consensus—was presented to the executive. Once a policy decision was reached, McNamara was loath to reexamine the particulars. "I know how you feel, Arthur," McNamara once told the dovish Ambassador Goldberg before a National Security Council meeting on Vietnam, "but it would be better if you didn't say anything. The president has already made up his mind and you would only embarrass him." When Ball first had the unmitigated gall to press his heretical views into a formal memorandum (October 1964), McNamara was "shocked by the document—less by Ball's apostasy than by his rashness in putting such thoughts on paper, which might leak to the press."[36] It also appears that McNamara did not fully trust Ball's discretion, as he once impatiently instructed him as to when and to whom he should make his private views on the war known.[37]

When Ball's October 1964 memorandum was first quietly circulated to the appropriate cabinet and White House offices (it was unpretentiously addressed to "Dean, Bob, and Mac"), McNamara was "absolutely horrified" and treated his copy "like a poisonous snake."[38] The general attitude of the paper's initial recipients (Rusk, McNamara, Bundy) was to consider it as something that really should not have been written—and "McNamara really just regarded it as next to treason."[39] Vance recalls that the paper received "very limited dissemination,"[40] even among McNamara's principal lieutenants. It is quite curious that this seminal memorandum (entitled "How Valid Are the Assumptions Underlying Our Viet-Nam Policy") never found its way into the hands of more than a very few cabinet and security agency department heads, and it is conspicuous by its absence in the collection of materials that came to be known as the *Pentagon Papers*—documents which were assembled at McNamara's direction, ostensibly to provide a *full* accounting of the options considered as policy evolved. What the secretary of defense did with his copy is uncertain. Although McNamara has very recently insisted that he "did not influence in any way" the disposition of the paper, it is prudent to conclude that he did not personally insure that Ball's dissent took its place among the significant documents related to the war.[41]

From the decidedly limited personal insights into the Vietnam era that Robert McNamara has disclosed,[42] the impression that emerges is that as he formulated his own views, he was not seriously detained by Ball's papers. Clearly, he did not take the substance of the October 1964 memorandum, or

Ball's dissent generally, very seriously. Indeed, he dismisses the entire body of the under secretary's arguments by reminding the author that "none of Ball's proposals were ever actively staffed-out." In almost belittling tones pointing to the conclusion that Ball's memorandums were not seriously considered as policy options by more thoughtful and responsible men, McNamara has urged the author to "examine carefully the degree to which they [Ball's memos] excited additional work along the same lines in the State Department, the Defense Department, the National Security Council, and the advisory staff." McNamara's analysis of Ball's dissent includes the caution that it is one thing for a paper to have been written—and even discussed—and quite another for it to have stimulated follow-up studies throughout the agencies.[43]

Of course, McNamara is correct. National Security Council and presidential advisory group records show that Ball's papers elicited sustained and excited debate within a very limited circle, but not much else. Meeting notes of key National Security Council meetings on Vietnam, in two corroborative, semiverbatim accounts recorded by Jack Valenti and NSC staffer Chester Cooper, clearly indicate that in talks during the period from February to July 1965—and particularly the critical discussions of July 21 and 28, 1965, after which Vietnam's civil war was effectively "Americanized"—Ball's papers were openly debated and he had his day in court.[44] Absent from the records of the Defense Department, State Department, and National Security Council, however, is any evidence whatever that Ball's papers initiated follow-up analyses or in any way affected policy. Indeed, William Bundy's paper of June 30, 1965, entitled "Holding on in South Viet-Nam" is the single memorandum to make a reference to a Ball paper. In it, Bundy recommended a "middle way" between precipitous abandonment called forth by Ball and precipitous escalation called forth by McNamara. In calling attention to the under secretary's dissent, Bundy merely concurred with Ball's analysis of the type of warfare the North Vietnamese would likely continue to wage against American forces.[45] In effect, Bill Bundy endorsed Ball's evaluation without endorsing his recommendation.

Although the security agencies may not have been stimulated by the dissident under secretary's Vietnam briefing book, Johnson was. The president had been particularly shaken by Ball's June 18 memorandum ("Keeping the Power of Decision Making in the South Viet-Nam Crisis"), in which he had written an impassioned appeal against committing troops above the 100,000 level. Ball believed that pledging American forces above that number would, by default, necessitate a commensurate escalation of Washington's political commitment to Saigon, narrow the U.S. negotiating position, and rapidly transform Vietnam's civil war into the long-dreaded "American land war in Asia." Immediately after Ball's June memo, Johnson took another hard look at the perilous course of action his advisers recommended. The president assigned the argumentative under secretary of state, the foremost advocate of restraint, and the pugnacious secretary of defense, the apostle of more aggressive policies, to more fully develop their analyses. Each was given an opportunity to assemble a more complete exposition of the views they had been arguing orally and in brief memorandums during the spring.

In early June the administration had announced that the number of American personnel in Vietnam would be frozen at 95,000. The Ball-McNamara debate within the administration centered on General William Westmoreland's request for an additional fifty battalions (200,000 troops). On June 21, Johnson issued Ball his marching orders through his young assistant Bill Moyers. "I want George to work for the next 90 days to work up what is going to happen after the monsoon season," the president told Moyers on the telephone. Johnson wanted it to be made clear to Ball that he was determined not to "go riding off in the wrong direction." Resigned to the approach that the United States might escalate the war "bit by bit," Johnson told McNamara "not to assume [he was] willing to go overboard." Referring to Ball and McNamara, the president confided to Moyers that "the fellow here with the best program is the way I will probably go"[46] and gave him the impression that he was, in early June at any rate, still undecided about whether or not to escalate above 100,000. Though Johnson ultimately made his decision for war on a much accelerated timetable (thirty rather than ninety days), the under secretary of state and the secretary of defense engaged each other in a direct competition for the president's ear throughout June and July. Whether or not Johnson "staged" this debate for political purposes, or whether he was in fact, during the month of June, genuinely undecided about a massive commitment of troops, is one of the more puzzling questions from the period and is examined in Chapter 5.

It was the second time in his curious career as a dissenter that Ball operated with an explicit presidential commission to develop his views on Vietnam. In rapid succession he drafted memos entitled "United States Commitments Regarding the Defense of South Viet-Nam" (on June 23), "A Plan for Cutting Our Losses in South Viet-Nam" (on June 28), and "A Compromise Solution" (on July 1). As previously noted, these papers argued that American policy was flawed by the absence of a specified and articulated rationale for extrication. Ball suggested one. Revealing his latent admiration for Eisenhower,[47] he based his formula on a precondition for American assistance to Vietnam established in 1954: "[the] ability of the South Vietnamese to use [American] assistance effectively."[48] Asserting that South Vietnam had not lived up to its end of the original bargain, Ball believed the Americans should fold their tent in Vietnam and come home. If the Americans stayed, the under secretary argued, they would lose the war.

Against these specific admonitions—and what were by then Ball's routinized recommendations to withdraw American forces—McNamara encouraged the president to hang on. During June and July the secretary of defense painted a sober picture of the deteriorating political and military conditions in South Vietnam. Arguing the flip side of Ball's reasoning, McNamara cited recent Vietcong successes, high ARVN casualty and desertion rates, loss of morale in Saigon, and the disappointing results from the bombing campaign as evidence that the United States should put more in. Resigned to "great difficulties ahead," McNamara offered the president, in his peculiar idiom, three options, the very framing of which precluded the acceptance of two: Option A (Ball's) was to withdraw under "conditions humiliating to the United States" and "damaging to our future effectiveness on the world scene"; Option B (Bill Bundy's) suggested that the Americans continue "at the present level" (which obviously did little to mitigate McNamara's June assessment that South Vietnam was near defeat); Option C (his own) endorsed a "substantially" expanded (175,000 to 200,000 troop level) American military input "to take the offensive" against the Vietcong/DRV and "to run them to the ground and destroy them." Predictably, McNamara advised that Option C promised "the course of action involving the best odds of the best outcome with the most acceptable cost to the U.S."[49]

The secretary of defense calculated that with this escalation, Americans killed in action could well exceed 500 per month, but he assured Johnson that public support for the war would continue. Coincidentally, McNamara was pressing hard at the very moment that events on the ground in South Vietnam were working against Ball's views. There had been a desperate call on June 18 from Air Vice Marshall Nguyen Cao Ky (who had become prime minister of a military regime the previous week) for more troops. Following this came news of the execution of an American prisoner-of-war, the bombing of a Saigon restaurant, and the disclosure of a Vietcong death list which included the names of Ambassador Taylor, Deputy Ambassador Alexis Johnson, and General Westmoreland. Johnson felt as though he was being intentionally provoked. Repeated crises in South Vietnam shocked the president into believing for the first time that he could lose the country to the Communists. In the end it was McNamara's advice which provided the "lighting rod" against which alternative courses of action were measured. Ball, Bundy, and McNamara were, as political scientist Larry Berman has pointed out, really "three unequal players." Though there was actually little doubt in anyone's mind as to whose arguments carried more weight with the president, after the June "debate" the secretary of defense emerged as the *"primus inter pares* among the principals."[50] McNamara would run the war. Until his own agonizing transfiguration from hawk to dove at the end of 1967, the secretary of defense would personally control the levers of technocratic combat in Indochina.

Adding to Ball's burdens as the only dissenter during the period in which the decisions were taken that Americanized the war was the fact that National Security Adviser McGeorge Bundy, like McNamara, was not measurably detained by his arguments. This should not have been surprising. On an intellectual level, Bundy honestly disagreed with Ball's analysis, gave greater strategic weight to Vietnam than the under secretary, and was, like Rusk, determined to meet what he saw as the Communist challenge to America's credibility. But there were also the problems of Bundy's professional and personal relationships with Ball. Though they have managed to maintain an outwardly cordial friendship since their government service,[51] the Ball-Bundy working accord was undermined by significant philosophical and political asymmetries. Bundy had been an Eisenhower Republican in 1952 and 1956 and Kennedy's personal first choice for under secretary of state in 1961. In Ball's view, Bundy typified what he referred to as the movers and shakers of the Kennedy administration and had been too easily seduced by the notion of extending American influence into the distant corners of the planet. Bundy, as Harvard dean and Yankee patrician, epitomized the Eastern Establishment from which Ball, the self-identified middle westerner, continued to feel alienated.

Clearly, their relationship lacked the abiding mutual affection which blunted Ball's disagreement with Rusk over Vietnam. Though they substantially overcame a "slightly prickly beginning,"[52] the under secretary's innate prejudice against NSC interference with the foreign policy machinery surfaced intermittently. Unlike many others in the Kennedy-Johnson coterie—including LBJ himself—Ball was "never in awe of McGeorge Bundy."[53] Unable to elicit the under secretary's deference, Bundy was suspicious of his methods, feeling that he was "too independent"[54] and prone to overstep bureaucratically defined roles. In his inimitable manner, Bundy once maligned what he thought to be Ball's egocentrism by telling him, "The trouble with you, George, is that you always want to be the piano player."[55] Bundy also appears not to have completely trusted Ball's conception of team play. In one notable episode in the summer of 1965, shortly after Ball's arguments against escalation had been debated and dismissed, Bundy suspected that the under secretary had leaked a self-aggrandizing account of his in-house dissent to columnist Joseph Kraft. Ball denied the allegation with ill-concealed indignation.[56]

Throughout their coinciding service to Presidents Kennedy and Johnson, the two antagonists weathered a number of excited procedural disagreements. A representative incident occurred in December 1963, when Bundy expressed dismay over mixed signals he had received from Rusk and Ball on a nomination for the post of deputy chief of mission in Saigon. Ball's personal choice had been William Sullivan, who, after traveling to Saigon with the Taylor-Rostow mission, began to doubt the wisdom of an American intervention. The White House candidate was David Nes, liked by Johnson and Bundy because they believed he "could go for the jugular."[57] After it became evident that Rusk was leaning toward Nes as the recommendation of the State Department, Ball began to backfill, reminding Bundy of earlier reservations the president had expressed about his own selection and repeating his high opinion of Sullivan. Bundy perceived Ball to be deviously trying to uproot a decision that had already been taken by the secretary of state. After the terse exchange Ball told Bundy, "You and I are getting at a place where we're getting rather quarrelsome with one another." Bundy shot back, "I really can only do business with one department at a time. I keep getting different signals from different parts of the seventh floor."[58] So he did.

Ball's relationship with Bundy was also compromised by a serious substantive dispute over the proposed Multilateral Nuclear Force (MLF), a project close to Ball's heart and closely linked to his aspirations for European unity.[59] Even today Bundy admits that it caused them real problems, and he has made, in light of the policy deliberations over Vietnam, the most remarkable statement that "George and I had our most sustained difference over the MLF."[60] In fact, Bundy went to considerable lengths to cut Ball off from the president on the idea of a collective European nuclear deterrent. Once, when Rusk ostensibly registered his support for the concept of a European-American nuclear arrangement (while not endorsing a precise blueprint), Bundy openly doubted the authenticity of the State Department memorandum. In a memo to the president covering the "Rusk paper," Bundy wrote, "The signature is the signature of Rusk, but the language is the language of Ball," suspecting that the under secretary had somehow taken advantage of Rusk's momentary distraction with other business to secure his signature on a memo that he did not wholly endorse. Bundy told Johnson that "George is pressing much too hard in a direction that does not make sense." As evidence of the national security adviser's considerable irritation, he wrote the president a second memorandum that same day stating, "I am sorry to say that this has become an obsession with George Ball, Robert Schaetzel and Henry Owen—they keep coming back to it by one means or another, and [the attached] memorandum is simply one more try."[61] In the end Bundy was able to persuade President Johnson not to endorse the MLF, and the project proposal for a collective nuclear deterrent sponsored by the United States died a slow, painful death.

In a sojourn that would further cement his convictions about an American presence in Indochina, Bundy toured South Vietnam. During his visit (on February 7, 1965), Vietcong forces attacked the American base at Pleiku, destroying helicopters and aircraft and killing eight American servicemen. The incident had a great impact on Bundy. "The polite debates around the highly polished conference table," as Johnson aide Richard Goodwin has observed, "were shockingly metamorphosed into real bodies, real blood, the audible moans of injured men. Bundy was horrified." Johnson later recounted that "all it took was a little taste of blood to turn him into a real hawk." Vietnam was, for the national security adviser, "no longer just a question of policy, it was a matter of honor and revenge." When he returned to Washington, Bundy began to advocate a campaign of "sustained reprisals" against the North Vietnamese and Vietcong. "We cannot assert," he wrote, "that [such] a policy will succeed in changing the course of the contest in Vietnam. [But] even if it fails, the policy will be worth it. At a minimum it will damp down the charge that we did not do all we could."[62]

Ideologies, bureaucratic personalities, and passions aside, Ball and Bundy harbored honest intellectual disagreements over Vietnam. Principally, Bundy did not believe that Ball's gloomy analyses took sufficient notice of the appalling casualties inflicted upon the Vietcong and NVA. "To accept Ball's argument," Bundy cautioned in oral and written arguments at a critical National Security Council meeting on July 21, 1965, called to debate the withdrawal option, "would be a radical switch in policy without visible evidence that it should be done." Unimpressed by Ball's strategic analysis, Bundy attempted to deflate his case against intervention by returning to the proven theme of American credibility. "George's analysis gives no weight to the losses suffered by the other side," Bundy stated, and he warned that "the world, the country and the Vietnamese people would have alarming reactions if we got out."[63]

Bundy also believed that Ball had simply failed to carefully think through the problem of what would happen to the country's global credibility if the Americans turned and ran. Sharing Ball's concern about maintaining the solidarity of the Western Alliance, Bundy had long felt, like Bobby Kennedy, that "the Americans might have to bleed a little in Southeast Asia to convince the Europeans they would bleed a lot on their continent." Ball ardently disputed this logic and was unalterably persuaded that the Europeans attached no significance to American forces being stationed in Southeast Asia. Simply stated, Ball would, and Bundy could not, accept the consequences of a precipitous American withdrawal from Vietnam. "George really didn't confront the difficulty with his ideas," Bundy has stated in a retrospective moment, and he recalls challenging him by retorting, "If you're not going to stay there what are you going to do about it?" Bundy recalls that, at the time, Ball's habitual answer, to "make peace," seemed a woefully inadequate response to the governing political and strategic realities. In the period before 1967, Bundy never discounted the strategic logic of the domino theory. "Either we go in there or the South falls to the North," Bundy argued, "and so do the associated Indochina states." More than once, in utter exasperation with Ball's unrelenting persistence in advancing what he considered an unacceptable formula for peace, Bundy would bark, "What are you going to say to the world about the people whom you have said that you'd never desert?"[64]

Thirdly, Bundy disagreed with a cornerstone of Ball's argument—that the United States was sorrowfully repeating a French tragedy. Full of guarded optimism, and directly challenging the under secretary's warnings, Bundy wrote a memorandum to the president on June 30, 1965, entitled "France in Vietnam, 1954, and the U.S. in Vietnam, 1965—A Useful Analogy?" in which he implored the president not to be deterred by Ball's histrionics. Bundy, like Walt Rostow who succeeded him as NSC director, held the view that South Vietnam was well along the road to becoming a stable capitalist democracy. At an NSC meeting on February 17, 1965, Bundy stated that "a non-communist society is struggling to be born," and he added that "there will be time to decide our policy won't work after we have given it a good try."[65] Unlike the French, the American people were "reconciled to our role in this conflict." The Americans, Bundy believed, had options and power available to them in 1965 which the French did not have in 1954.[66]

Finally, with regard to how Ball's dissent could be "managed," Bundy operated from a premise that was regrettably similar to Rusk's and McNamara's. As NSC director, Bundy was charged with monitoring opinions and presenting recommendations to the president in a politically sensitive manner. Bundy's self-defined role was to judiciously balance the separate, often incongruous, tasks of letting the president hear every argument from the bureaucracies and helping him forge conclusions from discordant opinions. A fact of life of the Johnson presidency from its inception in November 1963 to Bundy's departure in February 1966 was that the NSC director significantly influenced the manner in which the president processed advice. Indeed, Bundy meticulously orchestrated debates among the cabinet chiefs—who themselves canonized consensus—with a keen sense of bureaucratic hierarchy. It appears that to Bundy (and this was also the case for Rusk, McNamara, and the president), what was being advocated was often less important than the rank of the advocate. "It is certainly true," Bundy believed, "that if you are going to ask yourself what is the state [department] position [on Vietnam], you ask yourself first what is Rusk's position? That was a principle." In an enormously illuminating admission Bundy has also stated that he is quite certain that "if Ball had been secretary and Rusk a good hard-nosed under secretary, McNamara would have paid more attention—and I dare say so would the president."[67]

Personally in disagreement with Ball's brief on the war and hypersensitive to the uncomfortable political fact that Ball was complicating his task of consensus building within the top ranks of the administration, Bundy repeatedly engineered the dissemination and discussion of Ball's Vietnam papers so as to preordain their impact. The pattern was established at the outset with Ball's comprehensive memorandum of October 5, 1964. Two weeks after Ball circulated his paper Bundy wrote his own presidential memorandum—with Ball's paper attached to it—informing Johnson that "George Ball has sent this over as a personal memorandum." Bundy stated that he harbored "some reservations about it especially as a proposal in the height of the campaign," but conceded that he had "an obligation to George to make sure you get it."[68]

The president did not see the memorandum until February 24, 1965, and, as he barked at Ball on the telephone the same day, he "wanted to know why he had not read it before."[69] While not admitting to obstructing Ball's access to the president, Bundy reluctantly concedes that Ball "did not feel as though I was representing his views with the President adequately."[70] In explaining the manner in which the October 1964 memo was managed, Bundy has admitted that "it was extraordinarily clear that the president did not want to have an argument [within the administration] about Vietnam before the election" and has added that "I don't think George understood the substance of that point; he simply understood his argument wasn't being carried forward to the President." Bundy's objectionable methods did not keep Ball from finding alternative routes to the president, and the national security adviser knew of and apparently tolerated Ball's bureaucratic bypasses. "When he [Ball] thought that I wasn't representing his concerns sufficiently strongly," Bundy openly admits, "he went to the president via [Bill] Moyers instead of through me." Bundy concedes that "this was something Lyndon Johnson rather liked. From then on, George was part of the gang, and everyone knew he was part of the gang by the president's expressed desire. That made it all very manageable."[71]

As the options of June–July 1965 narrowed to three—Ball's proposal for a negotiated withdrawal, William Bundy's "middle way," and McNamara's recommendation to escalate—McGeorge Bundy pressed even harder against Ball's position. In a memorandum to Johnson in preparation for what turned out to be a critical July 1 meeting, Bundy wrote, "You will want to listen hard to George Ball *and then reject his proposal*. Discussion could then move to the narrower choice between my brother's course and McNamara's [emphasis added]."[72] Ever wary of Ball's ability to retard the tedious process of consensus building and particularly sensitive to the political fallout that would result from disclosure to the press of the under secretary's heretical views, Bundy repeatedly tried to cut him off by limiting the number of those privy to his arguments. A representative incident occurred before the July 1 meeting when Bundy told the president that "both Rusk and McNamara feel strongly that the George Ball paper should not be argued with you in front of any audience larger than yourself, Rusk, McNamara, and me." After canvassing the state and defense bosses, Bundy cautioned Johnson "that it is exceedingly dangerous to have this possibility [Ball's proposal for withdrawal] reported to a wider circle." Bundy concluded his forewarning to the president with the words, "In the light of Bob's and Dean's feeling . . . *I now recommend we keep this meeting small* [emphasis added]."[73] Clearly, argument about Ball's paper within that limited group preordained its fate.

Meanwhile, as Bundy was attempting to narrow the circle of advisers apprised of Ball's arguments (he even once recommended to Johnson that the under secretary of state be banished to Saigon as ambassador),[74] presidential assistant Bill Moyers worked to widen the readership of Ball's dissenting memorandums and conscript new voices into the ranks of dissenters. Though Moyers resists the temptation to describe Ball's superiors as willful impediments to the task of getting his views presented fairly to the president, he does concede the point that a pervasive sense of hierarchy blunted Ball's effectiveness. "They [Rusk, McNamara, Bundy] weren't obstructionist," Moyers has perhaps too generously stated, "they were men who felt keenly their official responsibilities to present the president with a considered consensus of the secretaries and the NSC." Noting that within the environment created by Johnson and the top cabinet officials, "a dissent was unlikely to have been treated by them as an acceptable way of doing business," Moyers adds, "Rusk and McNamara were not the type of men to say, here is our recommendation and attached is a fifty page paper from someone who disagrees with it. That's

not the way they construed their official duty." Despite the obvious exasperation with the process on so critical an issue, Moyers respects the fact that
"Rusk, McNamara, and Bundy had positions to defend and official responsibilities that made it unlikely they would be as hospitable to a contrary view." In
time, the permanence of this bureaucratic barricade led Moyers to openly
identify with Ball's position on the war, at considerable risk to his own base of
power within the administration as Johnson's trusted aide. By the spring of
1965, Moyers and Ball became "kindred spirits" in an inventive effort to
persuade Lyndon Johnson to reverse course.[75]

The two dissenters each possessed qualities and character traits that made
their collaboration effective. Moyers admits, for example, that his personal
admiration for the under secretary was a significant factor in explaining how
he was pulled out of Johnson's orbit and into Ball's. "It wasn't simply that he
had a position on Vietnam that made me admire him," Moyers concedes, "it
was that he had a way of thinking as well as a world view and a personality that
I found impressive." In the course of their association, Moyers slowly gravitated to Ball's position on the war. "I came to think he was right on Vietnam," Moyers recalls, "and the private conversations [we had] were very
persuasive."[76]

More than twenty years Ball's junior, Moyers credits him with being
"extremely helpful" to the younger men who came to the White House after
Kennedy's murder. The under secretary of state would generously spend time
briefing the new presidential aides brought in by Johnson on political and
economic issues concerning Europe. In time, Ball became Moyers's "tutor" on
Vietnam, and throughout Moyers's incarnation as Johnson's press secretary,
Ball would occasionally help him prepare for news conferences on Southeast
Asia. Moyers tactfully reciprocated by using his extraordinary influence with
the president to help Ball advance his position on the war. When Bundy proved
to be unreliable as a conduit to the president, Moyers oversaw the practical yet
delicate problem of insuring that the under secretary's papers were given to
Johnson at propitious moments. Ball quickly found that Moyers could be
trusted with these politically sensitive, "Top Secret" documents. As George
Springsteen notes, before Ball began working with Moyers, dissenting papers
were clandestinely delivered by Ball himself, or an emissary from his personal
staff, directly to their recipients.[77] The five extant copies of his October 1964
memorandum, for example, had been carefully numbered and signed and kept
in Ball's office safe on the seventh floor of the State Department. Insuring
confidentiality was a crucial part of the enterprise, to which Ball gave great
attention. But by the summer of 1965, Moyers had assumed responsibility for

Vietnam policy discussion, with participants, *left to right*, Assistant Secretary of State for Far Eastern Affairs William P. Bundy, Ball, Rusk, National Security Adviser McGeorge Bundy (with back to camera), President Johnson, and Secretary of Defense Robert McNamara. The countenances of the war managers are suggestive of the way Ball was received during his days in "court" in July 1965. (Photograph courtesy of George W. Ball)

managing the distribution of the papers and certain protocols as the under secretary's intercessor with Johnson.

Ball relied upon his young ally's judgment and political perspicacity to arrange effective ways for his papers to find their way into the president's "night reading."[78] Moyers exploited his intimate understanding of the rhythms of Johnson's schedule—and his enigmatic methods—and would often select the comparative calm of Camp David or the LBJ Ranch to show him a dissenting memo from Ball. It is clear that by June of 1965, Moyers—and not Bundy—was in complete control of Ball's Vietnam pipeline to the president. This was ironically illustrated on June 19 when Ball referred Bundy (special assistant to the president for national security affairs) to Moyers (special assistant to the president for domestic legislation) for a copy of his June 18 memorandum entitled "Keeping the Power of Decision in the Viet-Nam Crisis"—a paper that "had been requested of Ball by the president through Moyers."[79] The collusion worked. In contrast to the earlier episode in 1964 when the president did not see Ball's October memorandum until February when it was circulated through Bundy, both telephone and diary records show that the under secretary's June 18 paper—distributed via Moyers to the president—was read by Johnson the very next day.[80]

In discerning Johnson's motives in allowing—even encouraging—the collaboration of the two dissenters, Moyers credits the president with a sincere desire to know the most reasoned arguments for and against Americanization of the war. "Johnson knew that I hadn't made up my own mind about Vietnam," Moyers recalls, recounting the mood around the oval office in the spring and summer of 1965, "and that I would be a sympathetic corridor for Ball's access to him."[81] As the dovish alliance developed, Ball and Moyers increased the frequency of their telephone conversations and luncheon rendezvous in the White House mess. Ball's appointment calendar for the period February to June 1965 shows regular two-hour lunches with Moyers, unusually long for the under secretary's guarded schedule.[82] In these encounters—and in innumerable telephone conversations—Moyers apprised Ball of the president's shifting attitudes on a range of subjects related to the escalating American role in Southeast Asia, elicited Ball's reactions to specific presidential inquiries, and not infrequently acted as Ball's benevolent editor by pressuring the under secretary to revise what were normally overlong memorandums. With a perspicacious mind tuned intently to the political side of the Vietnam problem, Moyers established critical deadlines for presidential review of sensitive aspects of the war on which Ball was working.[83]

On the morning of April 24, 1965, Moyers called Ball to say that he "had a chat with the president over breakfast about the necessity of getting people doing nothing for 3–4 days but thinking about political and peaceful alternatives in SEA [Southeast Asia]."[84] At that time the State Department had been giving surprisingly little thought to developing strategies for a political resolution of the Vietnam conflict. Though the diplomatic corps had been reacting (usually cynically) to intermittent "peace offensives" initiated from outside Foggy Bottom's four walls, no deliberate effort, save for Ball's, was ongoing. Now, according to explicit presidential marching orders, Ball and Moyers were to assemble a study group of people from within and outside the government in order to develop new ideas about how the United States might leave Vietnam without surrendering. This was to be the under secretary's grand presidential commission, in Johnson's unique idiom, to "pull a rabbit out of the hat."[85]

Ball, at this time, was simultaneously working on two tracks. In addition to minding the "peace shop," he strove to coalesce the arguments and insights of those disposed against the war into a single brief against escalation, to be embraced by an august group of peace advocates. Empowered by an explicit presidential commission, in April 1965 Ball and Moyers began work to develop diplomatic and political alternatives to escalation. As others ultimately learned that the two apostles of restraint were operating with Johnson's blessing, a diverse and formerly silent gaggle of dissenters, once dispersed throughout the government, began to gravitate toward Ball. Though efforts were made to conceal the activity and the actors from the rest of the government and, particularly, the press, Ball's office became a center, and Ball himself a symbol, of dissent. In time, an interagency group was formed that included well-known and respected individuals from outside the government. Their decidedly limited charge was to develop "fresh thought";[86] they were *not* invited to organize a conspiracy to undermine the American commitment to South Vietnam. As State Department Asian analyst Allen Whiting described the situation, individuals moved about, literally in secret, in order to converse, share intelligence reports, and discuss their reservations about committing American troops to battle in Southeast Asia.[87] Within an atmosphere more analogous to a spy novel than to the normal functioning of the Department of State, Saigon deputy chief of mission William Trueheart met secretly with Ball to fill in the admittedly considerable gaps in his knowledge of South Vietnamese politics. On more than one occasion papers were surreptitiously lifted from Walt Rostow's policy planning office, used by Ball overnight, and returned the next day with no one (particularly Rostow) the wiser.[88]

Traveling across town to the vice-president's office via a "backstairs route," throughout the spring of 1965 Whiting periodically briefed Hubert Humphrey on Southeast Asia.[89] Secrecy was very carefully maintained during the collaboration with Humphrey. At the time, Ball felt that if he and Humphrey held face-to-face discussions on the subject of Vietnam they would both be rudely ostracized by Johnson, as Humphrey ultimately was. Contrary to his political convictions and deep personal affections, Ball found himself in the unenviable position of contributing to Humphrey's isolation. Prompted by a complex set of political and psychological motivations stemming from his own experience as vice-president, Johnson treated Humphrey poorly, shunning and even humiliating the vice-president. This established clear parameters for the manner in which Ball and Humphrey communicated about Vietnam. Ball likened LBJ's treatment of Humphrey to "hazing of a college freshman" and is baffled that Johnson, having been through it all himself under Kennedy and, in particular, Kennedy's White House staff, could be so cruel to his own vice-president.[90] As an admirer of Humphrey (he would resign as U.N. ambassador in 1968 to help salvage his flagging presidential campaign), Ball exercised extreme caution in his approaches to the vice-president. By the time of the spring deliberations over Vietnam, the clouds of discord between LBJ and Humphrey were obvious for all to see, and the deficient relationship between the president and vice-president in turn had a demonstrable effect on how information was processed at the top reaches of the government. On one occasion, when asked by the executive secretary of the State Department, Ben Read, to deliver one of his Vietnam memorandums to Humphrey, Ball demurred, stating that he personally did not mind the vice-president seeing the paper, "but the president was so sensitive about it."[91] And Humphrey was completely cognizant of the under secretary's quandary. "Ball's people clearly wanted to keep a safe distance from me," Humphrey later remarked, "and they did." Humphrey generously conceded that he "could not blame them."[92]

In order to insure that the "rabbit" Johnson so desperately wanted would materialize in the spring of 1965, Ball and Moyers enlisted the support of Dean Acheson, Lloyd Cutler, and Clark Clifford. Though the connection brought together three eminently able advocates, each with a greater or lesser degree of sympathy for Ball's central thesis, at that time neither Acheson, Cutler, nor Clifford joined Ball in arguing for an expeditious withdrawal.[93] But the Atlanticist orientation to world affairs which Ball shared with Acheson, as well as their close personal friendship, insured that they could at least harmonize as they developed an approach that might appeal to Johnson. In May 1965 (as reviewed in Chapter 3), Acheson, Cutler, and Ball wrote memorandums calling for a political resolution to the Indochina conflict. It was in connection with this work on a formula for negotiated withdrawal that Ball also personally approached the president's close friend and unofficial adviser, Clark Clifford. The son of a railroad official, Clifford was born in Kansas and reared in St. Louis. Near the end of World War II, as a junior assistant in the Truman administration, he became a presidential speech writer and part of Truman's "kitchen cabinet." Known as that administration's "Golden Boy," Clifford became one of the principal architects of the containment policy. In 1965, on a tour of South Vietnam as chairman of the Foreign Intelligence Advisory Board, Clifford wrote that "the optimism of our military and Vietnamese officials on the conduct of the war confirmed my belief in the correctness of our policy."[94]

Cooperation between the two middle westerners was enhanced by the fact that Clifford, also a Washington attorney of considerable reputation, "always admired George Ball" and thought him to be "an exceedingly able government servant." Recalling that they had gotten to know each other "as practicing lawyers in a number of matters together," Clifford acknowledges that their relationship was built on "a basis of mutual respect." Even before Clifford became secretary of defense in February 1968, he had worked on a number of interdepartmental Vietnam task forces for Johnson and was aware of Ball's dissent and intimately acquainted with his specific arguments. Despite the fact that Clifford supported the broad contours of Johnson's policies until about one month after his confirmation as secretary of defense in February of 1968, he recalls that "George felt that I was somewhat of a colleague of his."[95]

Clifford vividly reminisces about a plane ride out to the LBJ Ranch in the early summer of 1965 during which time he and Ball had what he describes as "a good chance to talk." Even at that time, as escalation was just getting under way, Clifford was "quite sympathetic" to the views Ball expressed. A tenuous alliance developed between them even though Clifford could not yet embrace Ball's position and had reservations about how well the under secretary of state was bureaucratically positioned for the fight. "Rusk was the number *one* from State and Ball was the number *two*," Clifford emphasizes. He believed that "if both Rusk and Ball had agreed, that would have a good deal more impact upon the president [emphasis in original]." Clifford was ever mindful of the transcending fact that "Rusk, physically, intellectually and in every way, one hundred percent supported Johnson's position on Vietnam."[96] Nevertheless, he discreetly indicated to Ball that he was willing to explore the matter at length with him, and Ball began feeding Clifford copies of his papers and notes. The alliance was cemented on July 23, 1965, when Clifford telephoned the under secretary of state to report that he had devoted the entire evening (until 2:00 A.M.) to his papers and had completed "a most careful study of what Ball had given him." At that time the cultivated hawk, Clifford admitted that he found the material "impressive and persuasive."[97] It was not until later, in December 1965, that he would publicly lock arms with Ball on an issue relating to the spiraling commitment in Vietnam. In the debates over the Christmas bombing pause, Clifford was one of the very few to side with the under secretary in recommending a standing down of the aerial attacks. Clifford recalls that during the winter pause debates Ball first expressed his appreciation for his assistance in "manning the ramparts" in the admittedly uphill effort to persuade Lyndon Johnson to begin to reverse course.[98]

Ball hoped that he had found his well-placed ally, but Clifford would not then go the extra mile. Though he had privately opposed troop increases in the summer of 1965, he could not then bring himself to argue for a negotiated withdrawal—the inevitable consequence of which he still saw as a patently unacceptable Communist victory. Though Clifford admired Ball's position on the war, he did not believe that he had completely confronted the alternative to staying on the course established by McNamara. "I didn't see how, at the time," Clifford has retrospectively stated, "that anything that George was offering was going to bring the conclusion of the war." This must have been quite frustrating for the man who as secretary of defense during the last eleven months of the administration would inherit a policy he then believed to be failing in stages. "I admired George for his courage. The President knew how he felt, and he just felt George was wrong. He was doing everything he could within the limitations that a president extends to you when he disagrees with you." Clifford agonized about what to do. There seemed to be no course that did not invite one kind of disaster or another. "Each time I went to Vietnam I came back less enthusiastic about it," Clifford reminisced. "Jesus, I hated it. I hated to go there."[99]

As later developments record, Clifford eventually embraced Ball's position on the war, and he generously credits the former under secretary of state with a prime role in his conversion. Clifford came full circle on the war. By the time of Nixon's inauguration in 1969 the once ardent advocate of intervention was advising the new president to extricate the country from the Vietnam bog. Quite charitably, Clifford admits that "George just saw it more accurately than the rest of us. I think he was very gratified when I came around."[100] Found among Ball's personal papers is a letter from Clifford dated July 9, 1970, the last two sentences of which read: "Not a week goes by but what I don't recall the soundness and accuracy of your views with reference to Vietnam. Would that you had prevailed."[101]

Nominally, Far Eastern Affairs Assistant Secretary William P. Bundy should also be counted among Ball's allies.[102] (As noted above, his was the single top-level memorandum to be founded on Ball's analysis of the war.) Like Clifford, Bundy was also reasonably well placed. Brother of the national security adviser, Dean Acheson's son-in-law, and closely identified with Mc-Namara while serving as assistant secretary of defense, Bundy was potentially a prime confederate in the prosecution of the case against escalation of the war. He was personally inspired by the under secretary's papers, saw great difficulty ahead for the United States in Indochina, and was particularly persuaded by Ball's reasoning that the front line against communism in Southeast Asia should be Indonesia or Thailand and not South Vietnam.[103] Bundy, like Ball, rejected McNamara's thesis that the North Vietnamese would, in the summer of 1965, begin to wage "positional" or "Third Stage" warfare with conventional units. He concurred with Ball and the intelligence community that, for the foreseeable future, the United States would confront primarily a guerrilla adversary.[104] Bundy was, in point of fact, in agreement with Ball's analysis and shared his doubts, but, like a growing list of advisers, he was not willing to accept the strategic or political consequences of the precipitous withdrawal Ball proposed. Bundy was admittedly in a state of "personal crisis." Bearing the burden—and a deepening sense of personal responsibility—for the policy up to that point, himself beset with ulcers, his wife beset by a nervous disorder known to be compounded by the war, Bundy pressed on.[105]

At critical junctures during the tense discussions among Johnson's principal war counselors, the apprehensive assistant secretary sided with McNamara. Bundy concedes that his position was largely a result of the confident and authoritative manner in which McNamara argued, against which he weighed Ball's comparatively haphazard approach to the Vietnam debate. McNamara won the decisive paper chase. Bundy personally felt that Ball's briefs on Vietnam "just didn't have anything like the argumentative force of a McNamara memorandum," noting that Ball's papers were written "at white heat."[106] (Ball himself admits that they were "dictated mostly late at night, and often without benefit of staff work.")[107] Bundy also emphasizes that "George did not devote a lot of time to it [Vietnam] in the '64–'65 period. He was not in the day to day stream, not reading the cables, not soaked in it the way the rest of us were."[108]

Admitting that Ball knew the story of the French experience in Vietnam quite well, Bundy has long felt that "it's always a little harder for the outsider, or semi-outsider, to argue with those who have been hearing the whole thing and litigating it. George was coming from a little outside the problem."[109] Ball's avowed Eurocentrism appears to have worked against any general acceptance of his Vietnam brief. Ball's antagonists continually reminded the president of the origins of the dissident under secretary's views. Once, after the critical July 21 NSC meeting during which Westmoreland's request for additional troops was debated, NSC secretary Horace Busby drafted a summary memorandum of the conference for the president. Busby stated that Ball had been "impressively clear-headed and organized in his argument" against sending more troops, but he added as a disclaimer that Ball's thinking was influenced by "two factors of a decade ago: (1) concern held over from the Stevenson campaign for adverse U.S. reaction to keep any Asian war limited, and (2) his strong personal involvement, i.e., with the French."[110] Ball undermined his own advocacy—at least in Bundy's eyes—with his chronic reiteration of an aggravating (yet ultimately prophetic) theme: "George was a little bit of a stuck record" in asserting that the Americans were doomed to repeat the French tragedy. Bundy has stated that "every now and then he overdid the comparison in a setting when we were so cross with the French for so many other reasons. Sometimes it was quite irritating to hear that argument." What is more, the fact that Ball "over-emphasized Europe" and "just put zero on the China factor," in Bundy's view, "rendered his analysis much less cogent than it might otherwise have been. The idea that he thought only Europe was important was a fact in the way people read him."[111]

To an account of Ball's "allies" in the cause of reversing the Johnson administration's thinking on Southeast Asia must be added a consideration of his personal acquaintances in the Washington press corps. Without exception, those members of the press associated with the State Department, including government personnel and working correspondents during the period, report that Ball maintained excellent press relations and that he developed warm friendships with a number of journalists during his tenure as under secretary.[112] Ball's press relations shaped, styled, and informed his dissent; they also became an irritation of considerable magnitude to the president. Because Lyndon Johnson, as his biographers universally agree, had an almost pathological fixation with loyalty in the ranks, the president ultimately was unnerved with the company kept by his under secretary of state.[113]

This was most apparent near the end of Ball's service when the president once quizzed him about his close ties with the administration's archcritic Walter Lippmann. At the outset of the administration, Lippmann had been a staunch defender of the progressive agenda advanced by the Texan, liked Johnson personally, and was not prone to the derogatory appellations so often overheard in cocktail circles at the new president's expense. Johnson deliberately cultivated a functional, if not warm, relationship with Lippmann by dispensing gifts, invitations to state dinners, personal visits to his Woodley Road home in Washington, private lunches, and plenty of "photo-ops." But Lippmann soon concluded that he had been flagrantly misled about Vietnam. Though he initially accepted that the mission of American military forces in Indochina was to bring about a condition favorable to a political settlement— what Lippmann referred to as a "Tito-style" resolution of the Southeast Asia problem—the precipitous "Americanization" of the war in the summer of 1965 left little reason to doubt that Johnson was pursuing an outright military victory. Lippmann quickly broke with the administration. His columns denouncing the war became progressively more strident, with the immediate result of utterly demolishing his once cordial relationship with Johnson— whom he ultimately referred to as "the most disagreeable individual ever to have occupied the White House."[114] It was not long before Ball would pay a price for his propinquity to Lippmann. Feeling the emotional and political heat from the escalating ordeal in Vietnam, and enraged with Lippmann's attacks in the pages of *Newsweek* magazine, Johnson challenged Ball's loyalty: "Is he [Lippmann] telling you what to say or are you telling him what to write?"[115]

Most significant among Ball's press contacts was the venerable *New York Times* columnist James "Scotty" Reston, with whom he has maintained a friendship of more than thirty years. Ball's relationship with Reston was qualitatively distinct from the solid personal relationships he kept with other journalists, including Chalmers Roberts and Murray Marder of the *Washington Post*. Ball communed often with, and confided in, Reston. They shared the intellectual benefit of an unqualified candor and implicit trust. In differentiating between his many friends among Washington's working correspondents and columnists and the affections he held for Reston, Ball has stated that "Scotty was another fellow altogether." Testifying to their unique relationship, Ball once flatly remarked, "I never was as candid with the others." Though at great peril to his own credibility and standing with Johnson, Ball found comfort in disclosing to Reston the most intimate details of his battle with the administration at each discouraging stage of escalation and protest. Because they lived in the same Washington neighborhood (at opposite ends of Woodley Road) and saw each other frequently during their leisure hours, Reston became a sounding board against which Ball could voice his discouragement with the flow of events in Southeast Asia. But he was much more than that. By the summer of 1965 Reston had become a formidable and independent critic of what he thought to be the Kennedy-Johnson tendency to inflate the geopolitical and strategic significance of South Vietnam. Ball and Reston shared a similar intellectual map of the world—in their minds Southeast Asia was a peripheral region. Sharing Ball's view of international relations as well as his trepidation about the escalating Indochinese war—and possessing an influential voice in Washington circles—Reston became a major force in shaping opinion against escalation. As part of the bargain he became a major annoyance to Lyndon Johnson.

Ball's telephone log shows that he and Reston were frequent conferees on Vietnam. Indeed, they exchanged more telephone calls on the subject than did Ball and the president, Ball and Moyers, or Ball and any other single individual.[116] Throughout the entire period, the under secretary's appointment calendar shows frequent "lunch with Scotty" entries.[117] Utterly ignoring the normal prohibitions to which an administration officer is subjected when speaking with members of the press, Ball and Reston openly discussed the most sensitive matters before the government. Testifying to the sensitivity of the information they exchanged and the level at which they discussed Vietnam, a half-dozen of the Ball-Reston TELCON transcripts in Ball's personal file are marked "Eyes Only—No Distribution" in a manner similar to the way information might be circulated among the intelligence agencies, the cabinet chiefs, or by the president himself.[118] (Though Ball and Reston often discussed matters of great gravity, their dialogue was not without its light side. Their "code" for the president of the United States was "His Nibs."[119] At particularly anxious junctures in the Vietnam debates, when Ball became somewhat of an insomniac as work on the dissenting memorandums drove him repeatedly from his bed, Reston would dispense the advice, "If you can't sleep—drink.")[120]

One recurring theme in the many tête-à-têtes Ball and Reston conducted on Vietnam was their commiseration with each other about McNamara's excessive exuberance. Ball once confided to Reston in January 1964 that the secretary's optimism "was to a considerable extent based on quite inadequate information," and he regularly attacked what he referred to as McNamara's "damn the torpedoes" posture.[121] As their conversations are traced from the winter of 1964 to the fall of 1966, it is evident that Ball clandestinely provided Reston with a running account of the government's deliberations as well as his own developing opposition to the expanding commitment to South Vietnam. Significantly, not a single Reston column ever exploited the privileged information he received from Ball. They contributed to each other's running criticism of Lyndon Johnson's war, as well as of what they judged to be the uncritical manner in which the United States was invoking the containment doctrine. Their Realist sensibilities, shared with Lippmann, were offended by the unlimited global agenda that the administration seemed to be pursuing. "We are in a disturbing position," Ball told Reston in the aftermath of the Tonkin Gulf incident. "Our relative power vis-à-vis the other Western nations is diminishing, but we still seem to be extending our responsibilities."[122]

In a remembrance that is substantially belied by the record—and one that probably says more about his concern for protecting the reputations of his two good friends—Ball has professed that "Scotty and Walter [Lippmann] were the only two who really knew my thoughts on Vietnam."[123] The fact of the matter is that Ball was less discriminating than he would like others to believe in scattering his arguments against the war around Washington. Other press insiders also came to know the details of his campaign within the government. Ball maintained a close personal relationship with journalist Marilyn Berger. In the summer of 1965, syndicated columnists Marquis Childs and Philip Geyelin were somewhat secretively invited by Ball (through his intermediary and confidant, Assistant Secretary of State for Political Affairs James L.

Greenfield) to an annex of his seventh-floor office to review his large blue three-ring "Viet-Nam Briefing Book." Ball had systematically compiled copies of his memorandums and notes so that any potential ally might conveniently and quickly peruse—"off the record" and "for background only"—his analysis of how escalation had proceeded and what he thought should be done. First Schlesinger, then Galbraith, then ultimately a gang of less intimate associates became familiar with the bound documents. In due course, select contents of the "secret" vinyl briefing book became public information. Childs invoked the prerogatives of a long personal friendship with Ball for continued access to the materials.[124] Keeping his privileged information a closely guarded secret for months, Childs finally published a column celebrating Ball's dissent on June 20, 1966, entitled "Ball on Vietnam: A Necessary Voice." In the broadside directed against Lyndon Johnson's conduct of the war, he wrote that "it has been no secret in Washington that for the last three years Ball has consistently opposed in the private councils of Government the escalation of the war." The article portrayed Ball as the single dissenter in what he called a "hermetically sealed" circle of presidential advisers.[125] Geyelin, who was then researching what would later become a history of the president's foreign policy entitled *Lyndon Johnson and the World*, pressed Ball for, and received, similar access. He was less discreet than Childs. Prior to the under secretary's resignation from government, Geyelin wrote that "Ball was a dogged and consistent 'devil's advocate' about almost everything the United States did in Vietnam from mid-1964 on," and, in fortifying his narrative, he was not at all bashful about paraphrasing Ball's "Top Secret" memos.[126]

With the president's senior cabinet officials unalterably fixed in their determination that America prevail militarily in Vietnam, Ball gravitated toward doubters at lower levels of, and even outside, the government. Inevitably the tension between his private convictions about the war and his perfunctory public support for what he thought to be a surefire recipe for disaster produced intriguing ironies and twists in the story of Ball's role as a dissenter. In June of 1966 Childs had sagely noted that Ball had been "playing a lonely and extraordinary role that only the historians can put in proper perspective."[127] The remainder of this study describes those ironies and provides the perspective called for by Childs.

Chapter 5

Opposition's Ironies

George Ball is the only man who I have ever really known
in government who, on five minutes instruction from the president,
can take either side of a proposition.
—Lyndon Johnson

George revelled in his unique and well-known role as in-house hair shirt;
I don't doubt that he believed in his devil's advocacy brief on Vietnam,
but I think at bottom it was a matter of ego.
—J. Robert Schaetzel

THE STORY of Ball's dissent is packed with paradox. Indeed, the mere existence of a top-level dissenter seems quite outlandish in an administration that elevated consensus building to a sacred principle. Given Lyndon Johnson's rigid strategic assumptions, his instinct for political harmony, and a complex psychological makeup that could not easily suffer criticism, Ball's running argument with the administration over Vietnam is among the more extraordinary episodes in an extraordinary decade. It is ironic that the cosmopolitan and Europe-focused under secretary of state would become best known for his analysis of a civil war in Indochina. It is equally ironic that Ball's ostensibly secret dissent was to become one of the few celebrated chapters in what has otherwise been an antiheroic period in American history. The irony is compounded by the fact that Johnson repeatedly called upon Ball, the administration's most notorious dove, to make his case for escalation to the Congress, to the press, and to foreign capitals. Finally, in light of history's confirmation of Ball's analysis of the American role in the Vietnamese civil war, it is the quintessence of irony that there should be so much conjecture about the origins of, and motivations behind, his dissent.

Though they were on opposite sides of a momentous debate, Johnson liked and respected Ball, and his affection and esteem were generously reciprocated. "There were two things about Ball which Johnson admired," recalls Jack Valenti. "One was that Ball had great courage—he was not a go-alonger—and the other was that Ball was a man of literate grace."[1] Johnson and Ball maintained warm relations until LBJ's death in 1972—a phenomenon exceedingly rare among those with whom the sometimes cantankerous president disagreed about Vietnam. This mutual affection was evident near the end of LBJ's life when, at considerable inconvenience in the summer of 1971, Ball loyally participated in the dedication of the Lyndon Johnson Presidential Library in Austin, Texas. Afterward, Johnson voiced his private sentiment that Ball had "meant so much to [him] over the years as a willing, as well as superior, partner." In a warm personal letter, Johnson lavishly expressed his appreciation to Ball for his attendance, assuring his former "colleague" that he was among those whose presence "meant the most" to him.[2]

It also should be noted that Johnson and Ball were genuinely moved by each other's analyses of the Indochinese problem. There is no doubt that the president shared the under secretary's fears about what could result from an Americanized war, and Ball was keenly aware of the political pressures with which Johnson wrestled as he searched for the best way to maintain the sovereignty of his besieged South Vietnamese ally. Ironically, for reasons which become clear below, they were each other's "best friend" during the ordeal of deciding to go to war.[3] The blunt reality was, however, that Johnson's cultural sensitivities, his preeminent concern for political survival, and his orthodox Cold War strategic calculus compelled him to launch the United States into its most ambiguous war—against Ball's most passionate warnings.

A parochial man who at one point in life considered the "East" to be anything east of Oklahoma and the "West" anything the other side of Johnson City, Texas,[4] LBJ slowly developed a keen interest in the world outside the American heartland. His visit to Australia during World War II and insights gained from his senatorial duties during the Korean conflict were benchmarks in that education. Like most politicians of the period, he was mesmerized by the rhetoric of a crusade against godless communism and was particularly sympathetic to the struggle of Asians to win political freedom and to develop modern capitalist economies.

But it was Johnson's role in the campaign for Hawaiian statehood that had the most direct bearing upon the development of his progressive racial attitudes, which would ominously surface during the Vietnam era. Having once considered Pacific peoples "alien in spirit and nationality,"[5] Johnson had worked against the admission of Hawaii for two decades. Then, as the Senate began new hearings at the end of the 1940s, he confessed that "the scales were removed from [his] eyes."[6] Lyndon Johnson became a Pacific statesman, not only an enthusiast for Hawaiian statehood but an advocate of a political and economic alliance of democratic Asian nations underwritten by the United States. Hawaii became for Johnson "a model of how men and women of different races and different cultures can come and live and work together; to respect each other in freedom and hope."[7]

The Hawaii statehood debates transpired within the larger context of the domestic civil rights movement, and the Texas senator considered these events as equally desirable and mutually reinforcing ends. In the course of his simultaneous involvement in both enterprises in the late 1950s and early 1960s, Johnson personally transcended the pervasive racial bigotry of his region and spearheaded the cause of racial reform in both the domestic and foreign policy arenas. His commitment to break down the walls of race hatred in America was extended beyond national boundaries. His outreach to "the little people of Asia," whom he believed to be struggling to develop political democracies and capitalist economies, complemented the prevailing strategic doctrines of the 1960s. American security and economic self-interest would be served by the manly containment of what Johnson uncritically perceived to be the Sino-Soviet Communist bloc. It was, for LBJ, a moral challenge. He would combat racism on a global scale. Johnson decried prejudice in any form, often boasting that his daddy had resisted joining the Texas Ku Klux Klan and that, as a boy, he was not allowed to express even an ounce of bigotry. Inspired by a Wilsonian conception of world order (absent Wilson's cultural-bound snobbishness), throughout the 1950s Johnson consistently supported schemes designed to weld the West to the East in trade, cultural exchange, political development, and technological assistance.

That the Vietnamese were racially dissimilar made LBJ an even more ardent advocate of their cause. The argument advanced by some of his critics in the late 1960s (particularly Minnesota senator Eugene McCarthy) that Vietnam was an alien land in which the United States had no business—a view which intimated that the Vietnamese were racially inferior and not worthy of an American blood sacrifice—made Johnson more, not less, determined.[8] In LBJ's view, the brown people of Cotulla, Texas, the black people of Selma, Alabama, and the yellow people of the Pacific Rim were not sharing in the twentieth century's promise of abundance. His courageous leadership on the momentous race issue in America merged with his conviction that peoples everywhere, regardless of color, shared common aspirations. Inside every Vietnamese, Johnson believed, was a good American waiting to get out. He sincerely felt that if America was to fulfill her role as a model of a liberal society she must provide global leadership in the attainment of those shared goals. His hugely ambitious Great Society agenda was the fulfillment of his liberal vision on the domestic front. He would feed the hungry, educate the illiterate, house the homeless, heal the sick, fight crime and poverty, and complete the truncated work of Reconstruction. Johnson's international vision—which he saw as supporting and legitimizing his domestic program—included no less than a broad scheme to economically modernize, politically democratize, and culturally integrate the toiling masses of the Far East.

Johnson's decisions for war in Vietnam must be understood within the context of his larger designs for what he called "Free Asia." Of the crucial months during the spring and summer of 1965 when escalation was being planned, Johnson wrote that "the whole exciting story of what was happening in Asia behind the shield of our commitment was largely neglected."[9] Johnson saw Vietnam as an emerging capitalist bastion, a potentially vital ally in a vital area of the globe. American presence in South Vietnam was not exclusively a response to aggression and political crisis, and U.S. assistance should not be understood exclusively as a military exercise. LBJ saw his policies as serving the larger end of advancing the economic and political integration of the region, a device similar to Kennedy's "Grand Design" for Europe or "Alliance for Progress" in Latin America. Ever conscious of and, by all accounts, immodest about his place in history, Johnson was intoxicated by the prospect of doing good works in Southeast Asia. He envisioned a New Deal and a Marshall Plan rolled into one and in 1965 initiated a "massive effort to improve the life of man in that conflict-torn corner of our world."[10]

Johnson believed that what could not be won with sticks on the battlefield could be achieved by wielding the carrots of technology transfer, education, medical assistance, aid, and credit. In his now famous address at Johns Hopkins University in the spring of 1965 (which is best remembered as a political white paper in defense of the American military presence in Vietnam), Johnson outlined his plans to reap "a rich harvest in a hungry land" through the construction of a vast Mekong Delta "TVA," allocation of farm surpluses, the distribution of food and medicine, literacy programs, and the creation of an Asian Development Bank—of which he was especially proud.[11] In Johnson's mind, the problems he faced in Asia were similar to those confronted by his Democratic predecessors in Europe. The national security— and the historic liberal vision of his party—were severely threatened by "communist aggression." Events during his presidency such as the nearly successful Marxist coup in Indonesia served to confirm his judgments. The domino theory was not merely an abstraction. In much the same way that the European

Recovery Program had blunted the sharp edge of the Communist advance in Europe, Johnson would combat disease, poverty, and ignorance—the most treacherous enemies of human freedoms—with a seemingly boundless development program for Southeast Asia.

Notwithstanding his munificence and noble aspirations for the forgotten peoples of the Pacific Rim, it was politics that drove Lyndon Johnson, and his attentiveness to domestic political factors in his decisions for war was ill concealed. He had long been hypersensitive to the charge, stemming from what was then commonly referred to as "the loss of China" in 1949, that the Democratic party was soft on communism. His "constant and unending fear was always the Right," presidential assistant Harry McPherson has emphatically stated, "never the Left."[12] He was manifestly phobic about his domestic political opponents—those "who never wanted to help the poor Negroes in the first place"[13]—attributing a Communist advance in Vietnam to a weakness in him.[14] Simply put, Johnson did not believe he could survive politically if he turned his back on what most everyone in 1964–65 unhesitatingly considered to be America's moral obligation to maintain the independence of South Vietnam. The final domino for LBJ was not, after all, some small Asian nation but his presidency. Without office, his progressive vision for civil rights and welfare democracy would grind to a halt.

As Johnson was to discover, however, the Great Society was just as seriously jeopardized by the political and material costs of the war. The president effectively used his unparalleled legislative skills to manufacture a marginally acceptable political and strategic compact with the leadership in Congress. Ardently hoping to avoid a destructive debate on either foreign or domestic policy, the president pursued both agendas aggressively, simultaneously—and discreetly. The military reserves would not be called up, there would be no tax increases to bankroll the Indochinese military operations, and the "presidential war" in Vietnam would be prosecuted with as little detailed public disclosure as permissible. Tragically, this "guns-and-butter" approach to governance, as the Bourbon kings of France had sorrowfully discovered, proved to be ruinous.

The prospect of a conservative backlash was ever present in his mind, and domestic political concerns significantly narrowed Johnson's tactical choices in Vietnam. "On this," presidential aide Richard Goodwin has stated, "he was a man possessed, wholly impervious to argument. The only thing he understood [and feared] was political opposition."[15] On the right flank, Johnson worried about the political costs of giving one inch of soil to the Communists. On the left flank, he was mindful of what he mistakenly interpreted to be

Kennedy's ironclad commitment to South Vietnam. If he abandoned Kennedy's initiatives and broke his implicit guarantees of South Vietnam's security, he believed he would lose the critical support of the Eastern Establishment for the Great Society. Haunted by pressures to prevail from the Right as well as the Left, with Rusk reminding him that the war was strategically necessary, with McNamara assuring him that the war could be won—and Bundy convincing him that in fighting the war he was doing what Kennedy would have done—Johnson "stayed the course."[16]

It is ironic, then, with strategic, cultural, and political instincts for the conflict in Vietnam seemingly in his blood, that Johnson would encourage Ball to develop his heretical views. LBJ was peculiarly enthusiastic about hearing Ball's advice and was even comforted by his dissent. Although Rusk and McNamara thought Ball was "completely misguided" in his analysis, they conceded—in McNamara's case somewhat reluctantly—that the president had a right to hear the under secretary's views.[17] Ball took full advantage of this license from his president and cabinet superiors and impressed Johnson with his cogent and persuasive arguments. Johnson became a careful student of Ball's memos, insured each was given a "full-dress discussion,"[18] and in meetings demonstrated "total familiarity"[19] with nearly every argument he advanced. Johnson welcomed Ball's recalcitrance and recalled in his memoirs that particularly during the critical debates over escalation in the spring and summer of 1965, "[the cabinet] discussed Ball's approach for a long time and in great detail, and all of us felt the same concerns and anxieties that [he] had expressed." There was, however, little movement. The logic stacked against Ball's position was bewilderingly simple. Johnson correctly recalls that "most of the men in the Cabinet Room were more worried about the results in our country and throughout the world, of our pulling out and coming home."[20]

Strangely enough, except for infrequent eruptions about Ball's close relationship with other dissenters that Johnson considered enemies, the under secretary's position on the war improved rather than diminished his rapport with the president. Ball has repeatedly emphasized that he and Johnson maintained a "very warm personal relationship."[21] The truth was that LBJ was a reluctant belligerent in 1965 and, like Woodrow Wilson in 1916–17, was loath to become mired down in the tangles of foreign military intervention. Within distinctly defined negotiating parameters, he was, in fact, constantly seeking a nonmilitary solution to what he knew might well be an intractable operational problem of tracking down and killing Vietcong. But the preponderance of counsel he received consistently called for deeper military involvement. "Not one time," Jack Valenti later declared, "did one White House aide or high-stationed public official say 'Mr. President, we ought to get our ass out.' The only man who said it was George Ball." Valenti laments that the under secretary of state "was never able to persuade the president that he could escape the opprobrium of the right if he had pulled out and ran." The president could not bypass political realities. "Design the plan," Johnson would say. "Hell, I want to get out, but somebody gotta tell me how to get out."[22]

Valenti energetically refutes what he admits is "the popular image of Johnson" as an executive who bullied his advisers into repressing their convictions in order to simply confirm his views—what political scientist Larry Berman has artfully dubbed "the Caligula Syndrome." Indeed, in disagreement with most observers of the Johnson presidency, Valenti portrays an executive who welcomed and was stimulated by dissent. "If Johnson knew what your counsel would be every time," Valenti asserts, "he would ask your advice less and less." Ball was not, in Valenti's view at any rate, Johnson's "token foil."[23] But notwithstanding Valenti's generous appraisal of LBJ's willingness to hear opposing viewpoints, considering the consensus at the top echelons of the cabinet supporting escalation during the "July decisions" of 1965, it is indeed surprising that LBJ seriously considered a dissent. Johnson had unbounded esteem and respect for Dean Rusk, calling him "one of the greatest patriots he had ever known," and often expressed "great faith in the quality of his opinions."[24] The president also had great admiration for Bundy, at least during 1965, because "listening to Bundy was like listening to Kennedy."[25] (When Bundy finally left the government in February 1966, Lady Bird Johnson had said that her husband would miss him "like a big front tooth."[26] By that time, however, LBJ and Bundy had begun to quarrel about how the war should be managed politically, with Bundy calling for greater candor and public disclosure of top-level intelligence to increase public support for the war.) And Johnson had "an almost apotheosis about McNamara; he thought McNamara was divinely inspired at times because his mind had this computer-like serenity."[27] Clearly then, the efficacy of Ball's advocacy was diminished by the exceedingly high regard in which Johnson held his other top advisers during the July deliberations.

Johnson cordially invited Ball into his private thoughts on Vietnam, then slammed the door in his face. As the under secretary developed his case against the war between October 1964 and January 1966, the president swiftly countered each of his arguments with firm rebuttals and sometimes even sarcasm. If Ball argued that the United States was not explicitly bound by the South East Asia Treaty to defend South Vietnam, Johnson might repeat what were nearly the last words of John F. Kennedy in Fort Worth, Texas, declaring

America's "duty" to maintain the balance of power between the Communist and Free Worlds.[28] When the under secretary argued that a bombing pause might open a diplomatic channel, the president might angrily retort: "Oh yes, a bombing halt, I'll tell you what happens when there's a bombing halt. I halt and then Ho Chi Minh shoves his trucks right up my ass. That's your bombing halt."[29]

Johnson was stimulated but not persuaded by Ball's argument against escalation and once stated that he "felt [that] the Under Secretary had not produced a sufficiently convincing case or a viable alternative."[30] Ball has metaphorically likened his dissent to a "Chinese water torture." He felt powerless to do much beyond insuring an "incessant dripping of what were becoming familiar arguments" in the hope of wearing down the resistance of his colleagues, "most of all, the President."[31] With disarming simplicity, Clark Clifford provided what may be the most accurate evaluation of Ball's impact on LBJ: "Johnson accepted George, he admired George, he respected him. Moreover, he thought it was courageous of Ball to speak up as he did and present that position. But the President just thought he was wrong."[32]

Johnson's open arms welcome of Ball's advocacy was not, however, without its perils. Though the president actively sought Ball's contrary views, the means by which the dissent was conducted were highly problematic. For Ball to operate effectively, utmost political sensitivity and unquestioned loyalty had to be sincerely and continuously demonstrated. Coming at the president with a dissenting brief on Vietnam during a moment of acute political crisis could severely weaken an argument. By proselytizing too aggressively for his views, Ball could easily destroy the rapport he had carefully cultivated with Johnson, undermine his credibility on other issues dearer to his heart, and, in the process, become a nuisance to the administration. Worse, if Ball were to indulge himself in a fit of self-righteous pique and publicly blazon his opposition by denouncing what he privately held to be a morally repugnant policy of military overkill, he would instantly put his influence with the president, and his job, at risk.

There were other critical elements to the anatomy of dissent. First, appreciating Johnson's respect for bureaucratic hierarchy, Ball avoided dealing with the president on an ex parte basis on Vietnam. Keenly aware that he enjoyed Johnson's confidence because he first enjoyed Rusk's, Ball insured that his presidential memorandums were circulated to and discussed with the secretaries of state and defense and, much of the time, the national security adviser. Just as importantly, as he would retrospectively relate to CBS correspondent Marvin Kalb, Ball had to argue wisely "within the limits of the possible."[33]

Ever judicious, he did not continue to fight lost battles for self-aggrandizing moralistic purposes. Cognizant of the dangers of dissent, the under secretary of state felt the president would listen to him only if he had something to say about the business at hand, and he exercised extreme caution when he did, on occasion, push for a reexamination of an issue.

For example, in October and again in November 1964 Ball made a strong strategic and political case against bombing North Vietnam. But when the decision was taken to strike above the 17th parallel, he quickly retreated to the tactical arguments for constricting the radius of the targets and for bombing pauses. Similarly, in July 1965 Ball argued passionately against committing 100,000 American troops to frontline engagements. But after the twenty-first of that month, when the decisions were taken to Americanize the fighting, he retreated to the argument for fewer troops in what was to be a vain attempt to limit the commitment and temper the risks of intervention. With such concessions, Ball's papers maintained their peculiar slot in Johnson's "midnight reading"[34]—those few memorandums on immediate procedural problems to which the president gave his greatest attention.

Ball was the quintessential Vietnam dove. He consistently recommended a policy of negotiated withdrawal while harboring no illusions about the political future of the Saigon regime. However, to have incessantly advanced his general view would have been irresponsible and, from his standpoint as the only dissenter in the senior advisory bodies on Vietnam, unwise. Indeed, events periodically shelved philosophical discussion and strategic review—in which the under secretary of state was regularly engaged—and opened complex deliberations over tactics, in which he was not regularly engaged. Meetings on Vietnam after the spring of 1965 very often took on a crisis atmosphere. This was the case on February 7, 1965, when Vietcong units rocketed an American army barracks and helicopter base at Pleiku, killing eight soldiers and destroying five aircraft. Meeting with the NSC, members of the cabinet, and the Senate leadership that evening, Johnson announced: "We have kept our guns over the mantel and our shells in the cupboard for a long time now. I can't ask our American soldiers out there to fight with one hand tied behind their backs." In the wake of Pleiku, a campaign of "sustained reprisal" against individual Vietcong attacks (Operation Flaming Dart) commenced.[35]

In a telephone conversation with National Security Adviser McGeorge Bundy immediately following the Pleiku incident, Ball expressed profound misgivings about where a tit-for-tat policy as called for by the NSC that day would ultimately lead. He called it "pragmatism at its worse." On this occasion, Bundy shared Ball's doubts.[36] But in the tempestuous atmosphere in the cabinet room on February 7, Ball eschewed calling for a grand reappraisal of American policy. A crisis had submerged his position, and the under secretary joined his colleagues in their response. Rusk, McNamara, Bundy, and the Joint Chiefs were all agreed that reprisal strikes were called for, and for the first time Ball identified himself with a military option. At the February 7 NSC meeting, as presidential aide Bromley Smith's notes show, Under Secretary Ball announced: "*We* are all in accord that action must be taken. *We* need to decide how to handle the air strikes publicly. *We* must make it clear that the North Vietnamese and the Viet Cong are the same [emphasis added]."[37]

Within the small community of Johnson's senior advisory staff on Vietnam, Ball thus affirmed his loyalty on the *inside*. Moreover, to register his loyalty on the *outside*, Ball sent a rebutting letter to *Washington Post* columnist Drew Pearson. Having recently credited the under secretary with "restoring sanity to our mouse-trapped thinking regarding Viet-Nam," Pearson had identified Ball as the lone dissenter in the government, bucking the tide of disaster but surrounded by undiscriminating hard-liners. In order to disclaim any hint of disharmony among Johnson's principal advisers on Vietnam, and with the avowed and expressed intention of maintaining his open channel to the president, Ball denied the perceptive and accurate characterization in the column. In a personal letter, part of which was published after Ball had made an "arrangement" with the *Post* (ostensibly a "backgrounder, off-the-record" briefing), he reminded Pearson that he had "personally joined in recommending the retaliatory response" after Pleiku.[38]

Subsequently, at another critical strategic juncture, Ball again exhibited his pragmatic approach to dissent and his loyalty to Johnson. On this occasion, during the intense discussions of July 1965, after which General Westmoreland's request for 100,000 combat troops was granted and the Vietnam war was effectively "Americanized," Ball personally associated himself with a policy he adamantly believed was doomed to failure. At the July 21 NSC meeting—at the very moment Johnson was weighing final arguments about General Westmoreland's request—Ball told Johnson that he foresaw a "perilous voyage," repeated his "grave apprehensions," and delivered his now routine epistle against escalation. "But," Ball added, "let me be clear. If the decision is to go ahead, I am committed. Qualifications I have are not due to the fact that I think we are in a bad moral position. I have had my day in court."[39]

To the degree that he could bring himself to trust any man, Johnson trusted Ball. He perceived his under secretary of state—unlike so many others outside the executive branch advocating similar views—to be an honorable public servant and was confident in his professionalism, sense of decency, and concept of fair play. Simply put, the president knew that Ball would not betray him. As reinforcing exercises, Johnson occasionally assigned Ball tasks that would serve the political ends of the administration and, at the same time, reaffirm his convictions about his under secretary's reliability. In 1964, when Ball was still avoiding the Vietnam problem as much as possible, Johnson gave him the delicate job of guiding the South East Asia Resolution, or more popularly, the Tonkin Gulf resolution, through Congress. The under secretary's pronounced public endorsement of the resolution—a document that he, ironically, had been instrumental in drafting—deeply impressed the then mildly skeptical chairman of the Senate Foreign Relations Committee, J. William Fulbright. Ball and Fulbright had always enjoyed "excellent relations," trusted each other, and could count on each other's political support. (It was Fulbright who had managed to unhinge Kennedy's appointment of Republican William C. Foster as economic under secretary and bring Ball into government in 1961.) Fulbright's own misgivings about the seemingly limitless authority requested by the executive were alleviated by his trusted friend's reputation for honesty and persuasiveness and by what he knew to be Ball's personal reservations with the concept of an American military intervention in Southeast Asia. Fulbright had worked to defeat the similarly proposed Middle East Resolution in 1957 but was convinced—ironically, by the administration's resident dove—that he should go along with the White House on this one. The Arkansas Democrat was persuaded—perhaps Johnson was too—that the Tonkin Gulf resolution was conceived to stop the spread of war and to preclude the need for American combat troops. Fulbright recently has written that it had been "a great mistake to be taken in by [the administration's] presentation" and claims that he was willfully deceived by Johnson, Rusk, and McNamara about the details of the alleged attacks in the Gulf of Tonkin in August 1964. He blames Congress for its tendency to acquiesce on foreign policy matters in deliberations with the executive branch and lambastes the "gullibility" exhibited by the legislature during the summer of 1964. Fulbright admits that he "clearly made a mistake" in voting for the resolution. As always, the Congress was "preoccupied," as Fulbright sees it, "with a resounding affirmation of [American] unity," with the disastrous effect of suppressing "considerations of legislative accuracy and precision."[40] After the Tonkin Gulf resolution was passed by a vote of 88 to 2 in the Senate, Ball kept Fulbright apprised of the most sensitive strategic and political discussion regarding Vietnam. Fulbright's biographer, perhaps too generously, credits Ball with being the senator's "main source of information." What Fulbright knew about the White House discussions on Vietnam he learned from Ball, and at least in part because of the under secretary's own skepticism, he would for two years give the administration the benefit of the doubt on Vietnam.[41] After Johnson rudely ostracized Fulbright for his criticism of the war, Ball would become his eyes and ears in the executive branch, and Fulbright's dissent was augmented not only by Ball's general line of reasoning but by hard intelligence data that the two secretively shared.

Ball's encounter with Fulbright over Vietnam was by no means his only exposure to the avowed "opposition." Indeed, as an officer of the executive branch charged with implementing the president's policies, he performed innumerable official tasks to explain and generate support for escalation. Moreover, and adding to his ironic role, he periodically took on extraneous outside duties to advance the very course he was, on the inside, fervently disposed against. Ball was motivated by three factors. The first was professional pride. He believed then (and his seemingly endless redrafting of the book he is presently writing affirms) that if an assignment was worth performing, it was worth performing well. Proud of his elocution and skills as an advocate, Ball once wrote that "a policy not carefully articulated is no policy at all."[42] Embarrassed by sloppy writing and speech making from the State Department, he would just as soon defend escalation in a speech or rebut a column written by an administration critic himself in order to insure that it was done effectively—despite the fact that he personally disagreed with his own message. Secondly, Ball believed he needed to take a pronounced position advocating escalation on the *outside* in order to cultivate his special calling to dissent on the *inside*. He instinctively understood that there would be friction with the president and his colleagues created by his views and worked hard to insure that his position on Vietnam did not diminish his effectiveness on issues dearer to his heart. Unqualified public support of Johnson's Vietnam policies served this end. Thirdly, LBJ's preoccupation with the public relations aspects of the expanding war complicated and conditioned Ball's dissent. By propagating a positive attitude, Johnson hoped to enlist the cooperation of the Congress and the American people and maintain a national focus on his domestic agenda. Believing that the under secretary of state, by virtue of his own reservations, would know what appeals to make and how to bend other skeptics to the administration position, the president sent him chasing around Washington, around the country, and around the world as a lobbyist for escalation.

In an effective if incongruous display of mainline Cold War rhetoric applied to Southeast Asia, Ball attacked foreign and domestic critics of Johnson's Vietnam policy with bombast that quickly earned him a reputation as a tough, articulate, and loyal administration spokesman. Between February 1965 and August 1966 the itinerant diplomat crisscrossed the United States and Europe, warning against an "expansionist China" while in Dallas,[43] applauding the "effective work toward creating a Vietnamese Great Society"[44] and promising to "resolutely fight to the end"[45] in Washington, linking America's Vietnam policy to "the Principles of '76" in Philadelphia,[46] "recalling the unpunished aggressions of the Rhineland" in Lake Como, Italy,[47] aggressively hinting that "Hanoi may be bombed" in Paris,[48] and (prematurely) declaring that the Vietcong were "losing heart" in London.[49]

Given Johnson's political and psychological idiosyncrasies, Ball's objective to maintain his dissenting voice within government councils was well served by his public posture. As it has been repeatedly echoed by his biographers, LBJ was almost paranoid about dissenters leaving the government and openly attacking him and would just as soon suffer disloyal bureaucrats than to have them quit and embarrass the administration. Of dissenters within the government Johnson would say, "I'd rather have them inside the tent pissing out, than outside the tent pissing in."[50] Having deep reservations himself about escalating the war—and intellectually stimulated by his under secretary's evocative arguments—Johnson embraced Ball with particular fervor. But the president would not allow him to become a loose cannon. Ball was too able, too articulate, and he had too many important and influential friends. Johnson would neutralize Ball by showering him with kudos, generosity, flattery—and responsibility. He would be kept in the family.

Toward "domesticating"[51] Ball, in the fall of 1965 Johnson assigned him the task of heading an interagency Vietnam working group, ostensibly designed to develop fresh thinking on Southeast Asia and to direct the nation's nonmilitary operations abroad. To employ his under secretary's considerable abilities in a important job—and to keep him on a short leash—the president gave him more profile, more power, and his unmitigated gratitude. Part of this personal ploy has been attributed to what *New York Times* columnist James Reston called "The Johnson System." Writing that LBJ did not want to be left alone with the hard-liners, Reston concluded that Johnson "created an advisory committee of hawks [of which there were plenty] presided over by a dove [of which there was one]" in order to condition what Johnson thought was "extremism" in the advice he was receiving on Vietnam.[52]

The Johnson system worked to the satisfaction of its maker. From the moment Vietnam became a first order problem in the late summer of 1964 and for several months thereafter, Ball played an important political role for the administration. He assisted in the drafting of the seminal Southeast Asia Resolution and, despite his serious misgivings about the intelligence analysis of the "so-called" attacks on two American destroyers, dutifully told NBC's "Today" show following the Tonkin Gulf incident in August 1964 that "it has been demonstrated that [American] forces are capable of dealing with any kind of action that might occur."[53] Ball dispensed political advice by routinely coaching the president and Moyers before press conferences,[54] and he regularly scolded authors of hostile columns.[55] On more than one occasion, he was sent to explain the rationale behind increments of escalation to Senate liberals Fulbright and Mike Mansfield of Montana.[56]

On May 3, 1965, Ball once again faithfully toed the administration's line on Vietnam. At a conference of SEATO ministers he disparaged Hanoi's insistence that America withdraw from Vietnam's private political struggle (a view with which he privately sympathized) as propaganda and a "hollow disguise."[57] On August 12, 1965, Johnson assigned Ball the job of responding to a peace appeal submitted by Nobel laureate Linus Pauling.[58] On October 6, 1965, Ball conferred with Attorney General Nicholas Katzenbach "about the possibility of invoking the Logan Act against leftist student groups in Berkley [*sic*]"[59]—whom he once called "placard carrying hysterics."[60] On November 16, 1965, Johnson ordered Ball to play the role of private investigator by researching a mysterious "midnight brandy conversation between [Adlai] Stevenson and [Eric] Sevareid" which led to stories that the administration was carelessly turning down opportunities to negotiate with North Vietnam.[61] On January 29, 1966, in an effort to regain Walter Lippmann's blessings for the administration, Ball sent his friend a memorandum on Johnson's behalf—to which he cynically referred as "a lawyer's effort to argue the Administration's position on Viet-Nam." (In a cover letter Ball admitted to his good friend and confidant that the memo was "more advocacy than analysis.")[62] On April 21, 1966, Ball drafted an eloquent defense of the American policy which was read by Rusk before the Senate Foreign Relations Committee (SFRC).[63] National Security Adviser Walt Rostow telephoned the under secretary to report that he found it "very helpful" when Ball told the SFRC on June 30, 1966, that there was "no other course to follow other than the one the Administration is following."[64] The day after Ball's appearance on the Hill (during which the SFRC seemed determined to give the Johnson administration a black eye), Moyers called Ball to tell him that "the President thought [he] had really given it back to them in an effective way."[65]

The under secretary of state performed innumerable impromptu tasks in support of his president. Although Ball's extracurricular efforts might well be

construed as normal political duties routinely performed by government officers, three episodes provide insights into Ball's peculiar situation and illuminate aspects of his ego, conception of service, and strategy of dissent. The
first, antedating the Johnson presidency, was a self-initiated address to the
Economic Club of Detroit. On March 26, 1962, Ball had elicited McGeorge
Bundy's advice on his proposed remarks on the Indochinese situation. Stating
that "we are long overdue for a public explanation in terms which we could
hand out to the public when asked," he specifically mentioned "cutting down
on the White House letter answering problem." Bundy was very cool to the
idea. He said that "Ball was a brave man to do it" but added the caution that
"the President [Kennedy] is eager to play this [Vietnam] as low key as possible, not excluding the notion that there would come a time when we could back
off."[66] Ball made the speech. Despite the cautionary words from the White
House, the under secretary of state told his Detroit audience on April 30, 1962,
that "Viet-Nam is one of the world's danger spots where a valiant people are
struggling to defend their freedom."[67] The speech—vintage Ball—was so well
crafted, so articulate, and so well received that the Department of State quickly
published it as a pamphlet. Ball shamelessly proffered to his Detroit audience
that which he privately felt was a flagrantly inflated account of Vietnam's
significance to U.S. security and utterly ignored the reservations which he
expressed to Kennedy in November 1961. *Herald Tribune* columnist Margue-
rite Higgins quoted Ball as saying that "American retreat or withdrawal from
Viet-Nam is unthinkable" and that the American commitment "is now irrevo-
cable."[68] Ironically, when newspaper accounts of the address were made the
following day, Kennedy was extremely "disturbed" that Ball had grossly
overstated the extent of the American commitment. Kennedy demanded to see
a copy of the address and began calling editors in order to retract portions of it
from their publications. Kennedy engaged in full-throttle damage control.[69] In
a paradoxical case of runaway rhetoric, Ball outran Kennedy's conception of
the American role in Vietnam.

In a similarly self-motivated manner in March 1965, Ball warned the
National Foreign Policy Conference for Non-Governmental Organizations in
Washington that "what we do in Viet-Nam will have a profound meaning for
people in the other outposts of freedom." In a surprisingly bellicose address,
he attacked the "beguiling doctrines" of nationalism and isolationism, then
resurgent in Europe and the United States, and roundly criticized French
president Charles de Gaulle for self servingly "maintaining a nationalist policy
in the allied world and a neutralist position in Communist-threatened Southeast Asia."[70] In what the *Christian Science Monitor* reported as an "extraordi-

narily frank and stern allusion," Ball lambasted President de Gaulle, stating "that it was not enough for a nation simply to offer advice on all aspects of world affairs. It should be prepared to back that advice with resources."[71] Since Ball was, in private, entirely in accord with the French position on America's intervention in Southeast Asia and drew repeatedly upon French analogues in developing his Vietnam memorandums, it is particularly ironic that he was acquiring a reputation as the foremost France-basher within the American government. The speech was widely reported in national newspapers and was, like his earlier address on Vietnam, published by the State Department as a pamphlet under the evocative title "The Dangers of Nostalgia."[72]

Confident of Ball's ability to deal forthrightly with the French, in September 1965 Johnson dispatched him to Paris in hopes of gaining de Gaulle's understanding for the American position in Southeast Asia. The president was also "eager to keep Western governments aware of his willingness to negotiate" and ordered his under secretary of state to London, Bonn, and Rome to drum up support on the international front.[73] In a ninety-minute talk benignly described as "warm and interesting" but yielding no "major changes in French policy," Ball and de Gaulle rehashed the inflexible positions of their respective governments: The United States would remain resolutely committed to maintaining the political freedom of South Vietnam; France would continue to call for a neutralist regime in Saigon—while openly trading with the North Vietnamese.[74] There was no discernible movement by either side. Ball delights in retelling the story of two monolinguists debating a disagreeable subject without the help of an interpreter, in what turned out to be an encounter noticeably prejudiced by his considerable affections for de Gaulle's archantagonist, Jean Monnet. Commenting on the paucity of results stemming from the meeting, de Gaulle's continued and openly expressed pessimism about prospects for peace, and France's continued commerce with Hanoi, Ball has rather cynically stated that he was "doing a chore, that's all," and was "basically rather sympathetic with him [de Gaulle]."[75]

In a similarly ironic encounter—and by effectively betraying his own political and strategic instincts—Ball attacked Bobby Kennedy for his "new approach" to the Indochinese crisis in January 1966. With regard to Vietnam, John and Robert Kennedy had thought along roughly parallel lines. After the assassination in November 1963, Bobby's first instinct was to fulfill what he interpreted to be his brother's objectives. But President Kennedy's Indochina legacy was at best, according to his most meticulous biographer, "dual and contradictory." Although JFK's rhetoric has given rise to an expansive interpretation of his intentions, he had in fact imposed "absolute limitations" on the commitment he envisioned for Southeast Asia. In particular, JFK confidants Arthur Schlesinger, Jr., and Roger Hilsman insist that Kennedy would never have committed American combat troops or ordered the bombing of North Vietnam. Because Kennedy had developed a contingency plan for extrication in 1965 if the South Vietnamese failed to show progress on the battlefield, Schlesinger flatly declares that Kennedy would not have escalated the war to the degree that Johnson ultimately did. Though admittedly highly conjectural, these views are generally supported by members of Kennedy's inner circle.[76]

Johnson, as noted above, interpreted his predecessor's Southeast Asian legacy in radically different terms. For LBJ, the war in Vietnam was a direct challenge to the reputation of the country—and to the manhood of the president. Particularly after Pleiku, Johnson seemed to personalize the conflict. Bobby Kennedy, on the other hand, thought that Johnson had become obsessed with military victory and failed to understand the political nature of the war. "The essence of counterinsurgency," Kennedy told the International Police Academy in July 1965, "is not to kill, but to bring the insurgent back into the national life."[77] Kennedy believed that "victory in a revolutionary war is won not by escalation, but by deescalation."[78] In the summer of 1965, while LBJ sought military victory, Bobby Kennedy began to advance a plan for a negotiated withdrawal based on power sharing with the National Liberation Front and a neutralist Saigon government.

On February 19, 1966, Kennedy boldly announced a "new approach" for the political resolution of the conflict. "A negotiated settlement," he declared at a staged press conference, "means that each side must concede matters that are important in order to preserve positions that are essential." His most significant disagreement with Johnson centered on the disposition of the Vietcong. "There are three things you can do with such groups: Kill or repress them, turn the country over to them, or admit them to a share of power and responsibility."[79] Advocating the latter course in an open break with the administration, Bobby Kennedy challenged Lyndon Johnson's rationale for war.

The very next day, on February 20, Ball appeared on ABC's "Issues and Answers" and lashed out at Kennedy, calling his plan "an unacceptable solution"[80] and arguing that a coalition in Saigon of the type that he envisioned "would quickly turn into a communist government."[81] The fact that Kennedy's conception of a negotiated withdrawal and the political reconstitution of South Vietnam coincided with the plan that Ball, Acheson, and Cutler had proposed a year earlier renders Ball's response to Kennedy's initiative quite peculiar—

and indeed brings his motives into question. Although Ball emphatically (but not persuasively) denies that Johnson had assigned him the task of attacking Kennedy, it was clear that administration officials had mounted a "united front"[82] (including rhetorical assaults by Bundy and Humphrey) against Robert Kennedy's proposals. In explaining his response to Kennedy's "new" proposals for Vietnam, Ball has simply stated that it was a matter of presidential politics: "I didn't want to encourage Bobby's candidacy. I didn't think he'd make a very good president." Ball adds that he "knew Bobby long before [he] knew Jack," and considered the younger Kennedy to be "a rather spoiled and petulant young man." Having defended Henry Wallace during the political witch hunts of the early 1950s, Ball "could never forgive Bobby for his McCarthy days." Disparaging Robert F. Kennedy as a "demagogue," Ball freely admits that his personal animosity probably conditioned his response to Kennedy's proposals for a political settlement of the Vietnam War.[83]

Between October 1964 and September 1966 Ball was in what he once grossly understated as "a position of considerable ambivalence." Contemplating the conflict between his patently contradictory roles inside and outside the government, he recalls his agonizing dilemma: "I had my private views and I also had my public views which I had to defend if I was to stay there [in the executive branch] at all." Ball had been a lawyer for thirty years and had seldom actually embraced intellectually or emotionally the positions and principles he was defending. Even though he was the number two policy officer in the State Department, he was unable—or unwilling—to transcend the conventions of his vocation. "As a professional with responsibilities for the policy," Ball recalls, he was quite willing, when called upon, to make the hawk's case for the administration.[84] An articulate lawyer and diplomat, he more than ably served as LBJ's hired intellectual gun.

When the American commitment deepened with the introduction of combat troops after July 1965, the tensions between Ball's private convictions and public responsibilities grew to nearly unmanageable levels. As his identity as the single administration dissenter became more widely known, it became progressively more difficult for him to publicly represent the administration's position on the war. As early as October 1964, Ball's colleagues had expressed concern about his public profile. That month it was apparent that James Reston and the *New York Times* had become aware of "a high level parley" on Vietnam in which there had been a "Devil's Advocate"—the first time that pregnant term was used with reference to the under secretary of state.[85] Reminding the president that Ball was "zealous in his loyalty to you," Bundy nevertheless wrote Johnson a memorandum in January of 1965 which summarized his own suspicions about the source of worrisome leaks and cited the considerable difficulties in identifying the leaker. Bundy reported to Johnson that columnist Joseph Kraft "had just completed a profile on [Ball]" and was, therefore, "in a very good position to know [his] views." Though concerned about the under secretary of state, the national security adviser also tried to convince the president that Kraft had "picked up his picture of the Ball memo [October 1964] from more than one source."[86] Johnson was not so sure.

The issue of Ball's "outside activities" subsided until a month later when, on February 15, a furious president called him to ask "if he had seen Tad Szulc's *N.Y. Times* article" which "states very closely the thoughts in [your] memo on V-N." Johnson "thought it incredible" that the article specifically referred to the details of what had been discussed the previous Saturday and demanded to know how the story had gotten out. Ball denied responsibility for a leak and reminded the president of how he had carefully impounded the extant copies of the memorandum. Unmollified, Johnson shot back that he "was going to put watches on the top people he deals with over there [referring to the State Department]" and that "if necessary [he would] make decisions by himself, or get one man alone with him in the room and bar all others." Johnson concluded the harangue by telling Ball that he had discovered some "shocking things" in tracking down leaks from within the administration and that he "was confident that either Ball, Mac Bundy, or McNamara let this get away from them."[87]

After February 15, the under secretary of state exercised considerably more discretion in his dealings with government bureaucrats and those members of the press with whom he did not have a close personal relationship. In fact, the record shows that after February 1965 Ball would regularly disassociate himself from his own views. He began deferring inquiries by journalists to other government officials—or, curiously enough, to other journalists—and disqualifying himself on sensitive questions. On one occasion when he won a dovish senator's praise for "raising a cautionary finger about the SVN [South Vietnam] business," Ball obsequiously replied that his views "were the same as the other people advising the president."[88] On February 22, 1966, journalist Barbara Kerr asked Ball, who she said was "well-known to be in opposition," to arrange "a series of private briefings for high ranking members of the press." He declined.[89] When his close friend and former business partner Clayton Fritchey was asked in April 1966 to write a feature story on him for the *New York Times Magazine*, Ball told Fritchey that he did not then want to "advertise" his Vietnamese position.[90] Later the same week, when *St. Louis Post-Dispatch* columnist Marquis Childs asked him "whether bombing North

Vietnam was having an effect on the will of the people," Ball retorted—in diametric opposition to his private analysis of the air strikes—that the air war was demonstrating tactical results and that "the assumption is wrong to look for the effect on the peoples' will."[91] This new discretion was demonstrated again when Ball responded to the charge by *Washington Post* editor Chalmers Roberts in July 1966 that "the accent is all on the war side and not much accent on the peace side." Ball firmly and simply rebutted the criticism of the administration by declaring that "what is going on is justified."[92]

Ball was obviously walking a tightrope and, as his dissent became more widely known, was only marginally successful at keeping his struggle within the government distinct from his public profile. The sharpness of his disagreement with the consensus behind escalation and the constancy and sheer mass of his oppositional papers and oral arguments make Ball's dissent an anomaly of American politics. There are few examples in American political history of high-ranking officers so long maintaining so contrary a position with their superiors on a paramount issue. Diplomatic historians Richard Neustadt and Ernest May note, as a historical pattern, that subcabinet officials in opposition with their superiors on *any* issue serve an average of just twenty months in office.[93] The norm would suggest that Ball should either have been silenced by his superiors, reassigned, fired, or, on his own volition, resigned in protest. None of these predictable eventualities occurred.

An equally likely outcome, as political scientist Irving Janis's compelling "groupthink" theory argues, would have been that Ball, consciously or subconsciously, accommodate himself to the consensus for intervention. "One of the main psychological assumptions underlying the hypothesis," Janis argues persuasively, "is that when a policy making group becomes highly cohesive [as Johnson's war cabinet was], a homogenization of viewpoints takes place."[94] Especially under the extreme emotional pressures of war, it is far more likely for a dissenter within the group to support, however reluctantly, his embattled colleagues. Janis has observed that within the Johnson administration, "everyone in the hierarchy was subjected to conformity pressures." Those who expressed reservations about escalation became suspect, and the epithet, "I am afraid he is losing his effectiveness," was threateningly applied with great effect to the dissenter. The so-called effectiveness trap, Janis tells us, "inclines its victims to suppress their criticisms" and "makes any member who starts to voice misgivings ready to retreat to a seemingly acquiescent position in the presence of perturbed superiors."[95]

Ball's sustained dissent appears to be even more aberrant when Johnson's philosophy of politics and his political talents are considered. Simply stated, LBJ lionized consensus and abhorred conflict. Politics was, for the Texas Democrat, operational and divorced from abstract dialogue. He had little patience with ideological discourse or with ideologues. Debate, he believed, was more likely to sharpen disagreement than to stimulate political action. Johnson's greatest gift as a politician was his celebrated and sometimes intimidating ability to forge a consensus for legislative action. He was, in his generation, the acknowledged master of the art of personal persuasion. Throughout his career in the House of Representatives, the Senate, and the White House, he had repeatedly demonstrated his craft of direct personal inducement in winning converts to causes. But the record fails to show a single instance of Johnson beguiling Ball with his most potent tactic, the intimate "one-to-one encounter,"[96] or any attempt whatsoever to win him over to his view of the war. Indeed, because the opposite is confirmed, because the president encouraged opposition from his under secretary, Ball's dissent cannot be understood apart from a consideration of LBJ's political strategy on Vietnam, his perception of Ball, and his real personal doubts about his policies.

First, during the political tumult which followed the precipitious escalation of July 1965, Ball's dissent permitted Johnson to state publicly that he had weighed both sides of the question of whether or not to Americanize the war. Ball was useful to the president in this way until he left the government in September 1966. As Robert L. Gallucci insightfully notes in *Neither Peace Nor Honor*, "Johnson's circle of close advisors narrowed as critics of the war proliferated,"[97] and save for Ball's assigned role the president would have been open to the charge of receiving one-dimensional advice. In the spring and summer of 1965, as North Vietnamese provocations narrowed Johnson's military and political choices, he insulated himself in order to concentrate on the tactical problem of punishing a determined and elusive enemy. At this point, Ball's dissent became a premium political commodity—a sort of managed, self-contained opposition to the war in pinstripes. Without reopening every question to bureaucratic review, Johnson employed—indeed directed—his under secretary to provide alternative judgments. "With the exception of George Ball in 1965," as Herbert Y. Schandler poignantly observed in *The Unmaking of a President*, "no one close to the president had questioned our basic Vietnam strategy, nor had the president welcomed or sought such questioning."[98] Johnson relied on Ball as a safe (meaning loyal) and cogent (the president always found his papers well reasoned) source of opposing viewpoints, and he regularly expressed his appreciation. "George," the president would say, "I can't tell you how grateful I am to you for disagreeing with me."[99]

Second, the under secretary was himself a political adornment. Ball was, in Johnson's own words, "inspiring, stimulating and shoving."[100] But mostly, the president admired Ball's elegance and reputation as a sagacious lawyer. Just days before his presidency expired, Johnson addressed a State Department reception for Dean Rusk. "I can't let this occasion go by," LBJ remarked, "without paying tribute to George Ball—one of the ablest, most loyal and most courageous men I have known in public life." That evening, Johnson told a story about a candidate for a teaching position in Johnson City, Texas. "The school board," he mused, "was divided on whether the world was round or flat" and asked the candidate how he taught it. "The poor fellow needed the job so much—he said: 'I can teach it either way.' George Ball," Johnson quipped in closing, "is the only man who I have ever really known in government who, on five minutes instruction from the President, can take either side of a proposition."[101]

Although Johnson thought Ball was wrong on Vietnam, he genuinely welcomed his "raising red flags."[102] Fearful of becoming mired down on the Asian mainland or precipitating World War III, Johnson appreciated Ball constantly reminding him of the perils of intervention. Without peer in his comprehension of domestic policy, Johnson realized he was out of his element when it came to planning a counterinsurgency operation in the Southeast Asian jungles. Ball accurately assessed the relationship between Johnson's uncertainties and his own dissent: "Johnson had graver doubts about the war than several other people around him. He was my best friend while I was urging [an] opposite course."[103] Although it is impossible to calibrate precisely the impact that Ball had on Johnson, his dissent at the very least prompted Johnson to pause, reflect, and demand greater proof from the advocates of an expanded U.S. commitment. Moreover, new insights show that Johnson kept what he called "The Ball Plan"[104] (the under secretary's disengagement formula delineated in Chapter 3) in the recesses of his mind and may have been prepared to act upon the proposals for a political resolution if a military breakthrough would allow him to do so without it appearing to be an act of desperation. Indeed, as Johnson's designated peace commissioner Averell Harriman disclosed shortly before his death in August 1986, "Johnson had decided to get out of Vietnam . . . to declare a cease fire and bring our troops home."[105]

Harriman's assertion certainly complicates the question of where Johnson

Ball, *left*, confers with President Johnson, 1965. Ball's dissent in regard to the president's Vietnam policy was, as the president told him, a valuable counterpoint. (Photograph courtesy of George W. Ball)

intended to go in Vietnam, and how he intended to get there. The most generous interpretation of Ball's role in relation to the president's intentions suggests that Johnson was sincerely looking for a way out or at least preparing for a cataclysmic new circumstance that would change the character of the war and allow him to get out. If the opportunity presented itself, the interpretation goes, he would have Ball's plan in hand and ready to execute. The least generous interpretation of Ball's role in relation to the president's intentions is that Johnson's bona fide aspirations for economic development in Southeast Asia, what he considered the unacceptable political risks of precipitous withdrawal, and the consensus for escalation among Rusk, McNamara, Bundy, and the Joint Chiefs, relegated Ball's dissent to a staged contrivance of personal manipulation and political maneuver. Johnson's repeated references to Ball as "*his* lawyer" and "*his* devil's advocate [emphasis added]," the Texas school board parable, and the fact that so much of Ball's work on Vietnam was specifically commissioned by the president certainly support this view.[106] Indeed, as McGeorge Bundy notes, "*George didn't invent his role, the president assigned it to him* [emphasis added]."[107]

But Bundy's uncharitable—and representative—evaluation must be qualified by a careful reconsideration of the decision-making chronology. Ball's most comprehensive memorandum, written in October 1964, was wholly self-initiated. He acted independently to produce a most penetrating examination of the assumptions upon which the Johnson administration was proceeding in Vietnam, and from that point forward the under secretary of state was the acknowledged torchbearer of the disengagement argument within the executive branch. The narrowly opened window of opportunity to fundamentally change the contours of American policy existed for Ball only during the spring and summer of 1965. Between the time of the Pleiku incident in February and the Americanization of the war in July, Ball's remonstrations were reasonably thoroughly debated—and then rejected. When debate over ends gave way to discussion of means after the July decisions, Ball's dissent became an innocuous fixture of Vietnam bureaucratic politics. Johnson read the dissenting papers with interest but could not act upon their recommendations. Ball continued to be a counselor but not a policy officer.

Johnson's senior advisory staff on Vietnam—those from whom suggestions were seriously considered for policy—was slowly reduced to what has been derisively referred to as "a tiny priesthood of the anointed participants in the mysteries of the war." In the caustic words of one observer, NSC meetings became a "charade, convoked to ratify decisions already made by Johnson and his steadily constricting inner circle." Examination of the documentary record is distressingly corroborative. The regularity with which the same arguments were repeated in the NSC causes one to conclude that the meetings were not forums for the discussion of widely varying alternatives but merely a place where tired officials continuously rationalized their analyses—and their prejudices. Because Johnson was irrevocably fixed in his belief that he could not act upon the under secretary of state's plan to extricate the United States from a war he believed should be waged, Ball's dissent may have merely served to stimulate his colleagues to a more precise exposition of their views. NSC meetings, therefore, simply served to enforce unanimity. The president "would let them know what 'decision' they were supposed to make." On one occasion, just minutes before an NSC meeting was convened in which the dovish U.N. ambassador Arthur Goldberg was asked to participate, this tendency toward "orchestration" was exhibited. Goldberg, who had (as described in Chapter 4) naively considered his invitation as an opportunity to voice his reservation about military escalation, was taken aside by the dutiful secretary of defense and reminded not to say anything that would "embarrass" the president.[108]

As the peace movement and organized congressional opposition to the war emerged after 1966, the president became isolated, secretive, and, as his insightful Boswell Doris Kearns suggests, "irrational."[109] Less than generous chroniclers of the Johnson presidency have repeatedly emphasized "the deterioration of [the president's] capacity to distinguish what was real—what his rational faculties knew to be real—from what he wished to believe." In time, LBJ's "paranoid disintegration" became a frequent topic of discussion among White House assistants. As he occasionally meandered through acerbic monologues about the swelling ranks of "enemies and conspirators" determined to wreck his presidency, Johnson would blast the "liberals, intellectuals, and communists," who, he believed, were all members of the same unpatriotic set. "Lippmann is a communist, so is Teddy White," Johnson would bellow. Orders to lash out at his political enemies by unleashing the FBI or the IRS that were barked in the midst of an irrational outburst—or angry directives to fire a person within the administration merely because of the friends he kept—were routinely ignored by the White House staff.

Johnson's transcendent concern with leaks to a progressively more inquiring and militant press prompted him to continuously narrow the number of individuals involved in top-level Vietnam discussions. McGeorge Bundy's personal notes from the spring of 1965 to his departure from government in February 1966 show that even as the meetings got smaller—and the under secretary's views became more estranged from the immediate agenda of escalating a military intervention he believed should never have been initiated—Ball nevertheless maintained his seat at the Vietnam conference table. Invariably, Johnson would check the box next to the under secretary's name on a list of potential conferees prepared for him by Bundy.[110] Unable—or unwilling—to heed his advice, Johnson ironically continued to value Ball's counsel. The president even once made the remarkable statement to his brother that he considered Ball "among the finest brains in this country" and among "the half-dozen most influential men" on Vietnam.[111]

In the right mood, Ball has admitted—albeit reluctantly—that Johnson "used" him.[112] Having stated that, he has found the frequently asserted "devil's advocacy" interpretation of his dissent to be an affront to his personal pride and a source of considerable irritation.[113] Assured that his colleagues "never once doubted the sincerity of [his] views"[114]—a conclusion that Rusk, McNamara, and Bundy have independently confirmed—Ball is noticeably exasperated by critical accounts of his role in the Vietnam drama, particularly those written by former NSC aide James C. Thomson and political scientist Hans J. Morgenthau. Thomson interprets Ball's intimacy with President Johnson to be evidence of the extent to which he had been "domesticated." Basing his interpretation on insights gained from his exposure to the dissident under secretary as Bundy's assistant, Thomson derisively remarks that "once Ball began to express his doubts, he was warmly institutionalized, and encouraged to become the in-house devil's advocate." Thomson caustically concludes that the "upshot" was preordained: "The process of escalation allowed for periodic requests to Mr. Ball to speak his piece; Ball felt good; the others felt good (they had given a full hearing to the dovish opposition); and there was minimal unpleasantness. The club remained intact."[115]

In his searching Realist critique of American foreign policy entitled *Truth and Power* (1970), Morgenthau argued that Ball's dissent was patently disingenuous simply because he was so closely identified with the administration as the war was being escalated. "Ball had doubts about some of the tactics of the war," Morgenthau wrote, "but [saw] eye to eye with Johnson on philosophy and strategy." Bitterly hostile to Johnson's policies, Morgenthau believed that "it was impossible to be a member of the Johnson administration and a dove at the same time."[116] In a *New York Review of Books* article the following year (suggestively entitled "The Wild Bunch"), Morgenthau celebrated the "deflation of the myth that Under Secretary of State George Ball was opposed to the Vietnam War" and quoted Dean Rusk as saying that "Ball only played the role [of dissenter] when he was assigned it."[117]

What, then, was the essence and intention of Ball's dissent? Was it a "devil's advocacy" or an unfeigned exposition of heartfelt convictions? Was it an exercise in bureaucratic politics or strategic analysis? "Was Ball," as journalist Henry Brandon rhetorically posed it, "simply writing memoranda for the record?"[118] Rowland Evans and Robert Novak sharpened these questions in 1971 when they determined that "George Ball was not taken at all seriously by policy makers or staff technicians on Vietnam." Evans and Novak observed (quite incorrectly) that Ball "seldom conferred personally with Johnson and drafted relatively few presidential memoranda." The dissent, they argued, was "lightly regarded by central figures making Vietnam policy, including presidential adviser McGeorge Bundy." They added that those responsible for the policy saw Ball's views as "stemming from dovish visceral reaction rather than hard-boiled cerebration." *Washington Post* editorialists concluded that "those close to the president felt he was irritated by dissents from his under secretary of state once policy had been made."[119]

Although there is plenty of documentary evidence to suggest that Johnson was more than "irritated" by dissents, and even more by dissenters, the weight of evidence with specific reference to Ball shatters the impression of an annoyed chief executive. Even though Ball's memorandums failed to significantly discredit the conventional wisdom on Vietnam in the period between February and July 1965, Johnson thought Ball's position on the war to be cogent and powerful. A Rand Corporation study supports the view that the under secretary's dissent was indeed "lightly regarded" by all but the president himself. As noted above, Ball anchored part of his argument against escalation on the prediction that, as U.S. casualties mounted, public support for the war would proportionally diminish. Ball had arrived at the crucial July 21 NSC meeting armed with a chart correlating the drop-off in public opinion polls with the rise in casualties during the Korean War to fortify his argument. A raft of "former senior advisers" interviewed by Rand researchers in 1983 "seemed not even to be able to recall Ball's presentation at all." The Rand study notes that although "Rusk expressed respect for Ball for speaking what he thought to be the case," he summarily discounted any estimates of predicted casualties as wholly unreliable. McNamara did not take them seriously either and even audaciously claimed he "had never seen Ball's casualty charts before." McGeorge Bundy merely recalls that "the question of casualty levels was not a large element in the discussions of 1965," and William Bundy simply "did not remember Ball's presentation."[120]

A useful illumination of the matter of Ball's opposition to the war has been offered by a fellow dissenter. In comparing presidential style on the particular problem of doves and Vietnam, State Department intelligence analyst Paul Kattenburg concluded in 1980 that "each President [JFK and LBJ] had his own style with dissenters." Kennedy, Kattenburg asserts, "tended to grill [them] on Indochina and then suggest that Robert Kennedy keep an eye on them." Johnson, on the other hand, "often showed direct irritation but managed to salve his conscience by literally training himself to listen to, and sometimes hear, George Ball." Even though Ball was given "frequent access to the President," he was, as Kattenburg laments, "carefully kept from actually playing a decision making role."[121]

Because Ball apparently had so little direct influence on policy, a gaggle of second-tier bureaucrats who observed him firsthand express the shared conviction that he was driven by ulterior motives. Though Rusk, McNamara, and Bundy dispute the thesis that Ball sought to exploit the Vietnam issue for professional advancement,[122] the frequency and vehemence with which this interpretation arises from those below the top echelon is compelling. Convinced that Ball "used" Vietnam to advance himself as Rusk's successor, Allen Whiting recalls a late night meeting in the late summer of 1965 during which, after two or three whiskeys, Ball remarked that the chart lines plotting rising casualties and diminishing public support would intersect around the time of the 1966 congressional elections. According to Whiting's interpretation of events, in making a case against escalation, Ball was positioning himself for the inevitability that Johnson would be compelled to reverse course and change horses. Ball would be, as the new secretary of state, positioned to orchestrate America's extrication from Indochina. Emphasizing how important it is "not to miss personal ambition as a driving and conditioning element in [Ball's] behavior," Whiting claims that "Ball saw Vietnam as his winning ticket," his bureaucratic trump card. "Dean will be wrong and I will be right," Ball boldly declared to Whiting.[123] Former assistant secretary of defense Adam Yarmolinsky, an early critic of Johnson's policies, concurs with Whiting: "Some men radiate virtue and some men radiate ambition." The former aide to McNamara stated that "none of us [Defense Department doves] felt that he was a help at all. He had no impact on John [McNaughton, assistant secretary of defense] or Bob [McNamara]. Ball's papers are more important today than they were in the 1960s."[124]

Similarly, J. Robert Schaetzel has suggested that Ball's character and personality traits are central elements in the story of his dissent. Though openly an admirer of Ball's talents and intellectual gifts, Schaetzel focuses attention on Ball's penchant for self-absorption in analyzing his profile on Vietnam and his behavior generally. He asserts that because he was cast in the role of dissenter by the president—at least part of the time—Ball rather liked to play the maverick in Vietnam bureaucratic politics. "George revelled in his unique and well-known role as in-house hair shirt; I don't doubt that he believed in his devil's advocacy brief on Vietnam, but I think at bottom it was a matter of ego."[125]

Most vitriolic in his denunciation of Ball is Roger Hilsman, who served as State Department intelligence analyst and assistant secretary of state for Far Eastern affairs under Kennedy. He claims that "Ball really got conned," and worse, "became an intellectual whore" by playing the role of "his majesty's loyal opposition." Otherwise complimentary of Ball, Hilsman laments that "he was a terrible disappointment" to those working at the lower rungs of the State Department in an effort throughout 1964 to demilitarize the commitment to South Vietnam. Hilsman has long believed that Ball "came to Vietnam for all the wrong reasons," had only "marginal influence on policy," "never intervened [in the State Department meetings] on his own volition," and failed to effectively tap the resources of the agencies of government over which he exercised control. Hilsman suggests that Ball never really took time to confer or be briefed adequately enough to fortify his advocacy. "Too often," Hilsman stated, "Ball shot from the hip on Vietnam."[126]

A truly balanced evaluation of Ball's dissent must include an accounting of his personal interests and professional preoccupations. An estimate derived from his appointment calendar during his six-year tenure as under secretary of state shows that he spent perhaps as little as 5 to 10 percent of his time on Vietnam.[127] Save for intermittent periods when he was thoroughly consumed by the subject, the Europe-focused under secretary mostly busied himself with the world far to the north and west of Indochina. (Ball is quick to remind his listeners that he spent a good deal more time working on a tangled meat import bill than he did on Vietnam.)[128] Former assistant secretary for political affairs Robert Manning notes that Southeast Asia "was something he almost compulsively wanted to stay away from—partly because he sensed trouble, and partly because he felt it was a second-rate problem, and a real pain-in-the-ass."[129] Something also must be reiterated about the world view from which Ball's perspective on Vietnam sprang. His dissent emanated primarily from his presuppositions about the world and only secondarily from his episodic and at times perfunctory investigation of the political and military crisis in Vietnam. Indeed, insights drawn from experience in private and public enterprises antedating his State Department tenure overwhelmed Ball's analysis of the Vietnamese problem and undermined his advocacy in critical circles by identifying it with a Realist world view that, in the 1960s, was not in vogue among the New Frontiersmen. When it came to Southeast Asia, as Hilsman has explained it, "George merely offered an ideology."[130]

It has already been amply demonstrated that Ball was patently uninspired by developmental economics and dubious about the prospect of "nation-building," that he cast a cynical eye at Third World foreign assistance, that he was Eurocentric to the point of ambivalence toward Indochina, that he was unmoved by the hyperbolic rhetoric of a Free World struggle against communism, and, most significantly, that he remained unconvinced that the Americans could defeat the North Vietnamese with the means contemplated. With this intellectual baggage, it is scarcely surprising that Ball demurred from the policies pursued by Lyndon Johnson. Affectionately known within the administration as the "in-house dove" (in part because of his personal aversion to war),[131] or "Ol' Stop the Bombing George" (most specifically for his diatribes against air strikes),[132] or "a Johnny-One-Note" (for his innumerable warnings that American involvement in Southeast Asia would undermine the Atlantic Alliance),[133] and a "charter member of the White Man's Club" (because of his hesitancy to assist the developing nations),[134] Ball spoke in a different idiom from those whose primary concern it was to wage a perplexing war in a distant Vietnamese jungle. Though he mastered an impressive array of intelligence materials and developed unique insights into the complex operational problems of counterinsurgency warfare, Ball's dissent was perceived as merely an ideological argument. As Johnson's eminent "Tuesday Cabinet"[135] and all manner of Vietnam task forces debated how victory could be achieved, Ball argued that the war should not be waged. The under secretary's ideology and world view, which rejected military intervention in Vietnam, were unconvincing to a president who embraced a countervailing ideology and world view that called for military intervention in Vietnam—and the war came.

In time, Ball managed to partially dissolve his connection to the Johnson administration. His tangled return to a not-so-private life, his continued and progressively more strident criticism of the war until 1973, and, most particularly, the maturation of his political philosophy and global strategy for the United States are the final topics of this volume. With a keen sense of what perils his country would confront if the lessons of the Vietnam experience were not articulated and heeded, Ball set about—sometimes by baldly partisan attacks and flagrantly embroidered interpretations of events—to force a reexamination of what too easily had passed as the conventional wisdom of the Cold War.

Chapter 6

A Wholly Partisan Critic

George Ball stood alone in winning the respect and admiration of
his presidents and secretary of state by the vigor and clarity of his
dissenting views in two administrations. When a person leaves public
office, he has the rights and privileges of a private citizen. It is
his privilege, not his duty, to go public [with his dissent], no
matter what the professors may say.
—Dean Rusk

The stage was set for an American extrication when Johnson withdrew.
Had Nixon and Kissinger learned anything at all from our agonizing
experience, they would have promptly ended the war. . . . The case
is a strong one, and if Kissinger was finally rewarded with the
Nobel Prize, that merely refutes the old canard that the Swedes have
no sense of humor.
—George Ball

BY THE SPRING OF 1966, Vietnam's internal civil conflict had been
effectively transformed into an Americanized technocratic war. At year's end
the number of U.S. combat forces in Southeast Asia would exceed 400,000,
and even the most conservative combat strategists called for dozens of thousands more. The new reality of massive U.S. casualties awakened the American people to their new "Free World challenge." With escalation advancing
rapidly, front-page news was dominated by reports of bloody military engagements. As visual images from the Vietnam killing fields finally became a daily
feature of network news, deep divisions over strategy surfaced within the
administration. With the war generally—and the pacification programs in the
South particularly—producing only marginal results, Johnson's Vietnam advisory staff was racked by dissension. As the year wore on an open break

developed between the civilian leadership in the Pentagon and the Joint Chiefs of Staff over the bombing campaign and the pace of escalation.

One by one, in varying intensities of apprehension, subcabinet bureaucrats identified with a failing policy began to quit the administration and run for the cover of private think tanks and universities, from which many sharply and impertinently denounced the war. By no means the first critical player to leave, the under secretary of state was by the spring of 1966 alienated from the war policy, thoroughly exhausted, and ready to quit. Although his arguments against military escalation were depleted and his zest for the fight with his colleagues over Vietnam nearly extinguished, Ball maintained the utmost cordiality with those still in the trenches, particularly Rusk and the president. Ever protective of the administration as he was asserting his views inside the government, Ball was equally concerned about embarrassing Johnson and adding to his already considerable political burdens with an impudent departure. Guarding his private plans from public discussion, throughout the spring and summer Ball maintained a heartening public image and the proverbial stiff upper lip as he regularly squashed reports that he was even considering resigning. In March he told a *Washington Post* correspondent that he had "no plans to leave anytime soon,"[1] and in June he forcefully rebutted a wire service story predicting his departure by flatly stating that he "did not have any intention of leaving the administration."[2]

On the eighteenth of July however, Ball stumbled in his effort to preserve a low profile. The under secretary's office telephone transcripts show that in the course of a private conversation with correspondent Marquis Childs, Ball confided that he "had been trying to negotiate himself out [of the administration] since February" and had already "made personal arrangements accordingly."[3] In fact, he had already planned to return to private life in the field of investment banking and had even finalized most accommodating terms of employment with his new Wall Street partners. Almost immediately, talk of Ball's imminent departure was commonplace around Washington. Journalists, who had scrupulously refrained from disclosing what they knew of Ball's dissent in exchange for candid "background only" briefings from a surprisingly forthcoming policy officer, began celebrating and analyzing his departure. Columnist Mary McGrory published a story revealing the existence of "a thick loose-leaf folder containing eloquent briefs against escalation" in Ball's office on the seventh floor of the State Department and applauded him as a stalwart voice of prudence within the administration. Senate Foreign Relations Committee chairman J. William Fulbright also expressed his alarm about the prospect of Ball's departure, as it would leave LBJ alone with the hawks; the under secretary's resignation, Fulbright remarked, would leave "only one or two bedraggled senators to carry on" against Johnson.[4] Admiring Ball's independent position on Vietnam, Joseph Kraft hoped, in print, that another "Doubting Thomas" might replace him and even presumptuously suggested that a "devil's advocate" be built into the executive branch and "given an institutional base."[5] Others speculated about whether Johnson would fill Ball's position with a "devil's advocate" to "give Dean Rusk a hard time" or a "Johnson advocate" who might exist within the administration simply to confirm the president's judgments about Southeast Asia.[6] Anticipating the under secretary's resignation, pundit Clayton Fritchey summed up a generally held sentiment among the Washington press corps—and the claque of antiwar liberals that was, by then, highly dubious of Johnson's Vietnam policies—when he wrote that "we can only hope that when George Ball leaves he will want to share his thoughts with us."[7]

Ball only partially fulfilled Fritchey's wish. Proud of, and confident in, his brief against the war which he had developed over the course of twenty-four months, Ball felt that time and events would vindicate him. But this certitude fostered serious personal dilemmas: Should he go public with what he thought was an exceedingly strong case against further escalation and for a negotiated settlement to a losing war? Should he lock arms with the "Bolshevik cluster"[8] of dissenters who had, in varying degrees of revulsion and frustration, quit the administration over Vietnam? Should he join with the Fulbright/Mansfield clique within the Democratic party and publicly denounce the war? Ball's Washington neighbors began to offer advice by the bushel. Walter Lippmann exhorted him to publicly vent his running argument with the administration with the express intention of discrediting the policies of Johnson, Rusk, and McNamara. Indeed, Lippmann felt that Ball should have raucously resigned in protest over Vietnam two years earlier. James Reston, who did not want the under secretary of state to "go off unsung"—and who looked forward to publishing his privileged insights—also urged him to take his case to the public. But Ball would have none of it. The unfailingly loyal and eminently discreet team player resisted the temptation to advertise his prophetic analyses of the war, partly because of his personal values and partly because of what he knew were the considerable hazards associated with confronting Lyndon Johnson. Ball told Reston in September that he "did not want to exit ungracefully"[9] and opted for a quiet return to private life. During the months that Ball was preparing to leave government for the fourth time, he often contemplated Dean Acheson's gentlemanly departure from the Roosevelt administration in 1933. "Abhorring vainglorious gestures," Ball once wrote admiringly of his mentor,

Acheson eschewed the temptation of a public confrontation with his superiors and "contented himself with a graceful letter of resignation."[10] To the greatest degree possible under the circumstances, Ball sought to replicate Acheson's departure.

Sympathetic to Ball's bureaucratic frustration and personal desires, the president readily accepted his resignation. Expressing "deep personal as well as official regret," Johnson wrote that Ball had "earned the right to private life after five and a half years in the line of fire."[11] Whether, at bottom, the president felt regret or relief over Ball's departure is unknowable. His valuable service to the administration in areas not related to Southeast Asia aside, by September 1966 Ball's views on Vietnam were no longer useful to an administration mired down in the most complex tactical discussions of a war that the under secretary merely keep repeating should not be waged. But, for the most part, Ball had played it straight with Johnson. His was a "by-the-book" internal bureaucratic dissent.

Although the president had once denounced him in the company of his personal assistants for "leaking documents to a hostile writer,"[12] Ball broke with the administration on excellent terms. There is every indication that the under secretary of state had earned the president's respect, trust, and genuine affection. Commemorating his diplomatic career at a State Department testimonial dinner in October 1966, Johnson exclaimed that "George Ball's achievements required no review" and that he had "distinguished himself in dozens of critical and sensitive situations." Johnson told his audience that he particularly appreciated Ball's "frankness of advice" and then roundly dismissed the then prevailing interpretation of his dissent. "If one were to believe only what we read in the press," Johnson cautioned, "we would think that George Ball's chief service to this administration was to play the role of devil's advocate. Well I don't know about that. In government, I have never known the devil to need an advocate. He usually makes his own case pretty well."[13]

It is ironic that Johnson, who had defined Ball's role in the Vietnam debates for two years, would, in a single commemorative oration, seek to allay the "devil's advocacy" image he had himself so carefully cultivated. At the end of September 1966 Ball exited quietly. He burned no bridges. Claiming not to have resigned on principle or in protest over Vietnam, he preserved years of faithful protocol. Not once did he violate a confidence or intentionally make life difficult for those on the inside whose continued burden it was to pursue an elusive victory. Although he continued to oppose military intervention, Ball was a cautious and wholly partisan critic. He went out of his way to be exculpatory in his public remarks, portraying Lyndon Johnson as a circumspect and prayerful decision maker and a decidedly reluctant belligerent, and he often expressed sympathy for the predicament in which the administration found itself. Indeed, Ball's behavior rudely disappointed those who were poised to embrace him as the leader of the opposition to the war in Vietnam. Otherwise acclaimed as the most sage among the "best and the brightest," Ball has been treated rather harshly by liberal academics who might have applauded his resignation, and, given the timing and manner of his departure, he has befuddled many who had admired his position on the war. He was scolded for identifying with the administration as long as he did and denounced for not more vociferously attacking Johnson's policies when he finally left.

Former NSC staffer James C. Thomson was among the first of the Vietnam-era dissenters to address the intricacies of principled resignation in a 1974 *Foreign Policy* magazine article entitled "Getting Out and Speaking Out." Close collaboration in the NSC with McGeorge Bundy put Thomson in close quarters with the archetypical believer in the sacrosanct principles of loyalty and team play. In describing how the principle is sometimes expressed, Thomson drew upon an anecdote from his association with Bundy: When Thomson quit and spoke out against the war, Bundy roundly scolded him with the rejoinder that "those who had been entrusted with responsibility by a president had been handed a pistol along with that trust. Those who later spoke about their period of service not merely broke that trust, but turned that pistol on the man who had trusted them and shot him in the head." Bundy once caustically queried Thomson, asking "what standard of decency could have caused a man to do what you have done?"[14]

Thomson was unnerved by what he considered to be an unwarranted vilification by Bundy and, perhaps as catharsis, embarked upon an academic study of the phenomenon. Analyzing why selected public officials opposed to the war did not resign in protest during escalation and why they kept quiet when they finally did leave, Thomson found five interrelated reasons, including (1) a sense of loyalty and the tendency to feel that they owed their president continued allegiance after returning to private life; (2) a very real "fear of retribution" and an anxiety that the Internal Revenue Service, FBI, or Justice Department might be turned against them; (3) a concern about a "barred return," more fully described as the probability that once a bureaucrat goes public with his opposition to an announced policy he is no longer suitable for membership in the "Club" (defined as the government or corporate establishment); (4) a genuine anxiety over security regulations, including the reticence the dissenter feels about disclosing classified information; and (5) the desire for continued access and influence, described as the conviction dissenters feel that, though they might disagree on a single issue (large or small), they must maintain their influence within the government to advance other policies more central to their responsibilities and interests. Dubbing the aggregate of these elements the "national security ethic," Thomson (incorrectly) asserts that Ball was among a group of dissenter-resigners—including Michael Forrestal, John Gardner, Townsend Hoopes, Chester Cooper, and, ultimately, Robert McNamara—whose visceral, dovish views were suppressed by the national security ethic as they "silently slipped back" into the private sector or were given another high profile government job in return for their continued loyalty and silence.[15]

In their provocatively entitled 1975 study, *Resignation in Protest: Political and Ethical Choices Between Loyalty to Team and Loyalty to Conscience in American Public Life*, Edward Weisband and Thomas M. Franck both implicitly and explicitly criticize Ball for identifying with the Johnson administration and the policy of escalation as long as he did and for leaving "with neither a feud nor a fuss." Disappointed in the statecraft exhibited by many during the Vietnam era, Weisband and Franck find that Ball's "ethical autonomy" gave way to his "concern about the loss of a painstakingly built and carefully projected image of eligibility for high office." Hypercritical of the tendency among "sycophantic ministers" in a presidential system to display unwarranted loyalty, the authors contend that Ball fell prey to the ethical traps of the American presidential system. The unwillingness of top executive branch appointees to openly disagree with their president, they forcefully argue, is abetted by an "atomistic bureaucratic concept of areas of responsibility." During the last year of the administration, for example, even though Health, Education, and Welfare Secretary Wilbur Cohen was utterly disposed against the war in Vietnam—expenditures for which were seriously undermining his domestic programs—he kept quiet, claiming that the policy was outside his area of responsibility and therefore none of his business. Having taken this particular issue up with Ball during an interview they conducted for their book, Weisband and Franck note the response he shot back as evidence of a patently "atomized" bureaucrat: "Why should I have resigned in protest over Vietnam," Ball asked? "My main responsibility and my principal interest was Western Europe."[16]

The two political scientists become even less generous by declaring that the "unwarranted loyalty" Ball displayed toward Johnson as well as his style of resignation epitomize a pernicious "legal ethic" in public service. Trained as an attorney, Ball was imbued with what the authors deleteriously refer to as the "anti-disclosure ethic." No matter how much he might personally disapprove of his client's behavior, as a lawyer Ball felt duty-bound to protect his client's interests. The inviolable rule of "professional confidence" is implicit in such relationships. Weisband and Franck deplore these "old habits" and believe that the antidisclosure ethic "is both fallacious and dangerous in a democracy."[17] The authors repeatedly assert that the British parliamentary system, in which dissenting ministers retain their political base in the House of Commons, is a superior institution—given as it is to frequent and audible dissent, accented by principled resignations. In the absence of checks imposed upon the chief executive in a presidential system, the antidisclosure ethic effectively nullifies one of the few meaningful checks on presidential power.

Claiming that "a cabinet of 'yea-sayers' is a profound danger in an era of wide presidential discretion," Weisband and Franck ask whether Ball might not have been more effective in checking Johnson's decision to escalate the war by resigning in protest and immediately going public with his cogent memorandums warning of the snares of escalation. They theorize that "the American executive style," characterized by "acquiescent public service followed by mute departures from government," has established a dangerous precedent. Only infrequently, the authors charge, is presidential discretion checked by meaningful opposition—either from within or outside the executive branch. When bureaucrats do quit on principle, they "generally avoid all contact with the members of Congress, voter groups, students, and others who publicly espouse the very cause that induced their resignations."[18] Such was the case with Ball.

In the distillation of their alarming and compelling conclusions at the close of the book, Weisband and Franck assert that a tradition of quiet resignation has polarized American society, particularly in times of crisis, by placing the burden of opposition on "outsiders." As was certainly witnessed between 1967 and 1973, political tension is exacerbated when the Establishment is challenged by those who inherently lack legitimacy. Their study found that during the Vietnam War many Americans felt their government was "hopelessly corrupting" when no single senior member of the Johnson administration (Ball and McNamara are the authors' principal whipping boys) came forth to assert publicly the views they were advancing inside the government. Opposition was left to "outsiders" with neither the expertise, prestige, or access to intelligence to provide plausible alternatives.[19] Arguably, because Ball had been in the business of opposition to the war for so long but refused to speak out, the antiwar movement was deprived of its most experienced, able, and articulate advocate.

Somewhat sanctimoniously, the authors contend that "for the sake of the republic" and "for the cause of Vietnam disengagement," Ball should have taken a leading role in the antiwar movement. They claim that the dissenting under secretary's open break with the policy of escalation "would have restored the faith of the young in the system," added desperately needed credibility to the antiwar movement, and stimulated more enlightened debate about a profound and highly complex foreign policy crisis. Americans, who in the turbulent 1960s would gladly have rallied behind leaders experienced in foreign and defense policy, found that none of that group was willing to lead. To be sure, Weisband and Franck admit that the personal "costs" to Ball "would have been enormous" and perhaps would have even led to his ostracism by the professional and social circles he inhabited. "We would be less than candid," the authors inveigh against the likes of Ball, "if we did not admit to a vast admiration for the few, like William Jennings Bryan, who spent themselves heedlessly for the public weal and for their principles, without concern for the costs to their careers."[20]

Ball himself is discernibly irritated, indeed insulted, by such interpretations of his methods. "The gentleman," James Thomson once remarked, "is still uneasy about the role that he played in that time, and I think he probably should be."[21] Although he remains defensive, Ball continues to believe that his was the morally and politically correct course. His largest and most frequently expressed complaint is that his loyalty to Johnson and quiet departure have inauspiciously become the phenomena against which his substantive strategic and diplomatic contributions during the Vietnam deliberations have come to be measured. Ball's style of resignation is the subject most frequently turned to by those critiquing his role in the government during the 1960s. Like it or not, he has become a symbol of the sometimes maligned principle of gentlemanly dissent. As former secretary of state Cyrus Vance (who indignantly resigned from the Carter administration as a protest against the ill-fated hostage rescue mission) simply stated, "George will have to live with his decision." Though as a general proposition Vance considers Ball among "the most talented public servants [he has] ever encountered" and "a truly extraordinary man," he harbors trenchant criticism of his failure to more boldly declare his opposition to the war. "I think the real question that George must ask himself is if he had resigned earlier would he have had more impact?" Admitting that "one can debate that old argument both ways" and that "to a point" the strategy of fighting political battles from an interior position holds obvious merits, Vance also believes that "there comes a point when you know you've done as much as you can, and the only way you're going to have more impact is to say, 'I'm going to resign and I am going to state why I resigned.'" Did Ball stay too long? "That," Vance has stated, "is the question George must ask himself." The former secretary of state concedes that Ball made a "full try" on the inside, but he also recognized, from his vantage point in the Defense Department during the mid-1960s and later in his role supporting Harriman at the luckless Paris peace talks in 1968, that "it became fairly evident after a period of time that it [escalation] really wasn't going to change, and I think that's the point at which George must ask himself."[22] The query to which Vance refers is nothing short of whether Ball could have made a significant contribution to the national interest by openly confronting the administration.

Eager to defend his behavior, Ball has missed few opportunities over the years to address the subject of protest resignations. He has repeatedly maintained that storming out of the administration in protest over Vietnam would have been foolish for the simple reason that Southeast Asia was only marginal to his comprehensive responsibilities as under secretary of state. When they interviewed him for their book, Ball was quick to remind Weisband and Franck that just "five percent" of his working time was spent litigating the Vietnam issue.[23] Continuing to believe that in resigning in protest over Vietnam he would have sacrificed his considerable influence on "more important concerns," Ball says that he never seriously considered quitting as a principled act. "By and large," Ball impatiently declared to another interviewer in the wake of the *Pentagon Papers* disclosures, "I was in total sympathy with almost every other aspect of policy, and Vietnam to me was not the central policy of the United States—it was an aberration."

Somewhat disingenuously, Ball maintains that, for him, "Vietnam was always a side-issue," and he has stated that "the more time that Rusk spent on Vietnam—and Vietnam increasingly absorbed his energies—the greater [his] responsibility was for problems in other parts of the world."[24] In one of its more mundane manifestations, the Vietnam crisis became, at least in Ball's analysis, a practical bureaucratic question about the division of labor between the top two policy officers in the State Department. As the secretary became progressively more involved in the political and tactical problems related to the war in Southeast Asia, the under secretary felt compelled to mind the store in strategic areas not directly related to Vietnam and in the administration of the department. The obvious weakness of that argument is that well before Ball so quietly resigned, Vietnam had become the preeminent issue related to the conduct of America's total foreign policy and one for which the consequences were conspicuous in virtually every other area of the world.

In analyzing Ball's resignation, it must also be noted that he sincerely felt "an old-fashioned aversion to undercutting [his] colleagues"[25] and would not add to their burdens with a self-aggrandizing public row with LBJ or Rusk. Ball's dissenting arguments were entertained precisely because the president had confidence that he "would never betray or embarrass" the administration,[26] and he had long ago accepted those implicit preconditions. In the summer of 1966, he admitted to Reston that, because of the recent secondary disclosures about his ostensibly secret dissent, he was "on a very warm wicket" with Rusk, McNamara, and the president.[27] Perhaps wrongly, the under secretary elevated loyalty above the substantive strategic principles of his dissent. Expressing "profound respect" and "very real affection" for his colleagues, Ball felt he could not further imperil confidences—or friendships. Proud of his "close and friendly relationship" with Johnson and his "extraordinarily close" association with Secretary Rusk, Ball broke from the administration as delicately as he dissented within it.[28]

A "most important consideration" to Ball was that he felt he "could always have his day in court," and he contented himself with arguing from an interior position. The president listened. "Were I to leave," he wrote, "[Johnson] would not hear the same views from anyone else."[29] A petulant resignation and public protest would have destroyed his carefully cultivated credibility on Vietnam as well as his considerable influence on what he felt were more salient issues. "To raise Hell merely for the psychic glow and the adulation of the already persuaded," Ball once stated, "[would be] mere self-indulgence and not worthy of a serious man."[30] He would not preach to the choir. He also doubted that a protest resignation would be effective, believing that it would have been at most "a one day wonder."[31] As he analyzed his options, Ball recognized the stark probability that the "official leakers" in the White House would intimate that he was a sorehead, could not play team ball, and was about to be fired anyway. The White House propaganda mill would quickly reduce his principled resignation to an exercise in "sour grapes."[32]

Professional aspiration, crass or otherwise, must also be considered as a factor in Ball's manner of dissent and resignation. Clearly, ego and ambition, prominently exhibited by most successful leaders and administrators, are among the more conspicuous aspects of his character. Even into the 1980s, he not so quietly harbored the desire to become secretary of state and considered himself—and others certainly did as well—worthy of mention on any Democratic presidential nominee's "short list" of Establishment luminaries to be seriously considered for the position. Further, as noted above, he had contemplated the possibility that he might someday preside over the United States's extrication from Vietnam. Wanting to preserve his career options and availability for high appointive office, Ball was simply loath to cross a Democratic president. If Johnson—or his successor—decided to change course in midstream, Ball fancied himself to be the horse that would pull the country out of the Vietnam bog. As he foresaw the future from the perspective of 1966, a resignation in protest would have seriously jeopardized his desire to play a major role at a propitious moment in the future.

In reflecting upon his options as a hired bureaucrat who was grievously disenchanted with the continued escalation of a war he felt would not be won, Ball momentarily addressed the question of where to turn if he did resign in protest. His options were limited. The under secretary of state passionately disdained and would in no way identify with the antiwar movement. He was repelled by what he considered to be the hysteria, crudity, anti-intellectualism, and the "Yahoo-outrage"[33] of the street protests, and he was offended by what he called the "obscene gibbering and caterwauling of moronic youths." He once flatly declared that he "did not want to be a hero of the yippies."[34] Although, as a lawyer with decidedly liberal persuasions, he revered "anyone's constitutional right to make an ass out of himself," he doubted that the protesters could stop the war "by carrying placards or burning draft cards."[35]

Affirming Ball's decision to resign quietly was his intellectual judgment that a surfeit of protest resignations is simply not desirable. As a former subcabinet officer of the executive branch, Ball prides himself on not becoming a "kiss-and-tell" bureaucratic of the type made popular by the advent of Reaganism. His loyalty was very much appreciated. In April 1977 Dean Rusk sent him a copy of the Weisband and Franck volume, along with a review he had just completed for the *American Journal of International Law*. Acknowledging receipt of the materials, Ball thanked Rusk for his "stalwart defense" of his Vietnam position and offered a revealing critique of his own behavior. "Anyone who has broad responsibilities such as you and I occupied," he counseled Rusk, "is compelled by the nature of his responsibilities to develop views on a wide spectrum of world issues." Ball concurred with his former boss that Weisband and Franck had failed to recognize that if "on 90 percent of the issues one might agree with [their] president, while having reservations or disagreements on the remaining 10 percent," the compulsion to noisily resign is significantly diminished. Ball criticized Weisband and Franck by stating that "since total agreement on every issue is likely to reflect little more than an indecisive character," dissent is a natural and organic element in the governing process. Ball dismissed as "nonsense" the suggestion that a policy officer is compelled to publicly vent each disagreement he might have with his colleagues and chastised the authors for ignoring "one of the central conditions that should precede a decision to resign." As Ball related to Rusk, if bureaucrats followed the Weisband and Franck prescription "American government would destroy its own effectiveness." In concluding his most private thoughts to Rusk, Ball remarked, "Someday I hope someone will write something sensible on this issue."[36]

The former diplomat is not alone in his defense, and Ball's letter file during the period of his resignation is rife with supporting and congratulatory correspondence. Representative is Democratic party stalwart Wilson Wyatt's comment: "Your exceptional performance as Under Secretary of State is equalled only by the splendor of your exit."[37] But perhaps the most significant affirmation of Ball's behavior was written by Rusk in his review of the Weisband and Franck volume. After expressing serious reservations about the thesis of the book, Rusk inverted the author's prescriptions by declaring that "George Ball stood alone in winning the respect and admiration of his presidents and secretary of state by the vigor and clarity of his dissenting views in two administrations. When a person leaves public office, he has the rights and privileges of a private citizen. It is his privilege, not his duty, to go public, no matter what the professors may say."[38]

In the fall of 1967, *Atlantic Monthly* editor Robert Manning (formerly assistant secretary for political affairs and privy to the dissent) invited Ball to set a portion of his views to print. In what was to become a curiously understated critique of American intervention in Vietnam, Ball began work on his first book. As he would later in his fulminations against the Nixon-Kissinger management of the war, Ball did not then center his discussion on individuals or in any way engage in ad hominem attacks on his former colleagues. As he would later in describing what he considered to be the darker crevasses of Nixon's character, Ball did not then factor personalities into his analysis of what he obviously considered egregious errors of political and strategic analysis during the Johnson administration. Even from the vantage point of private life, Ball continued to express sympathy for the predicament in which the Johnson war cabinet found itself and, oddly enough, did not even advance the arguments he had so eloquently developed inside the government at an earlier period.

Indeed, weighed against his memorandums written between 1964 and 1966, Ball's prescriptions for policy in 1967–68 seem banal and sterile. In a blueprint for American foreign policy entitled *The Discipline of Power: Essentials of a Modern World Structure*, which was, in the main, written in the later half of 1967 and completed before the Tet offensive of 1968, Ball credited Johnson with "a searching and prayerful study of all alternatives." He generously concluded that escalation was "the exercise of a judgment that he

[Johnson] was entitled, and indeed, obligated to make." Calling Vietnam "a hard case," Ball conceded that the political and military situation in Southeast Asia was "complex and confused." To those who railed against the brutality of the conflict, Ball dispassionately declared that "wars are, by definition, inhumane." With direct reference to the antiwar movement, what he called the "great body of the disenchanted," Ball declared that the American people "will not eliminate the inhumanity with incantation."[39]

As deeper Vietnam involvement throughout 1966 and 1967 had proportionally engaged American prestige, Ball had become more cautious about recommending a precipitous withdrawal. In a curious twist in his analysis, his position on the war in 1968—at least those views he put in print—in large measure refuted his views of the earlier period between May 1964 and July 1965. Against his assertion of 1965 that the United States should accept Vietcong power sharing in the South, he stated in 1968 that it should not, predicting that "the disciplined Communist element would quickly dominate the politically naive representatives of the soggy regime in Saigon." Against his 1965 argument that the United States was not obligated to defend South Vietnam pursuant to the South East Asia Treaty because the threat against her was not clearly "outside aggression," he is noticed in 1968 arguing against recognition of the Vietcong, stating that a policy so conceived would compromise the legal basis for the American intervention by admitting a de facto "internal revolt." Once willing to support virtually any expedient for American withdrawal, in 1968 Ball casually dismissed the entire peace process; indeed, he actually undermined United Nations peace initiatives by reminding his readers that because neither Red China nor North Vietnam were members, Hanoi was justified in rejecting any U.N. claim to legitimacy as an arbiter. A U.N. role, he stated, "would have little practical meaning." Ball did hitch his 1968 wagon to one old theme. Flatly stating that bombing had "seriously impaired the moral authority of the United States," he reiterated his arguments of 1964 and 1965 against aerial attacks. He openly concluded in 1968 that in bombing North Vietnam for three years, the United States had unwisely risked Chinese intervention and "frustrated any Soviet attempt toward peace-making," while having "little effect on the war in the South."[40]

With an air of resignation, and patently justified in the hope that he might succeed Dean Rusk as secretary of state, Ball carefully measured his criticism of the administration. "It comes as a shock to anyone who looks at the problem," he wrote in late 1967, "to discover how few options remain." Noting that political and military conditions on the ground in Vietnam "are not that bad" (again, writing immediately prior to the Tet offensive), he observed that "the key to a solution lies in patience and flexibility" and made the most outlandish remark that he had "nothing better to offer." In his private memorandums of 1964 and 1965 Ball had been the proponent of immediate and unqualified extrication. Quite curiously, his public declarations in 1967 and 1968 held that the United States had "no serious option but to continue the course [it is] presently pursuing" and counseled that, at this juncture, it was "far safer and sounder than would be the resort to either withdrawal or major escalation."[41]

Even from the relative serenity and immunities of retirement, Ball's loyalties to Johnson and Rusk remained rigidly intact while they were still in office. In point of fact, Ball maintained a very close association with the Johnson administration even after his departure from the State Department. In accepting his resignation in September 1966, Johnson told him that he "would like to think that [he] would be able to call upon him from time to time in the days ahead,"[42] and in the ensuing months and years he did so with great regularity. In one of his prototypical displays of personal manipulation, and mindful of the possibility that the once loyal dissenter's fidelity might wane, the president periodically summoned Ball to the White House. Now fifty-seven years old, well traveled, virtually without peer in his comprehension of complex economic and political matters relating to Europe, the retired under secretary was invaluable as a part-time presidential counselor.

But there is also compelling evidence to suggest that Johnson solicited Ball's advice and maintained a relationship out of a concern that he might, in time, develop an independent identity as a critic of the war outside the government. At a time in 1966–67 when reports from the battlefields and the chronically plagued pacification programs were anything but encouraging, and as it became obvious that the Great Society was imperiled by the unforeseen political and material costs of the war, Johnson shuddered at the thought of Ball joining the camp of his political enemies. Indeed, for over a year before Ball left, the president had agonized over the problem of appointees who might resign and turn against the administration. Immediately after the war was Americanized in July 1965, Johnson directed Abe Fortas, Clark Clifford, and McGeorge Bundy to concert a policy about how to "manage" the "problem" of "those who leave us" and attack the administration's policy in Vietnam. In an effort "to undercut the damage that any such individual might do," the committee of three assembled their collective wisdom in a memorandum dated August 12, 1965. At the next press conference, they advised, the president should issue a "standing rebuke" for any who might violate the "standards" often enunciated by the administration. On this score, Lyndon

Johnson was unambiguous: "I don't believe," he had once asserted, "that the special responsibility of a government official ends when he leaves office." Johnson emphasized that those who leave government "should exercise the utmost restraint" in reporting the inner workings of government so as to preserve "candid, cordial, and informal relationships among officials" so essential to effective government. Those working in government, he concluded, "are entitled to believe that their associates are loyal, understanding, and reliable."[43]

A brief digression into Ball's relationship with the Johnson administration after his resignation demonstrates that he faithfully upheld Johnson's explicit standard of confidentiality. Because of the disagreeable views he held on the war, and also because of the "liberal" company he kept, Ball knew that he would be subject to inordinately close scrutiny by an increasingly distrustful chief executive. As a general proposition, Johnson was concerned about dissenters; specifically, he was concerned about Ball and would continually tease him with sarcasm about his close personal relationship with the dovish Senator J. William Fulbright and liberal columnists Walter Lippmann and James Reston.

Subtle indications that the president was particularly sensitive to media attention given the nay-saying under secretary immediately after he left the government are scattered throughout Ball's White House personnel file. Presidential aides carefully monitored his television appearances for months after his departure. Johnson's press secretary, George Christian, dutifully managed responses to inquiries about Ball with the intent of minimizing the differences Ball had with the administration over Vietnam. In the last year of Johnson's presidency, during which storms of popular protest and embarrassing leaks induced Johnson to further constrict the number of assistants privy to top-level Vietnam discussions, word reached the White House that columnist Joseph Kraft was writing a feature story on Ball for the *New York Times Magazine*. Kraft wanted to see the president for a "backgrounder" interview. Christian told Johnson that he would not "ordinarily" recommend an appointment on such a matter but added that "on this specialized subject," he believed "it would be wise for the President to meet with him [Kraft]." In the wake of the politically disastrous Tet offensive of 1968, LBJ was plainly averse to letting an account of the administration's most celebrated dove be published without his side of the issue fully represented.[44]

Ball's "domestication" was to be a continuous process. Toward realizing the dual and complementary objectives of tapping Ball as a reservoir of wise counsel *and* maintaining a close "political" relationship with him, Johnson periodically sought the former diplomat's advice on trade and economic matters. In his new capacities as a private citizen and international banker, Ball briefed the president on his investment mission to Korea, helped the administration negotiate a wheat transaction with India,[45] was periodically asked for comprehensive memorandums on a great range of political and strategic issues,[46] and was even commissioned to chair the ex-comm-like crisis committee during the *Pueblo* incident of January 1968.[47] In a penultimate gesture of confidence and unflagging trust, Johnson also included Ball in two top-level Vietnam gatherings of the "Wise Men"[48]—ostensibly to perform his familiar role as the champion of moderation. Although "Citizen Ball" developed no new themes during the two Wise Men sessions in which he participated, he was clearly less decorous than "Under Secretary Ball" had been in advancing his dovish views. "Even after my resignation," he has written, "I could not free myself from the oppressive burden of the war." Harkening to a Johnson summons on November 1, 1967, he dutifully attended a meeting of the Wise Men or, as he likes to employ the appellation, "the usual suspects." Predictably, the record of this meeting shows that he made his "usual plea for extrication to the usual deaf ears." But on this day the character of his dissent dramatically changed. Formerly a model of circumspection while advancing his views, on this date for the first time he burst into a short but impassioned tirade. As he was leaving the cabinet room after hours of what he thought was a futile reiteration of a tired rationale for American intervention in Vietnam's civil war, Ball exhibited a profound emotional frustration stemming from three years of waging a failed effort to convince his colleagues of the folly of their war. His sense of futility was aggravated by the fact that the tragedy was, as they spoke, being escalated and compounded in Southeast Asia. He erupted. "I've been watching across the table," he barked to Wise Men Dean Acheson and John J. McCloy. "You're like a flock of old buzzards sitting on a fence, sending the young men off to be killed. You ought to be ashamed of yourselves." Ball was himself surprised and embarrassed by the intensity of his outburst.[49] Though it added unexpected drama and color to an otherwise banal seminar on what he considered to be the sterile doctrine of containment, Ball's impolitic effusion apparently did no permanent damage to his good relationships with the senior men.

When Ball left the State Department in September 1966 he endeavored, albeit unsuccessfully, to forget about the war. There were private matters that needed tending. The former diplomat made no attempt to conceal his grief about the fact that his private fortunes, by his standards as a six-figure Washington attorney at any rate, were lagging miserably during his years in the State

Department. Simply put, Ball had grown accustomed to the good life, and his family finances were in disrepair after six years at the annual salary of $22,000. Again a private citizen, Ball profited handsomely from his experience in government. A consummate *pantoufle*,[50] he already had held four different government jobs. Ball's professional career is a classic demonstration in how methodically federal appointees have been able to move back and forth between high-profile government positions and lucrative private-sector employment. As under secretary for economic affairs, he also held the titles of alternate governor of the International Monetary Fund, director of the International Bank for Reconstruction, and director of the American Development Bank. Ball was a recognized expert on international economic affairs. Upon retirement he accepted an offer to become the director of Lehman International, the newly formed division of Lehman Brothers Investment Bank, and spent most of 1967 traveling throughout Europe and the Far East in connection with his banking activities. Though an admiring journalist once quipped that Ball "wouldn't know a transaction if it bit him," his professional and personal intimacy with foreign industrialists and finance capitalists throughout the world was certainly a welcomed commodity at Lehman Brothers.[51]

The period from November 1967 to February 1968 was an acute transitional phase in the Vietnam War. For the first time, Johnson's top military and civilian commanders recognized and acknowledged that the war was stalemated. Making matters worse was the fact that Secretary of Defense McNamara and the Joint Chiefs of Staff conducted an open and running disagreement about how to turn the impasse into a victory. McNamara, near an emotional breaking point, began to publicly express his private conviction that it could not be done. Having lost, by his own admission, all credibility with the public and without a viable plan for winning the war, McNamara was gratuitously eased out of the administration to become president of the World Bank. Clark Clifford, a longtime Johnson confidant and an unofficial adviser who had been deeply impressed with Ball's dissenting arguments, became secretary of defense in February 1968. Within one month after he took over the Pentagon, Clifford reluctantly concluded that the war could not be won and that the United States should get out. The administration's Vietnam policy—indeed the administration itself—was rapidly unraveling.

In this hyperemotional political atmosphere, Ball again rallied to the service of a besieged president. Yet another presidential summons interrupted his apprenticeship in investment banking. On April 24, 1968, Johnson telephoned Ball to ask him—indeed compel him—to serve out the remainder of the year for retiring United Nations ambassador Arthur Goldberg. After determined but

Ball in 1968, the year in which he took his experience and expertise into private enterprise after retirement from his last government post. (Photograph courtesy of George W. Ball)

unavailing efforts to resist, Ball was pressured—in point of fact forced—into accepting. Without an appreciation of what columnist James Reston has labeled the "Johnson Style," it would appear that Ball was an odd choice for the appointment. It is ironic that, as a product of his close association with Adlai Stevenson, Ball prided himself on being "the only American ambassador to the United Nations who knew, in advance, the sterility of the job." Many of his closest associates have noted that he was barely able to conceal his contempt for the institution, and he once called the U.N. ambassadorship "the last post I wanted." Ball had little patience for what he referred to as the "scholastic nitpicking" and "ritualistic exercises" which the American permanent representative must endure.[52] After a somewhat turbulent confirmation hearing— during which South Carolina senator Strom Thurmond harangued him for his anti-Nixon hyperbole in the election campaign of 1960 and his dubious defense of State Department employees who had illegally furnished classified documents to a congressional committee—Ball was confirmed by the full Senate with two dissenting votes.[53] Though he played an instrumental role in condemning the behavior of the Soviet Union in crushing the short-lived "Prague Spring" in 1968, he was, for the most part, unfulfilled by the routinized procedures at New York. Even in what was a quite brief tenure (June to September 1968), Ball's patience withered away, and he admits to spending a "good deal of [his] time sharing frivolous verse" with the British representative, Lord Caradon.[54] Once again, Ball disavowed his political instinct not to identify with a wounded administration and a failed policy in Vietnam and faithfully served Lyndon Baines Johnson. With aspirations for high office in the future, Ball took a post he did not want, at a most unpropitious moment, to demonstrate the highest order of loyalty to his party and his president.

In the spring of 1968, the North Vietnamese Tet offensive profoundly altered the course of the war—and claimed its most celebrated victim. On March 31, LBJ stunned a nation already quaking from three years of intense military engagement in Southeast Asia by announcing that he would not seek reelection. With his armies still in the field, the commander-in-chief admitted that he was politically defeated at home. As a violent spring gave way to a summer of heated presidential politics, Ball watched from the sidelines as American objectives in Vietnam became ever more elusive and as the war became the focal point of the 1968 elections. Peace plans, secret strategies, and new negotiating formulas were as abundant as candidates. From a nomination process traumatized by the assassination of Robert Kennedy and violence in the streets outside the Democratic convention, Richard Nixon and Hubert Humphrey emerged as the Republican and Democratic party standard-bearers.

In the dark mood arising out of a national political crisis (and amid unsubstantiated allegations of influence peddling while at the U.N.),[55] Ball's sense of futility in New York conjoined with his sense of urgency about presidential politics and prompted his departure from a government post for the fifth and final time. Declaring that he left the U.N. to assist his "poor friend Humphrey"—who was then 17 percentage points behind Nixon in the most favorable national poll—and to repair his "sagging fortunes," Ball informed the president of his irreversible decision to quit at the end of September.[56] Johnson immediately accepted Ambassador Ball's resignation "as an act of conscience."[57] Realistic about Humphrey's chances of winning the presidency and revolted by presidential campaigning in what he called "the Age of Slobbism," Ball joined the vice-president's team.

Ball wore two hats in the presidential campaign of 1968. Because he believed that it was imperative for Humphrey to quickly establish an independent position on the war, his first, and decidedly delicate, task was to conceive a plan for a negotiated settlement—one which was "sufficiently distinguishable from Johnson's to satisfy the more reasonable anti-war factions, without, at the same time, driving the president into outright opposition." Ball and Humphrey announced that they would abandon Johnson's insistence that North Vietnam suspend troop movement as a precondition for a stand down on the bombing. Then, acting unilaterally and somewhat brazenly, Ball dispatched his Lehman Brothers associate Harry Fitzgibbons to Paris in order to clear a proposed statement with peace negotiators Averell Harriman and Cyrus Vance. With a go-ahead from Harriman, Humphrey announced that, if elected, he would immediately halt the bombing, without precondition, "as an acceptable risk for peace." Next came the hard part. Ball called the president to read him a draft of the statement. "George," Johnson replied, "I know you'll be able to persuade them [the press] that this doesn't mark any change from the line we've all been following." Ball hesitantly demurred, "I'm sorry Mr. President, but that's not quite the name of the game." The "domesticated dissenter" had finally publicly declared his opposition to Lyndon Johnson's conduct of the war.[58] Ball had broken with the administration.

Liberated from the political circumspection and obscuring vanities of high office, Ball instantaneously transformed himself into a political propagandist. By his own admission, his second—and decidedly indelicate—task was to "attack Nixon so outrageously as to force people to think." Believing that Nixon's defeat was "crucial to the interests of our nation and the Free World," Ball indulged himself in his own erudite brand of invective in a series of articles, interviews, and speeches throughout the fall of 1968 as he savaged

"Tricky Dick" Nixon and the "Fourth Rate Political Hack" Spiro Agnew. Citing Nixon's lack of "settled principles" and his "preposterous choice for a running mate," Ball wielded a razor-sharp political hatchet for the floundering Humphrey campaign. He caustically characterized Nixon as "slick and evasive" and called attention to the "extraordinary differences between Agnew's qualifications and those of other modern candidates for vice president." Ball charged that Nixon selected Agnew "purely for reasons of political expediency" and stated that "their responsibility displayed by this selection is deeply disturbing." Indeed, he continued, it was "the most eccentric political appointment since the Roman Emperor Caligula named his horse as consul."[39]

So brutal were Ball's attacks that shortly before the November election he was roundly chastised by the private, nonpartisan Fair Campaign Practices Committee and charged with wanton "vilification and defamation of the names and character of former Vice President Nixon and Governor Spiro Agnew." The committee alleged that Ball had made "dishonest and unethical statements" which tended to "prevent the full and free expression of the will of the voters." Responding in writing to the committee's allegations, Ball was anything but contrite. He drafted a fifteen-page statement providing support of his original characterizations—and even added blistering new attacks. Citing harsh characterizations of Nixon in the editorial columns of Lippmann, Reston, and Henry Brandon, Ball held that his initial statements, when compared to those of other respected commentators, "were marked by restraint and gentility." With his broad political experience in the Stevenson campaigns of 1952 and 1954 and varied political and diplomatic service under Kennedy and Johnson, Ball maintained that he had "a solid basis for judging the man [Nixon] and his attributes of mind and character." While believing the complaints filed against him should be "summarily dismissed as quite frivolous," Ball dauntlessly reported that he would be delighted to present additional testimony in open hearing. The committee took no further action.[60]

With the advent of the Nixon administration in January 1969, Ball's pronouncements on the war in Southeast Asia immediately became personal and acrimonious. Having focused his remarks before the election on Nixon's character, after the inauguration the former under secretary of state frontally attacked the substance of the new president's Vietnam policy as it soon became perfectly clear that Nixon had far fewer inhibitions than Johnson did about commissioning violence. When it was evident that Nixon's campaign pledge to bring the troops home would only be accomplished by precipitously raising the level of violence in Indochina far beyond what had been contemplated by the Johnson administration, Ball went on the offensive.

Believing that "a fourth-rate power like North Vietnam must have a break-ing point," Nixon and his principal foreign policy architect, National Security Adviser Henry Kissinger, set out to find it. Operating on what Defense Depart-ment analyst Daniel Ellsberg designated as "the Madman theory," Nixon purposefully sought to insure that Hanoi regarded him as an irrational anti-Communist who might, in frustration, resort to any means in pursuit of victory in Vietnam. Toward giving credence to the macabre identity he sought, in March 1969 Nixon threatened to unleash what he referred to in carefully staged leaks to the press as "savage, punishing blows" against North Viet-nam.[61] Although it is clear from McGeorge Bundy's recent investigation that Nixon has retrospectively exaggerated his role as a nuclear-threat maker, he let it be known that he was at least considering the use of tactical atomic weapons as part of his "psy-war" strategy for Vietnam. In contrast, for example, to Johnson's immediate order to squash all talk about use of nuclear weapons at Khe Sahn in 1968, Nixon wanted "the other side" to know that he was contemplating the use of tactical nuclear devices as part of his diplomatic brinkmanship.[62] While American troops were being ordered home, the war was sharply escalating geographically, psychologically, and in terms of ord-nance expended by American aircraft.

The Nixon administration hit the ground running in Vietnam. Vowing not to repeat the mistakes of the past—but candidly admitting they would make their own—Nixon and Kissinger privately boasted that they could end the war within six months.[63] Throughout the spring and summer of 1969 the adminis-tration's much touted "phased troop withdrawal" and "Vietnamization" pro-gram, which cynically proposed to turn the fighting over to the army of the Republic of Vietnam, evolved within the context of the larger "Nixon Doc-trine" formally enunciated in Guam on July 25. In time, the discordant ele-ments of the doctrine came to be understood as a broad reduction of U.S. military commitments and personnel deployed around the world and the incre-mental transference of security obligations to native forces. Nixon and Kis-singer, both strategic Realists, sought to bring American interests in line with a new awareness of the limitations of American influence and pursue what they hoped would be a modus vivendi with the great Communist powers. To advance the grand strategic agenda, Nixon sought to scale down America's tactical commitment in Indochina.

In the first year of the administration, Kissinger initiated a triangular and suspiciously secret diplomatic initiative in the hope of demonstrating to the Soviets and the Chinese that they had more to gain from the United States by stopping the war than by prolonging it. Nixon called for increased "protective reaction air strikes" throughout North and South Vietnam and, as part of a new doctrine of "no-sanctuary," ordered bloody raids into Cambodia and Laos to seek out NVA and Vietcong staging bases. The Phoenix Program (which has come to be understood by many as a euphemism for a bloody campaign of Vietcong assassination) was launched, and the transformation of South Vietnam into a military state through the unprecedented transfer of billions of dollars worth of arms was begun. In addition to the stick, Nixon brandished a diplomatic carrot in May by proposing the "simultaneous withdrawal" of American and North Vietnamese forces from South Vietnam.

To his great disillusionment, Nixon's grand strategy improved neither the military situation on the ground in Vietnam nor the political and public relations aspects of the war at home. The administration was barraged with domestic crises, all seemingly related to Vietnam. A massive antiwar demonstration erupted in Washington on October 15. The revelation of the My Lai massacre hit front pages on November 16. Tragedy struck at Kent State University in May 1970 as four student demonstrators were gunned down by Ohio National Guard troops. The forecast of peace within six months appeared to be a chimera. Throughout 1970 and 1971 Nixon fared only slightly better than Johnson had in pacifying the Vietnamese countryside, wearing down a determined Vietnamese enemy, or selling the war to the American people. Set against the growing sentiments of despair and frustration in both the United States and South Vietnam, the qualitative difference between the Nixon and Johnson "resolve" to achieve victory at any cost became brutally apparent. Unable to improve the political stability of the Saigon regime or subdue a tenacious enemy on the battlefield, Nixon indignantly sought to change the context of the negotiations. On May 8, 1972, he did what Johnson dared not do and ordered the mining of Haiphong Harbor. Throughout the year the war continued to spill over neutral borders that Johnson had been reluctant to cross. By the end of 1972, during the Christmas season that Johnson had reserved for symbolic bombing pauses, Nixon sent B-52s into the skies above North Vietnam to loose 40,000 tons of explosives on the industrial and residential districts of Hanoi and Haiphong. As Nixon continued to order home American forces, he bolstered the South Vietnamese with aid, credit, unprecedented military assistance, and "absolute assurances" of continued support, all at a time when opinion polls showed that 58 percent of the American people thought his conduct of the war immoral.[64]

For four years, as Ball watched from the sidelines, Nixon struggled in vain to achieve an elusive "peace with honor" and, as a decidedly subordinate objective, to salvage the nation of his languishing South Vietnamese ally,

President Nguyen Van Thieu. The tragic chronicle of the Johnson administration in Vietnam seemed to be repeating itself. Restrained by his loyalty to LBJ and Rusk, Ball had expressed his views on Vietnam with studied reticence through the end of their terms. When Nixon became president however, it was as if a dam inside him burst. He wasted no time in attacking the Nixon-Kissinger "peace strategy" as it came into view in the first months of 1969. By November he was on the lecture circuit. First, at the University of New Mexico, Ball declared there is no "sacred redoubt called the Alamo" in Vietnam and flatly called for immediate American withdrawal. The United States had already lived up to Eisenhower's original promise, he asserted, and it was time to leave the country. Ball blasted Nixon's policy of phased withdrawal, stating that it "effectively ruled out any serious hope for a negotiated solution at Paris"—since it was "giving away" outright that which the North Vietnamese cared about most—while it mindlessly adhered to what he had long considered the failed doctrine of air power. Events belied Nixon's continued utterances about victory and an honorable peace. "Withdrawal of combat troops," Barbara Tuchman wrote mockingly of the policy, "is an unusual way to win a war."[65]

Following his address at the University of New Mexico, Ball told an Albuquerque newspaper that the United States should prepare for the "real possibility that President Nixon's Vietnam policy will fail." In December 1969, Ball sent Kissinger an advance copy of his forthcoming *New York Times Magazine* article entitled "We Should De-escalate the Importance of Vietnam." Although somewhat sympathetic to the narrow choices Nixon faced, Ball again sharply criticized the policy of phased withdrawal, stating that it would "almost certainly snuff out any lingering possibility of a negotiated settlement." He cited "recklessness" in American policy and expressed dismay that the administration had "refused to prepare for the possibility that we might not fully succeed in our objective." The former internal dissenter rang a familiar note in stating that Nixon was guilty of "exaggerating the political costs of extricating ourselves from a situation which large numbers of our people find totally unacceptable." Recalling the specificity of Eisenhower's original commitment to Diem, Ball concluded that the American people had already done "all [they] contracted to do." It was 1969. It was time to come home.[66]

The *New York Times Magazine* piece was followed by a *Newsweek* column in which he wrote that the United States had "mistaken Tonkinese aggression for Chinese imperialism" and hence had grossly overreacted to what was merely a matter of "marginal relevance" to the balance of power in the region.

Waxing more philosophical on the war than he had to date, Ball wrote that by irresponsibly inflating the importance of Vietnam with "reckless hyperbole," the present generation of leadership has "misled our children because we have not been honest with them." Ball believed that the "wrong lessons" would be learned by a new generation. Citing the "classic case" of Oxford's students who in 1933 "voted not to fight for king and country," Ball disparaged the sentiment of "isolationism" and "non-involvement" growing in public opinion—particularly among the young.[67] The internal dissenter had now moved into the public information media to offer analysis and healing advice on America's nightmare in Indochina.

Having thoroughly savaged Nixon and Kissinger, Ball ironically came to the aid of the administration in the spring of 1971. A political rescue operation of sorts was launched when senior Montana senator Mike Mansfield called for the immediate withdrawal of one-half of America's European forces from the NATO command. Kissinger promptly assembled an august group of former government officials to lobby aggressively against what came to be known as the Mansfield Amendment. Included on a list of "worthies" who could be counted on to man the barricades to defend the integrity of the Atlantic Alliance (the group also included Dean Acheson, McGeorge Bundy, John McCloy, and Cyrus Vance), Ball was telephoned by Kissinger, who referred to him as his "old sparring partner." Recognizing the "deeply-felt differences" between the former "Democratic" under secretary and the present administration, Kissinger hoped and expected that a "spirit of bipartisanship" would prevail during the debate over the future of NATO. It did. In a classic inter-Establishment play, Ball found himself tending an oar in the Nixon White House. As a tribute, Kissinger confesses that "Ball loved a fight in a good cause" and that he "went to work with his effectiveness and characteristic passion."[68]

And passionate he was. In private meetings with Kissinger, Ball suggested a theme to be developed toward defeat of the Mansfield proposal: The withdrawal of American forces from Europe was "capricious" and "reckless." Ball recommended that the administration warn the Senate against such a drastic move at a moment when Britain's entry into the European Economic Community was being negotiated and Germany was rethinking its relationship to the Eastern bloc in a much heralded "Ostpolitik." Europe, Ball advised, was experiencing an "uneasy summer," and it seemed "too nervous a moment to disturb the confidence" of the Continent.[69] Privately telling Acheson the preceding spring that "a growing number of damn fools on Capitol Hill" might well imperil the very foundation of the Atlantic Alliance, Ball believed that "nothing could be more stupidly timed."[70] Persuaded by the testimony of the lobby that Kissinger had assembled, the Senate rejected the Mansfield Amendment on May 19, 1971, by a vote of 61 to 36.

An accomplished bureaucratic infighter, Ball was too wise and experienced not to exploit his ephemeral role in the Nixon administration for larger ends. While railing against the Mansfield Amendment, he invited Acheson to join him in what came to be a failed effort to persuade the administration to revise—and actually discard—the Nixon Doctrine. Deploring foreign policy doctrines generally, Ball felt that Nixon's could be applied only very selectively and should be abandoned. It had, Ball believed, aided and abetted the "Mansfield Rebellion." He and Acheson reminded the administration that when the United States held itself aloof from world affairs, it lost control of events and contributed to disastrous outcomes. The Nixon Doctrine—as it called forth a general reduction of American commitments around the globe— "[was] scarcely the lesson that should be derived from Vietnam." The lesson to be learned, Ball counseled, "is not to abdicate leadership, but to be more selective in the use of our power."[71] An American president should not enunciate a doctrinal prohibition about the use of power but should instead exercise good judgment in a case-by-case review of when American power should be employed. Consumed by the complexities of triangular negotiations over Vietnam, Nixon gave little thought to the prescriptions articulated by Ball and Acheson. Analyzed together, the Mansfield affair, during which Nixon and Kissinger sought to insure the integrity of the American force structure in Europe, and the simultaneous pursuit of the reduction of commitment throughout the rest of the world suggest (erroneously) that Nixon and Kissinger were in fact reorienting American foreign policy back to the Atlantic community. In the short term, this was quite satisfying to Ball.

With the Mansfield Amendment defeated, partisan politics reconvened. In the summer of 1971, as an embattled Nixon sought an injunction against publication of the *Pentagon Papers*, Ball played the more familiar role of thorn in the side of the administration by publicly declaring that he warmly welcomed release of the documents. "On the whole," Ball told the *Washington Sunday Star*, exposing the process of decision making was "a very healthy business," and he flatly rejected the administration's claim of "irreparable injury to national security" by their disclosure. Immediately thereafter, Ball opened a second political front against the Nixon administration in a *Wall Street Journal* column, arguing that "this is a useful time to be considering the procedures for the exercise of the nation's war making powers." He pointed to what he saw as a "constitutional breakdown, a failure of the system of checks and balances," which had created grave ambiguities as to where constitutional authority to make war resides. Deploring what he called "institutional free enterprise," Ball called upon Congress to "make precise what the Founding Fathers chose to paint only with a broad brush" and to assert their role and "gain a major voice in the decisions that result in sending our young men into war."[72]

Generous, perhaps to a fault, in his analysis of escalation during the Johnson presidency, Ball was unrestrained in his condemnation of Nixon. (It should also be noted that time has done little to moderate his harsh views and that he sharply dissents from the recent "Nixon revisionism.") In Ball's view, the Nixon-Kissinger objective in Vietnam was distressingly transparent: The United States was attempting to end its military intervention without appearing to have abandoned the Saigon regime. Nixon was merely playing for a "decent interval" of time between the moment the Americans would leave the country and what he, Nixon, knew to be the inevitable unification of Vietnam by Hanoi. Ball maintains that so immoderate an escalation of the violence was inexcusable because Nixon, as a Republican who had inherited a failed policy from a Democratic predecessor, was politically better positioned than Johnson to extricate the country from Vietnam. Nixon, in other words, should have faced the facts. In doing so, he could have save countless thousands of lives. Ball once summarized this view in a letter to his friend John Kenneth Galbraith during a period when they were both nearing completion of their memoirs and reflecting on the lessons of the Vietnamese travail: "The stage was set for an American extrication when Johnson withdrew. Had Nixon and Kissinger learned anything at all from our agonizing experience, they would have promptly ended the war as [French prime minister] Mendès-France did in 1954. The case is a strong one, and if Kissinger was finally rewarded with the Nobel Prize, that merely refutes the old canard that the Swedes have no sense of humor."[73]

Alas, Nixon succumbed to the same narrow political logic as Johnson when he stated that he would not be "the first American President to lose a war." [74] Throughout the Nixon presidency, Ball continued to argue that the United States, rather than demonstrating its credibility and power in Vietnam, was, by pursuing an elusive goal, compromising its position of moral authority in the world and disclosing its weakness. Throughout the conflict the North Vietnamese and Vietcong, although losing specific military engagements with American and South Vietnamese forces, demonstrated that they had a winning political strategy. Ball believed then that Nixon simply lacked the courage to confront this disturbing reality. The administration was sorrowfully failing to profit from past lessons. Indeed, Ball wondered aloud whether Nixon or Kissinger had learned anything from the agony of the Johnson administration. "For such an astute man," Ball once wrote, "Henry Kissinger seemed to have entered the government with an unrealistic view of the war. [His] initial assessments of our Vietnam prospects sounded as though he had been absent on Mars during the preceding three years. In failing to recognize that North Vietnamese obduracy far transcended the constraints of Western logic, the Nixon administration spurned the grim lessons Americans should by then have learned." Instead, Nixon perpetuated the fallacy that South Vietnam might prevail. The besieged president privately recognized but refused to publicly confront the fact that South Vietnam, "lacking the drive, legitimacy and common purpose of a nation," would be defeated by the "cruel, fanatical revolutionary clique in Hanoi."[75]

Ball has retrospectively stated that "Vietnamization" (the much touted policy of incrementally turning responsibility for combat operations over to South Vietnamese forces) was nothing more than a "Nixon Confidence game." He deprecated the president's "extravagant promises" of continued support, which he knew, given the political climate in the Congress and throughout the nation, could not possibly be kept. For Ball, Nixon's strategy utterly lacked the idealism and the prospect of nation building which, however muddled, had underpinned the original Kennedy-Johnson policy in South Vietnam. In Nixon's mind, Vietnam was little more than a trap from which America must be sprung if he were to achieve his broader diplomatic agenda of improved relations with the Soviet Union and the opening of China. Because Nixon was deluded about the eventual fate of South Vietnam, Ball cannot forgive him for sending so many people to their deaths in pursuit of a papier-mâché peace.[76]

Further, Ball considered it morally outrageous that Nixon was so willing to pay—or more accurately, to have others pay—so high a price for such a transitory result. In attempting to achieve his "decent interval," Nixon seriously compromised America's moral authority. "Only a man too self-centered to comprehend the anguish of the human condition," Ball once remarked, "could give an order sending hundreds to their deaths for such a trifling purpose." In Ball's long recollection of him, Nixon "had always been the archetypal hawk, ready at slight provocation to dispatch Americans to kill and be killed." Ball genuinely feared that without constitutional checks, Nixon "could have indefinitely used [America's] armed forces as his personal chattel in Vietnam without the need to consult anyone."[77]

Failing to heed the lessons of the Johnson years, Nixon became a prisoner of his own miscalculations and pursued what Ball criticized as a "tragically misconceived" negotiating strategy. The tactics employed to achieve "peace with honor" ignored two fundamental principles. Nixon's first error was lodged in his initial generous assessment of the military situation in South Vietnam. Declaring that Saigon might be saved was either an epic self-delusion or a thinly veiled deception. Operating from the premise, at least publicly, that South Vietnam could survive the revolutionary struggle, Nixon failed to distinguish between American and South Vietnamese interests. "A great power," Ball wrote, "should not link its own bargaining objectives to those of a client state." South Vietnam hoped—and, given Nixon's rhetoric, had every reason to expect—that the United States would continue to guarantee its territorial integrity and sovereignty. The United States, in its turn, wanted almost desperately to end the war on any reasonable terms. From 1969 on, Nixon was "schizophrenically" declaring his intention to stand by South Vietnamese President Thieu while at the same time conniving to abandon the country. Locked in this inconsistency, the administration found itself negotiating on behalf of Saigon when its real objective was to achieve a deal for itself with Hanoi. The result was a duplicitous and cynical strategy that merely postponed the inevitable at an even greater cost in human life.[78]

Nixon's second error was that he failed to play his strongest negotiating card at the most opportune time. Ball faulted Nixon for wasting time with the demand for mutual withdrawal of American and North Vietnamese forces from the South. The Communists, he argued then (and reemphasizes with the benefit of hindsight), "would never yield possession of the 25 percent of South Vietnamese territory they had gained by long years of fighting." Meanwhile, Nixon undermined the U.S. negotiating position by withdrawing large increments of forces "and announcing that the process would continue." In his more recent analysis of the war years, Ball has "absolutely no doubt" that, had Nixon been willing to withdraw unilaterally in exchange for American POWs when American forces were at full strength (575,000) in 1969, he could have achieved a year-long cease-fire—his "decent interval." For Saigon, Ball concludes, the consequence would have been the same. Unification of Vietnam under communism "was the preordained final act of the grisly drama."[79]

For four years, Nixon pursued an elusive "peace with honor." By settling the prisoner exchange problem, reestablishing a demilitarized zone, and calling for a "cease-fire-in-place," the Paris peace accords, signed on January 27, 1973, finally provided an acceptable formula for American withdrawal. The last U.S. forces left the country on March 27. But the Paris agreement did not end the war. Repeated violations and aggression by the North Vietnamese mocked the spirit of the document. As a resurgent Congress imposed checks on executive prerogative with the passage of the War Powers Act in November 1973—and then drove Nixon from office in the wake of the Watergate revelations in August 1974—Hanoi wasted no time in pursuit of its goal of national unification. In March 1975 the Communist forces overran the important provincial capitals of the South. By April they were poised on the perimeter of Saigon. On April 23, President Ford declared the war "finished." On April 29, the last American diplomatic personnel were lifted off the roof of the American embassy in Saigon. On April 30, the Communists occupied Saigon and christened it Ho Chi Minh City.

Most observers were stunned by the rapidity with which the collapse came. There was no serious movement to reintervene. The inevitable "Vietnam Syndrome,"[80] a backlash from failed involvement in a menacing world, had etched itself in the national mood. The very name "Vietnam" became a metaphor for all that was wrong with America. A divided and guilt-stricken country craved healing. During those spring days when the nation was recoiling from twenty-five years of political involvement and nine years of war, Ball penned a postmortem for America's Vietnam debacle which, he later stated, he cannot improve upon:

> However one may justify it, [Vietnam] was a tragic defeat for America. Not in the military terms of the battlefield, but a defeat for our political authority and moral influence abroad and for our sense of mission and cohesion at home. A defeat not because our initial purposes were unworthy or our intentions anything less than honorable, but because—in frustration and false pride and our innocence of the art of extrication—we were forced to the employment of excessively brutal means to achieve an equivocal objective against a poor, small, backward country. That is something the world will be slow to forgive, and we should be slow to forget.[81]

Chapter 7

George Ball and the Theorists

*We have used the vocabulary and syntax of Wilsonian universalism
while actively practicing the politics of alliances and spheres of
influence and it is now time that we stopped confusing ourselves
with our political hyperbole.*
—*George Ball, 1967*

*I know of few things more hopeful for the future than the growing
determination of American business to regard national boundaries
as no longer fixing the horizons of their corporate activity.*
—*George Ball, 1968*

AN INCONSONANT combination of factors compelled Johnson to listen
intently to and then reject outright Ball's arguments against escalation. Similarly, except insofar as Kissinger's appreciation of Ball's intellect stimulated
discussion between the two about Vietnam over lunches in the White House,
the Nixon administration essentially ignored the former under secretary's
polemics against the rising violence in Indochina. But it would be erroneous to
perceive Ball merely as a failed advocate, for as the American militarization of
the Vietnam civil war continued on into a fifth, sixth, seventh, then an eighth
year, Ball was a leading voice in what came to be a comprehensive reappraisal
of the strategic doctrines and assumptions that had led the United States to war.
In the late 1960s new theoretical approaches to the study and management of
international relations emerged. As it would for most Americans, the Vietnam
conflict served as a watershed event in the development of Ball's world view.
With the great difficulties confronted and the great costs incurred in Indochina,
the containment doctrine, having provided an unchallenged blueprint for
American foreign policy for a quarter-century since World War II, was called
into question. Particularly after the military and political disappointments of
1967–68, the bipartisan consensus among American foreign policy elites

about the nature of the international state system, the role of the United States in world affairs, and the constitutional framework within which foreign policy was formulated and administered appeared to disintegrate. In four major books, innumerable speeches, and dozens of trenchant editorial essays, Ball locked arms with a coterie of Realist foreign policy sages who were, in the wake of the Vietnam conflict, rethinking containment.

Thoughtful public debate about foreign policy had been a dubious enterprise between 1945 and 1968. Indeed, in an age that produced the McCarran Act and McCarthyism, the patriotism of dissenters would readily be challenged if they wandered too far from the theology of global anticommunism. From the political stump—and indeed, from the university presses—few alternatives to expansive globalism were even intimated in the 1950s and early 1960s. Most students and practitioners of foreign policy uncritically accepted the Anglo-American view of international relations, articulated by Winston Churchill and Harry Truman, that characterized the Soviet Union as the spearhead of an aggressive and evangelical Communist ideology. Iron and bamboo curtain symbolism profoundly conditioned the discernment of world events among the first generation of American foreign policy elites in the postwar era. Before 1968, images of an unremitting conflict between the capitalist and socialist worlds were sustained by a surprisingly resilient bipartisan foreign policy consensus in the executive and legislative branches of government, and by elite opinion makers including journalists, professional historians, and political scientists.

Leading diplomatic historians such as Thomas A. Bailey (in *A Diplomatic History of the American People* [1940 and rev. eds.]), John W. Spainer (in *American Foreign Policy Since World War II* [1960 and rev. eds.]), and Julius Pratt (in *A History of the United States Foreign Policy* [1954 and rev. eds.]) had endorsed the extension of American power throughout the world and applauded the expansive interpretation of Truman's containment policy as a timely corrective to a generation of appeasement and isolationism. These writers, comprising the so-called Nationalist School,[1] held that the "aggression" of Soviet and Chinese communism in the period immediately following the Second World War left the United States little choice but to act as it did in formalizing military alliances. American military power would intervene to save the Western industrial democracies and their clients from the rising tide of "Sino-Soviet communism." The Nationalist historians believed that the Russians could not be trusted, that world communism was a consolidated and aggressive force, and that constant vigilance and overwhelming power were the only means of checking the erosion of Western institutions.

To the Nationalists, the East-West struggle was a "zero-sum game"—a gain for "the Bloc" was a loss for the "Free World."[2] Scholars of the Nationalist School saw the Cold War as an unyielding competitive struggle between two mutually exclusive systems of political economy and social values. The Marshall Plan, the Truman Doctrine, NATO, and a host of secondary security arrangements were seen as prudent and necessary responses to imminent Soviet threats. In short order, a political and intellectual consensus formed around the institution of the Atlantic Alliance. "Cold War," "containment," "Red Tide," and "dominoes" quickly became rarefied neologisms of the foreign policy community. To the extent that there was debate at all about a global, anti-Communist policy, argument was over means, not ends. Throughout the 1950s, bipartisan congressional support, bolstered by the nearly universal affirmation of American intellectuals, undergirded the American commitments and transformed the Truman Doctrine, once narrowly interpreted as a local program of political support for Greek and Turk nationalists, into an open-ended covenant with the Free World to check the spread of communism.

Even before it reached its messy conclusion, the debacle in Vietnam prompted an agonizing reappraisal of American foreign policy. Fissures in the Cold War consensus had first appeared when the American escalation in July 1965 failed to bring about a swift military victory or a negotiated settlement; the consensus rapidly evaporated in the aftermath of the 1968 Communist Tet offensive.[3] Despite unprecedented use of firepower and expenditure of enormous human and material resources, victory in Vietnam remained elusive. The question "containment at what cost?" began to be asked. Dissent from the theology of anticommunism, once a morally suspect avocation, suddenly became intellectually and politically respectable. As concerns about the morality and viability of the war were raised, the doctrines and assumptions on which American policy in Indochina was based were challenged. The meaning of the war in Vietnam, as well as the East-West ideological struggle from which it sprang, was rethought. Toward the end of the politically hyperemotional 1960s, attacks upon the war and its antecedent of overmilitarized containment became a cottage industry. Discussion of the Vietnam conflict was soon an omnipresent fixture in national political life. The war became the window through which Americans began to view foreign as well as domestic policy. As the late Charles DeBenedetti so elegantly pronounced: "For Americans, the Vietnam War was most extraordinary in that it was not so much a fight against enemies abroad as it was an internal struggle over their own national identity. Vietnam in American history meant—and still means—a struggle among Americans over the nature of their interests, their values, and the very meaning of their country and their purpose."[4]

The sharpest attacks on the war were made by an emerging "Radical

Revisionist School"[5] of American foreign relations. Propelled by scholars such as the late William Appleman Williams (*The Tragedy of American Diplomacy* [1959]), Gabriel Kolko (*The Roots of American Foreign Policy* [1969]), and Richard J. Barnet (*The Roots of War* [1971]), this group initiated a fundamental reassessment of the origins and evolution of the Cold War. After publication of these pioneering monographs, a flood of Revisionist books and articles appeared, establishing an entirely new context within which the Vietnam intervention was evaluated. Intriguing theoretical models employed by the Radical Revisionists all but shattered the anti-Communist orthodoxy which had pervaded the immediate postwar generation. Though not immediately driving the Nationalist School scholars from the field, the Revisionists "forced all diplomatic historians to reassess the factors contributing to the Cold War and to explain this historical development in a more complex and satisfactory way."[6]

In varying degrees, the Radical Revisionists embraced an "economic" or "imperial" paradigm, arguing that the Americans must share equal responsibility with the Russians for the breakdown of the Soviet-American Grand Alliance and the onset of the Cold War. Radical Revisionists contended that zealous ideologues in the Truman and Eisenhower administrations had failed to recognize legitimate Soviet security interests in Eastern Europe and, by contesting an appropriate Soviet sphere of influence, had exacerbated international tensions. Their most novel assertion was that an "incestuous" relationship existed between American industrial capitalism and American foreign policy. The Radical Revisionists argued that American wars generally—and the Vietnam War particularly—may be understood only by more fully examining the American domestic political economy.

The Radical Revisionists suggested that the United States had long pursued a policy of "free-trade imperialism" (Williams)[7] as a "tactic for restructuring the world economy and facilitating American economic penetration" (Kolko),[8] with the inevitable result of creating a "permanent war economy" (Barnet).[9] With America cast into the role of aggressor bent on world capitalist hegemony, the Revisionists interpreted the containment policy and the decisions to assist South Vietnam as a morally suspect variant of traditional American Open Door imperialism. Within this context, the ethical justification for the Vietnam intervention was severely attenuated.

Even before the Radical Revisionists were storming the academic presses and university seminar rooms, a third theory had emerged to challenge the Nationalists. "Realist Revisionist" scholarship, typified by Walter Lippmann's numerous editorials criticizing the Vietnam War, Hans J. Morgenthau's *A New Foreign Policy for the United States* (1969), and George F. Kennan's

The Cloud of Danger: Current Realities of American Foreign Policy (1969), was also challenging the prevailing assumptions about America's role as the world's guarantor of peace and the then-accepted means of global containment. The Realists had long blanched at Woodrow Wilson's clarion call for a "war to end all wars" and viewed American policymakers in the aftermath of both twentieth-century global conflicts as idealists who focused too passionately on moralistic and unrealizable goals. Decrying Wilson, the Realists embraced Hobbes and accepted armed conflict and revolutions as immutable features of human society. Armed aggression, they believed, would not be eradicated from international politics. The United States was just as likely to make matters worse by attempting—and failing—to police the world in areas of marginal strategic importance.

Though they were in agreement with the Radical Revisionists that the Cold War orthodoxy of the National School was too simplistic, the Realists found little common ground with the Radicals and castigated the naive theories of political economy espoused by their usually younger brethren. The Realists challenged the Radical Revisionists' economic determinism, sharply criticized their methodological simplicities, and rejected their assumptions about capitalism's unremittingly expansive tendencies. Indeed, the Realists thought that the Revisionists were not only naive but menacing. Alarmed by the Radical potential to undermine a concept of limited containment which he advocated, Kennan even implored the Princeton University Press to publish more books and articles to debunk what he considered to be the heresies of the Radicals.[10]

As a general proposition, the Realists believed that American foreign policy in the twentieth century had oscillated recklessly between isolationism, with the expressed intention of shielding the United States from the corrupting influence of the "Old World," and missionary wars, fought to recast that same world into the image of the United States. As a specific proposition the Realists castigated the open-ended moralism of Wilson, the myopia and storm-cellar isolationism of "the early" Arthur Vandenberg (that is, before Dean Acheson worked him over and he became a forward-thinking advocate of the Marshall Plan), and the strategic universalism of John Foster Dulles. They believed that for a quarter-century American statesmen had raised expectations with inflated rhetoric and had not faced the costs of achieving such stated goals as global containment or the "rollback" of Communist frontiers. As an alternative, the Realists advocated a policy of measured containment, advising the application of American power only to maintain the critical balance of forces among the industrial states and military intervention only in areas of vital strategic significance.

Like the Radical Revisionists, the Realist critics of the Cold War were noticeably disturbed with the cultural simplicities and ethnocentrism of the Nationalist School. They contended that exuberant policy managers had over-reacted to a perceived threat to the sovereignty of Western European states at the end of World War II. They were, by and large, less alarmed than the Nationalists by Soviet ideology and more sanguine than the Revisionists about the realities of Soviet military power at the borders of Western Europe. The Realists believed that Truman had mistaken traditional czarist expansionism and Russian claustrophobia for evangelical communism and spun wholly false historical analogies to bolster requests for expensive military programs—particularly the hydrogen bomb project. Added to the list of cognitive errors that the Realists believed were made in the immediate postwar period were the neglect of professional and personal diplomacy, too great an affinity for military solutions to what they considered essentially political questions, and the evolution of a policy based on facile assumptions about Soviet power. The Realists attempted to shatter the illusion of a world Communist monolith. They believed that universalism was no answer to isolationism and, like Walter Lippmann, asserted that global containment "was but the other side of the isolationist coin."[11]

To the Realists, Vietnam was not, as the Nationalist School assumed, a central factor in the Cold War. They flatly and aggressively repudiated the assumption that a world Communist conspiracy motivated North Vietnam's goal of national unification and emphasized that endogenous anticolonialism and latent Asian nationalism were at the root of the conflict. The primary objective in waging the Cold War, according to the Realists, was not the maintenance of peripheral states like South Vietnam but the preservation of democratic capitalism in Western Europe. As sharp critics of the manner in which the Cold War had been managed, Realists were not seduced by "nation building" scenarios, nor did they subscribe to the zero-sum dichotomy of the Nationalist School; they doubted that a Communist Vietnam would apprecia-bly—or even necessarily—enhance the political or military power of the Soviet Union or Communist China or in any perceptible way weaken the West. Simply because Vietnam lay outside of the democratic and industrial world and had, in their appraisal, little strategic value, the Realists believed that a policy of military intervention to compensate for a host of unmanageable political problems within South Vietnam ascribed to it far too much impor-tance.

To the Realists, the Vietnam intervention was a gross intellectual error born of the arrogance of Wilsonian universalism and its legatee, the containment doctrine. But the Realist critics attacked neither the moral purpose of American foreign policy nor the logic of containment. Realists were liberal internationalists and advocated an activist foreign policy. With Kennan the notable exception, Realists favored increased defense budgets and a strong national and international strategic posture. They felt the decision to intervene in Vietnam, however, was a serious political and military miscalculation stemming from unwarranted deference to theories of credibility. To the Realists, those who advocated escalation displayed too little appreciation for the maintenance of the world's "real" balance of power—that is, the correlation of forces among the industrial nations—and unthinkingly overextended American power into an area of the world with dubious strategic significance.

Unlike most practitioners of American foreign policy (Schlesinger's assertion notwithstanding),[12] Ball was keenly aware of the historiography of the immediate postwar era, and his world views generally—and his Vietnam dissent specifically—were informed by the historical revisionism emerging during the 1960s. As has been made abundantly clear, Ball's acceptance of America's relative decline in power and an inexorably changing structure of international relations in the 1960s was a view shared by precious few scholars or practitioners of foreign policy. After September 1968, when he was no longer hemmed in by the protocols of appointive office, Ball's writing became highly theoretical and reflected a sober, Realist appraisal of the world's industrial, economic, and political power.

After his departure from the U.N., Ball, with no fewer than 250 speeches, as many editorial essays, formal interviews, eleven television appearances,[13] and the systematic exposition of his views in four books, joined a shadow government of Realist intellectuals who sought to revise American foreign policy objectives and align goals with resources. Rejecting the Nationalist School for its simplicity and offended by the iconoclastic anticapitalism of the Radical Revisionists, Ball is most fully understood by examining his writings within the context of the Realist hypothesis. Ball himself is forthright about the influence of select Realist writers upon his thinking. Claiming to be well acquainted with Hans Morgenthau's books, "particularly his long dissertations on the balance of power," having maintained a long friendship with Walter Lippmann, and having "read all that there was to read of George Kennan," Ball was immersed in the Realist strategic theories and in his own right became an eloquent and prolific Realist practitioner.[14]

University of Chicago political scientist Hans J. Morgenthau had originally made an academic reputation in the 1950s by rejecting utopianism (his synonym for Wilson's Fourteen Points), by baldly asserting that a nation's self-interest was narrowly defined in terms of its power, and by flatly declaring that the Cold War structure of international relations had lost its relevance. Corollaries were obvious: Power mattered more than international law in the real world, and policies tending to dissipate power should be discarded. Once dubbed "the pope of Realism,"[15] by the end of the 1960s Morgenthau had concluded that the containment doctrine had become an anachronism, unable, as he wrote, "to distinguish between what is desirable and what possible" and equally unable "to distinguish between what is desirable and what is essential." Morgenthau was convinced that the demands upon resources of a global anti-Communist policy exceeded capabilities, and he even dared to question the virtue of America's "instinctive opposition to communism."[16] In terms nearly identical to Ball's internal dissent, Morgenthau openly criticized Johnson's escalation of the Vietnam conflict, publicly announced in the summer of 1966 that "the Saigon government is hardly worthy of the name," called for a bombing halt, and proposed Vietcong participation in South Vietnam's government as a precondition for an expeditious American withdrawal.[17]

Like his Realist cousins who believed that "the world would be safer if Americans abandoned universalist crusades,"[18] Ball rejected utopianism and disparaged what he considered to be the immoderate rhetoric of American foreign policy. Belittling the view that the United States was the "New Jerusalem"[19] endowed with either unimpeachable virtue or infinite wisdom, Ball thought the Vietnam experience to be a sobering illustration of the limits of American influence. "What we have learned," he wrote in 1968, "is that international politics is both more and less than the art of the possible; it is the art of the practical."[20] Long concerned with obfuscation and hypocrisy embedded in the language of American foreign policy, immediately after leaving the U.N. he declared that a "sonorous universalist dogma" had, in conspicuous circumstances, contributed to bad policy-making, and, worse, that the American record belied American rhetoric. "We have used the vocabulary and syntax of Wilsonian universalism," Ball wrote in 1967, "while actively practicing the politics of alliances and spheres of influence and it is now time that we stopped confusing ourselves with our political hyperbole." Waxing theoretical, Ball found that American policy elites had deluded themselves: "While we have invented some new, high-flying abstractions—containment, liberation, halting of aggression, and so forth—these terms only blur and distort the ultimate purpose of the United States, which is to try to build peace not only by protecting our own interests but by recognizing the interests and the power of other peoples."[21] Emphatically renouncing unilateralism, Ball contended that for a quarter-century after the Second World War American foreign policy had been formulated and executed without the consent, and in some cases against the better judgment, of its principal allies—a tendency he found to be alarmingly reminiscent of America's isolationism in the 1930s.

Ball's first two books were concerned largely with the guiding theories of American statecraft, particularly the criteria that had been used for the exercise of American military power. In *The Discipline of Power: Essentials of a Modern World Structure* (1968) and *Diplomacy for a Crowded World: An American Foreign Policy* (1976), Ball developed a coherent theory of power which reconfirms his identity as a Realist—and which may be reduced to three maxims: The first is that "the possession of surplus resources and the political will to use them are what gives any nation the ability to exert a decisive influence on world politics"; the second is that "the ultimate arbiter of international conflict remains what it has been since the beginning of time, the possession of power"; and the third is that "power can be limited only by counter-balancing power."[22]

In the real world, Ball believed, there were few reliable checks on power, and he argued that the United Nations system has done very little to obviate the use of force in international disputes. (Although he once sardonically remarked that the U.N. had been reduced to mere service "as midwife for the birth of new nations," it should be noted that his once uncharitable criticisms of the institution have mellowed in the very recent past.)[23] For a quarter-century after its inception the U.N. system has been rendered impotent because neither the Soviet Union nor the United States has recognized its resolutions as binding international law. Since the creation of the United Nations, power, not principles of justice, has been the great weight in international affairs. (It is ironic that Ball—until very recently, at any rate—regularly inveighed against Wilsonian universalism and now serves on the Board of Governors of the Woodrow Wilson School of International Relations at Princeton University.)

Although he is quite sanguine about the perils of military conflict in the age of the atom, Ball reminds his readers that even the presence of vast nuclear arsenals has not nullified the use of force. In two episodes in which he was a frontline participant, Ball's theory of power was tested: The Soviets "blinked" during the 1962 Cuban Missile Crisis, he argues, because neither their interests nor their power was equal to that of the United States in the region. Conversely, during the 1968 Czech crisis, when the Russians had compelling interests and preponderant power in the region, they acted without hesitation or restraint.[24] The Russians haplessly backed down in 1962; the United States sat idly by while the brief "Prague Spring" froze over.

Like Morgenthau, Ball ardently advanced the view in the late 1960s that the most realistic strategy for the maintenance of peace is to insure a favorable correlation of forces among the major industrial states. To accomplish this the United States must, however reluctantly, allocate considerable political and material resources to its military establishment and develop a range of strategic options that are suitable for use in a wide variety of crises. Perhaps paradoxically, the liberal assumptions upon which Ball based his Vietnam dissent— including the acceptance of political and ideological change within the world order—must be understood within the context of his enthusiastic support for military preparedness, including a peacetime draft, compulsory military service, increased defense budgets, and the continued deployment of American forces in Europe. However, Ball has argued with equal vehemence that the United States must be careful not to squander its power. In a manner reminiscent of the eighteenth-century Prussian military doctrine, the army is an instrument of deterrence and not necessarily an instrument of foreign policy. In the last decade he opposed American military involvement in Angola, Afghanistan, Nicaragua, El Salvador, Grenada, and Lebanon by arguing that American power could not be used constructively in those environments and that the interests of the United States were not clearly engaged. Rejecting, indeed resenting, the label "neo-isolationist," Ball prefers to think of himself as "a military economist" willing to deploy American power only when a "clear and present danger" to a vital American interest exists and in a political and strategic arena where power might be used effectively and efficiently.[25]

An obvious question then arises: When, and to what end, *should* American military power be used? Theorist Ball summarily rejects neither a liberal global policy for the United States nor military intervention when it is necessary and proper. He recently even disclosed an incipient idealism which had existed somewhere between the lines of his Realist treatises of the 1960s and 1970s. "It is not enough," he told a 1987 Marshall Plan Conference in Bologna, Italy, "to discard an irrelevant tradition of universalism; we must, at the same time, develop a substitute framework, a new way of looking at the world." In the manner in which Kennan's Realism is defined by his abiding faith in the processes of diplomacy, Ball's is largely defined by what might be termed his institutional vision. He is a longstanding and dogged advocate of restructuring global political relationships to achieve what he has always considered to be the desirable end of free trade. American military power, in his analysis, is little more than a benign counterweight, serviceable merely as a deterrent to threats against Western institutions, not an instrument to be wielded in each and every crisis faced by the American government overseas. (He was once roundly criticized by Ambassador Averell Harriman for denying that the United States had to compete in the same league as the Almighty by watching after every little sparrow.) The essential goals of American foreign policy in the 1990s remain largely the same as those he endorsed a quarter-century ago. Calling for "a pragmatic test [for] Wilsonian principles," Ball continues to work toward the political integration of Europe and the advancement of the international economic open door as means to the end of enhancing Western security.[26]

It is a subtle yet significant distinction to note that while Ball has denigrated universalist doctrines, he has just as forcefully argued for idealistic and comprehensive institutions. Occasioned by a "Firing Line" encounter during which his conservative antagonist William F. Buckley, Jr., inflexibly endorsed the Monroe and Truman doctrines as unalterable assertions of American anticommunism, Ball renounced the universal application of any policy: "I don't think we ought to declare ourselves implacably against anything." It may be in the best interest of the United States, he suggests, to oppose communism in one setting and leave it alone in another. He has come to believe that the dual bogeymen of rhetoric and doctrine have plagued American policy, and he regularly pillories the use—and users—of hyperbole in foreign policy debate. Ball once argued that statesmen should forswear casual expiation of coldly reasoned policies and even once quipped that after-dinner speeches at state banquets should be banned—since they are "more likely to reflect either a dyspepsia or an inebriation" than a measured, well-reasoned policy. Believing that a comprehensive foreign policy is plainly not reducible to political simplification, Ball has concluded that presidential doctrines are more likely to cause rather than ameliorate international conflict, and he even once semifacetiously called for a "constitutional amendment" prohibiting them.[27]

But Ball does not embrace the bald doctrines of Realpolitik, which, he writes, "cannot permanently substitute for a sense of purpose." In what was, even for him, a surprisingly ethnocentric characterization, he once called the practices of shifting alliances and secretive diplomacy "un-American." Sympathetic to the plight of legislators obliged to explain international relations "to the home folks,"[28] Ball well understands the need to articulate idealistic ends. While renouncing the inflexibility of presidential doctrine, he concedes that a foreign policy formulated without some mature political principles is "simply a series of unrelated improvisations."[29] In one of his infrequent populist moods, Ball admitted that "a foreign policy that does not accord with the instinctive morality of Americans will not have a constituency."[30] The delicate balance between idealistic globalism and self-absorbed Realpolitik lies in a vital, formalized institutional structure within which the sentiments and concerns of the Western democracies may be respected. This requires open, multilateral consultations of the kind called forth by Monnet's vision of a United Europe or the American complement, Kennedy's "Grand Design."

Like Morgenthau, Ball has made a career of slaying the dragons of inflated foreign policy rhetoric, renouncing ends for which American power is unavailable or not rationally usable, and advocating the annulment of policies which have more symbolic than real value. His Vietnam dissent is ample testimony to this insofar as he had always felt that his colleagues had ascribed much greater symbolic importance to the Indochinese problem than it merited if coldly analyzed in strategic and economic terms. Employing the same Realist rationale, Ball criticized Nixon's much-heralded China initiative in 1971. While applauding the beginning of normalized relations with the People's Republic of China (PRC), Ball took exception to the style and manner of Nixon's mission and angrily vilified the president while most other commentators were tripping over each other in a race to praise him. The Nixon administration, Ball felt, had acted irresponsibly because it had acted unilaterally. Failure to consult Japan and the European allies compromised relationships that had real strategic and commercial value, in pursuit of a relationship with China that was, in his view, primarily symbolic.

In the wake of so much national euphoria about the "opening of China," Ball iconoclastically charged that while Nixon was "making history," he was also fomenting a serious crisis of confidence. Japan, for example, harbored justifiable fears that the United States might make secret agreements with China affecting its security. In the minds of other Asian leaders, Nixon's "request" for an invitation to China conjured up ancient images of subordination to the Middle Kingdom and, Ball states, created the perception of the American president's entourage as "supplicants bearing tribute."[31] In strictly economic terms, because "Japan's gross national product is two and a half times mainland China's," as he wrote in the *New York Times* in August 1971, it was "no bargain to trade a functioning friendship with a functioning superpower for the chance of a fragile arrangement with a potential one."[32]

Damning Nixon with faint praise, Ball did credit him with a sober appraisal of the China problem—particularly the need to normalize relations with the PRC and to revise America's anachronistic "Two China" policy. Though he openly doubted that Nixon had actually written the 1967 *Foreign Affairs* article attributed to him, Ball conceded the president's wisdom in identifying with the view that "any American policy toward Asia must come urgently to grips with the reality of China."[33] What Nixon appeared to be thinking made sense to Ball, and he granted that a new approach to China was required. However, as a professional diplomat with fitting respect for the professional foreign service and traditional protocols, Ball thought that the policy should be initiated at the level of "emissary diplomacy." When the China summit became an extravagantly publicized state visit—conducted, as he wrote, "in a Bearnaise sauce of intrigue and mystery"—it caused "substantial breakage" resulting from the neglect of multilateral consultation. In the end, Ball sadly concluded that the highly touted trip was merely a ploy "to offset [Nixon's] manifold delinquencies."[34] Europeans felt betrayed because they were not conferred with, and many Asian observers were simply puzzled by an American president pursuing a policy in a manner they interpreted as demeaning.

Also illustrative of Ball's penchant for disparaging policies with more symbolic than real value is his analysis of the presently intractable Arab-Israeli conflict. Invoking Morgenthau's Realist litmus test—"interest defined as power"—Ball has found much to be desired in the policy of the United States in the Middle East for the past three decades. Reminiscent of the manner in which he argued that South Vietnam possessed more psychological than actual value to the United States, in the past ten years Ball has courageously challenged the prevailing assumptions about Israel's strategic and political significance. Echoing his analysis of American–South Vietnamese relations in the 1960s, he has audaciously asserted that America's and Israel's interests are, at the moment, incompatible and has recently called upon the American government do nothing less than "systematically recast"[35] its relationship with its sister democracy. He vigorously dissents from the generally held thesis that Israel is an indispensable ally, asserts that the United States is undermining Israeli security by uncritically continuing to vote military support for what he considers her wrongheaded colonial policy, and will state in a forthcoming book entitled *The Passionate Attachment* that all this has occurred because the Jewish lobby exerts a disproportionate influence in American domestic politics.

Simply put, Ball believes that Israel is too small and in too precarious a strategic position in relationship to her neighbors to interminably occupy conquered lands. Worse, by automatically voting economic assistance and supporting her expansionist policies, the United States is unwittingly contributing to Israel's peril. A little more than a decade ago, in an exchange of wholly private thoughts from the sanctuary of retirement, Rusk and Ball concurred that a revision of American thinking toward Israel is necessary to avert calamity in the Middle East. "As one who spends most of his time west and south of the Hudson and Potomac Rivers," Rusk wrote Ball in the summer of 1977, "[I believe] an American role as the tail on Israel's kite would simply not go down here in the back country." Admitting that he was "talking on the edge of some very ugly things," Rusk reminded his still close confidant that "one of the causes of anti-Semitism is Semitism."[36] Ball's reply to Rusk's letter indicated that he was in full and complete agreement, adding the caveat that "our Eastern policy must be made in Washington and not Jerusalem."[37]

Since that exchange, Ball has traveled extensively in the Middle East, interviewed innumerable heads of state, policy elites, and academics, and has read and written extensively on the seemingly unmanageable Arab-Israeli quarrel. More recently, his apprehension—and rhetoric—were inflamed by Israel's 1982 invasion of Lebanon. "That Israel has great strategic value to the United States," he wrote to Senator Charles McC. Mathias in the aftermath of Israel's bloody incursion across the Litani River and on to Beirut, "is largely a delusion."[38] It is only a "glib assertion" that Israel is "America's most dependable ally in the Middle East"—a thesis, Ball propounds, which "cannot withstand the most elementary analysis."[39]

After a circuitous and frustrating search for a publisher, Ball put his ideas to print in a 1984 volume entitled *Error and Betrayal in Lebanon: An Analysis of Israel's Invasion of Lebanon and the Implications for U.S.–Israeli Relations*. In what has been accurately described as a "blunt and devastating essay,"[40] he roundly chastised the Reagan administration, which he states was "paralyzed by domestic pressures,"[41] for not dealing firmly with Israel. Ball's central thesis was unvarnished: Israel's invasion of Lebanon in 1982 was unwarranted, and the United States was an unthinking coconspirator for its compliant role during a crisis that resulted in atrocities against innocent Lebanese and Palestinians. America stood by while an international crisis was unnecessarily created which ultimately led to a failed American military intervention and a tragedy of death and destruction involving 243 American servicemen. Throughout the ordeal, Ball boldly declared that "Washington flaccidly let the Begin government, in effect, dictate America's policies and disregard America's interests."[42] After the dust settled on the tragedy, Ball intrepidly made the public declaration that the United States cannot "any longer afford to play the role of Israel's overly-indulgent guardian, uncomplainingly paying larger and larger bills and dutifully sweeping up the breakage produced by the ambitions of Israel's leaders."[43]

Abhorring what he calls Israel's "increasingly regressive rule" over its non-Jewish citizens, Ball is pessimistic about the future. "In the present atmosphere of hostility and violence," he writes, "there is no way one can reconcile an American-Israeli alliance with the maintenance of friendly Arab relations." Now a serious student of the Middle East political environment, Ball has set himself to the task of debunking the conventional wisdom which holds that because Israel has enjoyed enormous success on the battlefield it can remain a bulwark of democracy and a vital check on Soviet expansionism in the region. This, to Ball, is no more than "a slogan that passes for wisdom only because it escapes rigorous scrutiny." Israel is soon to be outgunned, and he asserts that the affinity Americans have for Israeli Jews and Israel's democracy must give way to the power realities and political pressures that will inevitably be brought to bear on the region. Israel, he warns, is a "tiny island in a hostile Arab sea." Her physical limitations constrain her growth and "deny [her] utility as a significant strategic asset."[44]

Ball repeatedly reminds his listeners that despite Israel's record of success on the battlefield in recent wars, Arab military and economic power is multiplying faster than Israeli by a factor of two. After each previous defeat, the Arab states have expanded the size and capabilities of their armies and have precipitously shrunk Israel's strategic advantage. In a sober assessment of the correlation of forces, accounting for the recruiting and training practices of the region's major states, he calculated in 1982 that "within four or five years, Israel's projected strength of 725,000 troops may be countered by at least a million Syrians and Jordanians; and this number does not include any troops from Iraq, Lebanon, the PLO [Palestine Liberation Organization], the Gulf states, or Egypt."[45] Despite these power realities, the United States continues to arm Israel and contribute to what the former under secretary of state caustically refers to as her "self-destructive ambitions."[46] It is his considered judgment that political pressure from an effective Jewish lobby—in combination with the sympathy Americans feel for the travails of modern-age Jews—has precluded an objective and realistic appraisal of American-Israeli relations and perilously contributed to the present quandary in the Middle East.

Ball has paid an exceedingly high price for his candor. Supremely rich in experience, on the correct side of the watershed Vietnam debate, arguably without peer in his insights into European economic and governmental institutions, and possessed of great personal force and political skill, Ball hoped that his long-felt private aspiration to become secretary of state would be realized with the victory of the Democratic party in the presidential election of 1976. It was not to be. Immediately after it became known that President-elect Jimmy Carter included Ball's name on a "short list" of serious contenders for the top position in the cabinet, an enraged public debate was triggered by what many considered to be his impolitic *Foreign Affairs* article, "The Coming Crisis in Israeli-American Relations" (Winter 1975/76). A storm of protest over the prospect of Ball's nomination gushed from the Jewish community. Carter vacillated. Ultimately, under serious political pressure, he removed Ball's name from consideration. Ball was denounced as an anti-Semite for his critique of American-Israeli relations (he has collected a thick file of hate mail from Jewish groups and individuals),[47] and his name eventually appeared on the Jewish Anti-Defamation League's "enemies list."[48] Indeed, anti-Ball passions within pro-Israel groups ran so high that when Carter's eventual secretary of state designate, Cyrus Vance, wisely sought his counsel on the Middle East and many other strategic issues, he was compelled to use an intermediary—namely, Dean Rusk—so as not to give even the appearance that the new administration might solicit his heretical views. Ball resigned himself to the temporary cloak of anonymity and admitted to Rusk that "it would be a bad idea for Cy to be seen conferring with me."[49] Vance and Ball contented themselves with personal correspondence and long-distance telephone discussions of the new president's foreign policy agenda.

Ball has certainly not been the only Realist Revisionist of the Cold War to challenge the strategic dogmas and political assumptions of the past quarter-century—or to taste the opprobrium of the Right in recent years. During the same period that he made his unique contributions to the reexamination of America's foreign policy doctrines, George Frost Kennan, Ball's friend and Princeton neighbor, has enlivened public debate on a great many issues. Like Ball, Kennan can be irritating, iconoclastic, exasperating. Perhaps not surprisingly, Ball has great reverence for Kennan and has openly admitted that the diplomat/scholar contributed immensely to his own strategic thinking and political sensibilities.

With very few peers in his comprehension of Russian history and Soviet-American relations, the much-scrutinized author of the pseudonymous "X-Article" in 1947 provided the original intellectual rationale for the containment policy. Though historians continue to debate what Kennan really meant as he wrote in the aftermath of World War II,[50] it suffices here to repeat Kissinger's kudo that Kennan "came as close to authoring the doctrine of his era as any diplomat in our history."[51] As State Department policy planning director, Kennan convincingly articulated how the Russians, driven by a Marxist-Leninist political creed, were committed to the expansion of their political frontiers and would continue to seek territorial aggrandizement until they were blocked by a superior political and/or military force. Perhaps unwittingly, Kennan convinced a generation of American foreign policy elites that the United States had little choice but to symmetrically apply "counterpressure" to Soviet political and military aggression. Although he called for an expanded

American role in protecting the security interests of the Western democracies, Kennan emphatically renounced globalistic dogmas or commitments to peripheral states—by which he ostensibly meant those nations not normally considered part of the industrially developed world. Critical of Woodrow Wilson's universalist diplomacy during World War I, Kennan argued in the period immediately after the Second World War that the American national interest would not be served by a grandiose unilateral attempt to restructure the international order.

Kennan somberly accepted that the world might not "be made safe for democracy." For many years he, like Ball, never put much stock in ubiquitous formulas like the Fourteen Points or institutions like the United Nations. Surprisingly, Kennan does not even applaud that institution's ultimate purposes; indeed, he rather misanthropically contends that the elimination of conflict among nations is neither possible nor desirable. "Unpleasant as [it] might be," he once told the National War College, "we many have to face up to the fact that violence somewhere in the world is more desirable than the alternative [of] global wars."[52] As these somewhat crude convictions were sharpened and expanded upon in no fewer than seventeen books and innumerable speeches and articles, Kennan earned a reputation as one of the foremost Realist theorists of the past forty years. But it also should be noted that in the fullness of his career Kennan developed a comprehensive critique of Western civilization by commenting on the world's demographic and environmental crises, the crass commercialism of Western capitalism, the pervasive moral decadence that he observes in America, and what he considers to be a patently irrational nuclear arms race.

At the same time Ball was advocating an immediate negotiated withdrawal from Vietnam from inside the executive branch of government, Kennan was writing conspicuously similar articles from his vantage point at the Institute for Advanced Study at Princeton University. In time, with the forum provided him by Senator Fulbright's televised hearings on the war, Kennan professed his Realist convictions as they related to the Vietnam problem. His dissent became part of the public record. On January 30, 1967, he warned the Senate Foreign Relations Committee of "an overreliance on military means" in Indochina and asserted that the "impersonal mass destruction of aerial bombardment" compromised the rationale for American intervention. Further, the former ambassador believed that, as an ally, the South Vietnamese "[had] in general much more to demand than they have to give." He testified that he "could personally not care less whether [a united Vietnam] calls itself communist" and told the Senate that Americans should not be asked to "shoulder the burden of determining the political realities in any other country—and particularly not one remote from our shores, from our culture and from our experience." Unknowingly echoing Ball's secretive brief against the war, Kennan called for "a resolute and courageous liquidation of unsound positions" in Southeast Asia.[53]

The scholar-ambassador's critique of the American role in Vietnam excited a considerable interest in the cultural and political values undergirding his Realist dissent. A theme recurring in Kennan's writing over the years is that a society should be measured less by its influence on international politics than by the quality of life provided its citizens. America's internal vitality, he believes, is a precondition to success in her global role. Having thought, written, and spoken on parallel tracks with regard to Vietnam, Ball embraces Kennan's concerns on a broad range of issues—particularly the view that foreign policy cannot be fashioned irrespective of domestic imperatives.

Gratuitously establishing an international agenda, the Ball/Kennan "critical list" includes the need to allay the once omnipresent Cold War mentality, work out an acceptable modus vivendi with the Soviet Union on those problems common to both empires, restore Western Europe's self-confidence, improve—without illusory expectations—North-South hemispheric relations with an eye on more rationally distributing the world's resources, and urgently address the critical business of the arms race. Long before *perestroika* became a household word, Ball and Kennan were among the first Realist Revisionists to declare that the Cold War paradigm of international politics had completely lost its relevance.

Less scholarly and deliberate in his exposition than Kennan, Ball developed an independent style that was fundamentally shaped by his careers in law and investment banking. In stark contrast to his Nationalist School contemporaries of the 1950s and 1960s for whom the falling dominoes metaphor was an intellectually respected strategic theorem—and sounding a good deal like Kennan—Ball rejected the view that the East-West struggle was a zero-sum game: "If a state where we have only a peripheral strategic interest engages in a flirtation with Karl Marx why should we be upset?" Reminiscent of his Anti-Imperialist League brethren of a century ago, Ball asserted that global hegemony—for either superpower—is just as likely to beget liabilities as assets. Conversely, Soviet power was not necessarily enhanced by the multiplication of sovereignties calling themselves socialist or Communist. "For the life of me," he mused in 1968, "I cannot see how we would be endangered by a Communist regime in Mali or Brazzaville or Burundi; its most likely effect would be to cost Moscow or Peking some money." He went further by declaring that the United States should simply accept the "fact" that in many areas of the world Western democracy was "quite powerless to bring about the essential modernizing measures that are prerequisite to progress." Indeed, he brazenly maintains that in certain instances only authoritarianism is able to "break up entrenched obstacles to development."[54]

More recently Ball has charged that the sobriquet "Cold War" has been little more than a "fixation" serving the purposes of politicians and industrialists who possess a vested interest in the term's continued usage. "The tags and slogans that passed for wisdom three decades ago," Ball coolly related to the 1983 West Point graduates, "are no longer appropriate."[55] He noted in his commencement address that the continuation of the Cold War mind-set has led to an "indulgence in paradox": American politicians ridicule the Leninist hypothesis that capitalism fosters war, while exploiting the fear of the Soviets and voting appropriations for larger nuclear arsenals. Ball is manifestly impatient with this type of policy-making. Guided by his keen sense of history (another trait he shares with, and genuinely admires in, Kennan), he looks forward to the day when the East and West "can regard each other very much as Protestants and Catholics now view one another four hundred years after the Reformation and its bloody doctrinal effects."[56]

Further, like Kennan, Ball believes that the concept of Cold War has lost its relevance because global security is presently threatened by far more ominous dangers. A "fanatical and widely destructive religious fundamentalism," a "vaulting demographic curve," rapid depletion of the world's nonrenewable energy resources, a wasteful Third World arms race, increasing pollution of the atmosphere and water, and the "sheer madness" of the nuclear arms race are problems of much greater magnitude than Soviet adventurism into areas of marginal political or strategic importance to the United States. In their contemplative retirements, Ball and Kennan have transcended the partisan political world and have become formidable spokesmen on ecological, social, and moral concerns. For years they have been advancing critiques of international relations that only very recently have become popularly accepted.

Russians and Americans, Ball believes, are far more likely to profit by finding common solutions to common problems than by menacing each other. He is convinced that the Soviets understand as much and since leaving government has expressed the view that America's historic fear of the Soviet Union warrants reconsideration. The once expansionist Marxist-Leninist ideology is "very largely drained out of the Soviet system," and the Russians have "lost effective control of the world-wide Communist Party structure." The Soviet Union, Ball adds, "cannot assume too much on the part of their client states and must adopt a more cautious foreign policy";[57] indeed, the Soviet empire might well be unraveling. In company with his Realist collaborator Kennan, Ball believes that the gravest danger to the world and to the superstates would be Soviet and American inattention to their shared plight. While on a private junket to Europe in 1987, Ball ambitiously proposed "an alliance of adversaries" to address the compelling dangers common to the United States and the USSR. Though he is not yet prepared to completely discard containment, a term which he told his Italian audience should be redefined "to accord with the original intention of its inventor," he asserts that the policy needs to be revised to be made more relevant to more immediate concerns.[58]

Ball's overriding concerns are, geographically and culturally, very easily discernible. Perhaps to a fault, his global perspective has been shown to be— and remains—almost inflexibly Eurocentric. While in the process of rethinking America's containment policy, he remains a consistent and tireless proponent of European integration. In countless forums, he has repeated the view that Europe is "the sensitive center of world power"[59] and the center of the world's trouble as well. The conflation of Ball's affinity for Realist theory and his ethnocultural prejudices fix Europe at the center of his strategic equation. He routinely notes that Western Europe's aggregate industrial product supersedes that of the Soviet Union, that Americans still rely on the "Old Continent for the good health and continued enrichment of our common civilization," and that "the solid bone structure of our law and institutions" is European.[60] Confident of Europe's eventual political consolidation—and a celebrant of 1992 before there was such a blueprint for the further reduction of commercial and legal barriers among the European Community membership—Ball's vision proceeds from the premise that a united Europe could constitute "a third force," a third superpower to check and balance the political influence of the Soviet empire.[61] In his view, American foreign policy was never more successful than when focused on "constructing a framework for the economic cooperation among the nations of the West" after World War II,[62] and he believes that logic impels Europe to continue to build upon the work accomplished by the 1958 Rome Treaty.

Ball is unapologetically Eurocentric. The single qualification in his general thesis respecting the geographic center of the world's industrial power is that, like Kennan, he includes Japan among the industrial powers of "the Northern latitude." This prompted one observer to remark that "Ball was a "trilateralist before there was a trilateral commission."[63] His writings repeatedly emphasize the fact that 80 percent of the world's goods and services are produced north of the 30th parallel. "If my analysis, directs itself largely to the industrialized North," he apologetically remarks, "it is only because that is where the power is. If, narrowing the lens further, my focus fixes largely on Europe, it is because that is where most of the danger is."[64]

Virtually ignoring Third World nations as factors in his grand constructs of the global economic and political structure, Ball claims to write "not from a lack of compassion" for the developing countries but "from a realistic sense of the limitations in American wisdom and comprehension" of their problems. In dissenting from Johnson's Vietnam policy he argued that American policy officers had too easily been seduced by developmental theories and had failed to appreciate the "crucial conceptual distinction between the problems of the Northern Zone and the peripheral Southern areas." The object of American policy should be to raise the standard of living of the South without naive illusions about eliminating "or even narrowing" the disparity of wealth between North and South. Ball is not optimistic about the likelihood of a speedy correction of the hemispheric imbalance of wealth—a condition, he notes, which has existed for thousands of years. "In spite of the hyperbole of political speeches," he states in an air of resignation, "we are not going to reduce the disparity."[65]

Among the intractable Third World problems which Ball considers ill-comprehended by the industrialized states is overpopulation. In the early 1970s, Ball's former staff chief George Springsteen has ruefully noted, demography became one of his "hobby horses."[66] Springsteen was kept busy supplying Ball with every conceivable type of analysis of world population trends. Predictably, Ball is wholly pessimistic about a solution. There is "nothing more grotesquely futile," he lamented in 1975, "than the effort to chase a vaulting demographic curve."[67] He absorbed Malthus and other theoretical literature, combed charts provided him by United Nations offices, and embraced what were then considered "alarmist" hypotheses including Padock and Padock's *Famine 1975*. The most that Western nations could hope to do in Third World countries, Ball reluctantly concluded, is to encourage family planning, support land reforms that will keep people on farms, and "make clear that we will not be eager to pour resources into hopeless situations."[68]

The final concern on Ball's critical list, one with perhaps less immediacy and far greater magnitude, is the nuclear arms race. The dreary strategic realities of the atomic age have become one of Ball's as well as Kennan's special interests in recent years. Although the two disagree on the wisdom of the "no first use" principle, which Kennan supports and which Ball believes is implied in American policy and requires no proclamation until the imbalance between conventional forces in Europe is further narrowed, they agree on one fundamental aspect to the problem of strategic nuclear weaponry: Given the possibility of massive, indiscriminate destruction of the planet, generalized radioactive fallout, and nuclear winter, debate over the doctrines governing nuclear weapons is reduced to disarmingly simple political and moral choices between national survival and suicide. Exceedingly impatient with protracted negotiations about force levels in recent years, Ball decries the seemingly limitless dialogue about numbers of missiles, delivery systems, and throw weights as so much "mischievous nonsense." The United States has indulged itself for too long in the assumption that it can maintain peace by stockpiling nuclear weapons. The security of the West, he argued recently, will not be won at "cosmic poker" but with rational political arrangements that respects the legitimate interests of the Soviet Union.[69]

Obfuscating the debate over nuclear weapons, in Ball's view, is "an elite group of economists, mathematicians, and political scientists, which has pre-empted the bomb as its special intellectual property," seeking "to impose logic on inherently irrational" scenarios.[70] These high priests of Nukespeak are unencumbered by rules of evidence, since there are no past nuclear wars against which to judge their scenarios. Centered in think tanks such as the Hudson Institute and the Rand Corporation, which Ball has satirized as their "monasteries," they write the nuclear doctrines for American politicians. In particular, he believes, the devotees of the once popular and now dubious Strategic Defense Initiative (SDI) and "limited war fighting" strategies in the Reagan administration employed a flawed rationale in rigidly basing their views on Soviet capabilities. Effective deterrence, he insists, exists far below the number of weapons to which the United States has been driven by an irrational fear of the Russian nuclear force. Even parity is rendered meaning-less by the swelling of arsenals above certain absolute numbers. The point at which it mattered how many missiles and delivery systems the United States and the Soviet Union possessed, Ball believes, has long since passed.[71]

In terms of nuclear doctrine, the 1980s were revolutionary. In Ball's view, the Reagan administration unthinkingly scrapped the constructive arrange-ments forged during the past quarter-century: SDI, if deployed, would mind-lessly abrogate the 1972 Anti-Ballistic Missile Treaty—which he considers one of the few effective brakes on the arms race. By so zealously promoting "Star Wars," Ball concluded, Reagan or his successors would unwittingly set in motion "forces that seem almost certain to trigger a furious acceleration of the nuclear arms race and seriously jeopardize the confidence and support of [America's] NATO allies." In decidedly passionate rhetoric, he has criticized Reagan's uncompromising attachment to SDI as the "whimsical antic" one might expect from an "absolute monarch." He has recently, and happily, conceded that George Bush and Defense secretary Richard Cheney appear to have more sense. Throughout the 1980s, however, discussion centered too much on technical speculation and too little on the political and strategic implications of "Star Wars." Suggesting that America's European allies would have every right to question the credibility of an American nuclear deterrent once SDI is deployed,[72] Ball was quite dubious that its technical assets would outweigh its political liabilities. Because "Star Wars" is "highly likely to fail"—if it is proven to be either technically unfeasible or too expensive—he believes that the United States would be wise to "bargain it away for some useful Soviet concession."[73]

Nevertheless, the former under secretary is far from being an advocate of unilateral disarmament. He has continually advised that in its bilateral relationship with the Soviet Union, the United States should concentrate on "maintaining and exploiting the political potential of the nuclear standoff with respect to those areas where there is a clear over-lapping of interests." Where the more serious political difficulties exist—that is, in the area of the world that would become a European nuclear battlefield—he reminds his readers of the profound differences in perspective within the Alliance: "Americans have been conditioned to regard nuclear weapons as a sword of Damocles precariously hanging over civilization." The fact remains, however, that many "informed Europeans" consider the nuclear forces "not as curses" but as blessings and believe that nuclear arms have finally delivered them from the cycle of wars that has plagued them for centuries. For fear of reinstating that cycle, he insightfully notes, Europeans "are not greatly impressed by the shrill demands of American politicians that they increase their expenditures for conventional forces." Joining others such as Henry Kissinger, Ball has called for the thorough redesigning of European conventional defense arrangements as part of the recently quickening nuclear arms reduction process. Without providing a detailed political formula for implementation, his vision suggests strengthening and modernizing of Europe's conventional capabilities in order to "raise the threshold for the use of nuclear weapons until it ceases to have meaning."[74]

Not normally given to populist impulses, Ball is delighted that so many private citizens have recently sought to reclaim nuclear policy from the self-styled nuclear nobility and "test it against their own pragmatic wisdom." While contending that foreign policy is primarily the business of elites, he concedes that "the loaf has to be leavened from time to time" with the objective participation of the unschooled. Despite the fact that those whom he disparages as "the scholastics" have attempted to trivialize the public's role in the discussion of a national nuclear arms policy, he gives the American people a great deal of credit for "intuitively understand[ing] that warheads are not weapons"—that nuclear weapons utterly lack utility as instruments of politics or war. Even presidents cannot claim meaningful expertise on the subject of atomic weapons. "Few come to office," he warns, "with profound comprehension of the implications of nuclear bombs." As innocents, chief executives routinely defer to the nuclear establishment types who, he believes, take themselves far too seriously and, worse, "have been enthralled by the conceptual fantasy of controlled escalation," a concept he believes is a "contradiction in terms."[75]

In "the world according to George Ball"—in which there is seemingly little hope of stemming the tide of overpopulation, averting ecological disaster, redressing disparities of wealth, or solving the contradictions of the nuclear age—how are peace, prosperity, and stability to be maintained? Surprisingly, for a man altogether devoted to more rational formulations of statecraft, the former diplomat finds the answer outside the purview of government. On more than one occasion he has reminded the author that he considers himself "preeminently a man of the private sector."[76] Although this curious self-conception has more than once been interpreted as a psychological ploy to shroud his considerable disappointment about never having become secretary of state,[77] it is true that Ball's conceptions of international relations are firmly rooted in his exceptionally rich experience as an international lawyer and investment banker. It is also true that the confluence of these two strands of thought—his theoretical Realism on the one hand and his embrace of a liberal capitalist internationalism on the other—have posed considerable problems of analysis. Attempting to reconcile his diplomatic Realism, particularly his position on Vietnam, with his unyielding aspiration for a "one world" economy can be perplexing. As historian and political economist David P. Calleo has noted, "There seems a rather considerable cleavage between George Ball, the realist critic of Vietnam, and George Ball, the rather exuberant enthusiast of functionalist integration and a new age of multinational corporations."[78] Though he has always been resistant to his identification as a dove, Ball has been most consistently reluctant to mix arms and diplomacy. But when his seasoned views on the international economy are considered, one finds that he is anything but an isolationist. Ball might most reliably be described as a theoretical cousin of the eighteenth-century European classical liberals or the American "dollar diplomatists" of a century ago. The former under secretary is an ardent exponent of "independent internationalism," which, as a mechanism of private capitalism, seeks to integrate the world's economic institutions.

Since the 1950s Ball has extolled the increasing interdependence of global economic institutions. In 1967 he coined the term "cosmocorp" to describe what he considers the desirable end of a completely integrated world economy. A champion of multilateral economic cooperation among the Western democracies, he has chastised audiences in the United States, Europe, and Japan by flatly stating that protectionism and self-interested economic nationalism (particularly currency devaluation) are the world's principal obstacles to general economic growth. He argued throughout the 1960s that a cardinal obligation of government is to insure the free exchange of goods and services across international frontiers. When in the late 1960s a raft of highly critical Radical Revisionist literature attacked the power of international capitalism, Ball staunchly rose to the defense of the primary institution of liberal internationalist capitalism—the multinational corporation. His astute defense of the power elite of the global economic system was both transcendent and quite controversial. He not only defended the remote and mysterious power of international capitalism's megacompanies but audaciously theorized that the multinational corporation will ultimately supersede the institution of the nation state—which he believes is "still rooted in archaic concepts unsympathetic to the needs of our complex world."[79]

In a 1967 *Fortune* magazine article entitled "The Promise of the Multinational Corporation," Ball confessed that he "[knew] of few things more hopeful for the future than the growing determination of American business to regard national boundaries as no longer fixing the horizons of their corporate activity." Simply put, he believes that most nations are inadequate as economic units and that global politics and global economics are "out of phase" with each other. He applauded the multinational for moving elements of production around the world with great facility and for "planning and acting in terms that are well in advance of the political ideas by which the world is organized." With a particular eye on European integration, he confidently forecast at the end of the 1960s that the significance of free trade principles and common markets "rests not only on their economic efficacy but also on the seeds of political unity they carry with them."[80]

From the platform of each of the five government offices he has occupied, Ball has argued that the United States desperately needs to rethink its economic destiny. His formula (for which, as we have seen, he has been roundly attacked) includes relinquishing the hope of competing favorably with cheap labor markets in the secondary manufacturing sector, more rigorously asserting the American comparative advantage in the high technology industries, opening American markets to the Third World producers, and more regular economic consultation and institutional cooperation with Europe and Japan. As a private attorney and as a U.S. trade representative during his career in the State Department, Ball has often been the target of popular outcry against the export of jobs to foreign states. He has sensed the powerlessness that consumers feel in relationship to the new economies of scale of the multinationals and knows well the "hypersensitivity to anything that suggests colonialism" in the host countries of American enterprise.[81] He is, nonetheless, insistent in his contention that the United States must set an example as a model liberal and free trading state, even while risking temporary dislocation in its own key industries (such as textiles). For too long, he has argued, Americans have failed to provide leadership and have unwisely engaged in shortsighted practices. "It was easier for a rich nation to appropriate public funds for foreign aid," he admonished in 1969 (with direct reference to U.S. trade policies toward Latin America), "than to grant foreign producers access to its markets."[82] Although Ball is proud of his ministerial role in GATT (General Agreement on Tariffs and Trade) during the Kennedy administration, he will clearly not be satisfied that the world has rationally ordered its economic house until each country can pursue its comparative trade advantages completely freely.

Otherwise an apologist for the international business community, Ball admits that there has been abuse and that "some kind of regulation"[83] of international capitalism is warranted. He is certainly not blind to the loathsome consequences of what Radical critics refer to as "economic imperialism." He is not averse, for example, to lambasting American companies for engaging in "bribery and kickbacks." These practices, he warns, "give substance to the Communist myth—already widely believed in Third World countries—that capitalism is fundamentally corrupt." The West "cannot have it both ways," glorifying the virtues of competition "and at the same time buy[ing] influence with under the table transactions." But it is also important to note that Ball dismisses the bulk of the criticism leveled against the institution of the multinational corporation as so much "irresponsible comment" from "the sages of the New Left." He writes that the capitalist countries "must strip the multinational corporation of the [negative] mythology that surrounds it," and he maintains that multinationals are still "the best mechanism we have so far developed for spreading private capital and know-how around the world."[84]

Keenly apprised of the complex scholarly debates over American foreign and economic policy of the past forty years, and having gained unparalleled experience from varied professional enterprises in the private sector, Ball remains a principal force in the foreign policy Establishment. Indeed, since the passing of John McCloy in April 1989, Ball is now widely understood to be the senior paragon in what is admittedly an ill-defined institution. As an author, frequent symposium discussant, occasional Princeton professor, speaker-in-demand, and, perhaps, a congenital contrarian, he continues to play a prominent role as an elite opinion maker, and his frequent commentary on foreign affairs and defense issues continues to instruct and compel. Ball's incisive analyses of world events still regularly appear on the pages of America's most influential publications. His forceful, and occasionally brazen, advocacy and elegant prose continue to irritate, cajole, and sometimes convince a new generation of foreign policy practitioners.

To his credit, Ball has not, like so many at his stage in life, become philosophically dogmatic. Indeed, analysis of his Vietnam dissent of the 1960s has been shown to be complicated by the fact that his convictions are drawn from a decidedly mixed intellectual bag. His middle western cultural roots, his immersion in classical literature, a disparate lot of mentors, thirty years in the private sector, and his varied government service are the diverse components of a hybrid mind. There is indeed, as Calleo noted above, "a considerable cleavage" in Ball's intellectual composition. A Realist, he dreams of global economic integration that transcends the crude balance of power predilections of orthodox Realism. A liberal internationalist, he is seemingly ambivalent about the underdeveloped world, causing one to resist ascribing to him a liberal's optimism. An ardent commercial "One Worlder," he is quite willing to accept sectors of the economic world being cordoned off with the rope of Marxism. A Vietnam dove and an apostle of restraint in innumerable crises where American power was applied, he has endorsed initiatives to precipitously strengthen conventional defenses in Europe and the United States and defies definition as a neo-isolationist.

This study has endeavored to discover the sometimes subtle—and sometimes not so subtle—relationship between ideology and analysis. As Chapter 3 described, Vietnam-dissenter Ball engaged the advocates of escalation with well-informed and well-reasoned arguments, but his rebellion against the prevailing winds of the containment doctrine was at least as much a reflection of a complex theoretical construct of the world which he continuously carried around in his head as it was a sustained and systematic examination of America's ordeal in Indochina. Put most simply, he believed that the United States would gain little ground in achieving the transcendent goals of an improved international trading structure and a more soberly defined balance of forces among the industrial powers by waging an ambiguous political war in Indochina. Ball once impertinently asked: "Have we learned [in Vietnam] or only failed?"[85] Americans may have to face the inhibiting fact that there will be crises and environments in which the application of their military power is inappropriate and counterproductive. As they confront future challenges, perhaps in the Baltic states, perhaps in the Middle East, perhaps in Central America, it would be wise for their warlords to carefully heed this story. They might well profit from a consideration of Ball's strategic Realism, his warnings against unilateralism, his conviction that regimes receiving American assistance must meet some meaningful standard of performance—and most particularly, his willingness to permit peoples to determine their own destiny. As Ball's good friend Adlai Stevenson once admonished, "It is often easier to fight for principles than to live up to them."[86] So it is.

Epilogue

GEORGE BALL is now in his eighties. At a time in life when most public figures would be content to indulge themselves in a private life which had so long been subordinated to the tangled affairs of state, he continues to be deeply engaged in the most complex issues of the day. He has, on more than one occasion, admitted to being too old for service in the American government—and too young for service in the Chinese government. Despite his seniority, he is still a significant force in the sometimes heated debate regarding America's role in the global village. Ironically, the force of his pen—which is now wholly unrestrained by politics—imparts him with considerably more intellectual license than he once had as a subcabinet officer of the government. Brushing aside the effects of transitory infirmities, Ball brusquely dismisses advice to slow down from those whom he disparages as his "quacks" and aggressively assaults his projects. Though with admittedly less stamina (and decidedly less self-criticism) than in times now past, he labors to insure that his voice continues to be heard.

Old habits die hard. Occasionally, in the process of investigating a colorful career and discovering the complexities of a man, I imagined what Ball's days must have been like in the spring of 1965 when, after twelve or fourteen hours at the State Department, he would work through the evening developing his case against escalation. As I came to appreciate nuances of his thought processes, I also noted important aspects of his physical and intellectual constitution, particularly his capacity to thoroughly immerse himself in an argument on behalf of a conviction. At the outset of my spring and summer visits to Princeton for research and interviews with Ball, a pattern developed. Typically, he would graciously—and, at first, somewhat formally—greet me at the office porch of his residence at 8:30 A.M. and we would very succinctly discuss one or two substantive questions from the previous day's encounter. Then, as I meandered down to his basement archive where file cabinets and notebooks line the interior walls, he would bore into his own work with a degree of intensity that all but precluded the slightest interruption. After laboring hours-on-end rummaging through papers, speeches, letters, newspapers clippings, keepsakes, and family business records, I would plod up the stairs at 5:00 P.M. to find a huge frame of a man still hunched over a grand French provincial desk utterly submerged in books and papers, still pecking away on a word processor keyboard. He always seemed to be in a rush, racing to meet a deadline—for publications as varied as the *Bulletin of Atomic Scientists* and the *Washington Post*—or working on his latest book. (In the time it took me to complete this volume, Ball wrote two of his own.) His zeal for work, the time he was willing to spend assisting me, his hospitality, and, at the cocktail hour, his good cheer—all seemed limitless. I was delighted to be able to study not just a strategic mind, but a whole man—brimming with humor, prejudices, appetites. Ball is not merely a man with a sense of duty: he has a passion for civilization that is most engaging.

Immersion in his personal effects and public papers (which he liberally borrowed from the government offices he held) quickly revealed a distinct pattern in his political and strategic thinking. Simply stated, Ball shows little regard for the opinion of the majority. Without behaving ostentatiously, he can be quite unconventional as a policy analyst. He absolutely deplores cliché mongers and almost axiomatically rejects the "bureaucratic view" of a problem, which he would define—and denigrate—as something believed but no longer examined. Despite having earned a reputation as a commonsense, Establishment sage, Ball is somewhat of an intellectual maverick. An audacious dissenter during the Vietnam era, disdainful of what he considers America's uncritical support of Israel, and prepared to lock arms and seek common cause with the "Evil Empire," he has regularly been identified with progressive, controversial, and unpopular positions which, in time, seem to prevail.

But prescience is not persuasion. Indeed, the great tragedy is that few politicians can afford to heed Ball's advice. While many agree with his analyses, they have often found his advice to be politically unbearable. At a point in his career when he might have moderated his views (or at least the manner in which he expressed them) in order to enhance his influence, Ball spoke out with frankness and passion. For his strident partisan attacks on Nixon in 1968 and, especially, his discomforting analyses on the Arab-Israeli quarrel, he is considered a pariah by his investment banking associates in New York—those to whom he once referred as "the presiding Deities on Wall Street." His unvarnished opinions have caused him to be thrown off the boards of directors of a dozen corporations, including Standard Oil, Singer, and the Upjohn Company. In the past ten years in particular, his intellectual honesty and defense of principle have caused a precipitous narrowing of his influence— and of his associations. In a representative episode, writing that he could not maintain membership in an institution "that would exclude Jesus Christ,"[1] Ball quit New York's prestigious Links Club after a thirteen-year affiliation when it refused to admit his Jewish friend, former Treasury secretary Michael Blumenthal. Not the least bit contrite, Ball puckishly regards these dislocations in the cause of veracity as "good fun." As we entered the Harvard Club together recently, Ball quipped that it was one of the few places in the city he could still join if he wished to.

For most of his career an avid correspondent and easily accessible to interviewers, Ball has recently become more reclusive. Deferring most inquirers to the distillation of events in his memoirs, he declines nearly all of the many requests for appointments he receives from scholars and journalists. Not normally given to sustained moods of nostalgia, occasionally he has shared his private thoughts about his colorful life and the lives of a number of his equally colorful cohorts. For the most part these conversations about his private insights into people and his own dreams and fantasies were, by agreement, "off-the-record" and are not mentioned in this work. One episode, however, was told without restriction and is pregnant with intriguing contemplations. Lamenting the uninspiring group of candidates at the outset of the 1976 presidential primary season, Ball was flattered when Blumenthal and Ambassador Averell Harriman offhandedly suggested that he seek America's highest office. Though he insists that it was really a "non-event," he speaks of his ephemeral presidential ambitions with ill-concealed glee—an emotion stemming much less from his viability as a candidate and much more from the certitude of his political and strategic convictions. Ball briefly considered, then dropped, the idea. Although nothing has been written about this episode, it has certainly stimulated the imagination of a curious Boswell.

How would candidate Ball have been perceived? Do his Vietnam dissent and other independent positions on major international issues suggest a standard of leadership by which he would have been favorably judged? How would his cosmopolitanism, "Northwesternism," and foreign policy Realism have fared under the bright lights of a populist event like an American presidential campaign? Where, and to what result, might he have led the country? These questions are of course unanswerable. Indeed, it is written somewhere in the canons of scholarship that historians should forswear such postulating and content themselves with finding and publishing "the facts." I find myself, however, irresistibly beguiled by the prospect of addressing the apparition of a George Ball campaign for the presidency.

Though he would be perceived primarily as "a foreign policy candidate," Ball's domestic political agenda for the 1970s and 1980s would most clearly have been faithful to the liberal vision of his party which had been evolving since the New Deal era. His open admiration of Franklin Roosevelt, his *pro bono* defense of Henry Wallace during the McCarthy era, a close political association with Adlai Stevenson, his practical experience under Kennedy and Johnson, and his close personal friendships with liberal stalwarts Galbraith and Schlesinger would have insured Ball's identification with the most progressive elements of the Democratic party for the past forty years. He would have campaigned for the "helping hand" agenda of his party because of what he felt was a moral obligation—and, most particularly, because it made good economic sense. He could reliably be counted on by labor for a higher minimum wage, by the retired for equitable social security benefits, by farmers for a compulsion to open foreign markets, and by students for a national educational plan. Indeed, Ball's great faith in education would most assuredly have shaped his campaign. He would have been "an education candidate." Solemn appeals to a country he perceived to be in the throes of a moral crisis would have punctuated his campaign rhetoric. He would have warned against the "the ordeal of modernity," which he would lament as the weakening of America's traditional institutions, and would have railed against "our anemic sense of community and common purpose." For all his urbane sophistication, Ball might have struck a quite conservative—though nonsectarian—chord as he mourned the loss of "certitude derived from religious conviction." Though himself a professed agnostic, candidate Ball would have quietly applauded the spiritual revival of the mid-1970s.

In sizing up this presidential aspirant touting his origins in the heartland of the country, the American people would have first considered what his prominent role in government during the 1960s revealed about his leadership assets and his approach to foreign and domestic policy. Though it will be recalled that Vietnam consumed only a fraction of his time, and as much as he would have liked it otherwise, Ball would have been perceived by the American people in 1976 as a Left liberal, a dove, and a model of gentlemanly dissent for his role in the Vietnam drama. This die was cast when the *Pentagon Papers* revelations secured his place in history as a symbol of what is now nearly universally considered to be the "right side" of the debate on the war and as the first to form judgments later confirmed by events. Voters would have regarded Ball as a supremely self-assured statesman and an independent thinker. Though he would not have stated it so flatly, he could claim that the course of history would have been profoundly altered had either of two presidents acted upon his recommendations, and he would have gained significant endorsements saying as much. As steadfast hawk Ellsworth Bunker, ambassador to South Vietnam, once wrote, "It is all so clear now that had [Ball's] advice been followed in 1961 much tragedy would have been averted."[2]

Because he was so uncompromising in characterizing the Vietnam War as an unmitigated error, candidate Ball would have campaigned in 1976 to align America's security commitments with her political and material resources. His public record would clearly demonstrate that he had not fallen prey to what Galbraith once called the "superpower complex," defined as the assumption that America can shape events in culturally remote areas of the world, or the "superpower anxiety," defined as the unconscious urge to try. He would have declared the Cold War competition for Third World hegemony finished and asserted that poverty and the forces of nationalism in the developing nations render pat ideological categories irrelevant. To those within earshot of his stump speeches, it would be abundantly clear that, as president, Ball would not engage American power in marginally significant areas of the world without the assured sanction of the American people, the Congress, and the country's principal allies. Though one can hardly imagine Ball making ad hominem attacks on McNamara, Rusk, or the ghost of LBJ, as a Democratic candidate in 1976 he would have sought to exorcise the Vietnam demon from his party by denouncing the war as "the dead end of unilateralism" and the indiscriminate use of "undisciplined power."

Ball's broad geopolitical views would have dominated discussion of his campaign, and he would have justifiably boasted international experience unmatched by any in the race from either party. His work in international law and finance, his frontline roles as a trade negotiator, his trials by fire as crisis manager during the Cuban, Congo, and Cyprus predicaments, and his intimacy with European elites would certainly have augmented his presidential résumé. Making international trade a campaign issue in 1976, and probably obsessive about instructing voters on the benefits of the Open Door, Ball would have searched (probably in vain) for a way in which to reduce the complexities of global commerce to salable political maxims.

But it was Ball's Vietnam dissent that disclosed his most fundamental strategic assumptions. For better or for worse, voters would have come to understand him as the cosmopolitan lawyer-diplomat who argued against the conventional interpretation of the South East Asia Treaty and who wrote well-reasoned briefs against the war. The essential contours of his world view were all in the memos, and the memos (some of them, at any rate) were in the *Pentagon Papers*. Power mattered. Ball would resolve not to dispatch American forces to corners of the planet where risks outweighed gains—where, for example, Chinese or Russian power, or the forces of independent nationalism, were more immediately engaged than American power. He would have respected the concept of "vital spheres-of-influence." Unlike others in the 1976 campaign for the Democratic nomination, Ball would have argued against linking issues of great magnitude, such as nuclear force reduction, to issues he considered secondary, such as human rights. This would not have been from any lack of sympathy but would have stemmed from his belief that much could be accomplished in the former area, where vital interests of states intersected, and very little in the latter area, where they did not.

Though Ball's fundamental conceptions would have appealed to liberal factions in both parties—and to a nation reeling from its longest war—his rhetoric would have been roundly attacked and perhaps willfully misinterpreted by the Right. He would no doubt have been labeled a "neo-isolationist" and characterized as "soft on communism." The consummate Establishment man, in 1976 Ball would have found himself in the ironic situation of having to take his case to the American people for the first time in his career. Though it has been privately remarked that "George would have difficulty knowing what populism was,"[3] he would have been forced by political necessity to broaden his message. Though he may have initially struggled to communicate with voters who were not devotees of *Foreign Affairs* magazine, he might also, with his very considerable gift for exposition, have been surprisingly successful.

A single artifact aptly illustrates why Ball's campaign could very well have been caricatured as "the politics of dual identity." On a bookshelf of his 12,000-volume personal library in his spacious office in Princeton sits David Halberstam's antiestablishment exposé, *The Best and the Brightest*. The volume is personally inscribed by the author in a most unusual—and telling—manner. On a half-sheet of Halberstam's personal stationary, folded and loosely placed in the inside cover of the book, are the words: "To George Ball with admiration and affection. . . . signed in detachable form in case any of the best and the brightest come by for dinner and check out your library."[4] In an otherwise antiheroic characterization of the bureaucrats who waged war in Vietnam, Halberstam celebrates Ball as a dissenter with wisdom and clairvoyance who also maintained his good standing within the Establishment. In the course of a presidential campaign, Ball would no doubt have profited from key Establishment endorsements but would at the same time have renounced the basic thrust of foreign policy espoused by the Establishment for the past quarter-century.

His stump speeches in 1976, including his distinctive metaphors, would have been laced with the discordant elements of Bryan-like populism and Kennan-like Realism. He might very well have stated in the campaign (as he would later):

As is so often the case in a democracy the people are proving wiser than their government. The American people have heard and are heeding the message. They do not envisage their country as the world's *gendarme* or even its nanny. And, it seems to me, they have given notice that if they are to support another major deployment of American forces, those in command will first have to show that the conflict at issue is of more than marginal relevance to our interests, that the regime we are seeking to support has deep roots throughout the countryside, that both the political and physical terrain are not hopelessly inhospitable, and that we can achieve limited objectives without committing disproportionately large forces or outraging world opinion.[5]

Ball would have sought to provide a blueprint for foreign policy leadership in the post-Vietnam era. Loath to fall back to policies that had emanated from an uncritical adherence to doctrine and equally disdainful of simple reactive pragmatism (witnessed more recently in the administrations of Reagan and Bush), he would have maintained that policy must be fashioned with clearly defined structures in mind. "It seems to me," he may have said from the stump,

> that many of our postwar policies have mixed a vague and irrelevant universalism with a new and transitional pragmatism, leading to improvised crusades and crusading improvisations. And what is bad can get worse. As we outgrow our old missionary habits we can easily fall into a mindless and automatic pattern of dealing with problems always for the short term, unless, quite self-consciously, we develop a satisfactory conceptual framework in which to fit the jagged edges of our day-to-day decisions. Great as it is, our power is finite, and we need a clear frame of reference to tell us how we can use it best—or whether in given situations we should use it at all.[6]

But while candidate Ball would have railed against the multisyllabic evils of universalism and pragmatism, he would in no way have campaigned against the basic moral assumptions of American foreign policy. In his own esoteric manner, Ball would have attempted to rekindle patriotism in an age when many Americans had lost confidence in their traditions, institutions, and leaders. While attacking globalism and the doctrines that gave rise to a generation of war in Vietnam, Ball would at the same time have maligned the war's more exuberant critics. For while there were painful lessons to be learned from the ordeal in Vietnam, Ball would have projected a very positive message about the inherent strength of American society—particularly its principles of political economy.

Candidate Ball would have characterized the late 1960s and early 1970s as a period during which sensible debate had given way to hysteria. Behind academia's ivy-covered walls, he had come to believe, "sober historians" were outshouted by their more youthful radical counterparts who "twist events like pretzels to fit them into the Marxist mold" and "strip the American experience of any glory or heroism." He would have renounced the period's pervasive nihilism with its emphasis on the antihero and called for a moral and even spiritual regeneration. He would have lashed out at pornographers "who confuse exhibitionism with liberty," sharply criticized the glorification of violence, and renounced the prevailing national mood which "substitutes a puerile cynicism for loyalty to the community or any actions beyond self-interest."[7]

Ultimately, the campaign would have turned to the question of character. Ball's challengers would have wondered out loud whether he behaved opportunistically by identifying for so long with the Johnson administration after the escalation, against which he was so passionately disposed, commenced in earnest. Who, after all, did the lawyer turned under secretary serve—the president, the American people, or his own professional calling? His dilemma of having to choose between career and conviction would have become a campaign issue. Though Ball has not second-guessed his behavior, the candidate might very well have found it difficult to answer repeated questions about his personal choices in the period between 1964 and 1966. He may have found campaigning uncomfortable and demeaning. Even his most stalwart admirers concede that he would have looked out of place shaking hands in factory shift lines or kissing babies. But though he may have been an unhappy candidate, with his considerable talents for analysis and explanation, he might well have been an inspiring president.

Notes

In a few instances, citations to items in journals and the popular press are incomplete, because these items were consulted in George Ball's personal scrapbooks, in which specific dates and page numbers were not always recorded.

Introduction

1. Michael Harris, "The Quiet Realist of Foreign Policy," *San Francisco Chronicle*, May 23, 1982.
2. Inaugural address of President John F. Kennedy, January 20, 1961, cited in Steven Cohen, *Vietnam: Anthology and Guide to "A Television History"* (New York: Alfred A. Knopf, 1982), p. 75.
3. Marquis Childs, "Ball on Vietnam: A Necessary Voice," *Washington Post*, June 20, 1966.

Chapter 1

1. George W. Ball to Dean Rusk, June 30, 1977, Personal Papers of George W. Ball, Princeton, N.J. (hereafter cited as PGWB).
2. John Osborne, "Unheretical Critic of Foreign Policy," *New Republic*, June 15, 1968, pp. 27–29.
3. Edward Hallett Carr, *What is History?* (New York: Vintage Books, 1961), p. 11.
4. U.S. Department of State, "Special Inquiry into George Wildman Ball, Results of Investigation," Freedom of Information Act Case No. 8600931. See also George W. Ball, *The Past Has Another Pattern: Memoirs* (New York: W. W. Norton & Company, 1982), p. 1–9.
5. George W. Ball to the author, January 10, 1989.
6. Ball, *Past*, p. 3.
7. George W. Ball interview, Princeton, N.J., April 17, 1986.
8. Ball, *Past*, p. 22
9. George W. Ball, *Diplomacy for a Crowded World, An American Foreign Policy* (Boston: Little, Brown & Company, 1976), p. 155.
10. Ibid., p. 171
11. Ball, *Past*, p. 23.
12. Ball, *Diplomacy*, p. 164.
13. Ball, *Past*, pp. 361–62.
14. J. Robert Schaetzel interview, Bethesda, Md., March 29, 1985; George S. Springsteen interview, Washington D.C., March 28, 1985; Lord Roll interview, Princeton, N.J., April 9, 1986. All respondents perceive Ball as "a European-American" and a man whose cultural affinities are decidedly "Western."

15. George W. Ball, *The Discipline of Power: Essentials of a Modern World Structure* (Boston: Little, Brown & Company, 1968), p. 259.

16. Ball, *Past*, p. 8.

17. George W. Ball and Douglas B. Ball interview, Princeton, N.J., April 17, 1986.

18. Ball, *Past*, p. 9.

19. Ibid., pp. 10–11.

20. Ibid., p. 426.

21. Ibid.

22. Ball, *Diplomacy*, p. 427 and p. 325.

23. Ball, *Past*, p. 11.

24. George W. Ball to Bernard De Voto, January 6, 1938, PGWB.

25. Found among Ball's personal papers is a box of papers from his undergraduate years at Northwestern, including syllabi from his literature courses, theme papers, and class notes.

26. Ball interview, April 17, 1986.

27. Ball, *Past*, p. 14.

28. George W. Ball, "Letter Addressed to Myself to be Read on the Day I Enlist," unpublished essay, PGWB.

29. Ibid.

30. Ibid.

31. Ibid.

32. U.S. Department of State, "Special Inquiry into George Wildman Ball, Results of Investigation," Freedom of Information Act Case No. 8600931.

33. Ball, *Past*, p. 17.

34. Ibid., pp. 15–19.

35. Arthur M. Schlesinger, Jr., interview, New York, N.Y., April 11, 1985; John Kenneth Galbraith interview, Cambridge, Mass., April 4, 1984. Both emphasized Ball's New Deal experience as a primary conditioning factor in his political development.

36. Columbia Typographical Union to Meyer Feldman, December 11, 1961, PGWB.

37. In Ball's personal letter file and papers are numerous correspondence and cancelled checks from campaign contributions—a normal sum being $1,000—to various Democratic candidates.

38. Schaetzel interview, March 29, 1985.

39. Ball interview, April 17, 1986.

40. William P. Bundy interview, Princeton, N.J., April 6, 1985.

41. Ibid.

42. Ibid.

43. Ball, *Past*, p. 20.

44. Ball interview, April 17, 1986.

45. U.S. Department of State, "Special Inquiry into George Wildman Ball, Results of Investigation," Freedom of Information Act Case No. 8600931. See also Ball, *Past*, p. 1–9.

46. Ball, *Past*, p. 21.

47. John Bartlow Martin, *Adlai Stevenson of Illinois* (Garden City, N.Y.: Doubleday & Company, 1976), pp. 644-45. Arthur Schlesinger, Jr., has told the author that "it is quite wrong to argue that the Kennedy group 'embraced Acheson's conception of unremitting Cold War.'" Schlesinger asserts that Kennedy "was much closer in his general views to the Harriman-Bowles-Stevenson line than to Acheson" and adds that

"too many historians are misled by the rhetoric of the inaugural address." Arthur Schlesinger, Jr., to the author, August 27, 1988. I responded to Schlesinger (David DiLeo to Arthur M. Schlesinger, Jr., September 12, 1988) by writing: "JFK has been interpreted as both a pragmatist (Schlesinger) *and* as a dogmatic Cold Warrior (Richard Walton). It is important to note that even essentially admiring accounts regard Vietnam as Kennedy's 'great failure in foreign policy' (Schlesinger, *A Thousand Days*, p. 910). Where Kennedy's sober realism served him well—i.e. Berlin and Cuba—it may have failed him in Southeast Asia. Again, as Professor Schlesinger concludes (*Robert Kennedy and His Times*, vol. 2, p. 758), 'Kennedy's Vietnam legacy was dual and contradictory.' "

48. William Bundy interview, April 6, 1985.

49. Ball interview, April 17, 1986.

50. Ball, *Past*, p. 21.

51. Ibid., p. 23.

52. George W. Ball, interview with William F. Buckley, Jr., "Firing Line," Subject #470, Southern Educational Communications Association, August 2, 1981.

53. Ball, *Past*, pp. 29–42.

54. Ibid., pp. 29–41 passim.

55. Ibid.

56. James M. Dougherty, *The Politics of Wartime Aid* (Westport, Conn.: Greenwood Press, 1978), p. 9.

57. Ball, *Past*, pp. 29–42 passim.

58. Ibid.

59. Ibid., p. 42.

60. U.S. Department of State, "Special Inquiry into George Wildman Ball, Results of Investigation," Freedom of Information Act Case No. 8600931.

61. David MacIsaac, *Strategic Bombing in World War Two: The Story of the United States' Strategic Bombing Survey*, 9 vols. (New York: Garland Publishing, 1976), 1:54.

62. Ibid., p. 95.

63. John Kenneth Galbraith, *A Life in Our Times: Memoirs* (Boston: Houghton Mifflin Company, 1981), pp. 201 and 205.

64. Thomas Ehrlich interview, Philadelphia, Pa., July 4, 1985. William Bundy, however, recalls that Ball did not explicitly refer to his USSBS experience in the text of his memorandums (and he is correct) or in oral arguments in Vietnam working groups and cabinet level encounters. And wisely so. All concerned well understood that targets in industrial Germany and rural Vietnam were not comparable, and to bridge the two would compromise the most effective argument Ball could make. This view is sustained by an analysis of Ball's memorandums and personal notes during the period. In virtually every forum since his resignation in 1966, however, Ball has explicitly connected his generic opposition to bombing in Vietnam to his World War II experience.

65. Ball interview, April 17, 1986.

66. Ibid.

67. Ball, *Past*, p. 195.

68. Ibid., p. 103.

69. George W. Ball, "The Period of Transition," in *Economic Unity in Europe: Programs and Problems* (New York: National Industrial Conference Board, January 21, 1960), pp. 9–34.

70. U.S. Department of State, "Special Inquiry into George Wildman Ball, Results

of Investigation," Freedom of Information Act Case No. 8600931.

71. Alfred Grosser, *The Western Alliance: European-American Relations since 1945* (New York: Vintage Books, 1982), pp. 103–4.

72. Cyrus Vance interview, New York, N.Y., April 3, 1985.

73. Arthur M. Schlesinger, Jr., *A Thousand Days: John F. Kennedy in the White House* (Boston: Houghton Mifflin Company, 1965), p. 769.

74. Jean Monnet, *Memoirs* (Garden City, N.Y.: Doubleday & Company, 1978).

75. Ball, Discipline, p. 40.

76. Monnet, *Memoirs*, pp. 227–28.

77. Helmut Schmidt, interview with author, Pomona College, March 15, 1986.

78. Monnet, *Memoirs*, p. 465, and Jean Monnet, "Remarks," December 5, 1974, PGWB.

79. Ruth Murdoch Ball interview, Princeton, N.J., April 6, 1985.

80. U.S. Department of State, "Special Inquiry into George Wildman Ball, Results of Investigation," Freedom of Information Act Case No. 8600931.

81. McGeorge Bundy interview, New York, N.Y., April 1, 1987.

82. Ball, *Discipline*, p. 49.

83. William Bundy interview, April 6, 1985.

84. James Reston interview, Washington, D.C., April 23, 1984.

85. Douglas B. Ball interview, Princeton, N.J., April 9, 1986.

86. George W. Ball, speech commemorating Walter Lippmann, September 23, 1979, PGWB.

87. Ball, *Past*, p. 100.

Chapter 2

1. Clark Clifford interview, Washington, D.C., July 5, 1985; Abram Chayes interview, Cambridge, Mass., August 5, 1986. Attorneys of considerable reputation in their own right, Clifford and Chayes regard Ball as an extremely able "Washington lawyer" and believe the mark of his profession is heavy on his Vietnam advocacy.

2. Arthur M. Schlesinger, Jr., *A Thousand Days: John F. Kennedy in the White House* (Boston: Houghton Mifflin Company, 1965), p. 23.

3. John Kenneth Galbraith to the author, September 10, 1984; Arthur Schlesinger, Jr., to the author, September 26, 1984.

4. Ronald Steel, *Walter Lippmann and the American Century* (New York: Vintage Books, 1980), pp. 523–24.

5. George W. Ball to Walter Lippmann, December 5, 1960, Walter Lippmann Papers, Yale University.

6. George W. Ball, *The Past Has Another Pattern: Memoirs* (New York: W. W. Norton & Company, 1982), p. 159.

7. Schlesinger, *A Thousand Days*, p. 155.

8. "Report to the Honorable John F. Kennedy from Adlai E. Stevenson," November 1960, Personal Papers of J. Robert Schaetzel, Bethesda, Md.

9. J. Robert Schaetzel interview, Bethesda, Md., August 14, 1984.

10. Schlesinger, *A Thousand Days*, p. 156.

11. George W. Ball interview, Princeton, N.J., July 9, 1985.

12. Schaetzel interview, August 14, 1984.

13. Ball, *Past*, p. 161.

14. Schaetzel interview, August 14, 1984.

15. "Report to the Honorable John F. Kennedy from Adlai E. Stevenson," November 1960, p. 5, Personal Papers of J. Robert Schaetzel.

16. Ibid., p. 7.

17. Ibid., pp. 1–20.

18. Ibid., p. 11.

19. Ibid., p. 12.

20. Ibid., Pt. 2, p. 2.

21. Ibid., appendixes.

22. Ball, *Past*, pp. 160–61.

23. George W. Ball interview, Princeton, N.J., April 16, 1984.

24. Schlesinger, *A Thousand Days*, p. 159.

25. Ibid.; Ball, *Past*, p. 161.

26. Schlesinger, *A Thousand Days*, p. 159.

27. Ibid., p. 161.

28. Schaetzel interview, August 14, 1984.

29. Jim F. Heath, *Decade of Disillusionment: The Kennedy-Johnson Years* (Bloomington: Indiana University Press, 1975), p. 119.

30. Schlesinger, *A Thousand Days*, pp. 148–49; David Halberstam, *The Best and the Brightest* (New York: Random House, 1972), p. 174.

31. Schaetzel interview, August 14, 1984.

32. Schlesinger, *A Thousand Days*, pp. 148–49.

33. Ibid.

34. U.S. Department of State, "Special Inquiry into George Wildman Ball, Results of Investigation," Freedom of Information Act Case No. 8600931.

35. Ball, *Past*, p. 152.

36. Schaetzel interview, August 14, 1984.

37. See Arthur M. Schlesinger, Jr., *Robert Kennedy and His Times* (Boston: Houghton Mifflin Company, 1978), 2:838, for a brief mention of the discord between Stevenson and Bobby Kennedy.

38. In a recent letter to the author, Ball demurs from the interpretation of his views about the United Nations, writing: "Schaetzel speaks of my 'latent contempt' for the United Nations. Left unqualified, this does not adequately represent my view. I was convinced at the time that the United Nations had been rendered so impotent by the Cold War *ment that* [*sic*] we might expect a veto in the Security Council regarding any significant initiative that the United States might launch. On the other hand, with the advent of Gorbachev and the Soviet rediscovery of the virtues of the United Nations, the whole situation has changed. So much so, in fact, that I am currently convinced that America should firmly discard its addiction to unilateralism which the Cold War has encouraged. We have an opportunity for the first time to test the Wilsonian thesis and we should avail ourselves of it to utilize the United Nations more effectively to solve the world's regional problems." George W. Ball to the author, January 10, 1989.

39. Schaetzel interview, August 14, 1984.

40. U.S. Senate, *Hearing before the Committee on Foreign Relations*, 87th Cong., 1st sess., January 24, 1961, p. 10.

41. Ibid., p. 14.

42. George W. Ball, *The Discipline of Power: Essentials of a Modern World Structure* (Boston: Little, Brown & Company, 1968), p. 224.

43. Ball, *Past*, p. 183.

44. Ibid. Walt Rostow told the author that his "knight in shining armor" approach to his study of Ball was "horseshit" and that "Ball was wrong on Vietnam and the developing world then [in the 1960s] and he's wrong today." Walt W. Rostow interview, Austin, Tex., May 18, 1987.

45. Ball, *Past*, p. 183.

46. McGeorge Bundy interview, New York, N.Y., April 1, 1987.

47. John Kenneth Galbraith interview, Cambridge, Mass., April 4, 1984.

48. Ball, *Past*, p. 164.

49. Ibid.

50. Ibid., p. 208.

51. Former secretary of state Dean Acheson was an oft-summoned adviser to Kennedy. As Arthur Schlesinger told the author, JFK "consulted Acheson because he wanted to hear the hard-line case, but he consistently rejected Acheson's advice (as over Berlin in 1961 and Cuba in 1962)." Arthur M. Schlesinger, Jr., to the author, August 27, 1988. John J. McCloy had been an adviser to Democratic and Republican presidents since World War II.

52. Quoted in John C. Donovan, *The Cold Warriors: A Policy-Making Elite* (Lexington, Mass.: D. C. Heath & Company, 1974), p. 81.

53. W. Averell Harriman, heir to the Harriman railroad fortune and former New York governor, is associated with "the most peaceful types" in the Kennedy administration; Connecticut governor Chester Bowles was also considered a liberal; Stevenson's liberal views on the Third World were by then well known. See Halberstam, *The Best and the Brightest*, for biographical and political mapping.

54. William P. Bundy interview, Princeton, N.J., April 6, 1985.

55. James Reston interview, Washington, D.C., April 23, 1984, and Jean Monnet, *Memoirs* (Garden City, N.Y.: Doubleday & Company, 1978), pp. 327–28.

56. Thomas L. Hughes interview, Washington D.C., August 11, 1986.

57. Examination of the "National Security File, Country File: Vietnam" shows that the bureaucracies were clearly engaged in Southeast Asia. The sheer volume of the file suggests that Vietnam was getting as much attention in 1962 as Cuba and Berlin. Prodigious documents by Bernard Fall and Roger Hilsman, in particular, distill many findings that were being made throughout the State Department, especially by the intelligence agencies. Papers of President Kennedy, John F. Kennedy Library, Boston, Mass. (hereafter cited as PJFK).

58. Schlesinger, *Robert Kennedy and His Times*, 1:437.

59. Ball, *Past*, p. 158.

60. Halberstam, *Best*, p. 11.

61. Ibid.

62. Ibid.

63. Schlesinger, *Robert Kennedy and His Times*, 1:437.

64. Ibid.

65. Ball, *Past*, p. 170.

66. Schlesinger, *Robert Kennedy and His Times*, 1:437.

67. Chester Bowles, Oral History interview, Ac 74–180, Papers of President Johnson, Lyndon Baines Johnson Library, Austin, Tex. (hereafter cited as PLBJ).

68. Hughes interview, August 11, 1986.

69. Ibid.

70. James C. Thomson interview, Cambridge, Mass., August 5, 1986.

71. Halberstam, *Best*, pp. 68–71.

72. "Thomson Thoughts on Bowles and State Department: A Provisional Balance Sheet on What Befell Liberals in the Kennedy Administration," Papers of James C. Thomson, Box 7, PJFK. Thomson wrote that "liberals have not been having a picnic under Kennedy" and commented that "Kennedy's single ideology is anti-Sovietism."

73. Ball, *Past*, p. 171.

74. Schlesinger, *Robert Kennedy and His Times*, 1:440.

75. *Washington Evening Star*, October 25, 1961.

76. James C. Thomson, "Random Musings about Chester Bowles and the Department of State," Thomson Papers, Box 7, PJFK.

77. J. Robert Schaetzel interview, Bethesda, Md., March 29, 1985. Schaetzel is not entirely unsympathetic to Ball's standards, however, and has made an avocation of finding talented and able people and bringing them into government service. George S. Springsteen interview, Washington, D.C., March 28, 1985.

78. George S. Springsteen interview, Washington, D.C., March 28, 1985.

79. Ibid.

80. Abram Chayes interview, Cambridge, Mass., August 5, 1986.

81. Ibid.

82. Springsteen interview, March 28, 1985. Springsteen cites an episode in which Ball asked Acheson's advice on staff work as an illustration of his boss's rhetorical compulsions: "Dean," Ball once petitioned his mentor, "when you were Secretary how did you handle your speeches? They [Ball's staff] give me these speeches and they're terrible. I have to rewrite them and it takes time." "Well George," Acheson said, "I got to the point where time was time and I just had to accept it whether I liked them or not. Some speeches were better than others." Springsteen laments that Ball never really acted upon Acheson's prescriptions.

83. George W. Ball interview, Princeton, N.J., April 18, 1984.

84. Springsteen interview, March 28, 1985.

85. Schaetzel interview, March 29, 1985.

86. Hughes interview, August 11, 1986; Thomson interview, August 5, 1986.

87. Testimony of Henry Wallace, *Hearings of the United States Senate Sub-Committee on the Internal Security Act*, Wednesday, October 17, 1951, PGWB.

88. *New York Times*, August 7, 1962.

89. Dean Rusk interview, Athens, Ga., March 27, 1985.

90. Hughes interview, August 11, 1986.

91. Meyer Feldman to General President, Amalgamated Clothing Workers of America, November 27, 1961. Feldman wrote: "I do not believe that Secretary Ball intended his speech to be construed as the acceptance of the expendability of any industry." TAG, FG 105, PJFK.

92. Alfred Grosser, *The Western Alliance: European-American Relations since 1945* (New York: Vintage Books, 1982), p. 104. Also, Ball's censure was called for because of his "lack of manners." *Congressional Record*, January 24, 1963, p. 981, PGWB.

93. Desk Calendar of the Under Secretary of State, PGWB.

94. Hughes interview, August 11, 1986.

95. Maxwell D. Taylor, *Swords and Ploughshares* (New York: W. W. Norton & Company, 1972), pp. 239–41.

96. Schlesinger, *Robert Kennedy and His Times*, 1:545.

97. Hughes interview, August 11, 1986.

98. Ball, *Past*, p. 410.

99. Desk Calendar of the Under Secretary of State, PGWB.

100. Ball, *Past*, p. 366.

101. Ball interview, April 16, 1984.

102. Robert S. McNamara, "Memorandum for the President," National Security File, Countries, Vietnam, Box 195, Vietnam, Memos and Reports, 11-1-61 to 11-16-61, November 11, 1961, pp. 1–2, PJFK.

103. "Memorandum from Secretary to All Posts," National Security File, Folder: Vietnam, 1-13-62 to 1-31-62, January 16, 1962, PJFK.

104. Kennedy is quoted in Guenter Lewy, *America in Vietnam* (New York: Oxford University Press, 1978), pp. 12–13.

105. Ibid.

106. Kennedy quoted in John Lewis Gaddis, *Strategies of Containment: A Critical Appraisal of Postwar American National Security Policy* (New York: Oxford University Press, 1982), p. 198.

107. Ibid., chap. 7 passim.

108. Ibid., p. 208.

109. Jonathan Schell, *The Time of Illusion* (New York: Vintage Books, 1975), p. 349.

110. Ibid., pp. 444–46.

111. Ibid., chap. 6 passim.

112. Schell, *Time of Illusion*, quoted in Stephen B. Oates, *Portrait of America* (Boston: Houghton Mifflin Company, 1978), p. 467.

113. Kent M. Beck, "The Kennedy Image: Politics, Camelot, and Vietnam," *Wisconsin Magazine of History*, December 1974, p. 53.

114. Presidential Appointment Book, PJFK.

115. Transcript, Vietnam Reel 3, WGBH Television, Boston, May 18, 1981, Sound Roll #2638, Personal Papers of Lawrence Lichty, Northwestern University.

116. Ibid.

117. Ibid.

118. Ball interview, April 16, 1984.

119. Ibid.

120. It should be noted that historian and Kennedy confidant Arthur M. Schlesinger, Jr., vigorously dissents from my interpretation and has written: "I do think there may be some misunderstanding of JFK and his attitude toward dissent. The discussion of 'Irish-style loyalty' implies that JFK punished and rejected dissenters. But Bowles was in trouble after the Bay of Pigs not because he opposed the policy but because he (or his people) were thought to have leaked his opposition to the press after the event. (I too opposed the Bay of Pigs, but, so far as I could tell, this did not bother or offend Kennedy.) . . . I never heard JFK object to Bowles on the ground of disagreements over policy. The problems with Bowles lay in other areas. I think too that Kennedy's remarks to George Ball about Vietnam on 7 November 1961 are misunderstood. When JFK said that Ball was 'crazier than hell' and that Americanization of the Vietnam war 'just isn't going to happen,' he meant that 'so long as I am president, you don't need to worry about 300,000 American troops in the rice paddies of Vietnam.' Kennedy, after all, *rejected* the Taylor-Rostow recommendations. His visit to Vietnam in 1951 had persuaded him of the folly of sending a white army into a Vietnamese civil war. Far from disagreeing with Ball's views, JFK (I am sure) was saying that George need not worry that anything like this would happen. The statement . . . that 'it was patently clear that Kennedy neither agreed with Ball's analysis . . .' seems to me wrong. He disagreed with Ball's prediction *because* he agreed with Ball's analysis." Arthur M. Schlesinger, Jr., to the author, August 27, 1988.

121. Presidential Appointment Book, PJFK.

122. Ibid.

123. Ball interview, April 16, 1984.

124. Ibid.

125. Hughes interview, August 11, 1986.

126. Ball interview, April 16, 1984; Roswell L. Gilpatric interview, New York, N.Y., April 1, 1987. Gilpatric adds that "Ball didn't have anywhere near the relation-

ship with Kennedy that he enjoyed with Johnson. He was not an intimate of Kennedy's."

127. TELCON (transcript of telephone conversation), George W. Ball and Roger Hilsman, September 23, 1963, PGWB.

128. Thomson interview, August 5, 1986.

129. TELCON, Ball and the President, January 28, 1962, PGWB.

130. Roger Hilsman interview, New York, N.Y., April 2, 1985.

131. TELCON, Ball and the President, February 14, 1962, PGWB.

132. Hilsman interview, April 2, 1985.

133. TELCON, Ball and the President, August 21, 1963, PGWB.

134. Ibid.

135. Ibid.

136. Papers of John Kenneth Galbraith, Box 12, General Correspondence, B General, PJFK.

137. Memorandum, Roger Hilsman to Secretary Rusk, National Security File, Vietnam Memos and Reports, Vietnam, Box 195, PJFK.

138. Hilsman interview, April 2, 1985.

139. "Untold Story of the Road to War in Vietnam," *U.S. News and World Report*, October 10, 1983, p. VN 7.

140. Hilsman interview, April 2, 1985.

141. "Untold Story of the Road to War in Vietnam," p. VN 7.

142. Ball, *Past*, p. 371.

143. Stanley, Karnow, *Vietnam: A History* (New York: Viking Press, 1983), pp. 283–84.

144. Ball interview, April 16, 1984.

145. Ibid.

146. Robert F. Kennedy, interview with John Bartlow Martin, 1:114, PJFK.

147. Ibid., p. 121.

148. Ibid., 8:945.

149. Hughes interview, August 11, 1986.

Chapter 3

1. George W. Ball, "We Should De-escalate the Importance of Vietnam," *New York Times Magazine*, December 21, 1969, p. 33.

2. Ruth Murdoch Ball interview, Princeton, N.J., April 6, 1985.

3. Douglas B. Ball interview, Princeton, N.J., April 9, 1986.

4. Ruth M. Ball interview, April 6, 1985.

5. Transcript, Vietnam Reel 3, WGBH Television, Boston, May 18, 1981, Sound Roll #2638, Personal Papers of Lawrence Lichty, Northwestern University.

6. George W. Ball, Memorandum: "How Valid Are the Assumptions Underlying Our Vietnam Policy," October 5, 1964, PGWB.

7. Thomas G. Paterson, *American Foreign Policy: A History* (Lexington, Mass.: D. C. Heath & Company, 1983), 2:529.

8. TELCON, Ball and the President, February 14, 1962, PGWB.

9. George W. Ball, Memorandum for the President: "United States Commitments Regarding the Defense of South Viet-Nam," June 23, 1965, p. 2, PGWB.

10. Ibid., p. 3.

11. Ibid., p. 5.

12. Ibid.

13. Ball, Memorandum: "How Valid Are the Assumptions Underlying Our Vietnam Policy," p. 43.

14. George W. Ball, "Memorandum to The Honorable Dean Rusk, Secretary of State," May 31, 1964, p. 2, PGWB.

15. Ball, Memorandum: "How Valid Are the Assumptions Underlying Our Vietnam Policy," p. 43.

16. Notebook, "1964–1965 Press Clippings," PGWB.

17. TELCON, Ball and J. Robert Schaetzel, March 17, 1965, PGWB.

18. Ball, "Memorandum to The Honorable Dean Rusk, Secretary of State," p. 2.

19. Ball, Memorandum for the President: "United States Commitments Regarding the Defense of South Viet-Nam," p. 2.

20. Ball, Memorandum: "How Valid Are the Assumptions Underlying Our Vietnam Policy," p. 43.

21. Ibid., p. 43.

22. Douglas Pike, "Comments: The Role of America's Allies in the Vietnam War" (Paper presented at the annual conference of the Organization of American Historians, St. Louis, Mo., April 8, 1989).

23. William P. Bundy interview, Princeton, N.J., April 6, 1985.

24. TELCON, Ball and McGeorge Bundy, March 15, 1965, PGWB.

25. Ball, Memorandum: "How Valid Are the Assumptions Underlying Our Vietnam Policy," p. 43.

26. Ibid.

27. Ibid.

28. Ibid.

29. George W. Ball, Memorandum for the President: "A Compromise Solution in South Viet-Nam," July 1, 1965, PGWB.

30. Ibid.

31. NSC and CIA findings cited in James William Gibson, *The Perfect War: The War We Couldn't Lose and How We Did* (New York: Vintage Books, 1988), p. 109.

32. Ball, Memorandum: "How Valid Are the Assumptions Underlying Our Vietnam Policy." p. 43.

33. Neil Sheehan, *A Bright Shining Lie: John Paul Vann and America in Vietnam* (New York: Random House, 1988), p. 123.

34. In candid remarks on the so-called Jordan Report (an effort by journalist William Jordan to convince the administration that the Vietcong were an autonomous force, independent of Hanoi's direct control) Ball admitted to being uncertain about the relationship of the Vietcong to the DRV. George W. Ball interview, Princeton, N.J., July 9, 1985.

35. Noam Chomsky, *For Reasons of State* (New York: South End Press, 1970), p. 129.

36. Tom Wicker, "The Debate on Bombing: Washington Divided on Resumption But Proponents Appear to Prevail," *New York Times*, January 26, 1965, p. 1.

37. Ibid. It should be noted that Arthur Goldberg argued for a pause but that "he was not then at the vital center of the decision making process."

38. Lyndon Johnson, Oral Histories, Interview with Lyndon Johnson, August 12, 1969, AC-661, p. 18, Lyndon Baines Johnson Library.

39. Wicker, "The Debate on Bombing," p. 1.

40. Jack Valenti, *A Very Human President* (New York: W. W. Norton & Company, 1975), p. 232. In his personal notes Valenti wrote that Ball made explicit reference to his experience on the United States Strategic Bombing Survey.

41. Ball, Memorandum: "How Valid Are the Assumptions Underlying Our Vietnam Policy," p. 43.

42. William Bundy interview, April 6, 1985.

43. Ball, Memorandum: "How Valid Are the Assumptions Underlying Our Vietnam Policy," p. 43.

44. Ball, "Memorandum to The Honorable Dean Rusk, Secretary of State," p. 2.

45. George W. Ball, Memorandum for the President: "Viet-Nam," February 1965, unidentified talking paper, PGWB.

46. McGeorge Bundy, Memorandum for the President: "Broodings on Viet-Nam," NSC Memos to the President, vol. 17, Tuesday, December 14, 1965, 7:45 P.M., Notes to President Johnson, NSC File, PLBJ.

47. During the 1982 libel litigation between William Westmoreland and CBS television in which it was charged that the Pentagon deliberately underreported rates of enemy infiltration in order to maintain congressional support for the war, Ball stated that the Defense Department reporting "didn't affect [him] because [his] mind had been made up for years. Events simply confirmed the fact that a lot of false impressions had been created by the reporting we were getting." George W. Ball interview, August 9, 1986, and Van Gordon Sauter (president, CBS News) to George W. Ball, June 15, 1983, with surreptitiously taped transcript enclosed.

48. McGeorge Bundy, Memorandum for the President: "Broodings on Viet-Nam."

49. McGeorge Bundy, Memorandum for the President, December 14, 1965, National Security File, Country File: Vietnam, Box 5, PLBJ.

50. George W. Ball, Memorandum for the President: "Viet-Nam: An Attempt to Achieve an Agreed Position," February 12, 1965, PGWB.

51. Ibid.

52. Ibid.

53. Allen Whiting interview, Laguna Hills, Calif., March 21, 1985.

54. Ibid.

55. Ibid.

56. Mark Lorell and Charles Kelley, Jr., "Casualties, Public Opinion, and Presidential Policy during the Vietnam War," Rand Corporation, Santa Monica, Calif., May 1983, unpublished draft document, PGWB.

57. Whiting interview, March 21, 1985; Lorell and Kelley, "Casualties, Public Opinion, and Presidential Policy during the Vietnam War."

58. Ball, Memorandum: "How Valid Are the Assumptions Underlying Our Viet-Nam Policy," p. 43.

59. Ball interview, July 9, 1985.

60. William L. Lunch and Peter W. Sperlich, "American Public Opinion and the War in Vietnam," *Western Political Quarterly* 32 (March 1979): 21–44.

61. George W. Ball, Memorandum for the President: "The Resumption of Bombing Poses Grave Danger of Precipitating a War with China," January 25, 1966, PGWB.

62. Ibid.

63. Ibid.

64. George W. Ball, Memorandum for the Secretary of State: "Bombing of Haiphong POL," May 5, 1966, PGWB.

65. Ibid.

66. Ibid.

67. Ibid.

68. Defense Department analyses of the American bombing campaign are reported in Gibson, *The Perfect War*, pp. 346–47.

69. Ibid.

70. George C. Herring, *The Secret Diplomacy of the Vietnam War: The Negotiating Volumes of the Pentagon Papers* (Austin: University of Texas Press, 1983), p. xvi.

71. Ibid.

72. Ball interview, July 9, 1985.

73. George C. Herring, *America's Longest War: The United States and Vietnam, 1950–1975* (New York: John Wiley, 1979), p. 164.

74. Ball interview, July 9, 1985. In his memoir, Ball gives surprisingly little attention to peace negotiations—less than a page in a lengthy chapter on Vietnam. As we will see in Chapter 6, he remarks that the agreement finally reached in 1973 was the one he advocated in 1965.

75. TELCON, Ball and the President, June 14, 1965, PGWB.

76. Bill Moyers interview, New York, N.Y., April 2, 1985. Moyers continued: "Well, he never cried ouch. The military tourniquet just kept being turned and finally there were no alternatives in Johnson's mind but to continue the course which had become too late for George's option to ameliorate."

77. Ball, Memorandum for the President: "A Compromise Solution in South Viet-Nam."

78. George W. Ball and Dean Acheson, Memorandum for the President: "A Plan for a Political Resolution in South Vietnam," May 1965, PGWB.

79. In the summer of 1965, Ball participated in what Herring has called "the mysteriously titled and long-secret XYZ contact in Paris." See Herring, *The Negotiating Volumes of the Pentagon Papers*, p. xxiv.

80. Ball and Acheson, Memorandum for the President: "A Plan for a Political Resolution in South Vietnam."

81. Ibid.

82. Ibid.

83. Ibid.

84. Thomas Ehrlich interview, Philadelphia, Pa., July 4, 1985.

85. Ellen J. Hammer, *A Death in November: America in Vietnam 1963* (New York: Oxford University Press, 1987), p. 180

86. State Department Telegram, DS-322, May 5, 1965, PGWB.

87. Ibid.

Chapter 4

1. Jack Valenti interview, Washington, D.C., July 5, 1985.

2. Dean Rusk interview, Athens, Ga., March 27, 1985.

3. Warren I. Cohen, *Dean Rusk* (New York: Cooper Square Publishers, 1980), p. 98.

4. Ibid., p. 94.

5. Rusk interview, March 27, 1985.

6. Robert Manning interview, Boston, Mass., August 4, 1986.

7. It should also be noted that the Foggy Bottom rumor mill is absent a single rumor or anecdote regarding any impairment of judgment. Though it was once quipped that "Ball's liver is the most over-worked organ in the Western World," it seems as though the affinity for libation that Ball and Rusk shared did not undermine their performance in their posts. J. Robert Schaetzel interview, Bethesda, Md., August 12, 1986.

8. *Washington Sunday Star*, June 27, 1971.

9. Rusk interview, March 27, 1985.

10. Ibid.

11. Ruth Murdoch Ball interview, Princeton, N.J., April 6, 1985.

12. Manning interview, August 4, 1986; James L. Greenfield interview, New York, N.Y., April 1, 1987.

13. George W. Ball, *The Past Has Another Pattern: Memoirs* (New York: W. W. Norton & Company, 1982), p. 168.

14. Manning interview, August 4, 1986.

15. Thomas J. Schoenbaum, *Waging Peace and War: Dean Rusk in the Truman, Kennedy, and Johnson Years* (New York: Simon & Schuster, 1988), pp. 431–32.

16. PGWB.

17. George S. Springsteen interview, Washington D.C., March 28, 1985.

18. Ball, *Past*, p. 384.

19. Ibid.

20. Rusk interview, March 27, 1985.

21. Cohen, *Dean Rusk*, p. 319.

22. Rusk interview, March 27, 1985.

23. Ibid.

24. Memorandum, Dean Rusk to the President, July 1, 1965, "Vietnam," Top Secret NSC History—Troop Deployment, quoted in Larry Berman, *Planning a Tragedy: The Americanization of the War in Vietnam* (New York: W. W. Norton & Company, 1982), p. 92, with citation, p. 167.

25. Rusk interview, March 27, 1985.

26. Ibid.

27. George W. Ball, interviewed by Paige E. Mulhollan (for the Lyndon Johnson Library), New York, N.Y., July 8, 1971, copy in PGWB.

28. Schoenbaum, *Waging Peace and War*, p. 432.

29. Ibid., pp. 422 and 466.

30. Cyrus Vance interview, New York, N.Y., April 3, 1985.

31. Ibid.

32. Ball's TELCON file shows that he and Secretary McNamara had a number of terse exchanges. One transcript is representative: On June 28, 1965, Ball told McNamara that he "would like to see the American Air Force stay out of north-east North Vietnam for a while" (for reasons not unlike those discussed in Chapter 3), to which McNamara replied, "We should do the same thing as we have done in the past two weeks." In the ensuing dialogue, Ball retorted that the past two weeks had been "pretty harry [*sic*]—having scrambled with MIGS and losing one plane over China." McNamara reiterated that he "saw no reason to change." In closing, Ball replied that "this was the exact conversation that had taken place in 1950 and then suddenly the 'boys' [Red Chinese] appeared." TELCON, Ball and McNamara, October 7, 1965, PGWB.

33. Richard N. Goodwin, *Remembering America: A Voice from the Sixties* (Boston: Little, Brown & Company, 1988), p. 375.

34. Ball, interviewed by Paige E. Mulhollan, July 8, 1971.

35. Ibid., pp. 27–28.

36. Stanley Karnow, *Vietnam: A History* (New York: Viking Press, 1983), p. 405.

37. In the fall of 1965, McNamara told Ball he had "no objection to raising the subject of cutting the bombing program, but he would rather it would be done at some time when [Admiral William F.] Raborn was not present." McNamara then asked Ball to say that he agreed with the secretary of state [which of course he did not] if the question came up. TELCON, Ball and McNamara, September 29, 1965, PGWB.

38. Ball, interviewed by Paige E. Mulhollan, July 8, 1971.

39. Ibid.

40. Vance interview, April 3, 1985.

41. Robert McNamara to the author, October 19, 1988.

42. See Paul Hendrickson, "The Night the Vietnam War Came Home to Robert McNamara," *Washington Post Magazine*, September 6, 1987, pp. 16–23, for a synopsis of the former secretary of defense's tribulations over Vietnam and an account of his self-imposed silence.

43. Robert S. McNamara interview, Washington, D.C., August 12, 1986.

44. NSC Meetings Notes File, PLBJ. Sets of notes taken by NSC staffer Chester Cooper and presidential assistant Jack Valenti are near verbatim accounts, printed and analyzed in George McT. Kahin, *Intervention: How America Became Involved in Vietnam* (New York: Alfred A. Knopf, 1986), pp. 368–78.

45. *The Pentagon Papers*, Senator Gravel, ed. (Boston: Beacon Press, 1974), 4:611.

46. TELCON, Ball and Bill Moyers, June 21, 1965, PGWB.

47. Arthur Schlesinger, Jr., has balked at the notion that Ball is possessed of any "latent admiration" for Eisenhower, as I record, and suspects that "[Ball] felt an Eisenhower citation would strengthen his case." Arthur M. Schlesinger, Jr., to the author, August 27, 1988. I responded: "This view has been confirmed in my talks with Ball, who feels that Eisenhower exercised good judgment in not providing air support to the French during the 1954 Dienbienphu crisis when pressed by Nixon and Dulles to do so, and I would also cite Ball, *Error and Betrayal in Lebanon* (pp. 23, 37, 58, 67, & 94) for evidence of his considerable admiration for Eisenhower's position on Israel and the Middle East." David DiLeo to Arthur M. Schlesinger, Jr., September 12, 1988.

48. George W. Ball, Memorandum for the President: "United States Commitment Regarding the Defense of South Viet-Nam," June 23, 1965, PGWB.

49. Document is printed in appendix to Berman, *Planning a Tragedy*, and analyzed in Kahin, *Intervention*, p. 365.

50. Berman, *Planning a Tragedy*, pp. 91–94.

51. The MLF "rub" apparently did not destroy a friendship. When asked by the publisher of Ball's memoirs to critique the manuscript, Bundy wrote: "I have tried to find a way to say that not even George is perfect, but it doesn't come out right, and anyway, who is?" PGWB.

52. Ball, *Past*, p. 173.

53. David Halberstam, *The Best and the Brightest* (New York: Random House, 1972), p. 494.

54. McGeorge Bundy interview, New York, N.Y., April 1, 1987.

55. Halberstam, *Best*, p. 494.

56. TELCON, Ball and McGeorge Bundy, August 8, 1965, PGWB.

57. Halberstam, *Best*, p. 372.

58. TELCON, Ball and McGeorge Bundy, December 12, 1963, PGWB.

59. George Ball has told the author that his "passionate attachment to the MLF has been grossly over stated," which, when repeated in a discussion with McGeorge Bundy, elicited laughter. George W. Ball interview, Princeton, N.J., April 6, 1986; McGeorge Bundy interview, April 1, 1987.

60. McGeorge Bundy interview, April 1, 1987.

61. McGeorge Bundy, Memorandum for the President, January 28, 1966, NSC File, Memos to the President, McGeorge Bundy, Box 6, PLBJ.

62. Quoted in Goodwin, *Remembering America*, p. 377.

63. Quoted in Berman, *Planning a Tragedy*, p. 110.

64. McGeorge Bundy interview, April 1, 1987. One of the period's ironies is that Bundy, like McNamara, was ultimately reconciled to Ball's position on the war. At a

meeting in November 1967, after they had both left the government, Bundy stated: "For the first time in my life I find myself agreeing on this issue [Vietnam] with George Ball." Chalmers Roberts, *Washington Post*, July 5, 1970. In another instance (June 27, 1965), Bundy sided with Ball. Atop Ball's SEATO paper arguing that America's commitment to South Vietnam under the South East Asia Treaty was not decisive, Bundy attached a memo of his own to the president: "My own view [exactly the one Ball expressed in the memo] is that if and when we wish to shift our course and cut our losses in Vietnam we should do so because of a finding that the Vietnamese themselves are not meeting their obligations to themselves or to us." NSC File, NSC History Deployment of Forces, Vietnam, July 27, 1965, vol. 5, Tabs 314–325, Box 4, PLBJ. In a less formal manner, Bundy and Ball exchanged views about how the U.S. government (USG) should react to atrocities. Bundy was persuaded that Ball was making important arguments. In a discussion about reprisals in the aftermath of the publication of a death list of South Vietnamese and American leaders, Bundy called Ball to tell him that the president was "getting hard-nosed." Ball thought that the decision to build a policy out of piecemeal reactions to confrontations was "dreadful," to which Bundy added that his "personal judgment runs with Ball's" that the USG had not developed a strategy for reprisal for incidents like Pleiku. TELCON, Ball and McGeorge Bundy, June 6, 1965, PGWB.

65. Meetings Notes File, Box 1: February 17, 1965, PLBJ.

66. Kahin, *Intervention*, p. 352.

67. McGeorge Bundy interview, April 1, 1987.

68. NSC File, McGeorge Bundy, October 20, 1964, vol. 7, Box 2, PLBJ. A second, and more subtle, example of the Bundy imprint occurred on January 20, 1966, when, as a cover to a Ball memorandum against resumption of the bombing, Bundy wrote that it was a paper "you may wish to read" and contrasted it with another attached paper which in his view was—in contrast to Ball's—"a quite careful estimate of probable reactions of the Communists and others to various possible lines of decision on this issue." NSC File, Memos to the President, McGeorge Bundy, January 20, 1966, Box 6, PLBJ. It should not be concluded that Bundy was one-dimensional about Ball's advocacy; on one occasion, in fact, he shared Ball's thoughts with the president on his own volition. Responding to Johnson's instructions to discuss a cease-fire and peace mission with Ball and Bill Moyers, Bundy wrote a memo the postscript to which reads: "George Ball made an interesting argument this afternoon to the effect that it would be a very good thing for us all if we could get out of bombing in the North all together. He was talking from rough notes, and I asked him to leave them with me for my instruction. Because of your interest in every aspect of this problem, I think they may interest you too, and I attach them at Tab A." NSC File, McGeorge Bundy, December 14, 1965, PLBJ.

69. TELCON, Ball and Bill Moyers, February 25, 1965, PGWB.

70. McGeorge Bundy interview, April 1, 1987.

71. Ibid.

72. McGeorge Bundy, Memorandum to the President, July 1, 1965, 9:00 A.M., NSC File, vols. 12–14, Box 4, PLBJ.

73. McGeorge Bundy, Memorandum to the President, July 1, 1965, 5:30 P.M., NSC File, vols. 12–14, Box 4, PLBJ. On another occasion, Bundy similarly tried to narrow the circle of those exposed to Ball's heretical views. Attaching a Ball paper as a tab to his own memorandum, Bundy wrote: "I think the Ball proposal needs a lot of thought . . . and should probably not be discussed in a large NSC meeting. It must be a very tight circle—limited perhaps to Goldberg, Rusk, Ball, McNamara, and whichever of

your own people you want." NSC File, Memos to the President, McGeorge Bundy, January 5, 1966, Box 6, PLBJ.

74. Jack Valenti, *A Very Human President* (New York: W. W. Norton & Company, 1975), p. 141.

75. Bill Moyers interview, New York, N.Y., April 2, 1985.

76. Ibid.

77. Springsteen interview, March 28, 1985.

78. James C. Thomson interview, Cambridge, Mass., August 5, 1986.

79. TELCON, Ball and Bill Moyers, June 19, 1965, PGWB.

80. Ibid.

81. Moyers interview, April 2, 1985.

82. Appointment Calendars, Appointment Books, PGWB.

83. TELCONS, Ball to/from Bill Moyers, May 1964 to September 1965, PGWB.

84. Moyers interview, April 2, 1985.

85. Ibid.

86. Ibid.

87. Allen S. Whiting interview, Laguna Hills, Calif., March 21, 1985.

88. George W. Ball interview, Princeton, N.J., July 9, 1985.

89. Whiting interview, March 21, 1985.

90. Albert Eisele, *Almost to the Presidency* (Minneapolis: Piper Company, 1972), p. 234.

91. TELCON, George Ball and Benjamin Read, February 14, 1965, PGWB.

92. Hubert Humphrey, *The Education of a Public Man: My Life and Politics* (Garden City, N.Y.: Doubleday & Company, 1976), p. 327.

93. In the aftermath of the Tet offensive (January–March 1968) both Dean Acheson and Clark Clifford began to argue for negotiated withdrawal.

94. Clark Clifford interview, Washington, D.C., July 5, 1985.

95. Ibid.

96. Ibid.

97. TELCON, Ball and Clark Clifford, July 23, 1965, PGWB.

98. Clifford interview, July 5, 1985.

99. Ibid.

100. Ibid.

101. Clark Clifford to Ball, July 9, 1970, PGWB.

102. Ball is not at all warm to the idea of including Bill Bundy among the dissenters. In an interview for the Lyndon Johnson Library Ball stated: "I was *alone* in the top councils. If Bill Bundy tells me he had lots of reservations—he never argued them in any direct way. I remember saying to Bill Bundy once on a certain measure of escalation that, 'I don't think this has a chance. I think it is absurd to be putting this up and seriously going for it.' I said, 'What do you think the chances are?' 'Oh,' he said, '10 or 15 percent.' I said 'That's absolute nonsense for a great government to go ahead on as potentially costly a program of this kind in terms of lives, in terms of ancillary breaking that might occur on that kind of risk. It's a lousy business judgment. You can't do it.'" George W. Ball, Oral History transcript, Lyndon Baines Johnson Library, copy found in PGWB.

103. William P. Bundy interview, Princeton, N.J., April 15, 1984.

104. Berman, *Planning a Tragedy*, p. 137.

105. Walter Isaacson and Evan Thomas, *The Wise Men: Six Friends and the World They Made* (New York: Simon and Schuster, 1986), p. 657.

106. William Bundy interview, April 15, 1984.

107. George W. Ball, "How Valid Are the Assumptions Underlying Our Viet-Nam Policy," October 5, 1964, PGWB.

108. William Bundy interview, April 15, 1984.

109. Ibid.

110. Horace Busby, Memorandum for the President: "Impressions, Vietnam Discussion," July 21, 1965, Office Files of Horace Busby, "Vietnam," Box 3, File Copy, PLBJ.

111. William Bundy interview, April 15, 1984.

112. In interviews with the author, James L. Greenfield (*New York Times*), Robert Manning (assistant secretary of state for political affairs), James Reston (*New York Times*), and Murray Marder (*Washington Post*) have all emphatically concurred that Ball maintained unusually good press relations.

113. Ball's personal friends in the press included Murray Marder and Chalmers Roberts of the *Washington Post*, James Reston of the *New York Times*, and Walter Lippmann, then a columnist for *Newsweek*. George W. Ball interview, Princeton, N.J., August 12, 1986. Ball was also said to have maintained an "unusually close" relationship with Marilyn Berger of the *Washington Post* and NBC Television—who is "reputed to have very good sources in the State Department." Gene Bird to the author, May 18, 1989.

114. Ronald Steel, *Walter Lippmann and the American Century* (New York: Vintage Books, 1980), pp. 547 and 572.

115. Ball, *Past*, p. 430.

116. It is significant to note that Ball kept his office TELCON file, organized chronologically, and collated two binders entitled "Vietnam TELCONS," examination of which shows that Reston has more entries than any other individual. PGWB.

117. Appointments Calendar of the Under Secretary of State, PGWB.

118. TELCON, Ball and James Reston, May 27, 1965, PGWB.

119. TELCON, Ball and James Reston, August 5, 1964, PGWB.

120. Ibid.

121. TELCON, Ball and James Reston, January 28, 1964, PGWB.

122. Ibid.

123. George W. Ball interview, Princeton, N.J., April 17, 1986.

124. Philip Geyelin interview, Washington, D.C., April 2, 1987.

125. Marquis Childs, "Ball on Vietnam: A Necessary Voice," *Washington Post*, June 20, 1966.

126. Philip Geyelin, *Lyndon B. Johnson and the World* (New York: Fredrick A. Praeger, 1966), pp. 210–13.

127. Childs, "Ball on Vietnam: A Necessary Voice."

Chapter 5

1. Jack Valenti interview, Washington, D.C., July 5, 1985.

2. Lyndon B. Johnson to George W. Ball, June 7, 1971, PGWB.

3. British Broadcasting Company, "Trying to Win with LBJ," July 5, 1977, Transcript of Tape #2040-2155, PGWB.

4. Walt W. Rostow, *The United States and the Regional Organization of Asia and the Pacific, 1965–1985* (Austin: University of Texas Press, 1986), p. 31.

5. Ibid.

6. Ibid., p. 32.

7. Ibid.

8. Walt W. Rostow, *The Diffusion of Power: An Essay in Recent History* (New York: Macmillan, 1972), p. 496.

9. Lyndon Baines Johnson, *The Vantage Point: Perspectives of the Presidency, 1963–1969* (New York: Holt, Rinehart, and Winston, 1971), p. 356.

10. Rostow, *Regional Organization*, p. 7.

11. Lyndon Johnson, "Peace Without Conquest," April 7, 1965, cited in Steven Cohen, *Vietnam: Anthology and Guide to "A Television History"* (New York: Alfred A. Knopf, 1982), p. 108.

12. Merle Miller, *Lyndon: An Oral Biography* (New York: G. P. Putnam's Sons, 1980), p. 488.

13. Doris Kearns, *Lyndon Johnson and the American Dream* (New York: New American Library, 1976), p. 265.

14. Ibid., p. 275.

15. Arthur M. Schlesinger, Jr., *Robert Kennedy and His Times* (Boston: Houghton Mifflin Company, 1978), 2:773.

16. Johnson, *Vantage Point*, p. 42.

17. Transcript, Vietnam Reel 3, WGBH Television, Boston, May 18, 1981, Sound Roll #2638, Personal Papers of Lawrence Lichty, Northwestern University.

18. Ibid.

19. Ibid.

20. Johnson, *Vantage Point*, p. 147.

21. "Johnson Grateful for Dove's Advice," *San Francisco Chronicle*, June 28, 1971.

22. Valenti interview, July 5, 1985.

23. Ibid. See also Larry Berman, *Planning a Tragedy: The Americanization of the War in Vietnam* (New York: W. W. Norton & Company, 1982), p. 3.

24. Valenti interview, July 5, 1985.

25. Ibid.

26. Quoted in David Halberstam, *The Best and the Brightest* (New York: Random House, 1972), p. 625.

27. Valenti interview, July 5, 1985.

28. Johnson, *Vantage Point*, p. 42.

29. Quoted in Halberstam, *Best*, p. 624.

30. Johnson, *Vantage Point*, p. 147.

31. George W. Ball, *The Past Has Another Pattern: Memoirs* (New York: W. W. Norton & Company, 1982), p. 396.

32. Clark Clifford interview, Washington, D.C., July 5, 1985.

33. Transcript, CBS Television Network, "Face the Nation," June 27, 1971, p. 12.

34. Philip Geyelin interview, Washington, D.C., April 2, 1987.

35. George C. Herring, *America's Longest War: The United States and Vietnam, 1950–1975* (New York: John Wiley, 1979), p. 129.

36. TELCON, McGeorge Bundy and George Ball, February 7, 1965, PGWB.

37. National Security File, Meeting Notes File, vol. 3, Tab 27–28, PLBJ.

38. Drew Pearson, "White House Answers Viet Critics," *Washington Post*, March 6, 1965.

39. National Security File, Meeting Notes File, Box 1, File Name: July 21, 1965, Meetings on Vietnam, PLBJ.

40. J. William Fulbright, *The Price of Empire* (New York: Pantheon Books, 1989), pp. 104–9.

41. William C. Berman, *William Fulbright and the Vietnam War: The Dissent of a Political Realist* (Kent, Ohio: Kent State University Press, 1988), p. 30

42. Ball, *Past*, p. 232.
43. *Dallas Morning News*, February 28, 1965.
44. *Baltimore Sun*, April 4, 1965.
45. *Washington Post*, April 11, 1966.
46. *Washington Post*, July 5, 1966.
47. *New York Times*, April 4, 1965.
48. *Herald Tribune*, Paris ed., July 14, 1965.
49. *The Times*, London ed., September 9, 1965.
50. Clifford interview, July 5, 1985.
51. James C. Thomson interview, Cambridge, Mass., August 5, 1986.
52. James Reston, "Washington: The Johnson System," *New York Times*, March 6, 1966.
53. Transcript, NBC Television, "The Today Show," August 5, 1964, PGWB.
54. TELCON, Ball and Bill Moyers, January 29, 1964, PGWB.
55. Ibid.
56. TELCON, Ball and the President, January 12, 1966, PGWB.
57. *Washington Post*, May 3, 1965.
58. McGeorge Bundy, Memorandum for the President, August 12, 1965, NSC File, Memos to the President, McGeorge Bundy, vols. 12–14, August 1965, Box 4, PLBJ.
59. TELCON, Ball and Nicholas Katzenbach, October 6, 1965, PGWB.
60. Donald Katz, "The Grand Designer," *New Republic*, January 13, 1979.
61. TELCON, Ball and the President, November 16, 1965, PGWB.
62. George W. Ball to Walter Lippmann, January 29, 1966, PGWB.
63. Draft Statement for Secretary Rusk, April 21, 1966, PGWB.
64. TELCON, Ball and Walt Rostow, June 30, 1966, PGWB.
65. TELCON, Ball and Bill Moyers, July 1, 1966, PGWB.
66. TELCON, Ball and McGeorge Bundy, May 3, 1962, PGWB.
67. George W. Ball, "Viet Nam: Free World Challenge in South East Asia," U.S. Department of State Publication 7388, Far East Series, no. 113, April 30, 1962.
68. Schlesinger, *Robert Kennedy and His Times*, 2:742.
69. TELCON, Ball and McGeorge Bundy, May 1, 1962, PGWB.
70. George W. Ball, "The Dangers of Nostalgia," U.S. Department of State Publication 7858, March 16, 1965.
71. *Christian Science Monitor*, March 18, 1965.
72. Ball, "The Dangers of Nostalgia."
73. *New York Times*, August 31, 1965.
74. *Herald Tribune*, Paris ed., September 1, 1965.
75. George W. Ball interview, Princeton, N.J., August 9, 1986.
76. Schlesinger, *Robert Kennedy and His Times*, 2:758; Abram Chayes interview, Cambridge, Mass., August 5, 1986; Roger Hilsman interview, New York, N.Y., April 2, 1985.
77. Schlesinger, *Robert Kennedy and His Times*, 2:763–64.
78. Ibid., p. 764.
79. Ibid., p. 769.
80. *Washington Post*, February 21, 1966.
81. *New York Times*, February 22, 1966.
82. Ibid.
83. Ball interview, August 9, 1986.
84. Ibid.
85. TELCON, Ball and McGeorge Bundy, October 8, 1964, PGWB.

86. NSC File, vol. 8, Memos to the President, Box 2, January 19, 1965, PLBJ.

87. TELCON, Ball and the President, February 15, 1965, PGWB.

88. TELCON, Ball and James Greenfield, June 14, 1965, PGWB.

89. TELCON, Ball and Barbara Kerr, February 22, 1966, PGWB.

90. TELCON, Ball and Clayton Fritchey, April 4, 1966, PGWB.

91. TELCON, Ball and Marquis Childs, April 12, 1966, PGWB.

92. TELCON, Ball and Chalmers Roberts, July 1, 1966, PGWB.

93. Richard E. Neustadt and Ernest R. May, *Thinking in Time: The Uses of History for Decision Makers* (New York: Free Press, 1986), p. 171.

94. Irving Janis, *Victims of Groupthink: Psychological Study of Foreign Policy Decisions and Fiascos* (Boston: Houghton Mifflin, 1972), p. 116.

95. Ibid., p. 119.

96. Kearns, *Lyndon Johnson and the American Dream*, p. 132.

97. Robert L. Gallucci, *Neither Peace nor Honor: The Politics of American Military Policy in Vietnam* (Baltimore: Johns Hopkins University Press, 1976), pp. 132–34.

98. Herbert Y. Schandler, *The Unmaking of a President: Lyndon Johnson and Vietnam* (Princeton: Princeton University Press, 1977), p. 324.

99. British Broadcasting Company, "Trying to Win With LBJ," July 5, 1977, Transcript of Tape #BLN27/103Y325, PGWB.

100. TELCON, Ball and the President, December 28, 1965, PGWB.

101. Lyndon Baines Johnson, Remarks at a State Department Dinner, 8th Floor, January 16, 1969, PGWB.

102. TELCON, Ball and the President, June 14, 1965, PGWB.

103. Transcript, Vietnam Reel 3, WGBH Television, Boston, May 18, 1981, Sound Roll #2638, Personal Papers of Lawrence Lichty, Northwestern University.

104. TELCON, Ball and the President, June 14, 1965, PGWB.

105. Don Cook, "Harriman: When LBJ Lost His Nerve," *Los Angeles Times*, August 31, 1986.

106. TELCON, Ball and the President, December 28, 1965, PGWB.

107. McGeorge Bundy interview, New York, N.Y., April 17, 1984.

108. For illustrations of this theme see Richard N. Goodwin, *Remembering America: A Voice from the Sixties* (Boston: Little, Brown & Company, 1988), pp. 350, 379, 382, and especially p. 410.

109. Kearns, *Lyndon Johnson and the American Dream*, pp. 324–50 passim.

110. National Security File, Memos to the President, M. Bundy, vols. 12–14, Box 4, August 12, 1965, PLBJ.

111. *New York Times*, November 18, 1969.

112. Miller, *Lyndon: An Oral Biography*, p. 413.

113. In scatological terms, Ball has disputed the devil's advocacy hypothesis. Ball interview, August 9, 1986.

114. Ibid.

115. James C. Thomson, "How Could Vietnam Happen?: An Autopsy," *The Atlantic*, April 1968, p. 49.

116. Hans J. Morgenthau, *Truth and Power: Essays of a Decade, 1960–1970* (New York: Praeger Publishers, 1970), p. 202.

117. Hans J. Morgenthau, "The Wild Bunch," *New York Review of Books*, February 11, 1971.

118. Henry Brandon interview, Washington, D.C., April 2, 1987.

119. *Washington Post*, June 30, 1971.

120. Mark Lorell and Charles Kelley, Jr., "Casualties, Public Opinion, and Presi-

dential Policy during the Vietnam War," Rand Corporation, Santa Monica, Calif., May 1983, unpublished draft document, PGWB.

121. Paul M. Kattenburg, *The Vietnam Trauma in American Foreign Policy, 1945–1975* (New Brunswick: Transaction Books, 1980), p. 233.

122. Robert S. McNamara interview, Washington, D.C., August 12, 1986; Dean Rusk interview, Athens, Ga., March 27, 1985; McGeorge Bundy interview, New York, N.Y., April 1, 1987.

123. Allen Whiting interview, Laguna Hills, Calif., March 21, 1985; Whiting to the author, December 12, 1984.

124. Adam Yarmolinsky interview, Catonsville, Md., August 13, 1986.

125. J. Robert Schaetzel to the author, December 13, 1986.

126. Hilsman interview, April 2, 1985.

127. Desk Calendar, Office of the Under Secretary of State, PGWB.

128. Ball interview, August 9, 1986.

129. Robert Manning interview, Boston, Mass., August 4, 1986.

130. Roger Hilsman interview, April 2, 1985.

131. Thomson interview, August 5, 1986.

132. Ibid.

133. Hilsman interview, April 2, 1985.

134. Chayes interview, August 5, 1986.

135. Henry F. Graff, *The Tuesday Cabinet: Deliberation and Decision on Peace and War under Lyndon B. Johnson* (Englewood Cliffs, N.J.: Prentice-Hall, 1970).

Chapter 6

1. *Washington Post*, March 3, 1966.

2. *Washington Capitol News Service*, June 27, 1966.

3. TELCON, Ball and Marquis Childs, July 18, 1966, PGWB.

4. *Philadelphia Evening Bulletin*, October 4, 1966.

5. *Chicago Daily News*, June 4, 1966.

6. *Boston Globe*, October 2, 1966.

7. Clayton Fritchey, undated article, without attribution, PGWB.

8. James C. Thomson, "Getting Out and Speaking Out," *Foreign Policy Magazine* 13 (Winter 1973–74): 63.

9. TELCON, Ball and James Reston, September 22, 1966, PGWB.

10. George W. Ball, *The Past Has Another Pattern: Memoirs* (New York: W. W. Norton & Company, 1982), p. 19.

11. Lyndon B. Johnson to George W. Ball, September 21, 1966, PGWB.

12. Jim Heath, *Decade of Disillusion: The Kennedy and Johnson Years* (Bloomington: Indiana University Press, 1975), p. 262; Richard Harwood and Haynes Johnson, *Lyndon* (New York: Praeger Publishers, 1973), pp. 128–29.

13. Lyndon B. Johnson, "Remarks of the President at Farewell Reception Honoring George W. Ball," October 6, 1966, Office Files of John Macy, PLBJ.

14. James C. Thomson interview, Cambridge, Mass., August 5, 1986.

15. Thomson, "Getting Out and Speaking Out," pp. 57–63 passim.

16. Edward Weisband and Thomas M. Franck, *Resignation in Protest: Political and Ethical Choices Between Loyalty to Team and Loyalty to Conscience in Public Life* (New York: Grossman Publishers, 1975), pp. 58, 138–39, 153–54.

17. Ibid., p. 163–64.

18. Ibid., p. 165.

19. Ibid., p. 191.

20. Ibid.

21. Thomson interview, August 5, 1986.

22. Cyrus R. Vance interview, New York, N.Y., April 3, 1985.

23. Weisband and Franck, *Resignation in Protest*, pp. 139 and 225.

24. *Washington Sunday Star*, June 6, 1971.

25. Ball, *Past*, p. 432.

26. Ibid.

27. TELCON, Ball and James Reston, September 22, 1966, PGWB.

28. *Department of State Newsletter*, October 1966, PGWB.

29. Ball, *Past*, p. 432.

30. Ibid., p. 431.

31. George W. Ball interview, Princeton, N.J., August 9, 1986.

32. Ball, *Past*, p. 432.

33. Ibid., p. 442.

34. Ibid., p. 447.

35. Ball, *The Discipline of Power: Essentials of a Modern World Structure* (Boston: Little, Brown & Company, 1968), p. 311.

36. Ball to Dean Rusk, June 30, 1977, PGWB.

37. Wilson Wyatt to Ball, September 22, 1966, PGWB.

38. Dean Rusk, review of *Resignation in Protest*, by Weisband and Franck, *American Journal of International Law* 71 (April 25, 1977): 160–63, Personal Papers of Dean Rusk, Athens, Ga.

39. Ball, *Discipline*, pp. 308–11.

40. Ibid., pp. 331–32.

41. Ibid., pp. 329, 331–32.

42. Lyndon B. Johnson to Ball, September 21, 1966. PGWB.

43. National Security File, Memoranda to the President, McGeorge Bundy, vol. 13, August 1965, Box 4, PLBJ.

44. Name File, George W. Ball, Box 45, PLBJ.

45. Memorandum, Marvin Watson to the President, February 18, 1967; Letter, Lyndon Johnson to George Ball, September 11, 1967, Name File, George W. Ball, Box 46, PLBJ.

46. Memorandum, Joseph Califano to George Ball, May 3, 1968, Confidential Name File, George W. Ball, Box 1, PLBJ.

47. Ball, *Past*, p. 436.

48. The so-called Wise Men—an ad hoc nonpartisan group that served as an unofficial advisory board for Vietnam—varied in composition but normatively included former secretary of state Dean Acheson, Ball, General Omar Bradley, Mac Bundy, Arthur Dean, former Treasury secretary Douglas Dillon, Ambassador Henry Cabot Lodge, retired diplomat Robert Murphy, General Matthew Ridgway, General Maxwell Taylor, former assistant secretary of defense Cyrus Vance, and others.

49. Ball, *Past*, p. 407.

50. Ezra N. Suleiman, *Elites in French Society: The Politics of Survival* (Princeton: Princeton University Press, 1978), pp. 226–28.

51. Ball interview, August 9, 1986; Donald R. Katz, "The Grand Designer," *New Republic*, January 13, 1979, p. 21.

52. Ball, *Past*, pp. 436–44 passim.

53. Confidential Memorandum, Federal Bureau of Investigation, May 15, 1968, Subject: George W. Ball and *Congressional Record* of May 13, 1968, Freedom of Information Act Case No. 262,289, PGWB.

54. Ball, *Past*, p. 443.

55. See John M. Ashbrook, "Reflections on the Departure of Mr. George Ball," *Congressional Record*, October 15, 1968 (E9165), PGWB. Congressman Ashbrook stated: "Although Mr. Ball gave as his reason for resigning his desire 'to help assure the election of Hubert Humphrey and the defeat of Richard Nixon,' *The Wall Street Journal* of October 4 suggested another possible reason for his departure: GOP Senators consider airing 'moonlighting' charges against Humphrey advisor, George Ball. They say he continued to maintain an office at Lehman Brothers investment banking firm while serving as Ambassador to U.N. Some critics suggest that fear of embarrassing disclosures caused Ball to quit the U.N. post."

In addition to the suspicions raised in the House of Representatives, the FBI was given a copy of an anonymous letter written to Sidney Goldberg of the Government Employees' Exchange and dated August 22, 1968. The author of the letter contended that while he/she was "an admirer of Mr. Ball's ability [they were] shocked and sickened by the cynical and flagrant use of government relations by Lehman Brothers." Additionally, the letter charged that Ball had been "able to exploit his government relations not only for himself but for his banking and law firms." U.S. Department of Justice, Federal Bureau of Investigation, Conflict of Interest Matter, George Wildman Ball, Former United States Ambassador to the United Nations, September 27, 1969, PGWB. Ball has quite gleefully admitted to, and denigrated as "naive and frivolous," all of the charges in the letter. Ball interview, August 9, 1986.

56. Ball to President Johnson, September 25, 1968, PGWB.

57. President Johnson to Ball, September 25, 1968, PGWB.

58. Ball, *Past*, pp. 444–48.

59. George W. Ball, "Answer of George W. Ball to 'Complaint and Petition for Hearing on Violation of the Code of Fair Practices,'" undated document, PGWB.

60. Ibid., passim.

61. George C. Herring, *America's Longest War: The United States and Vietnam, 1950–1975* (New York: John Wiley, 1979), p. 223 and chap. 7 passim.

62. McGeorge Bundy, *Danger and Survival: Choices about the Bomb in the First Fifty Years* (New York: Random House, 1988), pp. 538–41.

63. Herring, *America's Longest War*, p. 221.

64. *Miami Herald*, November 16, 1969.

65. Barbara Tuchman, *The March of Folly* (New York: Ballantine Books, 1984), p. 360.

66. George W. Ball, "We Should De-escalate the Importance of Vietnam," *New York Times Magazine*, December 21, 1969.

67. *Newsweek*, [1970], undated and untitled article with Ball's personal handwritten notes, PGWB.

68. Henry Kissinger, *Years of Upheaval* (Boston: Little, Brown & Company, 1982), p. 372.

69. George W. Ball, "Europe's Uneasy Summer," *Washington Post*, May 19, 1971.

70. Ball to Dean Acheson, March 3, 1970, Dean Acheson Papers, Yale University.

71. Ibid.

72. *Washington Sunday Star*, June 27, 1971; *Wall Street Journal*, August 5, 1971.

73. Ball to John Kenneth Galbraith, October 31, 1980, PGWB.

74. Ball, *Past*, p. 422. Nixon once stated, "I'm not going to end up like LBJ, holed up in the White House afraid to show my face on the street. I'm going to stop that war. Fast." Quoted in Herring, *America's Longest War*, p. 219.

75. Ball, *Past*, pp. 411 and 422.

76. Ball interview, August 9, 1986.

77. Ball, *Past*, pp. 420–21.
78. Ibid., pp. 415–17.
79. Ibid., pp. 414–17.
80. George C. Herring, "The 'Vietnam Syndrome' and American Foreign Policy," *Virginia Quarterly Review* 57 (Fall 1981): 594.
81. George W. Ball, *Diplomacy for a Crowded World: An American Foreign Policy* (Boston: Little, Brown & Company, 1976), pp. 82–83.

Chapter 7

1. Jerald A. Coombs, "Cold War Historiography: An Alternative to John Gaddis's Post Revisionism," *Society for Historians of American Foreign Relations Newsletter* 15, no. 2 (June 1984): 9.
2. Mariana P. Sullivan, "The Foreign Policy Consensus after Vietnam," *Peace and Change* 9, no. 2//3 (Summer 1983): 80.
3. Ibid., p. 81. Sullivan cites the inconclusiveness of the Vietnam struggle as straining, then shattering elite agreement on the war.
4. Charles DeBenedetti, "Lyndon Johnson and the Antiwar Opposition," in *The Johnson Years*, ed. Robert A. Divine (Lawrence: University of Kansas Press, 1987), 2:23.
5. Richard A. Melanson, *Writing History and Making Policy: The Cold War, Vietnam, and Revisionism*, vol. 6 (New York: University Press of America, 1983). See chap. 4, "Cold War Revisionism Subdued," for breakdown of the Revisionist School into Radical and Post Revisionist scholars.
6. Robert Divine to Richard Melanson, quoted in ibid., p. 96.
7. William Appleman Williams, *The Tragedy of American Diplomacy* (New York: Dell Publishing Co., 1972), p. 96.
8. Kolko is quoted in Melanson, *Writing History and Making Policy*, p. 75.
9. Barnet is quoted in ibid., p. 76.
10. Ibid., p. 87
11. Lippmann is quoted in ibid., p. 46.
12. Ibid., p. 127. In Melanson's account of the postwar foreign policy debates, Schlesinger claims that "Kennan, Morgenthau, Lippmann, Niebuhr, and Ball were *not* Cold War revisionists." Although in the broadest sense he is correct—that the group did not echo the hypothesis that the requirements of American capitalism fundamentally shaped the doctrine of expanding the Open Door—the group shared a great many common assumptions with the revisionists, including the view that the United States did not hold a monopoly on virtue and moral authority in the world. In this sense, Ball shared common ground with even the Radical Revisionists. Professor Schlesinger also claims that practitioners of foreign policy during the 1960s were mostly unaware of the scholarly debates about the Cold War. An examination of Ball's papers, however, particularly since his son was working toward a Ph.D. in history and assisting with the development of the dissenting memorandums, reveals keen insights into the debate over the character and evolution of the Cold War.
13. Speech File, Tables of Contents, PGWB.
14. George W. Ball interview, Princeton, N.J., April 17, 1984.
15. Stanley Hoffmann, "Realism and Its Discontents," *Atlantic Monthly*, November 1985, pp. 131–36. The term "Realist" is not without its critics. In commenting on papers given on Ball and Kennan to the Organization of American Historians, Professor Lloyd C. Gardner remarked: "Indeed, the papers this morning should make us

ponder the mystifying and mythmaking tendencies latent in terms like realist. The term enjoys such a persistent vogue, one supposes, because no one wants to be known as an *un*realist. Fortunately, since the term is so imprecise, almost anyone can rent the *sobriquet* especially while writing about themselves." Lloyd C. Gardner, remarks to the annual conference of the Organization of American Historians, Philadelphia, Pa., April 4, 1987.

16. Hans J. Morgenthau, *A New Foreign Policy for the United States* (New York: Praeger Publishers, 1969), pp. 3–12.

17. *Look Magazine*, August 1966, p. 24.

18. Keith L. Nelson and Spencer C. Olin, Jr., *Why War? Ideology, Theory, and History* (Berkeley: University of California Press, 1979), p. 29.

19. George W. Ball, review of *Fragments of My Fleece*, by Dean Acheson, Personal Papers of J. Robert Schaetzel, Bethesda, Md..

20. George W. Ball, *The Discipline of Power: Essentials of a Modern World Structure* (Boston: Little, Brown & Company, 1968), pp. 300–301.

21. Ibid., p. 301.

22. See Ball, review of *Fragments of My Fleece*; Ball, *Discipline*, pp. 16–17 and 20.

23. George W. Ball, *The Past Has Another Pattern: Memoirs* (New York: W. W. Norton & Company, 1982), p. 175. A discussion of Ball's views of the United Nations system would be incomplete and intellectually dishonest without at least a consideration of his most recent reappraisal of the system. Admitting that he "must be getting old" to have rediscovered the idealism and inherent workability of the organization, Ball has recently modified his once considerable misanthropy directed against the U.N. On April 22, 1988, Ball made the following remarks to the American Society of International Law in Washington: "These days it is easy to forget that, when its framers drafted the United Nations Charter against the background of experience with the Concert of Europe and the League of Nations, they centered the peacemaking function in the Security Council. They empowered that body to adopt resolutions binding all members and made those resolutions enforceable through the imposition of a specified range of sanctions, not excluding military action.

"But, unfortunately, this machinery was never tested, for, soon after the UN Charter was adopted, the emerging Cold War contest between the Soviets and West undercut the basic assumption that the great powers would be able to make common cause; and for four decades thereafter Cold War calculus has led each superpower to use its veto to block initiatives by the other, thus rendering the Security Council of only marginal utility.

"Confronted with the Council's impotence, our government mindlessly yielded to the easy option of preempting for itself the role of world policeman, while at the same time trying assiduously to exclude the Soviet presence and influence from large proportions of the world.

"The result was easily predictable. By letting itself be represented as what some Congressmen sanctimoniously called the 'conscience of the world,' America has by its appearance of presumptuous imperialism created antagonism and resentment. Such resentment might have been avoided—or at least substantially mitigated—had our actions and policies been invariably fair and evenhanded, based on considerations more uplifting than mere anti-Communism combined with a slavish support of a variety of despotic regimes whose only discernible distinction was that they were not Russian henchmen. But we all too often adopted a posture of self-righteous unilateralism even when our actions violated Thomas Jefferson's commandment that we should show 'a decent respect for the opinions of mankind.'

"It is time to put aside our unilateral posturing and begin once again to use the United Nations in the manner its framers originally intended. Even for our own countrymen such an abrupt change in our national conduct would pose a considerable challenge but it would also open vast new possibilities. We Americans have become so addicted to unilateralism that the practice of resorting to the United Nations would require a major reorientation in our thinking and a substantial reconsideration of our strategy. It is a truism of physiology that when a human organ ceases to fulfill its intended function, it tends to atrophy, and, because the East-West conflict has for four decades effectively paralyzed the principal organ of the United Nations—the Security Council—that whole institution has fallen into disrepute among wide sectors of American opinion.

"But that does not mean, as many academic critics solemnly assert, that the Wilsonian concept of institutionalized diplomacy is unworkable. It means rather that it has never been tried under conditions where it could possibly be effective; first, because the United States failed to ratify the League of Nations and, second, because the Cold War has, up until now, precluded the super powers from making common cause. Now, by finding areas of common interest with the Soviet Union—creating, as it were, an alliance of adversaries or concert of the powerful—we at last have the chance to test Wilsonian principles pragmatically."

24. Ball, *Discipline*, p. 10.

25. Ball interview, April 17, 1984.

26. George W. Ball, "Comments at the Marshall Plan Conference," The Bologna Center, Italy, November 11, 1987, PGWB.

27. Transcript, "Firing Line," Southern Education Communications Association, August 2, 1981.

28. George W. Ball, *Diplomacy for a Crowded World: An American Foreign Policy* (Boston: Little, Brown & Company, 1976), p. 312.

29. Ibid.

30. Ibid., p. 27.

31. Ibid., p. 310.

32. Ibid., p. 25.

33. George W. Ball, "A Venture in Symbolic Diplomacy," *New York Times*, August 2, 1971.

34. Ball, *Diplomacy*, p. 20.

35. Ibid., p. 23.

36. Dean Rusk to Ball, July 6, 1977, PGWB.

37. Ball to Dean Rusk, July 20, 1977, PGWB.

38. Ball to Senator Charles McC. Mathias, Jr., March 26, 1986, PGWB.

39. George W. Ball, *Error and Betrayal in Lebanon: An Analysis of Israel's Invasion of Lebanon and the Implications for U.S.–Israeli Relations* (Washington, D.C.: Foundation for Middle East Peace, 1984), p. 124.

40. Stanley Hoffmann, Preface to Ball, *Error*, pp. 17–19.

41. Ball, *Error*, p. 23.

42. Ibid., p. 123.

43. George W. Ball, "Prophets of the Holy Land," *Harper's Magazine*, December 1984, pp. 35–36.

44. Ibid. Ball adds: "At the end of 1984, Israel should still be able to marshall 675,000 troops against 600,000 for its probable opponents, Syria (with 500,000) and Jordan (with 100,000). But President Assad recently announced that Syria would expand its forces to 800,000 troops by 1986; and King Hussein of Jordan, amid widespread speculation in Israel that in any future war with Syria Israeli troops would

be forced to pass through Jordan, is increasing the size of his regular army and establishing a 200,000-man militia."

45. Ibid., p. 36.

46. Ball, *Error*, p. 131.

47. Ball keeps a manila file of "hate mail" which is, to date, approximately four inches thick. PGWB.

48. Paul Findley, *They Dare to Speak Out: People and Institutions Confront Israel's Lobby* (Westport, Conn.: Lawrence Hill & Company, 1985), p. 35.

49. Ball to Dean Rusk, July 20, 1977, PGWB.

50. "Containment: 40 Years Later," *Foreign Affairs* 65, no. 4 (Spring 1987): 827–90.

51. John Lewis Gaddis, *Strategies of Containment: A Critical Appraisal of Postwar American National Security Policy* (New York: Oxford University Press, 1982), p. 26.

52. George F. Kennan, "Planning of Foreign Policy," War College Lecture, Box 17, George F. Kennan Papers, Seely G. Mudd Manuscript Library, Princeton University.

53. Walter L. Hixson, "Containment on the Perimeter: George F. Kennan and Vietnam" (remarks to the annual conference of the Organization of American Historians, Philadelphia, Pa., April 4, 1987).

54. Ball, *Discipline*, pp. 234–35.

55. George W. Ball, "Comments: West Point Military Academy," West Point, N.Y., June 3, 1983, PGWB.

56. Ball, "Comments at the Marshall Plan Conference," November 11, 1987.

57. George W. Ball, unpublished editorial remarks addressed to Meg Greenfield, *Washington Post*, September 4, 1981, PGWB, and Transcript, "Firing Line," Southern Education Communications Association, August 2, 1981.

58. Ball, "Comments at the Marshall Plan Conference," November 11, 1987.

59. Ball, *Discipline*, p. 19.

60. Ball, *Diplomacy*, p. 154.

61. Ball, *Discipline*, p. 67.

62. Ball, *Diplomacy*, p. 278.

63. Cyrus Vance interview, New York, N.Y., April 3, 1985.

64. Ball, *Discipline*, p. 18.

65. Ibid., pp. 222–23 and 235.

66. George S. Springsteen interview, Washington, D.C., March 28, 1985.

67. Ibid., p. 229.

68. Ball, *Diplomacy*, p. 256.

69. Ball, "Comments: West Point Military Academy," June 3, 1983.

70. George W. Ball, "White House Roulette," *New York Review of Books*, November 8, 1984, p. 5.

71. Ibid.

72. George W. Ball, "The War for Star Wars," *New York Review of Books*, April 11, 1985, p. 3.

73. Ball, "Comments at the Marshall Plan Conference," November 11, 1987.

74. Ball, "Comments: West Point Military Academy," June 3, 1983.

75. Ibid.

76. Ball interview, April 17, 1984.

77. Doris Kearns interview, Concord, Mass., August 3, 1986. In borrowing liberally from her Freudian analysis of LBJ (*Lyndon Johnson and the American Dream*, [New York: New American Library, 1976]), Ms. Kearns has interpreted Ball's self-conception of a "private sector personality" as a projection of his disappointment over never having achieved the highest diplomatic office in the land. With the publication of his

second book in 1976—somewhat presumptuously entitled *Diplomacy for a Crowded World: An American Foreign Policy*—Ball made what may be said to be his most concerted bid to become secretary of state. Having tactically "switched" from Independent candidate John Anderson to Jimmy Carter, Ball sent Carter lengthy memorandums—then a bound copy of his book. As Edward Luttwak wrote in *The New Republic* on June 26, 1976, "George Ball's quest for office long ago ceased to be discreet." Inside the Carter campaign, Zbigniew Brzezinski frankly observed that "as far as Ball's book [was] concerned, I doubt that anyone in the campaign actually read it. But it was interpreted as a bid by Ball to be considered for the post of Secretary of State." Zbigniew Brzezinski to the author, April 27, 1987.

78. David P. Calleo to the author, April 4, 1986.

79. George W. Ball, "The Promise of the Multinational Corporation," galley proof reprint of article that was published in *Fortune*, June 1, 1967, PGWB.

80. John M. Ashbrook, "Reflections on the Departure of Mr. George Ball," *Congressional Record*, October 15, 1968 (E9165), PGWB.

81. Ball, "The Promise of the Multinational Corporation," p. 9.

82. Ball, "Trade Favors for Latins Could Open Pandora's Box," *Washington Post*, December 14, 1969.

83. Ball, *Diplomacy*, p. 293.

84. Ibid.

85. George W. Ball, "Have We Learned or Only Failed?" *New York Times Magazine*, April 1, 1973, p. 13.

86. Quoted in J. William Fulbright, *The Price of Empire* (New York: Pantheon Books, 1989), p. 123.

Epilogue

1. George W. Ball to Landon Hillard (chairman, Committee on Admissions, The Links Club), March 13, 1981, PGWB.

2. Ellsworth Bunker to George W. Ball, November 1, 1982, PGWB.

3. John Kenneth Galbraith interview, Cambridge, Mass., April 4, 1984.

4. PGWB.

5. Statement of George W. Ball before the Congress of the United States, Committee on Foreign Affairs, House of Representatives, Subcommittee on Asian and Pacific Affairs, April 29, 1985, PGWB.

6. Ball, *Diplomacy*, p. 345.

7. Ibid., p. 325.

Bibliography

Collections of Papers

Dean Acheson Papers, Yale University.
George W. Ball Papers, Princeton, N.J.
John Kenneth Galbraith Papers, John F. Kennedy Library, Boston, Mass.
Lyndon Baines Johnson Papers, Lyndon Baines Johnson Library, Austin, Tex.
George F. Kennan Papers, Seely G. Mudd Manuscript Library, Princeton University.
John F. Kennedy Papers, John F. Kennedy Library, Boston, Mass.
Walter Lippmann Papers, Yale University.
Bill Moyers Papers, Lyndon Baines Johnson Library, Austin, Tex.
J. Robert Schaetzel Papers, Bethesda, Md.
Arthur M. Schlesinger, Jr., Papers, John F. Kennedy Library, Boston, Mass.
Adlai E. Stevenson Papers, Seely G. Mudd Manuscript Library, Princeton University.
James C. Thomson Papers, John F. Kennedy Library, Boston, Mass.

Interviews with the Author

Ball, Douglas B. Princeton, N.J., April 9, 1986; April 17, 1986.
Ball, George W. Princeton, N.J., April 16–20, 1984; July 9–12, 1985; April 6, 1986; April 17, 1986; August 9–13, 1986; March 21, 1990; and periodic telephone conversations, 1984–90.
Ball, Ruth Murdoch. Princeton, N.J., April 6, 1985.
Brandon, Henry. Washington, D.C., April 2, 1987.
Bundy, McGeorge. New York, N.Y., April 17, 1984; April 1, 1987.
Bundy, William P. Princeton, N.J., April 15, 1984; April 17, 1984; April 6, 1985.
Chayes, Abram. Cambridge, Mass., August 5, 1986.
Christopher, Warren. Los Angeles, Calif., March 6, 1985.
Clifford, Clark. Washington, D.C., July 5, 1985.
Cutler, Lloyd. Washington, D.C., April 6, 1989.
Ehrlich, Thomas. Philadelphia, Pa., July 4, 1985.
Evans, Barbara. Washington, D.C., April 7, 1989.
Fulbright, J. William. Washington, D.C., July 5, 1985.
Galbraith, John Kenneth. Cambridge, Mass., April 4, 1984.
Geyelin, Philip. Washington, D.C., April 2, 1987.
Gilpatric, Roswell. New York, N.Y., April 1, 1987.
Goodwin, Richard. Concord, Mass., August 3, 1986.
Graff, Henry. New York, N.Y., April 2, 1985.
Greenfield, James L. New York, N.Y., April 1, 1987.
Hilsman, Roger. New York, N.Y., April 2, 1985.
Hughes, Thomas L. Washington, D.C., August 11, 1986.
Johnson, U. Alexis. Washington, D.C., July 5, 1985.

249

Kearns, Doris. Concord, Mass., August 3, 1986.
Kindleberger, Charles A. Washington, D.C., April 6, 1989.
McNamara, Robert S. Washington, D.C., August 12, 1986.
Manning, Robert. Boston, Mass., August 4, 1986.
Marder, Murray. Washington, D.C., April 2, 1987.
Martin, Ed. Washington, D.C., April 6, 1989.
Moyers, Bill. New York, N.Y., April 2, 1985.
Owen, Henry. Washington, D.C., July 5, 1985.
Reston, James. Washington, D.C., April 23, 1984.
Roll, Lord. Princeton, N.J., April 9, 1986.
Rostow, Walt. Austin, Tex., May 18, 1987.
Rusk, Dean. Athens, Ga., March 27, 1985.
Schaetzel, J. Robert. Bethesda, Md., August 14, 1984; March 29, 1985; and August
    12, 1986.
Schlesinger, Arthur M., Jr. New York, N.Y., April 11, 1985.
Sheehan, Neil. Orange, Calif., November 19–20, 1989.
Springsteen, George S. Washington, D.C., March 28, 1985.
Steel, Ronald. Los Angeles, Calif., April 25, 1986.
Thomson, James C. Cambridge, Mass., August 5, 1986.
Trueheart, William C. Washington, D.C., August 11, 1986.
Vahey, Helen. New York, N.Y., April 2, 1985.
Valenti, Jack. Washington, D.C., July 5, 1985.
Vance, Cyrus. New York, N.Y., April 3, 1985.
Whiting, Allen S. Laguna Hills, Calif., March 21, 1985.
Yarmolinsky, Adam. Catonsville, Md., August 13, 1986.

Government Publications

Ashbrook, John M. "Reflections on the Departure of Mr. George Ball." *Congressional
    Record*, October 15, 1968.
Ball, George W. "The Dangers of Nostalgia." U.S. Department of State Publication
    7858. March 16, 1965.
Ball, George W. "Viet Nam: Free World Challenge in South East Asia." U.S. Depart-
    ment of State Publication 7388. Far East Series, no. 113. April 30, 1962.
Cleveland, Harlan. "Great Powers and Great Diversity: The Perceptions and Policies of
    President Kennedy." *Department of State Bulletin*, December 1963.
"Under Secretary Ball Should Be Censured." *Congressional Record*, January 24, 1963,
    p. 981.
U.S. Congress. *Congressional Quarterly Almanac*. Washington D.C.: GPO, 1970,
    1971, 1972, 1973, 1974, 1975.
U.S. Congress. House. Committee on Foreign Affairs. *Hearings on Termination of
    Hostilities in Indochina*. 92d Cong., 2d sess., May 16, 18, 23, and June 1, 1972.
    Washington, D.C.: GPO, 1972.
U.S. Congress. Senate. Committee on Foreign Affairs. *Background Information Relat-
    ing to Southeast Asia and Vietnam*. 6th rev. ed. Washington D.C.: GPO, June
    1970.
U.S. Congress. Senate. Committee on Foreign Affairs. *U.S. Involvement in the Over-
    throw of Diem, 1963*. Staff study based on the Pentagon Papers. Washington,
    D.C.: GPO, 1967.

U.S. Department of State. "Special Inquiry into George Wildman Ball, Results of Investigation." Freedom of Information Act Case No. 8600931, January 14, 1987.

Books

Ambrose, Stephen E. *Rise to Globalism: American Foreign Policy since 1938*. New York: Penguin Books, 1985.

Austin, Anthony. *The President's War*. New York: J. B. Lippincott, 1971.

Ball, George W. *Diplomacy for a Crowded World: An American Foreign Policy*. Boston: Little, Brown & Company, 1976.

————. *The Discipline of Power: Essentials of a Modern World Structure*. Boston: Little, Brown & Company, 1968.

————. *Error and Betrayal in Lebanon: An Analysis of Israel's Invasion of Lebanon and the Implications for U.S.–Israeli Relations*. Washington D.C.: Foundation for Middle East Peace, 1984.

————. *The Past Has Another Pattern: Memoirs*. New York: W. W. Norton & Company, 1982.

Baritz, Loren. *Backfire: A History of How American Culture Led Us into Vietnam and Made Us Fight the Way We Did*. New York: William Morrow & Company, 1985.

Barnet, Richard J. *The Alliance: America, Europe, Japan, Makers of the Postwar World*. New York: Simon & Schuster, 1983.

————. *Roots of War*. New York: Penguin Books, 1972.

Berman, Edgar M. D. *Hubert: The Triumph and Tragedy of the Humphrey I Knew*. New York: G. P. Putnam's Sons, 1979.

Berman, Larry. *Lyndon Johnson's War*. New York: W. W. Norton & Company, 1989.

————. *Planning a Tragedy: The Americanization of the War in Vietnam*. New York: W. W. Norton & Company, 1982.

Berman, William C. *William Fulbright and the Vietnam War: The Dissent of a Political Realist*. Kent, Ohio: Kent State University Press, 1988.

Braestrup, Peter. *Big Story*. 2 vols. Boulder, Colo.: Westview Press, 1977.

Brzezinski, Zbigniew. *Power and Principle*. New York: Farrar, Straus, Giroux, 1983.

Bundy, McGeorge. *Danger and Survival: Choices about the Bomb in the First Fifty Years*. New York: Random House, 1988.

Campbell, John Franklin. *The Foreign Affairs Fudge Factory*. New York: Basic Books, 1971.

Carr, Edward Hallett. *What Is History?* New York: Vintage Books, 1961.

Chomsky, Noam. *For Reasons of State*. New York: South End Press, 1970.

Cohen, Steven. *Vietnam: Anthology and Guide to "A Television History."* New York: Alfred A. Knopf, 1982.

Cooper, Chester. *The Lost Crusade*. New York: Dodd and Mead, 1970.

Crabb, Cecil V. *The Doctrines of American Foreign Policy: The Meaning, Role and Future*. Baton Rouge: Louisiana State University Press, 1982.

————. *Policy Makers and Critics*. New York: Praeger Publishers, 1976.

————. *Presidents & Foreign Policy Making: From FDR to Reagan*. Baton Rouge: Louisiana State University Press, 1986.

Dallek, Robert. *The American Style of Foreign Policy: Cultural Politics and Foreign Affairs*. New York: New American Library, 1983.

Divine, Robert A., ed. *The Johnson Years*. 2 vols. Lawrence: University of Kansas Press, 1987.

Donovan, John C. *The Cold Warriors: A Policy-Making Elite*. Lexington, Mass.: D. C. Heath & Company, 1974.

Draper, Theodore. *Abuse of Power*. New York: Viking Press, 1967.

Dubofsky, Melvyn, and Athan Theoharis. *Imperial Democracy: The United States since 1945*. Englewood Cliffs, N.J.: Prentice-Hall, 1983.

Esterline, John H., and Robert B. Black. *Inside Foreign Policy: The Department of State Political System and Its Subsystems*. Palo Alto, Calif.: Mayfield Publishing Company, 1975.

Estes, Thomas S., and E. Allan Lightner, Jr. *The Department of State*. New York: Praeger Publishers, 1976.

Evans, Rowland, and Robert Novak. *Lyndon B. Johnson: The Exercise of Power*. New York: New American Library, 1966.

Findley, Paul. *They Dare to Speak Out: People and Institutions Confront Israel's Lobby*. Westport, Conn.: Lawrence Hill & Company, 1985.

Fitzgerald, Frances. *Fire in the Lake: The Vietnamese and the Americans in Vietnam*. New York: Vintage Books, 1972.

Fulbright, J. William. *The Arrogance of Power*. New York: Random House, 1968.

––––––. *The Price of Empire*. New York: Pantheon Books, 1989.

––––––. *The Vietnam Hearings*. New York: Random House, 1966.

Gaddis, John Lewis. *Strategies of Containment: A Critical Appraisal of Postwar American National Security Policy*. New York: Oxford University Press, 1982.

Galbraith, John Kenneth. *How to Get Out of Vietnam*. New York: Signet Books, 1967.

––––––. *A Life in Our Times: Memoirs*. Boston: Houghton Mifflin Company, 1981.

Galloway, John. *The Gulf of Tonkin Resolution*. Rutherford, N.J.: Fairleigh Dickinson University Press, 1970.

––––––. *The Kennedys and Vietnam*. New York: Facts on File, 1971.

Gallucci, Robert L. *Neither Peace nor Honor: The Politics of American Military Policy in Vietnam*. Baltimore: Johns Hopkins University Press, 1975.

Gardner, Lloyd C. *Approaching Vietnam: From World War II through Dienbienphu*. New York: W. W. Norton & Company, 1988.

––––––. *Imperial America: American Foreign Policy since 1898*. New York: Harcourt Brace Jovanovich, 1976.

Gellman, Barton. *Contending with Kennan: Toward a Philosophy of American Power*. New York: Praeger Publishers, 1984.

Geyelin, Philip. *Lyndon B. Johnson and the World*. New York: Fredrick A. Praeger, 1966.

Gibson, James William. *The Perfect War: The War We Couldn't Lose and How We Did*. New York: Vintage Books, 1988.

Gitlin, Todd. *The Sixties: Years of Hope, Days of Rage*. New York: Bantam, 1987.

Goodman, Allan E. *The Lost Peace: America's Search for a Negotiated Settlement of the Vietnam War*. Stanford: Stanford University Press, 1978.

––––––. *Politics in War: The Bases of Political Community in South Vietnam*. Cambridge: Harvard University Press, 1973.

Goodwin, Richard N. *Remembering America: A Voice from the Sixties*. Boston: Little, Brown & Company, 1988.

Graebner, Norman A. *America as a World Power: A Realist Appraisal from Wilson to Reagan*. Wilmington, Del.: Scholarly Resources, 1984.

Graff, Henry F. *The Tuesday Cabinet: Deliberation and Decision on Peace and War under Lyndon B. Johnson*. Englewood Cliffs, N.J.: Prentice-Hall, 1970

Greenstein, Fred I. *Leadership in the Modern Presidency*. Cambridge: Harvard University Press, 1988.

Grosser, Alfred. *The Western Alliance: European-American Relations since 1945*. New York: Vintage Books, 1982.

Halberstam, David. *The Best and the Brightest*. New York: Random House, 1972.

_____. *The Making of a Quagmire: America and Vietnam during the Kennedy Era*. Rev. ed. New York: Random House, 1988.

Halle, Louis J. *The Cold War as History*. New York: Harper Colophon Books, 1967.

Halperin, Morton H., and Arnold Kanter, eds. *Readings in American Foreign Policy: A Bureaucratic Perspective*. Boston: Little, Brown & Company, 1973.

Hammer, Ellen J. *A Death in November: America in Vietnam 1963*. New York: Oxford University Press, 1987.

Hammond, Paul Y. *The Cold War Years: American Foreign Policy since 1945*. New York: Harcourt Brace Jovanovich, 1969.

Harwood, Richard, and Haynes Johnson. *Lyndon*. New York: Praeger Publishers, 1973.

Heath, Jim F. *Decade of Disillusion: The Kennedy-Johnson Years*. Bloomington: Indiana University Press, 1975.

Herring, George C. *America's Longest War: The United States and Vietnam, 1950–1975*. New York: John Wiley, 1979.

_____. *The Secret Diplomacy of the Vietnam War: The Negotiating Volumes of the Pentagon Papers*. Austin: University of Texas Press, 1983.

Hersh, Seymour M. *The Price of Power: Kissinger in the Nixon White House*. New York: Summit Books, 1983.

Hilsman, Roger. *To Move a Nation: The Politics of Foreign Policy in the Administration of JFK*. Garden City, N.Y.: Doubleday & Company, 1967.

Holsti, Ole R., and James N. Rosenau. *American Leadership in World Affairs: Vietnam and the Breakdown of Consensus*. Boston: Unwin Hyman, 1984.

Hoopes, Townsend. *The Limits of Intervention*. 3d ed. New York: W. W. Norton & Company, 1970.

Humphrey, Hubert H. *The Education of a Public Man: My Life and Politics*. Garden City, N.Y.: Doubleday & Company, 1976.

Hung, Nguyen Tien, and Jerrold L. Schecter. *The Palace File: Vietnam Secret Documents*. New York: Harper & Row, 1986.

Isaacs, Arnold R. *Without Honor: Defeat in Vietnam & Cambodia*. New York: Vintage Books, 1983.

Isaacson, Walter, and Evan Thomas. *The Wise Men: Six Friends and the World They Made*. New York: Simon & Schuster, 1986.

Janis, Irving. *Victims of Groupthink: Psychological Study of Foreign Policy Decisions and Fiascos*. Boston: Houghton Mifflin, 1972.

Johnson, Lyndon Baines. *The Vantage Point: Perspectives of the President, 1963–1969*. New York: Holt, Rinehart, and Winston, 1971.

Kaiser, Charles. *1968 in America: Music, Politics, Chaos, Counterculture, and the Shaping of a Generation*. New York: Weidenfeld & Nicolson, 1988.

Kalb, Madeline G. *The Congo Cables: The Cold War in Africa from Eisenhower to Kennedy*. New York: Macmillan, 1982.

Kalb, Marvin, and Elie Abel. *Roots of Involvement: The U.S. in Asia, 1784–1971*. New York: W. W. Norton & Company, 1971.

Karnow, Stanley. *Vietnam: A History*. New York: Viking Press, 1983.

Kattenburg, Paul M. *The Vietnam Trauma in American Foreign Policy, 1945–1975.* New Brunswick, N.J.: Transaction Books, 1980.

Kearns, Doris. *Lyndon Johnson and the American Dream.* New York: New American Library, 1976.

Kendrick, Alexander. *The Wound Within: America in the Vietnam Years, 1945–1974.* Boston: Little, Brown & Company, 1974.

Kennan, George F. *American Diplomacy, 1900–1950.* New York: New American Library of World Literature, 1951.

––––––. *The Nuclear Delusion: Soviet-American Relations in the Atomic Age.* New York: Pantheon Books, 1982.

––––––. *Realities of American Foreign Policy.* New York: W. W. Norton & Company, 1966.

Kennedy, Robert. *Robert Kennedy in His Own Words.* New York: Bantam Books, 1988.

Kissinger, Henry. *White House Years.* Boston: Little, Brown & Company, 1979.

––––––. *Years of Upheaval.* Boston: Little, Brown & Company, 1982.

Kolko, Gabriel. *Anatomy of War: Vietnam, the United States, and the Modern Historical Experience.* New York: Pantheon Books, 1985.

Komer, Robert W. *Bureaucracy at War: U.S. Performance in the Vietnam Conflict.* Boulder, Colo.: Westview Press, 1986.

Kraslow, David, and Stuart H. Loory. *The Secret Search for Peace in Vietnam.* New York: Random House, 1968.

LaFeber, Walter. *America, Russia, and the Cold War, 1945–1971.* New York: Alfred A. Knopf, 1972.

Landau, David. *Kissinger: The Uses of Power.* New York: Thomas Y. Crowell Company, 1972.

Langer, Paul F., and Joseph J. Zasloff. *North Vietnam and the Pathet Lao: Partners in the Struggle for Laos.* Cambridge: Harvard University Press, 1970.

Lewy, Guenther. *America in Vietnam.* New York: Oxford University Press, 1978.

Lukacs, John. *A New History of the Cold War.* Garden City, N.Y.: Doubleday & Company, Anchor Books, 1966.

McLellan, David S., and David C. Acheson, eds. *Among Friends: Personal Letters of Dean Acheson.* New York: Dodd, Mead & Company, 1980.

McQuaid, Kim. *The Anxious Years: America in the Vietnam-Watergate Era.* New York: Basic Books, 1989.

Martin, John Bartlow. *Adlai Stevenson of Illinois.* Garden City, N.Y.: Doubleday & Company, 1976.

Matusow, Allen J. *The Unraveling of America: A History of Liberalism in the 1960s.* New York: Harper & Row, 1984.

May, Ernest R. *Imperial Democracy: The Emergence of America as a Great Power.* New York: Harper & Row, 1961.

Melanson, Richard A. *Writing History and Making Policy: The Cold War, Vietnam, and Revisionism.* Vol. 6. New York: University Press of America, 1983.

Miller, Merle. *Lyndon: An Oral Biography.* New York: G. P. Putnam's Sons, 1980.

Morgenthau, Hans J. *A New Foreign Policy for the United States.* New York: Praeger Publishers, 1969.

––––––. *Truth and Power: Essays of a Decade, 1960–1970.* New York: Praeger Publishers, 1970.

Nelson, Keith L., and Spencer C. Olin, Jr. *Why War? Ideology, Theory, and History.* Berkeley: University of California Press, 1979.

Neustadt, Richard E., and Ernest R. May. *Thinking in Time: The Uses of History for Decision Makers*. New York: Free Press, 1986.

Nunnerley, David. *President Kennedy and Britain*. New York: St. Martin's Press, 1972.

Oberdorfer, Don. *Tet!* Garden City, N.Y.: Doubleday & Company, 1971.

O'Donnell, Kenneth P., and David F. Powers, with Joe McCarthy. *"Johnny, We Hardly Knew Ye": Memories of John Fitzgerald Kennedy*. Boston: Little, Brown & Company, 1972.

Osgood, Robert Endicott. *Ideals and Self-Interest in America's Foreign Relations: The Great Transformation of the Twentieth Century*. Chicago: University of Chicago Press, 1953.

Paterson, Thomas G. *Kennedy's Quest for Victory: American Foreign Policy, 1961–1963*. New York: Oxford University Press, 1989.

The Pentagon Papers: The Defense Department History of U.S. Decision-Making on Vietnam. Senator Gravel, ed. 4 vols. Boston: Beacon Press, 1974.

Pfeiffer, Richard M., ed. *No More Vietnams? The War and the Future of American Foreign Policy*. New York: Harper & Row, 1968.

Porter, Gareth, and Gloria Emerson. *Vietnam: A Definitive Documentation of Human Decisions*. Vol. 2. New York: Coleman Enterprises, 1979.

_____. *Vietnam: A History in Documents*. New York: Times Mirror, 1979.

Ravenal, Earl C. *Never Again: Learning from America's Foreign Policy Failures*. Philadelphia: Temple University Press, 1978.

Reedy, George. *Lyndon B. Johnson: A Memoir*. New York: Andrews and McMeel, 1982.

Rostow, Walt W. *The Diffusion of Power: An Essay in Recent History*. New York: Macmillan, 1972.

_____. *The United States and the Regional Organization of Asia and the Pacific, 1965–1985*. Austin: University of Texas Press, 1986.

Rusk, Dean. *Winds of Freedom*. Boston: Beacon Press, 1963.

Rust, William J. *Kennedy in Vietnam*. New York: Charles Scribner's Sons, 1985.

Salisbury, Harrison E. *Vietnam Reconsidered: Lessons from a War*. New York: Harper & Row, 1984.

Santoli, Al. *Everything We Had: An Oral History of the Vietnam War by Thirty-three American Soldiers Who Fought It*. New York: Random House, 1981.

Schaetzel, J. Robert. *The Unhinged Alliance: America and the European Community*. New York: Harper & Row, 1975.

Schandler, Herbert Y. *The Unmaking of a President: Lyndon Johnson and Vietnam*. Princeton: Princeton University Press, 1977.

Schell, Jonathan. *The Time of Illusion*. New York: Vintage Books, 1975.

Schlesinger, Arthur M., Jr. *The Imperial Presidency*. Boston: Houghton Mifflin Company, 1973.

_____. *Robert Kennedy and His Times*. 2 vols. Boston: Houghton Mifflin Company, 1978.

_____. *A Thousand Days: John F. Kennedy in the White House*. Boston: Houghton Mifflin Company, 1965.

Schoenbaum, Thomas J. *Waging Peace and War: Dean Rusk in the Truman, Kennedy, and Johnson Years*. New York: Simon & Schuster, 1988.

Sheehan, Neil. *A Bright Shining Lie: John Paul Vann and America in Vietnam*. New York: Random House, 1988.

Small, Melvin. *Johnson, Nixon, and the Doves*. New Brunswick: Rutgers University Press, 1988.

Smith, Michael Joseph. *Realist Thought from Weber to Kissinger*. Baton Rouge: Louisiana State University Press, 1986.

Smith, R. B. *An International History of the Vietnam War: Revolution versus Containment, 1955–61*. New York: St. Martin's Press, 1989.

Steel, Ronald. *Imperialists and Other Heroes*. New York: Random House, 1971.

———. *Pax Americana*. Rev. ed. New York: Penguin Books, 1970.

———. *Walter Lippmann and the American Century*. New York: Vintage Books, 1980.

Sullivan, Mariana P. *France's Vietnam Policy: A Study in French-American Relations*. Westport, Conn.: Greenwood Press, 1978.

Sullivan, Michael P. *The Vietnam War: A Study in the Making of American Policy*. Lexington: University Press of Kentucky, 1973.

Taubman, William. *Globalism and Its Critics: The American Foreign Policy Debate of the 1960s*. Lexington, Mass.: D. C. Heath & Company, 1973.

Thomson, James C., Jr., Peter W. Stanley, and John Perry Curtis. *Sentimental Imperialists: The American Experience in East Asia*. New York: Harper & Row, 1981.

Thompson, Kenneth W. *Cold War Theories*. Vol. 1. Baton Rouge: Louisiana State University Press, 1981.

———. *Masters of International Thought*. Baton Rouge: Louisiana State University Press, 1980.

———. *Morality and Foreign Policy*. Baton Rouge: Louisiana State University Press, 1980.

———. *Political Realism and the Critics of World Politics*. Princeton: Princeton University Press, 1960.

Thompson, W. Scott, and Donaldson Frizzell, eds. *The Lessons of Vietnam*. New York: Taylor & Francis, 1977.

Trewhitt, Henry. *McNamara*. New York: Harper & Row, 1971.

Uphoff, Norman, ed. *The Air War in Indochina*. Boston: n.p., 1972.

Valenti, Jack. *A Very Human President*. New York: W. W. Norton & Company, 1975.

Van Dyke, Jon M. *North Vietnam's Strategy for Survival*. Palo Alto, Calif.: Pacific Books, 1972.

Walton, Richard J. *Cold War and Counterrevolution: The Foreign Policy of JFK*. New York: Pelican Books, 1972.

Weisband, Edward, and Thomas M. Franck. *Resignation in Protest: Political and Ethical Choices between Loyalty to Team and Loyalty to Conscience in Public Life*. New York: Grossman Publishers, 1975.

———. *Secrecy and Foreign Policy*. New York: Oxford University Press, 1974.

Westmoreland, William C. *A Soldier Reports*. New York: Dell Books, 1980.

Williams, William Appleman. *The Tragedy of American Diplomacy*. 2d ed. New York: Dell Publishing Co., 1972.

Williams, William Appleman, Thomas McCormick, Lloyd Gardner, and Walter LaFeber. *America in Vietnam: A Documentary History*. New York: Anchor Press, 1985.

Articles

Allison, Graham, Ernest May, and Adam Yarmolinsky. "Limits to Intervention." *Foreign Affairs* (January 1970).

Ball, George W. "Block That Vietnam Myth." *New York Times*, May 19, 1985.

_____. "Fear Opens Another Door for Peace." *Washington Post*, August 1970.
_____. "Flaming Arrows to the Sky: A Memoir of Adlai Stevenson." *Atlantic Monthly*, May 1966, pp. 41–45.
_____. "Have We Learned or Only Failed?" *New York Times Magazine*, April 1, 1973.
_____. "The Period of Transition." In *Economic Unity in Europe: Programs and Problems*. New York: National Industrial Conference Board, January 21, 1960.
_____. "The Promise of the Multinational Corporation." *Fortune*, June 1967, p. 80.
_____. "The Prophecy the President Rejected." *Atlantic Magazine*, July 1972, pp. 36–49.
_____. "Reagan Should Come In Out of the Rain." *Los Angeles Times*, December 12, 1983.
_____. "We Should De-escalate the Importance of Vietnam." *New York Times Magazine*, December 21, 1969.
"Ball Fears Vietnam War." *Milwaukee Sentinel*, April 28, 1967.
"Ball Urges West Europe to Increase Foreign Aid." *Stars and Stripes*, April 1962, p. 1.
Barnet, Richard J. "The Illusion of Security." *Foreign Policy* 3 (Summer 1971): 71–87.
Beck, Kent M. "The Kennedy Image: Politics, Camelot, and Vietnam." *Wisconsin Magazine of History*, December 1974, pp. 45–55.
Brandon, Henry. "A Disarray of Diplomats." *London Times*, August 1966.
Bundy, McGeorge. "The Presidency and the Peace." *Foreign Affairs* 42 (April 1964): 353–65.
"Cabinet Index to the Kennedy Way." *New York Times Magazine*, April 22, 1962.
Clifford, Clark M. "A Viet Nam Reappraisal." *Foreign Affairs* 47 (July 1969): 601–22.
"Common Market Neighbors." *Washington Post*, April 5, 1962, p. A24.
"The Cuban Crisis Revisited." *Time*, November 7, 1983, p. 50.
"Devil's Advocate Leaves Post." *Evening Bulletin*, October 1, 1966.
Fairlie, Henry. "A Cheer for American Imperialism." *New York Times Magazine*, July 1965.
"Foreign Trade, Foreign Relations, the Presidency." *Time*, March 30, 1962, pp. 11–12.
Galbraith, John Kenneth. "The Plain Lessons of a Bad Decade." *Foreign Policy* 1 (Winter 1970–71): 31–35.
"Harriman: When L.B.J. Lost Nerve." *Los Angeles Times*, August 3, 1986.
Hartley, Anthony. "John Kennedy's Foreign Policy." *Foreign Policy* 4 (Fall 1971): 77–87.
Hendrickson, Paul. "The Night the Vietnam War Came Home to Robert McNamara." *Washington Post Magazine*, September 6, 1987, pp. 16–23.
Herring, George C. "American Strategy in Vietnam: The Postwar Debate." *Military Affairs*, April 1982, pp. 57–63.
_____. "'Peoples Quite Apart': Americans, South Vietnamese, and the War in Vietnam." *Diplomatic History* 14, no. 1 (Winter 1990): 1–23.
_____. "The Vietnam Syndrome and American Foreign Policy." *Virginia Quarterly Review* 57 (Fall 1981): 594–612.
"High Priority Given Plans for Atlantic Partnership." *Washington Daily News*, July 10, 1962.
"Historic Victory for Freer Trade: To Meet the Challenge of Europe, Congress Grants the President Vast Powers." *Newsweek*, October 1, 1962, p. 17.
Hodgson, Godfrey. "The Establishment." *Foreign Policy* 10 (Spring 1973): 3–40.
Katz, Donald R. "The Grand Designer." *New Republic*, January 13, 1979, pp. 21–25.

Kraft, Joseph. "George Ball's Exit Leaves Hole for Devil's Advocate." *Chicago Daily News*, June 1966.

Kristol, Irving. "American Intellectuals and Foreign Policy." *Foreign Affairs* 45 (July 1967): 594–609.

LaFeber, Walter. "Kennedy, Johnson, and the Revisionists." *Foreign Service Journal* (May 1973).

Leuchtenburg, William. "President Kennedy and the End of the Postwar World." *American Review* (Winter 1963).

Liefer, Michael. "Vietnam and the Premises of Intervention." *Pacific Affairs* 45, no. 2 (Summer 1972): 269–72.

"Losing George Ball." *Washington Post*, September 23, 1966, p. A24.

Lunch, William L., and Peter W. Sperlich. "American Public Opinion and the War in Vietnam." *Western Political Quarterly* 32 (March 1979): 21–44.

Luttwak, Edward N. "Mr. Ball's World." *New Republic*, April 1980, pp. 12–14.

McCardle, Dorothy. "George Ball Decorated." *Washington Post*, April 1967.

McGrory, Mary. "Katzenbach: He's Not George Ball But Has President's Ear." *Boston Sunday Globe*, October 1966.

_____. "My Six Years in the Fudge Factory." *Evening Bulletin*, October 1966.

Morgenthau, Hans, Arthur M. Schlesinger, Jr., Herman Kahn, Henry Kissinger, Hanson Baldwin. "Suppose the President Asked You, What Should We Do Now?" *Look Magazine*, August 9, 1966, pp. 24–32.

Morris, Roger. "Thomson, Moyers and Ball: Prophets without Office." *Washington Monthly*, 1977.

Roberts, Paul Craig. "Morality and American Foreign Policy." *Modern Age* 21, no. 2 (Spring 1977): 153–59.

Sellen, Robert W. "Old Assumptions versus New Realities: Lyndon Johnson and Foreign Policy." *International Journal* (Spring 1973).

Siracusa, Joseph M. "Lessons of Viet Nam and the Future of American Foreign Policy." *Australian Outlook* 30 (August 1976).

"A Slap at De Gaulle, High U.S. Official Critical." *U.S. News and World Report*, February 4, 1963.

"Study Says Kennedy Backed Viet Coup." *Los Angeles Times*, October 3, 1983.

Sulzberger, C. L. "The Dove Who Kept Cool." *New York Times*, March 1971.

Thomson, James C. "Getting Out and Speaking Out." *Foreign Policy* 13 (Winter 1973–74): 49–69.

_____. "How Could Vietnam Happen?: An Autopsy." *The Atlantic*, April 1968, pp. 47–53.

"Urbane Underground Flees the 7th Floor." *Washington Star*, September 30, 1966.

"Viet Policy Failure 'Real Possibility.' " *Miami Herald*, November 16, 1969.

Dissertations

The following dissertations are found at the John F. Kennedy Library, Boston, Mass.

Buckwalter, Doyle W. "The Gulf of Tonkin Crisis and Resolutions: Myth or Reality." University of Michigan, 1968 (#237).

Goldberg, Ronald. "The Senate and Vietnam: A Study in Acquiescence." University of Georgia, 1972 (#241).

Hurley, Robert. "President John F. Kennedy and Vietnam, 1961–1963." University of Hawaii, 1970 (#243).

Lewis, William F. "Reappraisal of Appeasement Fallacy of Munich as Justification for Decision in Southeast Asia." American University, 1967 (#244).

McCarthy, Joe E. "The Concept and Evolution of American Foreign Policy toward Vietnam, 1954–1963." University of Maryland, 1965 (#246).

Roskin, Michael G. "Turning Inward: The Effects of Vietnam on United States's Foreign Policy." American University (#248).

Index